DEVELOPMENT PERSPECTIVES FOR THE 1990s

Development Perspectives for the 1990s

Edited by

Renee Prendergast
Lecturer in Economics
The Queen's University of Belfast

and

H. W. Singer
Emeritus Professor and Fellow of the Institute of Development Studies
University of Sussex

St. Martin's Press   New York

First published in the United States of America in 1991

Printed in Great Britain

ISBN 0–312–06803–4

Library of Congress Cataloging-in-Publication Data
Development perspectives for the 1990s / edited by Renee Prendergast
and H. W. Singer.
p.   cm.
Includes bibliographical references and index.
ISBN 0–312–06803-4
1. Economic development—Congresses.   2. Developing countries–
–Economic policy—Congresses.   3. Developing countries—Commercial
policy—Congresses.   4. International economic relations–
–Congresses.   I. Prendergast, Renee, 1952–   .   II. Singer, Hans
Wolfgang, 1910–   .
HD73.D47   1991
338.9—dc20   91–24054
                                                           CIP

In memory of
John Blacking
Professor of Social Anthropology, 1970–90
The Queen's University of Belfast

Contents

Notes on the Contributors

Dina Abbot, Tutor and Research Student, Faculty of Technology, Open University, Walton Hall, Milton Keynes, England.

Razaq A. Adefulu, Lecturer, Faculty of Social and Management Sciences, Ogun State University, Ago-Iwoye, Ogun State, Nigeria.

Haleh Afshar, Lecturer in Politics, University of York, Heslington, York, Y01 5DD, England.

Shanti George, formerly Reader in Sociology, University of Delhi, currently holder of a Bernard Conyers Rural Communications Fellowship from the Arkleton Trust and resident in The Hague, The Netherlands.

Jim Fitzpatrick, Economic Consultant, Jim Fitzpatrick and Associates, 58 Haddington Road, Dublin 4, Ireland.

Margaret E. Harrison, Senior Lecturer in Geography, Cheltenham and Gloucester College of Higher Education, Shaftsbury Hall, St George's Place, Cheltenham, Gloucestershire, GL50 3PP, England.

John S. Henley, Senior Lecturer in International Business, University of Edinburgh, William Robertson Building, 50 George Square, Edinburgh, EH8 9JY, Scotland.

David Hulme, Senior Lecturer, Institute for Development Policy and Management, University of Manchester, Oxford Road, Manchester, M13 9QS, England.

Wang-Taek Jun, Research Student, Department of Economics, The Queen's University of Belfast, BT7 1NN, Northern Ireland.

Tony Killick, Senior Research Fellow, Overseas Development Institute, Regent's College, Inner Circle, Regent's Park, London, NW1 4NS, England.

Robert E. Maguire, Foundation Representative, Inter-American Foundation, 1515 Wilson Blvd., Rosslyn, Virginia, USA, 22209.

John E. Maynard, Lecturer in Economics, Napier Polytechnic, Sighthill Court, Sighthill, Edinburgh, EH11 4BN, Scotland.

J. H. McAdam, Lecturer/Agricultural Scientist, Department of Agriculture for Northern Ireland, Agriculture and Food Science Centre, Newforge Lane, Belfast, BT9 5PX, Northern Ireland.

Deborah McGurk, Economist, Department of Economics, University of Exeter, Exeter, EX4 4RJ, England.

Robin Mearns, Research Fellow, Institute of Development Studies, University of Sussex, Falmer, Brighton, BN1 9RE, England.

Desmond Norton, Senior Lecturer in Economics, University College, Belfield, Dublin 4, Ireland.

Trevor W. Parfitt, Lecturer, Department of Humanities, The Polytechnic, Queensgate, Huddersfield, HD1 2DH, England.

Michael Pretes, Research Associate, The Arctic Institute of North America, The University of Calgary, Alberta, Canada, T2N 1N4.

Renee Prendergast, Lecturer in Economics, The Queen's University of Belfast, Belfast, BT7 1NN, Northern Ireland.

S. M. Shafaeddin, Officer in Charge, Trade Policy Analysis Section, UNCTAD, Palais de Nations, Geneva, Switzerland.

H. W. Singer, Professor, Institute of Development Studies, University of Sussex, Falmer, Brighton, BN1 9RE, England.

Christopher Stevens, Research Fellow, Overseas Development Institute, Regent's College, Inner Circle, Regent's Park, London, NW1 4NS, England.

Andy Storey, Economist, Jim Fitzpatrick and Associates, 58 Haddington Road, Dubin 4, Ireland.

Andy Thorpe, Senior Lecturer in Economics, Portsmouth Polytechnic, Locksway Road, Portsmouth, Hants, England.

Talib A. Younis, Reader in Public Sector Management, Glasgow College, Cowcaddens Road, Glasgow, G4 OBA, Scotland.

List of Tables

List of Figures

Preface

The Development Studies Association (DSA) was set up in 1977 to promote the advancement of knowledge of international development issues and to facilitate communication and cooperation between those engaged in this field. In addition to its Annual Conference, the Association organises and supports a series of Study Groups on particular aspects of development. The Association disseminates information though its Newsletter which is published three times a year.

This volume contains a selection of the papers presented at the DSA Annual Conference held at The Queen's University of Belfast in September 1989. It is the intention of the Association's Council that the present volume should be the first of a series of DSA publications. The series will include selections from the proceedings of the DSA Annual Conference and, where appropriate, volumes on specific themes based on the work of the DSA Study Groups. A refereeing system for volumes in this series is currently being developed.

Given the nature of its subject matter, development studies is both a multidisciplinary and an interdisciplinary field. The Study Groups organised and supported by the DSA provide a unique organisational forum for bringing many different disciplines to bear on particular issues. It is hoped that the publications in this series will enrich our understanding of development processes by combining the benefits of a variety of approaches with the rigour associated with particular disciplines.

The editors of this volume wish to thank Georgina Holmes for secretarial assistance, Mary Trainor and Colin Coulter for editorial assistance, Katherine Orme for compilation of the index, and Frances Condick for her copy-editing.

Renee Prendergast
Series Editor

Introduction: Development Perspectives for the 1990s

Renee Prendergast and H. W. Singer

For many developing countries, the 1980s were a decade lost for development. Towards the end of the decade, real GNP per capita in Latin America and the Caribbean was lower than it had been ten years previously. In Sub-Saharan Africa, the situation was even worse with real incomes per capita in many countries lower than in the late 1960s. In Asia, however, the picture was rather different. Most Asian economies experienced modest but positive rates of growth of real per capita incomes while a small number of East Asian economies had growth rates in excess of the world average. Overall, world income inequality has sharply increased.

The weak performance of Latin American and African economies relative to the Asian economies may be partly explained by the differential impact of two external shocks: the sharp fall in primary commodity prices and the rise of real interest rates. Because of measurement difficulties, there is some dispute about the precise magnitude of the losses due to commodity price falls. According to UNCTAD estimates, total losses for all LDCs in the period 1981–6 were $42 *billion* with 1979–80 taken as base year. Due to their greater dependence on primary commodity exports, these losses were felt most keenly in Latin America and Africa, particularly in the latter.

Of the seventeen most highly indebted countries, twelve are in Latin America. These countries were extremely vulnerable to the rise of real interest rates in the early 1980s because much of their debt was borrowed from private sources at floating rates of interest. With the exception of Nigeria and Cote d'Ivoire, the debt of Sub-Saharan African (SSA) countries is mainly from official sources and at low fixed rates of interest. The debt problems of SSA spring not so much from rising real interest rates as from the magnitude of the debt itself (100 per cent of GNP as opposed to 60 per cent for Latin America) and the stagnation of export earnings during the 1980s.

As we move into the last decade of the century, developing countries, particularly in Africa and Latin America, find themselves confronted by a hostile external environment. Commodity prices are expected to remain low for the foreseeable future. The debt overhang and reduced flows of capital to the developing world mean that, without significant debt reduction, there will continue to be a net outflow of resources from LDCs. There is now a growing recognition that debt reduction is necessary if there is to be a return to growth and the Washington Institutions have undertaken to support and fund debt reduction programmes provided such reduction forms part of a strong and effective structural adjustment programme (SAP).

STRUCTURAL ADJUSTMENT

Restoration of external balance

The immediate task of any structural adjustment programme is to create the conditions for future viable growth, but they are tied through cross-conditionality to IMF stabilisation programmes which aim at the restoration of external balance. Theory suggests that, in conditions of full employment, the restoration of external balance requires a combination of expenditure-switching and expenditure-reducing measures. Expenditure reduction involves the use of fiscal and monetary policy to reduce all elements of government and private expenditure. Used on its own as a means of restoring external balance, it will require massive deflation of the economy with consequent costs in terms of output loss and unemployment. Expenditure switching is achieved by means of a real devaluation of the exchange rate which increases the domestic price of tradeable goods relative to that of non-tradeables. This should increase the profitability of tradeables production relative to that of non-tradeables and at the same time reduce domestic consumption of tradeables, thereby reducing imports and increasing the proportion of output available for export. There are, however, a number of factors which cloud this neat scenario. First, there is the difficulty that simultaneous expansion of traditional commodity exports by a number of countries will result in falling international prices, with the consequence that export volume increases will not be matched by revenue increases. Secondly, it has to be borne in mind that short run supply elasticities for export sectors such as mining and tree crop production may be extremely low. Consequently, there may be a long time lag before the benefits of expenditure-switching policies are felt. Thirdly, as shown by Shafaeddin's study (Chapter 5 of this volume), in low-income countries with a small industrial base, short-run supply elasticities in manufacturing may also be low. In addition, the dependence of the manufacturing sector on imported inputs may mean that in situations of import compression, output may fail to respond to expenditure-switching measures.

Since expenditure-switching measures are unlikely to produce substantial results in the short-run, it is evident that attempts to restore external balance within a short time scale will require greater reliance on deflationary measures with severe consequences in terms of social costs, as documented by Adefulu (Chapter 3). There is now a growing recognition that the three to five-year adjustment period envisaged in the first generation of SAPs was far too short and the EC approach embodied in Lomé IV anticipates a more gradual adjustment process over a time period of ten years or more. Aspects of the EC's approach to structural adjustment as well as the more general relationship between the EC and the associated ACP countries are discussed by Stevens and Killick (Chapter 1) and Parfitt (Chapter 2).

Creating a more responsive environment

While there is considerable dispute about the extent to which the present crisis in Latin America and Africa is the product of external shocks or internal mismanagement, there is widespread acceptance that excessive intervention and institutional failures have contributed significantly to the problem. Typical structural adjustment programmes prescribe a greater reliance on the market mechanism; removal of price controls, subsidies and other forms of market distortion; large-scale privatisation and trade liberalisation. Although the benefits to be obtained from a more responsive and competitive economic environment, from reduced political interference and greater accountability, are not in dispute, it is widely held that the first generation of SAPs went too far in downgrading the role of the state. Furthermore, as Stevens and Killick argue, the programmes were theory-based and standardised and failed to take due account of the institutional and socio-economic specificities of the economies concerned. At least partly for this reason the speed at which adjustment could take place was overestimated, and the size and duration of the social costs incurred severely underestimated.

In the design of the new generation of SAPs, greater attention must be given to the tailoring of programmes to meet the needs of specific countries. Provision must also be made from the outset for some mitigation of the social costs of adjustment. As Singer (Chapter 8) emphasises, this is not only necessary on humanitarian grounds but is a political prerequisite for the acceptance and, even more, the implementation of adjustment programmes. In addition, as Adefulu and Singer point out, failure to cushion vulnerable sections of the population from austerity may involve destruction of human capital and damage the long-term growth prospects of the countries concerned. If adjustment programmes are to lay the basis for sustainable growth, shock treatment which undermines the very foundations of such growth through the large scale destruction of human and physical capital must be avoided. This requires not only a longer-term perspective but also substantial additional financial and other aid flows for the relief of poverty and import strangulation. The positive role of food aid in this context is discussed by Singer while Fitzpatrick and Storey (Chapter 7) emphasise that the avoidance of potential negative side effects of food aid depends heavily on proper planning and management.

The market and the state

It was noted above that the first generation of SAPs placed heavy emphasis on reduced state intervention and greater reliance on market forces. As Stevens and Killick note, this was not simply a matter of the ideological predilections of the Washington Institutions, but also a well-founded response to real deficiencies. Examples of the way in which institutional failures have frustrated the achievement of desirable objectives are documented in Henley and Maynard's paper on development finance institutions (Chapter 15). Similarly, in their chapter on Sandinista agrarian reform, Thorpe and McGurk show that overambitious state intervention contributed to the Nicaraguan economic crisis of 1988. These examples demonstrate the need for governments to set realisable objectives and above all to develop institutional competence but, just as the existence of market failure does not lead to the conclusion that markets should have no role in allocation, so also, instances of 'state failure' should not lead us to advocate an end to all government intervention.

Experience, in any case, seems to show that in the most successful developing economies, the state and market played complementary roles. Shafaeddin (Chapter 5) shows that successful East Asian economies such as South Korea used selective trade strategies involving differential levels of protection on the one hand and export incentives on the other. The degree of protection or promotion, and the commodities to which they applied, varied depending on the level of development and the priorities and needs of the time. Similarly, in their chapter on Korean multinationals, Jun and Prendergast note that the Korean government's approach to inward investment was also selective. At any given point in time, policy was geared to attracting firms which strengthened domestic production capability and discouraging those which did not contribute positively to development priorities.

SUSTAINABLE DEVELOPMENT

For an economic system to be viable, it must at a minimum be capable of reproducing itself in the same form year after year. This means that the output of the system must be sufficient to provide the labour force with means of subsistence and replace all the inputs used in the process of production. For sustainable growth to be possible, an economic system must be capable of reproducing itself with a surplus, which if invested may be used to expand the scale of the system. With given technology and in the absence of resource constraints, the rate of growth of the system will depend on the size of the surplus and the proportion of the surplus which is used for investment. Improvements in technology reduce the amount of resource and reproducible inputs required for the production of a given output. The existence of scarce resources in fixed supply places limits on the expansion of certain lines of business or, if they are basic resources such as land, the continued expansion of the system will require the introduction of techniques of production which economise on the fixed resource.

In economies with high levels of dependence on primary production, achieving sustainable development is no easy matter. As noted by Pretes (Chapter 11), regions where primary commodities are produced or exploited for export tend to be characterised by booms and slumps. As documented in the Dutch disease literature, the existence of a substantial booming sector tends to produce dislocations elsewhere in the economy. Labour tends to be attracted away from the production of other tradeables and into the booming sector. Rising incomes in the booming sector allow increased consumer and government spending and may lead to the expansion of non-tradeables production, including social services. Resource depletion or terms of trade collapse may bring an end to the boom. The economic structure built up in the boom period is no longer viable and restructuring becomes necessary. As noted by Harrison (Chapter 14) social services financed by booming sector revenues may come under intense strain. Norton (Chapter 4) analyses the response of a labour-abundant developing economy to the collapse of a booming sector. His analysis suggests that in economies suffering from 'the Zambian disease', agriculture is likely to be the key growth sector in the long run, and that the re-structuring of such economies may take several decades. In this context, it is appropriate to mention McAdam's discussion of the consequences of the declaration of the Falkland Islands Conservation Zone in 1986 (Chapter 13). Revenues from fishing increased so dramatically that GNP increased by 180 per cent in a single year. This resource boom is likely to have profound consequences for the islands' traditional agricultural economy.

Perhaps a more fundamental issue from the point of view of the sustainability of development is the question of environmental degradation. While, with the exception of low-income countries other than China and India, the average annual growth rate of the population in most developing countries is declining, absolute populations continue to increase and will do so well into the next century. In some countries, the pressures of high population growth have led to more intensive exploitation of ecologically-sensitive lands or to pressure to open up forested frontier areas such as Amazonia. While higher levels of exploitation need not lead to ecological deterioration if they are accompanied by investment in appropriate infrastructure and farming systems, many developing areas are currently experiencing soil erosion or desertification and a consequent loss of land fertility. Large-scale deforestation such as that currently taking place in Amazonia and in parts of Indonesia also contributes to global warming, and destruction of vegetative cover in areas where farming has been intensified gives rise to woodfuel shortages.

Although population pressure is an important factor in environmental degradation in many parts of the developing world, it is not the sole cause of environmental damage. As Pretes shows, 60 per cent of land clearance in the Amazon region was done by large-scale developers and ranchers, and only 17.6 per cent by peasant farmers. Furthermore, it is important to stress that the relationship between population and the environment is by no means simple. As Mearns (Chapter 12) shows in his paper on the woodfuel crisis, problems relating to the environment have to be seen in a dynamic context embracing economic, social and cultural factors. Given the diversity of biophysical and cultural 'landscapes' of developing countries, Mearns argues that problems, and the opportunities to solve them, may be specific not only to place but also to social groups in each place. While emphasising that solutions to the woodfuel crisis require participation by local people at each stage, Mearns stresses that this does not exclude the need for economic, legal and political initiatives at the macro level to improve the broad context for local changes.

A BOTTOM-UP APPROACH

Like Mearns, several of the contributors to this volume stress the importance of the bottom-up approach to economic development. George (Chapter 18), in her paper on women and dairying in India shows that, while the practices and technology used by women in rural India are different from those of formal dairy science, they are in themselves scientifically, economically and ecologically sound. She also shows that, while the extension of commercialised dairying improves the lot of some women, it tends to further marginalise women from subordinate castes and classes even when women-only co-operatives are involved. On the other hand, Abbott shows that women's organisations developed and run by poor women can not only enable them to gain access to much-needed credit but also have the potential to address and represent their members other needs and concerns. The Grameen bank in Bangladesh, with 87 per cent female membership, represents another highly successful exercise in institutional innovation. The bank evolved out of an explicit action-research project which experimented with organisational structures and procedures to overcome the challenge of lending to the poor. As Hulme (Chapter 17) shows, it has an outstanding repayment rate record and the incomes of its members are substantially higher than those of comparable non-members.

Hulme analyses the prospects of replicating the bank in other countries and finds that there is a case for cautious optimism with regard to the bank's transferability.

While institutional innovations may play an important role in improving access to credit and the earning capacity of borrowers, cheap accessible credit will only improve the welfare of borrowers if it enables them to take advantage of investment opportunities. Younis' analysis of agricultural credit institutions in Jordan suggests that although institutional innovations could lead to some improvement in agency performance, the most serious problems contributing to loan default lay outside the realm of the agencies. He identifies inadequacies in water resources, research on land resources and marketing as key impediments to development in the agricultural sector.

Welfare-enhancing institutional innovation at grassroots level requires a facilitating macro environment. This is brought home forcefully by Maguire's discussion of food crop storage and marketing in Haiti (Chapter 10). Efforts by Haitian peasants to gain greater control over their farm economy involved co-operative programmes built around grain storage, marketing and credit activities. These programmes were intended to improve food security, to increase the revenues from grain sales and to reduce dependence on moneylenders and grain speculators. As such they were seen as a threat to the economic power of the corrupt elites who had dominated and exploited the countryside under the Duvalier regimes. As these reactionary elements fight for their political and economic survival, they have sought to thwart bottom-up development programmes by terrorising their membership and destroying their physical capital. The lesson here is that the overcoming of socio-political constraints is a vital aspect of development. Since, as noted by Parfitt (Chapter 2), corrupt regimes have often received outside support for strategic reasons, there are grounds for some optimism that this will be a less frequent occurrence as the intensity of the cold war lessens.

A LEARNING PROCESS APPROACH

In his discussion of the international transfer of institutional innovations, Hulme argues that, rather than using successful experiences as blueprints for establishing new institutions on a large scale, a learning process approach should be adopted. This involves the introduction of the institutional innovation on a small-scale experimental basis and its modification to suit the new environment. This organic approach recognises the rich variety of human socio-economic and cultural forms and the specificity of different locales, but, while respecting cultural values, it also emphasises the need for openness to learning and change. This emphasis on an adaptive evolutionary approach also characterises much of the recent literature on the development of technological capability in LDCs, and it is also implicitly or explicitly a hallmark of many of the contributions to this volume.

Development is a complex phenomenon embracing all aspects of human life. The value of an evolutionary approach is that it recognises that existing structures and cultures have an important influence on the way in which individuals, groups and societies respond to economic and social processes and events. Part of any such response may involve modification of existing structures or an emphasis on a particular aspect of culture (on the latter, see Afshar's account of the attempt by Muslim fundamentalist women to re-interpret Islam in favourable ways). Acceptance of an evolutionary approach does not imply an attitude of *laissez faire* or an absence of critique, but, it does imply an acknowledgement that ready-made solutions based on different structures and value systems may not be appropriate in the specific context of individual developing countries.

1 The EC and Structural Adjustment

Christopher Stevens and Tony Killick[1]

INTRODUCTION

Co-ordination between agencies engaged in policy-based lending is essential. With traditional project aid a lack of co-ordination may be wasteful but it need not vitiate the efforts of donors; with policy-based lendings this degree of tolerance disappears. A recipient government can only follow one set of recommendations for a given policy variable; if those providing advice do not proffer the same prescriptions it will be forced to reject some of them.

But such 'co-ordination' implies a narrowing of the range of policy advice. If all donors subscribe to the same prescriptions the adverse consequences of any errors in their analysis are increased. Moreover, what appears to donors as 'co-ordination' may seem to recipients more like 'ganging-up'. This is the more likely because of two factors: the 'advice' typically associated with structural adjustment lending involves a major encroachment on the sovereignty of the recipient; and the prescriptions offered are often controversial.

The co-ordination issue has not yet surfaced in an acute form because of a similarity of approach between those agencies active in the field. Until now the World Bank and the International Monetary Fund (IMF) (the international financial institutions or IFIs) have been the leading agencies for lending related to broad economic policies. Whilst there are important differences between them, the general thrust of their programmes is similar.

With the emergence of the European Community (EC) as a significant source of balance of payments support, the situation has become more complex. The EC's position is ambivalent: it has asserted both that it will avoid any open conflict with the IFIs and that its approach differs significantly from theirs. If EC funds are applied in support of the same policy agenda as those of the IFIs they will add significantly to resources available to underpin the changes and, hence, tend to increase the pressure on African, Caribbean and Pacific (ACP) states to follow the recommended path, for good or ill. By contrast, if they are applied in support of other policies they will act as a powerful counterweight to the influence of the IFIs. Hence, the policy stance of the EC will affect both the nature of

1

'structural adjustment' and the success of IFI activities.

The principal objective of this chapter is to use the EC example as a first step in identifying broader issues of donor co-ordination on policy based lending. It identifies the ways in which the approaches of the EC and IFIs are likely to be in concord or conflict and it examines the evidence of past collaboration and current plans. Further details can be found in Stevens and Killick (1989).

THE EC'S SHIFT TOWARDS STRUCTURAL ADJUSTMENT

The involvement of the EC (as opposed to the member states) in balance of payments support will be limited to aid to the sixty-eight ACP signatories of the Lomé Conventions. The period since Lomé I was negotiated has seen a gradual movement of the EC away from an exclusive emphasis on traditional projects as, like the World Bank, it has tried to adjust to changing circumstances in its partners.

The shift in Lomé policy reflects the fact that adjustment lending has increasingly focused on the countries of the ACP, and especially Sub-Saharan Africa. The economic situation of the ACP has continued to deteriorate and this has had a profound impact upon the working of the Conventions. Thirty of the fifty-two structural adjustment loans (SALs) and thirty-six of the seventy sectoral adjustment loans (SECALs) approved by the World Bank between 1979 and 1987 (financial years) were to ACP states (see Tables 1.1 and 1.2). By 1988, eighteen Sub-Saharan African countries had initiated structural adjustment operations and a further fourteen had borrowed to support sectoral reforms.

In these circumstances structural adjustment is an issue that impinged unavoidably on the implementation of Lomé III and will do so on its successor. This is because Lomé aid has had to take account either implicitly or explicitly of the economic policy changes undertaken by ACP states as part of a SAL. These typically involve decisions on policies that profoundly affect the implementation of traditional aid projects. Either Lomé projects will have to be tailored around these policies (thus implicitly accepting them) or there will have to be an explicit EC involvement in the SAL debate to safeguard project interests.

The EC Commission has urged the cause of explicit involvement and persuaded first the member states and then the ACP to accept some moves in this direction. An initial step was taken in December 1987 with the adoption of a 'special Community programme to aid certain highly indebted low-income countries in Sub-Saharan Africa'. This has been built upon in the current Lomé IV Convention.

A hallmark of Lomé III was sectoral policy dialogue which, for some of its supporters, represented a way out of the problem of relating EC-ACP

TABLE 1.1 *World Bank structural adjustment lending to the ACP, 1980–7*[a]
($ million)

Country	IBRD	IDA	SFA[b]	SJF[c]
Burundi		15.0	16.2	19.3
C.A.R.		14.0	16.0	
Côte d'Ivoire I	150.0			
II	250.7			
III	250.0			
Dominica		3.0		
Gambia		5.0	11.5	4.5
Ghana		34.0	81.0	
Guinea		25.0	17.0	42.2
Guinea Bissau		10.0		
Guyana	14.0	8.0		
Jamaica I	76.2			
II	60.2			
III	55.0			
Kenya I		55.0		
II	60.9	70.0		
Malawi I	45.0			
II		55.0		
III		30.0	40.0	39.1
Mauritania		15.0		
Mauritius I	15.0			
II	40.0			
Niger		20.0	40.0	
Sao Tome		4.0		
Senegal I	30.0	30.0		
II		20.0	44.0	7.0
III		45.0		
Togo I		40.0		
II		27.8	10.0	30.0
Zaire		55.0		
Total ACP	1 047.0	580.8	275.7	142.1
ACP as % of total of all recipients	20	82	100	100

Notes:
(a) World Bank financial years 1980–87;
(b) Special Facility for Africa;
(c) Special Joint Financing

SOURCE: World Bank (R88–15, 25.1.88).

TABLE 1.2 *World Bank sectoral adjustment lending to the ACP, 1979–87*[a]
(*$ million*)

Country	Loan/Credit	IBRD	IDA	SFA[b]	SJF[c]
Burkina	Fertiliser		13.7		
Ghana	Recon. import I		40.0		
	Export rehab.		76.0		
	Recon. import II		60.0	27.1	15.8
	Industrial sector		28.5	25.0	
	Education sector		34.5		
Guinea Bissau	Recon. import		10.0	5.0	
Jamaica	Export dev. fund I	31.5			
	Export dev. fund II	37.0			
	Export dev. fund III	30.1			
	Public enterprises	20.0			
	Trade and finance	40.0			
Kenya	Agriculture sector		20.0	40.0	12.5
Madagascar	Ind. assistance		40.0	20.0	
	Agriculture sector		20.0	33.0	8.9
	Ind. and trade policy		16.0	80.8	3.2
Malawi	Smallholder fert.		5.0		
Mauritania	Public enterprises		16.4		
	SNIM rehabilitation	20.0			
Mauritius	Industry sector	25.0			
Niger	Public enterprises		60.0	20.0	
Nigeria	Fertiliser	250.0			
	Trade policy	452.0			
Sierra Leone	Agriculture sector		21.5		
Somalia	Agriculture sector		30.0	32.6	13.5
Sudan	Ag. rehab. I		65.0		
	Ag. rehab. II		50.0		
Tanzania	Export rehab.		50.0		
	Multi sector rehab.		50.0	46.2	36.7
Uganda	Agriculture rehab.		70.0		
Zaire	Industrial sector		20.0	60.0	5.4
Zambia	Export rehab.	75.0			
	Agriculture rehab.		25.0	9.6	3.9
	Ind. reorientation		20.0	42.4	15.0
	Recovery credit		50.0		
Zimbabwe	Manu. export prom.	70.6			
Total ACP		1 051.2	891.6	441.7	114.9
ACP as % of total of all recipients		13	72	100	100

Notes:
(a) World Bank financial years 1979–87;
(b) Special Facility for Africa;
(c) Special Joint Financing.

SOURCE: World Bank (R88–15, 25.1.88).

agreements to those reached with the IMF/World Bank. It seemed to offer an avenue for the EC to discuss policy issues with the ACP without becoming embroiled in macroeconomic conditionality.

But the EC's subsequent response to the ACP's problems led it to broaden its approach by entering the realm of general import support and introduced it to the issue of macroeconomic conditionality. The 'special Community programme to aid certain highly indebted low-income countries in Sub-Saharan Africa' extended the scope of spending. Under it the EC made available during 1988 and 1989 Ecu 500 million in the form of quick-disbursing aid for import support to the poorest and most debt distressed African states. The funds were derived from several sources. One portion (Ecu 60 million of recycled funds) was available to be used for general import support. And there was an expansion in the funds for sectoral import programmes already legitimised by Article 188.

The issue of structural adjustment figured prominently in the Lomé IV negotiations, which reinforced the shift in aid practice. The new Convention both includes a special fund for structural adjustment (of Ecu 1150 million) and provides that aid from the normal country programmes will also be available under Article 188 for additional import support if required. This outcome represents a compromise between those EC member states that wanted a high proportion of funds to be available for structural adjustment (notably UK and Netherlands) and those favouring traditional projects (especially Italy, Ireland and Belgium).

These initiatives have brought to the fore the relationship between Lomé activities and those of the IFIs. The Commission's communication to the Council proposing the special Africa programme noted explicitly that general import programmes support would be framed taking into account 'the adjustment programmes and reforms decided upon in agreement with the World Bank or the IMF' (EC, 1987, para 14). The EC position was formally defined in a Council resolution of 31 May 1988 which *inter alia* calls for collaboration between the Community institutions and the Bretton Woods organisations.

The criteria for establishing the eligibility of African states to benefit from the programme were established in March 1988. Two of the criteria were uncontroversial, but the third relates directly to conditionality. States must have intoduced policies that are considered adequate to deal with their economic problems. By implication, an understanding with the IFIs is taken as evidence of such adequacy.

If a state has agreed a SAL with the World Bank then the EC money can be used for a general import programme. If no SAL is in place the EC will form a judgement as to whether policies with respect to a particular sector are adequate. If the judgement is positive, funds will be made available for a sectoral import programme.

Subsequent events suggest that co-ordination will extend to the EC member states both in their bilateral aid programmes and in their actions as members of the IFIs. In May 1989 the Council resolved that in the provision of support for adjustment there should be an attempt 'to increase consistency and convergence between the approach of the Commission and the Member States at all levels . . .' (EC, 1989, p. 5). To the extent that this effort succeeds it would result in a very large share of adjustment aid being made available under identical, or at least very similar, policy conditions. In 1987 the EC states provided around two-thirds of net ODA disbursements to Sub-Saharan Africa. To a significant extent this aid has been focused on countries undertaking programmes of structural adjustment bearing the seal of approval of the IFIs (World Bank, 1989).

DILEMMAS OF CONDITIONALITY

How will the EC affect key areas of structural adjustment? One set of issues concerns the policy prescriptions that are typically associated with a SAL. Another relates to the volume of resources available for structural adjustment. This section examines critically the existing IFI conventional wisdom on structural adjustment as a prelude to an assessment of the possible impact of the EC.

Four principal dilemmas affect both donors and recipients when designing structural adjustment policies:

- the provisions derived from mainstream policy theory are sometimes an inappropriate technology; yet the donor community is constrained in making it more appropriate;
- the design of effective economic policies is a highly complex matter and heavily dependent on the specifics of the economy in question; yet there is a strong institutional imperative for off-the-peg solutions and standard recipes;
- the measures contained in conditionality agreements are undermined by their externally-driven nature, and the fact that they are usually undertaken in crisis conditions further reduces the likelihood of successful implementation;
- the adjustment, which is the objective of the conditionality, is most needed where it is most difficult.

Typical conditions

Despite the wide range of multilateral and bilateral donors imposing policy conditionality, and the variety of country circumstances to which it is applied, there is a close similarity between the terms of the various agreements. A survey of major donor and IFI statements on the design of adjustment found a clear consensus (Killick, 1987). This can be labelled the '*new orthodoxy*'. Its components include:

- increased use of market mechanisms and the forces of competition for resource allocation and co-ordination, as against planning and controls. This finds examples in the substitution of rationing by price for administered rationing, and in the phasing out of consumer subsidies;
- an increased role for the private sector, including privatisation;
- measures to raise domestic saving; these include interest rate reform and the development of financial markets;
- liberalisation of trade and payments;
- maintenance of a realistic exchange rate, and other measures to encourage foreign investment;
- correction of other price/incentive distortions (*e.g.* improved agricultural producer prices);
- reduction of budget deficits (largely via expenditure cuts) and other demand management measures.

The homogeneity of the credit agreements, despite the heterogeneity of the countries being assisted, reflects the fact that conditionality has become a key instrument for translating into LDC practice the policy recommendations of Western-based economists. This gives rise to a danger that conditionality may incorporate elements of 'inappropriate technology', with the IFIs/donors facing intellectual, political and resource constraints in adapting this into more appropriate forms.[2]

The influence of theory

At the core of the new orthodoxy is a disillusionment with the efficacy of state interventions. In substantial part, this disillusionment is a well-founded response to real deficiencies. But the reaction has gone too far partly because there are strong but often unstated *value biases* in much contemporary policy theory. They adopt, for example, a negative view of liberty (as the absence of coercion, or *laissez-faire*) as against a positive view (relating it to a person's ability to realise his own goals and implying in economic life some minimal access to basic needs) and an emphasis on allocative efficiency *vis à vis* distributional concerns. More generally, there is a distinct affinity between recent trends in policy theory and the 'conservative revolution' that has been under way in economic policy in major OECD countries in the 1980s. This similarity includes the reassertion of the superiority of market solutions and a rejection of Keynesian approaches to economic management.

There are two important points to note concerning these value biases. First, the distributional concerns which underlie the positive view of liberty are more central issues in LDCs than in the OECD, for merely ensuring the absence of constraints is a quite inadequate approach in the face of malnutrition, poor access to quality education, avoidable ill-health and absence of other basic needs. Second, there is no clear parallel in many LDCs to the shift in public attitudes and electoral results that has heralded the conservative revolution in the OECD. These considerations suggest that there will sometimes be a mismatch in terms of values and objectives between OECD-based theory and LDC views.

Moreover, the foundations of much policy theory are decidedly shaky. Mainstream economics is divided against itself even more than usual, especially in the realm of macroeconomics. It is excessively preoccupied with the efficiency with which resources are allocated at a given time to the near-exclusion of other considerations. The consequence is a neglect of dynamics, with growth theory having become a backwater with little relevance to LDCs.

The role of the state

One consequence of bias in mainstream theory is that the reaction against the state has gone too far. Theoretical attempts were made in the early 1980s to prove the state to be inevitably impotent in macroeconomic management or to substitute fixed monetary rules for discretionary actions, but these were unsuccesful. Although there has since been a partial rehabilitation of the state, the danger is that conditionality still reflects too strongly the over-reaction. One can easily identify examples of the biases that result:

- when donors urge rapid liberalisation of financial systems, without giving enough thought to the market imperfections which are likely to result and their adverse effects;
- pressure for privatisation with insufficient attention to the competitiveness of private market alternatives, and the rival merits of rehabilitating public enterprises;
- neglect of environmental damage, which is a classic example of markets not producing socially desirable outcomes.

The greater degree of market imperfection in many developing countries is of particular importance in this context. Dualistic markets remain commonplace, where asymmetries in production and organisation prevent productivities from being equalised at the margin and resources from moving freely. One illustration of this is the large differences which commonly exist between interest rates in the formal and informal credit markets, implying both different sources of loanable funds in the two sub-markets and that different groups use these sub-markets to meet their credit needs. Labour markets in LDCs are also often marked by dualism, with non-equalising relationships between the formal and informal segments. While there is no longer any doubt that people in LDCs respond 'normally' to pecuniary incentives, this is not to say that traditional or institutional factors – such as extended family arrangements or divisions of labour based on gender, race or caste – do not sometimes dampen or modify that response.

In other respects too markets are more imperfect than in DCs. It is still common for widely differing prices to exist for the same product in outlets geographically close to each other, implying failures of information and/or competition. There is considerably greater industrial concentration in LDCs, with an associated probability of larger monopoly powers. Substantial imperfections still exist in many labour markets. And while much emphasis has been placed in recent years on financial repression in many LDCs, much state interference in capital markets has been prompted in part by monopolistic or oligopolistic behaviour by banks, or by other major imperfections in those markets.

In such circumstances market failures will be more widespread and serious than in a typical industrial country. Even allowing for the costs of policy interventions, and granting that there have been many 'state failures' too, there is a potentially larger role for the state to play – both in safeguarding against market failures and in providing the policy and infrastructural framework which will help markets work better – than is allowed for in the new orthodoxy.

Practical limits to conditionality

Biases in theory are not the only limitations on the efficacy of policy conditionality. Those who would make credit conditional upon the implementation of policies that would not otherwise have been adopted face a set of practical obstacles.

The first relates to the *externally-driven* nature of adjustment. Although it remains ill-defined, the meaning of 'structural adjustment' has moved on from the simple strengthening of a state's balance of payments to the current World Bank definition of 'reforms of policies and institutions'. This comes perilously close to saying that structural adjustment consists of those policy changes of which the donor community approves. The EC's rules for the Special Africa Programme are no exception. This ensures that adjustment will continue to be externally-driven.

A related problem arises from the fact that adjustment programmes are often associated with *crisis*. It is in a crisis that the decisions are most likely to be taken. But policy changes are most likely to be adhered to when they emerge organically, gradually through the existing political and bureaucratic structures. Since conditionality-related reforms are not likely to pass this test they are likely to be fragile. A final dilemma is that *adjustment is most needed where it is most difficult*. The capacity to adjust is a rising function of development (at least up to a point). It is particularly weak in the least developed. These considerations help to explain the weaker adjustment experiences of Sub-Saharan Africa and the difficulties that the IFIs have experienced. The problems are exacerbated because the creditor countries are reluctant to provide the financial support necessary for their approved policies to succeed. This and other unfavourable factors in the world economic environment are undermining LDCs' adjustment efforts. Because of their disadvantages the least developed are in particular need of longer-term programmes and more supporting resources.

Evidence of success

The controversial nature of the policies associated with structural adjustment in the ACP, and especially Africa, is exacerbated because of the paucity of evidence on the effectiveness of past efforts. (On this see the chapters by Adefulu and Parfitt in this volume.) The furore that surrounded the World Bank's report on *Africa's Adjustment, Recovery and Growth* underlines the problem (World Bank, 1989). To an extent the dispute between the World Bank and critics such as the UN Economic Commission for Africa is the result of differences over the most appropriate methodology and the priority to be accorded to various indicators of economic health. Such differences are made more difficult to resolve at present because too short a period of time has elapsed to identify clearly differences in economic performance between 'reformers' and 'non-reforr·ers', given the many extraneous factors affecting both sets of states, the wide diversity within each group, and the limited resources actually applied in support of African structural adjustment.[3]

The most that can be stated is that the recent economic performance of Sub-Saharan Africa is a cause for guarded optimism rather than pessimism, and that it provides evidence that tends to support the arguments in favour of adjustment conditionality rather than the reverse. But what it does not do is to give any reason for modifying the view that the remedies based on Northern economic experience should be applied only with great caution and modesty.

THE POTENTIAL IMPACT OF THE EC

Attitudes towards the IFI conventional wisdom

The Commission characterises the difference between its own style and that of the IFIs in terms of pragmatism versus text book theory. It argues that although some of the policies advanced by the IFIs may be correct according to the current conventional theoretical wisdom, they may not work in practice, either because LDC governments do not give them wholehearted support, or because of fundamental design flaws due to the different circumstances found in LDCs. With its lengthy experience of the ACP and the fundamentally different political relationship that exists between the Lomé partners, compared to the IFIs and their debtors, the Commission claims that it can bring to structural adjustment a missing element of political and economic realism.

Underlying such disagreements on policy details is a significant difference of approach between the EC and the IFIs. The EC will tend to be more tolerant than the IFIs to a *dirigiste* economic style in its ACP partners. The dominant economic philosophy within the Lomé section of the EC Commission is influenced strongly by the French intellectual tradition. Moreover, since the Lomé Convention is a legal text that accords the ACP *governments* an unusually high degree of control over the use of aid funds, the extent to which the EC can encourage privatisation (even if it wishes so to do) is limited. Because of these fundamental differences between the EC and the IFIs, the disagreements on detail may be more difficult to overcome than might be expected.

Stated in this way the Commission's critique has strong resonances with the preceding analysis, but it is far from clear how the Commission's involvement in structural adjustment would operate in practice. The Commission has acknowledged the need not to present the ACP states with two conflicting sets of policy recommendations. But this implies that those agencies involved in structural adjustment must either agree *ex ante* a compromise package of conditionality, or agree *ex post* to operate their separate programmes in such a way that they do not interfere with each other. It is inherent in the idea of compromise that there is give and take on both sides. Hence, co-ordination implies that to a certain degree the Commission will alter its approach to fit in with the requirements of the IFIs as well as the reverse.

The Commission's response to such arguments is that it does not envisage having its own 'policy package' to impose upon the ACP. Rather, it would tend to support ACP governments when they seek to amend the proposals of the IFIs to make them more politically acceptable and development-oriented. The question-mark that must hang over this position concerns the extent to which ACP states are able to articulate a coherent rejoinder to the conditionality proposed by the IFIs. Without such an autonomous policy package to relate to, the Commission will be left with a choice between accepting the IFI approach, becoming associated with ACP country attempts to dilute the IFI programmes, or devising its own.

Not the least of the obstacles in the way of the latter alternative is the absence of any convincing and systematic alternative to IFI orthodoxy. Neo-structuralist attempts are most relevant to economic conditions more common in Latin America and little in evidence in ACP countries. They are not, in any case, as radically different as sometimes presented. The 'African Alternative Framework' launched by the UN Economic Commission for Africa similarly does not meet the need. It appears to be predicated on political changes within Africa and improvements in the global economic environment which are unlikely to materialise, and is very ambivalent about the efficiency of government interventions and the desirability of macroeconomic balance (ECA, 1989). Also, the experiences of countries which have attempted to devise their own alternative approaches have been singularly discouraging.

There exists already a certain amount of evidence to judge the extent to which the EC and ACP can present a coherent alternative to IFI prescriptions. There have been a number of instances in which policy changes sought by the IFIs as part of a SAL have conflicted with the requirements of projects funded under the Lomé Convention. The Commission claims that it has been able to influence initial IFI prescriptions to modify text book remedies in the light of practical realities the better to relate to recipient government priorities and development interests. These examples are drawn largely from the food sector, and in particular from Cameroon, Niger, Senegal and Mali. It is no coincidence that the examples cited of succesful co-ordination all involve the food sector. This is both the area of focus for Lomé III activities in many ACP states and the sector in which the staff administering the Lomé Convention have the greatest expertise. A shift into general import support and macroeconomic dialogue would require new skills. A start has already been made within the Commission on providing some training and orientation to the new requirements, but these changes hardly seem adequate in themselves to prepare the Lomé Convention bureaucracy for a significant shift in emphasis on aid policy.

The problem would be mitigated to a certain extent if the World Bank continues to shift away from broad SALs to more narrowly focused SECALs. Co-ordination (as opposed to domination) would be easier to achieve if both actors were operating in the agricultural sector. But the problem is unlikely to disappear altogether, not least because the World Bank has itself to take note of the IMF's position on the macroeconomic issues. As is suggested by Parfitt's chapter in this volume, early evidence suggests that on issues outside the food sector the EC has so far tended to follow the lead of the IFIs.

Can Lomé add critical mass?

It is widely accepted that a major failing of past structural adjustment is that it has been attempted with inadequate funds and over too short a time horizon. Bearing in mind the IFIs' desire for greater co-financing of adjustment programmes, would the application of Lomé aid funds to the process make a significant contribution to easing these constraints? There is an opportunity cost in utilising Lomé aid funds for structural adjustment rather than in other ways. The assessment of whether this is a cost worth bearing must take account of the value to ACP states of linking Lomé and structural adjustment. This, in turn, is influenced by the extent to which Lomé funds could have an impact out of proportion to their own size by enabling the structural adjustment exercise to reach critical mass.

The grants that the EC will provide for *quasi* balance of payments support could be quite large in relation to World Bank structural and sectoral adjustment lending to the ACP. Any estimate of the relative size of Lomé aid funds must be speculative because the proportion of the country programmes to be available for import support is uncertain, as is the level of future World Bank structural adjustment lending. However, an impression can be obtained by using the aid figures for Lomé III and assuming alternative proportions available for structural adjustment.

The broad picture is clear. Lomé III aid could add substantially to the funds available for structural adjustment in many of the ACP. For sixteen of the twenty-nine ACP states that received SALs/SECALs between 1979 and 1987 the grant element of their Lomé III national indicative pro-grammes (NIPs) exceeded 100 per cent of their World Bank credits. Even if only 40 per cent of their NIPs had been applied to structural adjustment (in line with the World Bank's limit for IDA), it would have added 75 per cent or more to the World Bank's funds in six cases, and 50 per cent or more in a further six.

On closer examination these figures suggest other facets of the EC's involvement in structural adjustment. In almost all of the cases in which the Lomé III NIP represented a high proportion of SALs/SECALs, World Bank loans were relatively few. In fifteen of the sixteen ACP states in which NIP grants were equivalent to 100 per cent or more of World Bank loans, there were no more than two SALs/SECALs. By contrast, in nine of the ten ACP states receiving more than two SALs/SECALs the NIP was very small in relation to their World Bank loans.

There are, of course, several reasons why a state should have received only a small number of SALs/SECALs, but one explanation is that it failed to reach agreement with the IFIs on policy conditionality. To the extent that this explanation applies to the ACP, it suggests that Lomé aid for structural adjustment would be a significant addition mainly in states that are in policy dispute with the IFIs.

This must colour thinking on both the positive and negative potential features of donor co-ordination in this area, i.e. achieving critical mass and presenting a monolithic, insufficiently flexible front to the ACP. The lesson from the recent past seems to be that Lomé funds could make only a modest step towards critical mass in those states that satisfy IFI conditions, and would provide an alternative (rather than a supplement) to World Bank funds in countries that do not satisfy such conditions unless the EC interprets 'policy adequacy' as requiring agreement with the IFIs. Hence the impact will be felt less in terms of achieving critical mass than in terms of its potential for influencing IFI positions.

Will it increase politicisation?

A related consideration concerns the possibility that the EC's entry into structural adjustment could increase the politicisation of the exercise. Already evidence exists of increased politicisation of IFI decisions in the case of certain programmes: such politicisation undermines the legitimacy and effectiveness of the adjustment movement. The resulting lack of uniformity of treatment across countries has been near-scandalous in some cases and, in particular, has led to the diversion of major amounts of scarce resources to governments with little serious intention of implementing rigorous adjustment policies.

Consider the procedure likely to be adopted to deal with structural adjustment requests to the EC by ACP states that are in policy disagreement with the IFIs. Like traditional aid projects, they will be assessed by a committee representing the EC member states. Some EC states (notably the UK and the Netherlands) are much keener to impose IFI-type conditions than are others (notably France and Italy). It is likely that requests from ACP states with close political relations with France, Italy or like-minded states will receive an easier passage than those closer to the UK.

CONCLUSIONS

There are at least three major difficult issues for Lomé IV. First, how should the EC address the practical and theoretical deficiencies in IFI structural adjustment lending? Second, what should be the position with respect to those ACP states that have not reached agreement with the IFIs? Third, how should the total aid package be distributed among states which have and have not reached an understanding with the IFIs?

The link with the IFIs

The notion of a comprehensive 'EC conditionality' does not appear to be a practical option. It is ruled out by the non-availability of any convincing ready-made alternative, by the non-existence of the necessary EC cadres, by the existence of at least some evidence that the approach of the IFIs is having beneficial effects and by the desirability of additional resources with which to co-finance IFI programmes.

Yet it is clearly desirable for the EC to make some input to the design of conditionality. The EC should seek to exert influence on the IFIs to correct the weaknesses that have been identified in order to strengthen the adjustment process and thereby to raise aid effectiveness.

This implies that the EC must be willing at least to invest sufficient additional resources in its own policy-analysis capabilities to be able to monitor and evaluate the policies of the IFIs, and to contribute on approximately equal terms to discussions with IFIs on aspects of conditionality, both generally and as it relates to specific ACP countries. This is likely to involve a much more substantial investment in new skills than appears to be envisaged within the Commission. Without this investment good intentions are likely to remain untranslated into practice.

It also implies that the modalities must exist through which its influence can be brought to bear on the IFIs – and here we wish explicitly to include the IMF – at both these levels. Some such devices already exist, e.g. informal consultations on early drafts of Fund-Bank Policy Framework Papers, meetings in Washington between Commission and member state officials, and attachments to Bank country missions. But we are not convinced that these yet meet the need. This matter needs to be taken up in the IFIs' policy-making bodies.

Allocation of aid

An implication of a fully-fledged shift into structural adjustment is that the EC would have to be willing to refuse credits to countries which did not negotiate an adjustment programme with the IFIs. A policy of supporting IFI adjustment programmes would not be very meaningful without this negative sanction.

But this is clearly an extremely difficult area for the EC. It would make a clear break with the philosophy and practice of the Lomé Convention if aid were to be withheld completely or in large part from ACP states that were at loggerheads with the IFIs. For this reason it is unlikely to happen in a formal way. But just as structural adjustment affects traditional aid, so the reverse is true. Because of fungibility, 'sectoral' import support under Lomé and even projects could be regarded with some justification by the IFIs as undermining their attempts to persuade governments to accept reform.

The EC will have to steer a delicate balance between promoting improvements in the processes of policy dialogue so as to increase the sense of programme 'ownership' by LDC governments and the temptation to 'take sides' in favour of those governments in disputes with IFIs. The logic of its position (as a representative of a major group of countries within the IFIs) is that the Commission will ultimately identify with the collective donor position whatever its initial intentions.

The EC's ability to link aid to negotiations with the IFIs will be most pronounced in relation to the structural adjustment fund that, unlike the country programmes, will not be pre-allocated at the start of the Convention to each state under its NIP. As the 'Special Programme for Africa' illustrated , the Commission has some discretion on the use to which funds outside of the NIPs are put. The existence of the separate fund gives the EC scope to apply negative pressure on those ACP states that are in disagreement with the IFIs by withholding access to a part of the aid to which they would otherwise have been entitled.

NOTES

1. The authors are, respectively, Research Fellow and Senior Research Fellow at the Overseas Development Institute, London.
2. This argument and the following paragraphs are based on Killick, 1989.
3. Stevens and Killick, 1989, provides a more extensive analysis of the World Bank report.

REFERENCES

ECA (1989), *African Alternative Framework*, E/ECA/CM/ 15/6/Rev.3 (Addis Ababa: Economic Commission for Africa).

EC (1987), COM (87) 418 final, 11 September, para 14 (Brussels: European Commission).

EC (1989), 1319th Council meeting – Development Co-operation – Presse 82–G; (Brussels: European Commission, 16 May).

Killick, T., (1987) 'Unsettled Questions about Adjustment with Growth', in UNCTAD, *International Monetary and Financial Issues for the Developing Countries* (New York: United Nations).

Killick, T., (1989) *A Reaction Too Far: Economic Theory and the Role of the State in Developing Countries* (London: Overseas Development Institute).

Parfitt, T., (1989) 'Lomé IV: The Convention of Structural Adjustment', *Lomé Briefing No 9* (Brussels: EC-NGO Liaison Committee, June).

Stevens C., and T. Killick, (1989) *Development Co-operation and Structural Adjustment: The Issues for Lomé IV* (London: Overseas Development Institute; Dublin: Trócaire, Centre for Development Research).

World Bank (1988), *Report on Adjustment Lending (R88–199)* (Washington: World Bank, 8 August).

World Bank (1989), *Africa's Adjustment, Recovery, and Growth: Trends and Perspectives in the 1980s* (Washington: World Bank).

2 New Trends in EC-ACP Relations: Lomé IV and Structural Adjustment[1]

Trevor W. Parfitt

In December 1989 the EC and sixty-seven African, Caribbean and Pacific states (the ACP) signed the fourth Lomé Convention in Togo. The Lomé trade and aid arrangements have become a firmly established element in North-South relations since their inception in 1975. One of the central benefits offered under the Lomé regime is concessional aid. Much of the funding disbursed by the European Development Fund (EDF) is in the form of grants and low interest loans. It also entails relatively low conditionality, the EDF's only stipulation being that it should be spent on EC goods and services.

However, this benefit has been put at risk in Lomé IV. The central innovation of the new convention is the introduction of further conditionality into Lomé aid in the form of 'structural adjustment' programmes (SAPs). This paper will assess how this is likely to affect the operation of the Lomé aid regime. Initially the curent operation of the Lomé Convention will be examined to determine how far it actually benefits the ACP. The Community's reasons for introducing SAPs into Lomé IV will also be addressed. After a brief review of the structural adjustment debate the paper will analyse how the EC is likely to implement SAPs and examine alternative policies.

LOMÉ AND A DECADE OF DECLINE

The Lomé Convention offers the ACP states various benefits. First, the ACP have tariff-free access to the EC market for all but a few of their goods which are covered by the Common Agricultural Policy (the EC is fond of pointing out that over 90 per cent of ACP goods can enter Europe tariff-free). There are also special arrangements to facilitate the sale of certain ACP goods on the European market, notably sugar and beef. The benefits of EC aid have already been mentioned. The aid allocation for Lomé I (running from 1975–80) was Ecu 3462 million, whilst that for Lomé II (1980–5) was Ecu 5409 million. The total aid package for Lomé III (1985–90) was agreed at Ecu 8500 million and the global allocation for the first five years of Lomé IV (1990–2000) was raised to Ecu 12 000 million (negotiations for new aid will take place in 1995). Most of this aid is administered by the EDF and as noted above it consists of grants and soft loans. Some 70 per cent of EDF finance takes the form of project aid that is allocated to the National Indicative Programmes (NIPs) for each of the ACP states (details from Commission of the European Communities, 1986a). At the beginning of each convention an EC mission visits each ACP state to agree its NIP (this is the 'programming process'). The amount of aid allocated to each state is decided by the EDF alone, this being a controversial issue. The remainder of 'non-programmed' EDF aid is divided amongst various mechanisms, including Stabex, which compensates ACP states for shortfalls in their export receipts from agricultural products. Under the terms of Lomé II a fund to compensate for declining mineral export receipts was introduced, this being Sysmin. Whereas Stabex provides monetary compensation (any EC currency), Sysmin provides support in the form of a project, which may be aimed at restoring productive capacity for the mineral affected or at economic diversification. Perhaps the major innovation of Lomé III was the use of a proportion of non-programmed aid (together with funding from other sources) to finance fast-disbursing Sectoral Import Programmes (SIPs) for the import of necessary inputs for a particular economic sector, whether it be agriculture or industry. These programmes will be discussed below.

Clearly, the Lomé regime presents the ACP with a comprehensive battery of aid mechanisms. Indeed, Lomé aid represents a substantial input into many ACP economies. A number of states are heavily dependent on Stabex funding, even to the point where it represents a substantial proportion of their recurrent budgets. Unfortunately, each mechanism has certain weaknesses. Under-funding is a central problem, particularly for Stabex. In 1980 and 1981 Stabex was unable to cover valid claims made by the ACP states (Parfitt, 1983). In 1980 the shortfall was Ecu 123 million, rising to a deficit of Ecu 341 million in 1981. The EC had to reduce payments to the claimant states in both years. One might argue that these were exceptionally bad years for the fund due to the recession, but it ran into problems again in 1987 when legitimate claims amounted to over Ecu 803 million, whilst Stabex could only find Ecu 375 million. This necessitated further reductions of the payments made by the fund. Furthermore, the per capita value of the total aid package has declined over the years. There was a 30.9 per cent drop between Lomé I and Lomé II and a 12.5 per cent fall between the second and the third conventions (European Report, 30 July 1988, pp. 4–6).

With regard to the programmed (predominantly project) aid the most common complaint is that the disbursement rate is slow. During Lomé I Hills estimated that the time taken from initial presentation of a project for consideration by the EDF to the commitment of funds varied from eight to sixteen months (Hills, 1978, p. 2). However, evidence from Sierra Leone suggests that the EDF is not exceptional in taking so long to process projects (Parfitt, 1989). Few aid agencies seem to distinguish themselves by the speed of their bureaucracy. It is rather more worrying to find that the EDF's bureaucracy appears to be slowing down. After five years of Lomé I the rates of commitment and disbursement were 88 per cent and 46 per cent respectively, whilst the same rates were 77 per cent and 43 per cent after five years of Lomé II (Commission of the European Communities, 1986a, pp. 18–19). It is thought that this trend has worsened under Lomé III. Sysmin seems particularly prone to problems of slow disbursement. By the end of Lomé II less than half the finance available had been allocated to projects, and commitment rates have been slow under the third convention also.

However, certain projects are complex to design and mount whilst others, notably those in the social sector, have a long lead time and need to have funding allocated to them over a period before they can be expected to start showing results. One such example is the EDF contribution to the rehabilitation of the health system in Chad after its virtual destruction during that nation's civil war. The EC allocated Ecu 10.1 million during Lomé II to finance the renovation of health centres, supply of essential medicines, development of maternity and infant care programmes and the establishment of health centres and dispensaries throughout the country (Commission of the European Communities, 1986a, p. 55). This will be a long-term programme by its very nature, but to the extent that it is well-designed and effeciently managed it could make an essential contribution to the well-being of the ordinary Chadian. Critics have pointed out that under Lomé I and II most aid was not spent on projects that would help people at the grass-roots of society, but on infrastructural and other large-scale ventures, which on the one hand satisfied the demands of ACP elites for prestige projects and on the other hand supplied EC businesses with lucrative contracts to supply services and inputs. However, this balance seems to have been redressed somewhat under Lomé III where the EC put an emphasis in the programming process on supporting the rural sector, particularly with a view to promoting self-sufficiency (though this was a controversial move given that the ACP group interpreted it as a first step towards imposing greater conditionality on Lomé aid).

Many commentators have argued that the Lomé trade regime is not actually as liberal as the EC likes to pretend. ACP exports to Europe have to surmount an array of non-tariff barriers. The Rules of Origin stipulate that no less than 50 per cent of the value added in ACP goods must have originated in the ACP states and/or the EC. Given that few ACP states have the capacity to produce industrial goods incorporating so much value added this is a disincentive to economic diversification (Ravenhill, 1985). Additionally, the 'Safeguard Clause' allows member states to make derogations from the guarantees of free access if their market is threatened. The EC asserts that this clause has never actually been used. This is correct. However, the United Kingdom used the threat of the clause to force Mauritius to conclude a voluntary export restraint agreement restricting its textile exports to the Community (Parfitt, 1981, p. 90). Indeed, the Community's trade concessions have not resulted in any increase in the ACP share of the European market, which actually declined by one-fifth in the decade after 1975 from 20.5 per cent to 16.6 per cent. However, this bleak overall picture is modified by Stevens' (1989) findings that up to twenty-eight ACP states have managed to diversify into production of some seventy new exports including wood and leather products, clothing and out of season vegetables. The value of these exports in 1987 was Ecu 826 million, or 6.9 per cent of all ACP non-fuel exports to the EC. Whilst this may be a small amount in absolute terms it represents substantial growth from a very small basis. Stevens' results suggest that the Lomé trade regime has been conducive to at least a limited process of diversification.

It might also be argued that the overall decline of the ACP share of the European market is not attributable to any shortcomings of the Lomé regime. The EC asserts that the Convention represents one of the most liberal trading regimes to be found anywhere, and despite the qualifications made above there is some merit in this claim. An alternative explanation is to be found in a study undertaken for the Commission by the Kiel University International Economics Institute in 1984. The Commission commented:

> The chief conclusion of the Kiel study is that the obstacles to expansion of ACP trade lie first and formost in the ACP countries themselves, since it is structural distortions in their economies which make their exports uncompetitive. On the whole, seeing that most ACP countries have been unable to profit from Lomé trade preferences, the Commission's services would agree with that view. (Commission of the European Communities, 1985, p. 13)

Amongst the distortions that the Kiel study identifies as central to ACP uncompetitiveness are overvalued exchange rates that retard export growth (particularly of primary commodities); protective barriers that featherbed inefficient import substitution industries whilst disadvantaging other sectors including agriculture; low interest rates and high wage rates which combine to divert investment into unproductive capital-intensive schemes and away from traditional exports in which the ACP states have a comparative advantage; and high inflation. These conclusions are similar to those of the influential 1981 World Bank report, *Accelerated Develop-*

ment in Sub-Saharan Africa (the Berg Report). This also focuses on overvalued exchange rates and tariff barriers as factors that distort African economies, and adds for good measure that public sectors have frequently become overextended and inefficient. The Berg Report has been central in the development of a donor consensus on the nature of Africa's economic malaise. To the extent that the EC has accepted the Kiel report it would be reasonable to perceive it as joining that broad consensus.

It is not the purpose of this paper to enter into a rigorous analysis of this consensus. However, it is worth noting that many observers would agree with elements of the Berg/Kiel analysis, particularly in recognising that African exchange rates have often been overvalued and that the public sector in many states is inefficient. Equally, it should be remembered that both the Berg and the Kiel analyses understate the influence of the depressed commodity markets of the eighties in precipitating Africa's crisis. Furthermore, many observers have reservations about the applicability of neoclassical analyses to the African context. The Commission itself noted of the Kiel study:

> The analysis is based on the theory of comparative advantage and a classic concept of the allocation of production factors by the laws of the market. While such an approach is widely accepted, one may query its ability to account successfully for all the economic mechanisms at work in the ACP states; in most of those countries some of the preconditions for the operation of a market, such as freedom of access, monetization or the untramelled movement of goods and information, are lacking and the regulatory action of the market is partial and imperfect. (1985, p. 12)

It is also worth remembering that the state has played a crucial role in the development of most, if not all of the advanced nations.

Notwithstanding its own reservations, the conclusions of the Kiel study have been widely accepted within the Commission (this is the author's impression on the basis of several interviews with Commission staff). To this extent it has joined a donor consensus on the nature of ACP (and particularly African) economic problems that has been largely shaped by the Washington institutions. Having accepted this consensus on the nature of the problem it followed that the Community was likely to accept the Bank/Fund strategy for solving (or at least managing) Africa's crisis, namely structural adjustment.

It might be thought that the Lomé tradition of low conditionality combined with the principle that the ACP should retain their 'acquis' (the rights and privileges that they have attained under previous Lomé Conventions) might constitute an obstacle to any imposition of structural adjustment conditionality. Indeed, this has limited the Community's room for manoeuvre (as we shall see). However, during the first two conventions the Community became convinced of the need for more conditionality. They were unhappy about the uses to which Stabex transfers were being put and wanted greater control over how ACP recipients could spend this aid (there was evidence that certain states had misused this funding). They also wanted more control over the type of project funded with EDF aid, and so they instituted what was termed a 'policy dialogue' during the programming exercise for Lomé III. This entailed putting pressure on ACP states to focus their aid on a particular sector, usually the rural sector. This was not entirely welcomed by the ACP, despite the fact that it can be seen as a productive move away from prestige projects to a more grass-roots oriented approach. The ACP feared that this was the thin end of the conditionality wedge, and that once they conceded to policy dialogue more conditions would follow. They may well have been right.

Although the Lomé Convention can be criticised, the ACP states have gained real benefits in the form of concessional aid and some degree of economic diversification. Having examined how the Community has moved towards the adoption of SAPs, the next section shall discuss what these policies are and comment on their effects.

SHOCK THERAPY OR JUST SHOCK?

The concept of structural adjustment is usually associated with the IMF and the World Bank which generally insist that before any country can draw on their assistance it must mount a SAP. These two organisations trace Third World economic problems to misguided internal policies, notably over-reliance on an interventionist state and maintenance of an over-valued exchange rate rather than reliance on the market. SAPs are designed to correct these tendencies by reorientating the Third World away from state-centred planning models towards a market strategy of development based on exporting the primary commodities in which they have a comparative advantage. Thus, IMF/Bank SAPs tend to focus on such measures as reduction of protective practices, tighter control of public spending to leave room for the private sector and devaluation to give an incentive to agriculture. Indeed, such measures have been central to many of the SAPs sponsored by the Bank and the Fund throughout Africa (see Killick and Stevens in this volume).

The debate on the efficacy of the SAPs reached an unprecedented pitch of fury with the publication of the World Bank/UNDP report, *Africa's Adjustment and Growth in the 1980s*, which elicited a furious response from the ECA (1989a). The Bank's report seeks to demonstrate that those

African states that have most consistently followed SAPs have experienced the beginnings of a recovery in the late eighties. They have experienced higher GDP growth, increased agricultural output and higher exports according to the Bank's statistics. The ECA attacks this argument by taking the same statistics and using them to argue that the so-called 'strongly reforming countries' have actually suffered an even steeper economic decline than that of countries which have been less assiduous in embracing SAPs. In a review of this debate Parfitt argues that both the Bank and the ECA use these statistics in a dubious manner (1990). However, it is notable that the Bank biases its sample of strong reformers by including certain countries that had not observed SAPs for much of the decade (e.g. Zaire, Nigeria, Tanzania), whilst excluding countries that had undertaken successive SAPs in the early eighties (e.g. Sierra Leone and Zambia). UNCTAD observes that the 'performance of the twelve LDCs (Least Developed Countries) which have had consecutive programmes throughout most of the 1980s does not differ significantly from that of the LDCs as a whole' (1989, p. 28). The Bank's evidence as to the efficacy of SAPs does not stand up to examination. Furthermore, UNICEF has found considerable evidence to suggest that deflationary SAPs have adversely affected the living standards and health of vulnerable groups, including women and children (e.g. Cornia *et al.*, 1987). It is for such reasons that Washington-sponsored SAPs have been criticised as 'shock' treatment. UNICEF and other organisations have proposed an alternative model of 'adjustment with a human face' that will operate on a gradualist basis and take account of the interests of vulnerable groups.

It is also worth questioning the assumption underlying the SAPs that the best development path for the Third World is to concentrate on exporting primary commodities. The IMF has forecast a fall in prices in 1990 and its tentative projection for the mid-1990s is of a small rise that is 'unlikely to be sufficient to improve in any appreciable way the terms of trade of those countries primarily dependent on exports of non-fuel primary commodities for their earnings of foreign exchange' (IMF Survey, 24 July 1989, p. 239). Stevens (1989) argues that long-term structural factors will tend to depress commodity prices. These include the decline of manufacturing in the OECD countries, technical changes leading to lower consumption of raw materials and the saturation of markets, which is partly due to the problem of 'fallacy of composition' (i.e. the Bank and the Fund simultaneously advise individual Third World states to maximise their output of the same raw materials, resulting in over-supply).

These points raise considerable doubts as to the effectiveness of SAPs in stimulating growth and development. The next section will analyse how the Community proposes to incorporate structural adjustment into the Lomé regime.

ADJUSTMENT WITH HUMAN RHETORIC . . .

It might be asked how the EC intends to implement SAPs. The central statement on this issue is the European Council Resolution of 31 May 1988. This states that SAPs should be adapted to the particular circumstances of each country, their impact on different social groups should be taken into account and they should be implemented at a rate that is compatible with the capacities and resources of each country. Such an approach would be quite different from the shock treatment administered by the IMF and the Bank. The Community has apparently endorsed a gradualist approach of adjustment with a human face.

It has also been suggested that the Community will coordinate its structural adjustment efforts on a regional basis. This is to be welcomed as it will enable the Community to avoid the 'fallacy of composition' problem by regional coordination of its SAPs to ensure that different ACP countries or groups are engaged in complementary rather than competing productive activities. Such coordination could also be used to promote intra-ACP trade with the EC helping states in one region to identify potential markets in another area of the ACP. However, it is unclear how this regional coordination will be implemented and the details of what it will mean in practice are yet to be defined by the Commission.

More reassuringly for the ACP states conditionality will not be directly applied to all Lomé aid. The EC-ACP Ministerial Negotiating Session held in Brussels from 3–5 June 1989 decided that 'the bulk of resources will remain "acquis" within the programming and the dialogue' (Commission of the European Communities, 1989, p. 6.). In other words, the preferences of those EC member states that would have liked to see all Lomé aid made subject to conditionality (such as the United Kingdom) have apparently been overriden. The traditional Lomé aid mechanisms, notably the EDF, will not be directly tied to SAPs. Such conditionality will be applied via a new aid facility worth only Ecu 1.15 billion. It will be responsible for the aforementioned SIPs to finance imports for particular economic sectors in the ACP states. The facility may also finance General Import Programmes (GIPs) to cover general ACP needs for essential imports. The decision to apply conditionality only to this new facility seems to preserve the principle that the 'acquis' should be left intact.

However, the Community envisages that EDF aid, inclusive of Stabex, will be used in support of SAPs. It has been suggested within the Commission that up to 20 per cent of traditional programmable aid might be diverted in this way. Whilst this arrangement may add a valuable element of flexibility to the working of the Lomé aid programme, it may also lead to problems. The heavily indebted ACP states may well be tempted to maximise the amount of finance they can obtain in the form of the quick disbursing funding that will accompany the SAPs. This will be especially the case if the Community goes ahead with its plans for the introduction of GIPs which can be used to finance any imports deemed economically necessary to the ACP recipient. The Commission is all too likely to accept this situation in view of its anxiety to encourage the ACP to embark on what it sees as an essential process of economic restructuring. To the extent that this represents a growing trend towards making Lomé aid into quick disbursing finance there is a danger that long-term developmental priorities (e.g. social development as represented by the Chadian health project) could be forgotten. This raises the question as to how far SIPs, and especially GIPs, can be integrated into a long-term development strategy. It would be most unfortunate if increasing proportions of EC funding were to be spent on relieving short-term import needs (e.g. for petroleum) without helping to stimulate the development that could enable the ACP states to earn the foreign exchange to pay for such imports in the future.

The obvious way of reconciling ACP needs for short-term relief and long-term development would have been to ensure that the SAP facility was sufficiently funded to satisfy the majority of ACP demands for quick disbursing aid without drawing on the traditional facilities. However, the new facility is miniscule at Ecu 1.15 billion (Ecu 1.2 = US \$1 at 2 February 1990). The inadequacy of this sum can be gauged from a recent World Bank estimate that Africa will need a net transfer of US \$22 billion per year by 2000 (World Bank, 1989b, pp. 13–4).

This raises the question as to how these limited funds will be divided amongst the ACP states. The EC has specified certain eligibility criteria for its SAPs. The Commission will have to be satisfied as to 'the size and sustainability of the process of reform and adjustment undertaken by the ACP State concerned'. It will also take into account

the ACP State's economic situation, assessed in a flexible way, using indicators such as the level of development, the debt burden, balance of payments difficulties, the budget of the state and of the public sector, monetary and fiscal policies, the rate of inflation, dependence on commodity imports and the degree of poverty (Commission of the European Communities, 1989, p. 7).

ACP representatives at the Lomé IV negotiations were unhappy with this criterion because it indicated that certain categories amongst the ACP states could be denied SAP funding on economic grounds. The ACP side wanted to ensure that all states should have equal access to SAP funding irrespective of whether they are middle-income or lower-income countries. However, it is difficult to see how this could be achieved given the limited finance that is available. Consequently, it is not surprising to find that the EC member states and the Commission are in agreement that only certain states will be given SAPs, although they have not given any more detailed elaboration of the criteria to qualify for such aid.

. . . BUT A LESS HUMAN PRACTICE?

It is doubtful whether the Community will have the political will and the capacity to develop its own model of structural adjustment. Commission representatives stress that whilst they will coordinate their support for SAPs with the IMF and the World Bank, this will not detract from the humane and gradualist nature of the EC approach to structural adjustment. Indeed, it is implicit in the statements of some officials in DG8 that the Community can play a role in moving the Washington institutions towards adopting such a model of adjustment. Such an outcome would be very desirable, but there are reasons for doubting that it can be achieved. Firstly, Stevens and Killick (see their paper in this volume) observe that the Commission lacks the macro-economic expertise to influence the Washington institutions in any discussions aimed at aid coordination. Secondly, the EC lacks the economic clout to influence the Bank and the Fund. The Community has allocated Ecu 1.15 billion to finance SAPs during the first five years of Lomé IV, whilst the World Bank Group contributed some US $2 billion per year to Africa over 1986–7. One might reasonably expect that the larger donors will have the final say in deciding what kind of conditionality should be attached to aid.

It is also well known that certain member states, notably the United Kingdom and Holland, want the EC to stay fairly close to the Washington line on adjustment. There is evidence to suggest that such states are endeavouring to ensure that the Commission is not given too much latitude to develop its 'fanciful' ideas about adjustment. The European Council Resolution of 16 May 1989 stresses the need for effective coordination between the member states and the Commission on adjustment, but apparently the United Kingdom insisted that the minutes of the Council meeting include the qualification that this be done 'as far as possible' (Bullock, 1989, p. 51). Clearly, this represents an escape route from the commitment to adhere to a more humane model of adjustment.

Those states that wish to observe the Washington orthodoxy seem willing to use their influence on the Programming and EDF Committees (the former plays a major part in formulating each ACP state's NIP, whilst the latter takes the final decision on whether or not to finance any project submitted for consideration to the EDF by the ACP) and the Development Council to obstruct projects and programmes that stray too far from the straight and narrow path of *laissez-faire* virtue. Such was evidently the case with regard to a SIP for Tanzania worth Ecu 24.5 million. When the programme was submitted to the EDF Committee in September 1988 West

Germany, the United Kingdom and Holland blocked it on the grounds that Tanzania had failed to reach agreement with the IMF about how much it should devalue its currency, this being an element of the conditionality attached to a Fund programme then under negotiation. In fact this disagreement was the result of a technical misunderstanding between Tanzania and the IMF which the parties were in the process of settling. The Commission had to approach the World Bank to establish that this was the case, upon which West Germany withdrew its opposition to the programme. Consequently, the United Kingdom and Holland no longer had sufficient votes to hold up the programme and it was unblocked in November 1988 (Bullock, 1989, pp. 30–3). Whilst the SIP was only held up for a brief period, it is significant that several member states were so eager to tie EC aid to IMF conditionality that they did not even pause to establish the exact circumstances under which the Tanzanian disagreement with the Fund had occurred. Thus they contrived to punish Tanzania not so much for failing to observe the Washington line as for having the temerity to have misunderstood its finer details. It is worth noting that the EC member states' blocking power is not restricted to the funding designated for SAPs. Through their power on the Programming and EDF Committees they have the power to block any EDF project. This could well prove to be a mechanism for covertly introducing conditionality to all Lomé aid through the back door.

The Community's current approach to conditionality gives further reason to fear that in fact EC aid will be made contingent on following Fund/Bank 'shock' programmes. There has been a tendency for the EC to link the SIPs granted under Lomé III to Washington conditionality. The then UK Secretary of State for Commonwealth and Foreign Affairs, Mr Patten, revealed on 4 April 1989 (in answer to a parliamentary question from Mr A. Bennett, MP) that out of a total of twenty-five SIPs agreed with the ACP states thus far, seven had been explicitly linked to Fund/Bank SAPs, whilst many others had been in support of such programmes, although there was no explicit linkage. This leaves some doubt as to whether or not the latter group of SIPs would be suspended in the event of ACP non-compliance with Fund/Bank conditionality. However, a Commission Memorandum on SIPs states: 'Without creating any formal link between such [Fund/Bank] programmes and SIPs, their existence or the fact that one is being negotiated should be taken into consideration when deciding whether or not to finance a SIP' (Commision of the European Communities, 1986b, p. 5). It would seem that ACP states have to show willingness to accept IMF/Bank conditionality in order to obtain a SIP.

One can gauge what this means for the ACP states from the example of the SIP to finance industrial product imports into Malawi. This programme was made conditional on the World Bank-sponsored Industry and Trade Policy Adjustment Programme (ITPAC), which stipulates that the

Malawian Government must take such measures as reduction of the fiscal deficit, flexible exchange rate management, reduction of protection, price decontrol and a tax reform aimed at shifting the burden of taxation from international trade and production to domestic purchases and consumption. Essentially, this is a fairly typical Fund/Bank austerity programme. It may be noted that the Malawian people will have to endure the rigours of this programme at a time when their living standards have already been eroded by deteriorating export crop prices and commodity price rises. The latter have been caused by the activities of the South African-backed Mozambique National Resistance, which has sabotaged Malawi's rail link to the Mozambican port Nacala, thus raising transport costs. None of this is suggestive of the gradualist and flexible approach to structural adjustment advocated in the European Council's May 1988 Resolution. No account seems to have been taken of the very particular difficulties caused to Malawi by South African destabilisation. Indeed, there is nothing to indicate that the EC tried to influence the Bank to take a more nuanced approach. Even more remarkably, the Commission accepted the ITPAC as the basis on which the SIP should be disbursed before it was finally agreed. In the Financing Proposal for the SIP it was noted that the conditionality stipulated by the Bank was indicative (Commission of the European Communities, 1988). Not only did the Commission uncritically accept Bank conditionality as the basis for its own programme, it did so without actually knowing what form that conditionality would finally take. This raises fears that EC rhetoric about gradualist conditionality will prove to be an unconvincing mask for a slavish observance of the Fund/Bank model of structural adjustment.

To the extent that the Community actually links itself to the Washington line on conditionality it seems all too likely that it may also take on board the ideological baggage associated with those institutions. Hitherto, the EC has been largely apolitical in determining how its aid is to be distributed, making no obvious distinctions between regimes of the left, right or centre. The Washington institutions are not troubled by such scruples. The Bank in particular has denied aid to various leftist states, including Nicaragua, Vietnam, Allende's Chile and Mengistu's Ethiopia. Often it has acted under duress from the US administration of the day. By linking itself too rigidly to conditionality that is decided in Washington the Community will not only be committing itself to a 'shock' model of adjustment that it purports to disagree with, but also making Lomé aid into yet another foreign-policy tool for the United States.

Certain EC member states may not be dismayed by the idea of linking Lomé aid to US foreign policy, to the extent that it means opposition to left-wing regimes. However, they should bear in mind the fact that US intervention in Bank/Fund conditionality has not always been aimed at directing miscreant states back onto the path of *laissez-faire* righteousness.

Indeed, the Reagan and Bush administrations have exerted considerable influence on the IMF to protect Zaire from the worst rigours of structural adjustment despite the Mobutu regime's unrivalled reputation for corruption and economic mismanagement. Mobutu's status as one of America's most reliable allies in Africa has won him considerable latitude in the sphere of economic policy. The influence of the Bush administration helped to win him a new agreement with the IMF (signed on 9 June 1989) despite the fact that reports by the Fund and the Bank show that between US $300–400 million were misappropriated from Zaire's export receipts in 1988 (*Africa Analysis*, 23 June 1989, p. 3). Significantly, the announcement of Mobutu's agreement with the IMF was closely followed by an EC decision to award Zaire a SIP. It seems all too possible that the Community has simply endorsed a licence granted in Washington enabling Mobutu and his cronies to continue in the systematic plunder of their country.

STRUCTURAL ADJUSTMENT OR TRANSFORMATION?

It is the contention of this paper that the EC is in danger of turning down a blind alley in making Lomé IV the convention of structural adjustment. At worst, the Commission's lack of experience in dealing with structural adjustment and its lack of weight in negotiations with the Washington institutions will lead the Community simply to follow the line currently set by the Fund and the Bank. The arguments outlined above provide grounds for concluding that this will indeed be the case. There is of course a more optimistic scenario in which the Community will help to provide the impetus to push the Washington institutions towards a more humane model of adjustment with a human face.

This still leaves a question-mark over whether or not a free market strategy based on encouraging the ACP to rely on their traditional primary commodity exports will stimulate the economic diversification so badly needed by those states. It therefore seems reasonable to argue that if the Community is genuinely concerned about ACP development it might consider moving beyond the concept of adjustment and adopting a structural tranformation strategy as advocated by the ECA (1989b). The essence of such a strategy would be to combine elements of traditional adjustment policy with initiatives designed to diversify Third World economies. Thus, it would entail modifying (though not entirely dispensing with) some of the measures advocated by the Fund and the Bank such as devaluation, public sector cuts, reliance on traditional imports, credit squeezes and doctrinaire privatisation. Amongst the measures aimed at development and diversification are the following: diversion of government spending from the military and from all parastatals other than those in the social sector to the agrarian and social sectors; development of the rural infrastructure and of human capital through this increased social and rural spending; investment codes to help small industries; selective trade policies to tax conspicuous consumption; differential export subsidies and incentives for processed goods and carefully-chosen primary commodities; sectoral allocation of credit to benefit food and other productive sectors; limitation of debt service ratios to levels consistent with continued growth; and bilateral and multilateral commodity agreements. Through such measures traditional sectors would be maintained whilst new ones were developed.

Detractors might argue that all the ECA has done is draw up a rather ambitious shopping list of policy objectives that lack overall cohesion. However, the ECA proposal confronts a central issue in arguing that democratic reforms are essential to African economic recovery and advocating the promotion of popular political participation. Parfitt and Riley (1989) argue that one of the central factors in creating the environment that allowed many African states to misallocate and misappropriate public funds at will has been a lack of governmental accountability to the people. An extension of political participation to the majority of the people is the most effective safeguard against the wasteful policies that have helped to impoverish many African countries. Rather than attempting to minimise the state's economic involvement as the Washington institutions attempt to do, the ECA has recognised that it should be reformed, enabling it to play its necessary role in economic development. However, it is essential that any reforms should allow a genuine voice for the grass-roots in policy-making, thus providing an effective restraint on governing elites.

The role that the EC might play in a structural transformation strategy has been elaborated by ex-ACP Secretary-General Carrington. The key-note in EC activity would be to assist ACP economic diversification by enhancing most of the Lomé trade and aid facilities. Notwithstanding the liberalism of the trade regime, modification of the value-added provision of the Rules of Origin (i.e. lowering the 50 per cent minimum) would provide an impetus to the diversification process identified by Stevens. Similarly, Stabex could be extended to cover some processed as well as primary commodities. Thus, it might be revised to cover cocoa paste and butter as well as cocoa. This would encourage agro-industrial diversification. Sysmin already includes a clause enabling recipients to use its aid for diversification, but disbursement rates are so low that in practice this has had no impact. However, the EC intends to speed up the working of Sysmin and this will enhance its efficacy in assisting countries like Zambia in their attempts at diversification.

A central part of any structural transformation strategy must involve direct aid and assistance to achieve industrial development in the ACP states. The EC made guarantees of such assistance as early as Lomé I. However, they were never put into practice. The Centre for Industrial

Development (CID) remains under-funded in the context of Lomé IV and is very much a poor relation of DG8. Whilst it has done some good work, it has never been able to stimulate any substantial amount of private investment in the ACP states. Ex-ACP Secretary-General Carrington has noted that the European Investment Bank (EIB) has a lamentable record of investment in the ACP states, having placed only one-third of Ecu 600 million over a five-year period, whilst the African Development Bank invested US $1 billion over a similar period. Clearly, the CID and the EIB must play a much enhanced role in ACP development. The CID should be strengthened so that it can play its role of mobilising private investment in the ACP. The EIB for its part could help in this task by entering into joint ventures with private capital. The Commission could play a valuable role by helping the ACP to provide incentives for private investers.

However, there are risks entailed in this development path. There is evidence that influential forces within the EC have promulgated a strategy for a limited form of ACP diversification within a context of European economic control. This strategy stems from the Eurafrican idea of promoting a model of EC-African relations based on the exchange of European processed commodities for African primaries. Most commentators are agreed that the Yaounde Conventions that preceded Lomé I were based on this model. However, by the mid-seventies a feeling was abroad that the old Eurafrican order was no longer viable. The OPEC price hike and the subsequent primary commodity boom had radicalised broad sections within the Third World who increased their demands for assistance in diversifying their economies. The industrialised states had been made all too aware that their resource dependence on the Third World gave the latter considerable potential leverage. It was necessary to make some response that would defuse these demands. Europe's response was to adapt the Eurafrican model to accomodate a limited and European controlled process of diversification in the ACP signatories of Lomé I. Influential forces within the EC began to advocate a development strategy based on the transfer of the intermediate branches of European industry to the ACP states, whilst European business diversified into the more profitable high technology branches of production. The ACP development process was to be fuelled by European capital and inputs.

The imprint of this Eurafrican idea can be seen in various aspects of the Lomé regime. The Rules of Origin can be seen as serving a dual purpose. As we have noted the 50 per cent minimum puts limits on any autocentred process of ACP diversification. However, the cumulative clause in the Rules encourages ACP cooperation with European capital (as opposed to Japanese or American capital) by allowing work done in the Community to count in determining whether or not a commodity complies with the conditions for free entry. We have also seen that the 'Safeguard Clause' enables the EC to protect the European market from ACP goods if it deems such action necessary. The EDF has always practiced a policy of refusing to fund industrial projects because it sees this sector as the province of private capital. Rather than giving direct aid to industry, the Community hoped to use the CID as a device for identifying opportunities for European capital in the ACP states.

The Eurafrican development strategy would certainly result in a limited form of ACP development, but Europe would still occupy a superior niche in the international division of labour. The Community would maintain control of the high-profit advanced industries and ACP development would be either directly dependent on European capital, or reliant on European inputs. Thus, the EC hoped to maintain its privileged economic position in the ACP states. In fact, a full-blooded Eurafrican strategy was never implemented partly due to opposition from such forces as the European textile industry, which was not willing to relocate to the ACP states, or diversify. Perhaps a more decisive factor was the onset of international recession, which had the dual effect of making ACP states less attractive economically just as European investors were becoming less willing to take risks. (See Parfitt, 1987 for a full explication of the Eurafrican argument.)

Notwithstanding these points, it can be seen how easily the Eurafrican enterprise could be grafted on to a development path based on structural tranformation. The aim of increased European investment in the ACP states is at the centre of both strategies. Most ACP governments would welcome the prospect of a European multinational opening a branch or a factory in their country. Indeed, one might argue that the Eurafrican ideal would deliver substantive benefits to the ACP states in such forms as enhanced employment, some transfer of technology and an increase in receipts for the state from taxes, etc. (However, the last two must be regarded as dubious given that any enterprise that was set up in the ACP under Eurafrican terms would almost certainly be based on low technology, and would also expect to be accorded the battery of tax and other concessions that Northern capital is able to command throughout most of the Third World.) What Eurocentred development would notably fail to do is give the ACP states any measure of control in the development process.

The latter point enables us to identify crucial lines of distinction between the two strategies. Whereas the Eurafrican model utilises such devices as the Rules of Origin and the Safeguard Clause to block any autocentric process of ACP development, the stress of the transformation strategy is to create the conditions for such development. Thus, it entails such measures as lowering the 50 per cent minimum in the Rules of Origin and extending the coverage of Stabex to processed products in order to facilitate ACP diversification. Rather than relying solely on the CID to mobilise funds for industrial investment, a transformation strategy would entail a more active role for the EIB and the EDF, involving direct investment in industry. Perhaps the central difference between these two development paths is in the role that they envisage for European capital. Whereas the Eurocentric model involves the maintenance of European control, with ACP development taking place directly under the tutelage of European multinational capital, the emphasis of the transformation model is on joint ventures between EC and ACP businessmen and on facilitating the emergence of an ACP business sector that has its own dynamic of development. An initial move towards the latter goal might involve improving the capacity of the CID to undertake tasks such as transfer of technology and the preparation of feasibility, or market identification studies for ACP businesses. In short, the obstacles that the Eurafrican strategy places in the path of any auto-centred development would be disposed of under the transformation model. Instead, measures would be taken to encourage such development.

It might be asked why EC member states would undertake the substantial investment entailed in a policy of structural transformation aimed at least in part at emancipating the ACP states from European economic dominance. In fact it can be argued that structural transformation will not only benefit the ACP states, but also the EC. It is worth remembering that SAPs designed to trim Third World balance of payments deficits have resulted in the stagnation of Western exports to that area. The *Economist* (1 October 1988, p. 95) has pointed out that in 1987 OECD exports to the less developed countries (LDCs) amounted to US $300 billion down from a peak of US $386 billion in 1980, a decline that was attributed in part to the adoption of austerity policies by the LDCs. R. H. Green notes that in current dollar terms Africa's imports have fallen every year since 1981 and that 'Africa's share of total Third World imports has dropped by almost one-third' (Green, 1988). It is not surprising therefore to find that over the period of Lomé EC exports to the ACP have nosedived, falling in value from Ecu 19.3 million in 1985 to Ecu 16 million in 1986 and then to a low of Ecu 13.8 million in 1987 (Eurostat, External Trade; Monthly Statistics, 3, 1988, p. 4 and p. 53). Indeed, Green characterises Africa's crisis as an 'import strangulation' crisis. The nations of SSA are unable to import essential inputs for industry and agriculture due to the interaction of two factors, the first being their poor export performances, which are to a considerable extent attributable to stagnant markets for their goods. The squeeze on foreign exchange caused by this factor is exacerbated by their unmanageable debt burdens, which most African states are unable to service. The resultant inability to import inputs causes declining output, which reinforces the downward trend in African exports, thereby worsening the foreign exchange situation and further depressing the capacity to import. Thus import strangulation takes the form of a vicious circle of stagnation. A structural transformation strategy has the potential to reverse this tendency. By assisting the ACP states to boost their exports not only of primaries, but also of industrial goods, the EC will be helping to relieve the squeeze on foreign exchange that prevents the ACP from obtaining the inputs necessary to fuel their development. To the extent that this enhances ACP demand for European goods and services it will also be of benefit to the EC. In this sense structural transformation is not an act of charity, but a strategy for mutual EC-ACP development.

Nor would the EC be completely isolated in supporting such a strategy. As the debate on structural adjustment has worn on, a school of thought has apparently emerged within the World Bank that doubts whether adjustment policies can solve the problems of Africa. This viewpoint is reflected in a Bank report entitled *Beyond Adjustment: Towards sustainable growth with equity in sub-Saharan Africa*. Amongst its recommendations are support for the informal sector in order to boost industry and net financial transfers of US $20 billion per year by 2000. Progressives within the Community that want to influence the Washington institutions to adopt a more humane development policy may well find that the best contribution they can make is to try and move the EC beyond the dubious panacea of adjustment and towards structural transformation. By allying itself to an existing school of thought within the Bank the EC would enhance its chances of exerting some influence to moderate the neo-classical hegemony that currently holds sway in Washington. There are forces in the Community that would resist such an initiative, not least Thatcherite Britain. However, the active pan-European development lobby that has coalesced around the EC can help progressive elements in the European Parliament and the Commission to move EC policy towards a sympathetic stance to structural transformation. In this way the Community might make a positive contribution to the development of a more progressive community of ideas.

NOTE

The research for this paper was funded by a grant from the Nuffield Foundation for which the author would like to express his gratitude. Thanks are also due to Sandy Bullock who generously shared his research findings with the author and Colin Stoneman who was most helpful in obtaining copies of ECA documentation.

REFERENCES

Bullock, S., (1989) 'Structural Adjustment and Conditionality in European Community Aid to Sub-Saharan Africa: The Record of Lomé 3 and the Prospects for Lomé 4' MA dissertation submitted to the University of East Anglia.

Commission of the European Communities, (1985) *Study by the Kiel University International Economics Institute of the impact of and prospects for EEC-ACP relations in the field of trade and trade policy: Summary and comments* (Brussels: European Commission).

Commission of the European Communities, (1986a) *Ten Years of Lomé: A Record of EEC-ACP Partnership 1976–1985* (Brussels: European Commission).

Commission of the European Communities, (1986b) *Memorandum: Sectoral import programmes under Lomé 3* (Brussels: European Commission).

Commission of the European Communities, (1988) *Financing Proposal: Special Community Programme to Aid Certain Highly Indebted Low Income Countries in Sub-Saharan Africa: Programme for Industrial Products Imports, Republic of Malawi* (Brussels: European Commission).

Commission of the European Communities, (1989) *Ministerial Negotiating Session (Brussels, 3–5 June 1989), Ministerial Group 'C': Structural Adjustment, EC Statement* (Brussels: European Commission).

Cornia, G. A., et al, (1987) *Adjustment with a Human Face*, 2 vols (Oxford: University Press).

Economic Commission for Africa, (1989a) *Statistics and Policies: ECA Preliminary Observations on the World Bank Report 'Africa's Adjustment and Growth in the 1980s'* (Addis Adaba: ECA).

Economic Commission for Africa, (1989b) *African Alternative to Structural Adjustment Programmes (AA-SAP): A Framework for Transformation and Recovery* (Addis Adaba: ECA).

Green, R. H., (1988) 'The Lomé's in economic context; Whither now?', *Lomé Briefing*, No. 1.

Hills, J., (1978) 'The European Development Fund; Proposals for the Renegotiation' in CIIR, *The Renegotiation of the Lomé Convention: A Collection of Papers*, (London/Dublin: CIIR/TROCAIRE).

Parfitt, T. W., (1981) 'The Lomé Convention and the New International Economic Order', *Review of African Political Economy*, 22.

Parfitt, T. W., (1983) 'The First Lomé Convention and its Effects on Sierra Leone', PhD thesis, University of Manchester.

Parfitt, T. W., (1987) 'Equals, Clients, or Dependents? ACP Relations with the EC Under the Lomé Convention', *Journal of Modern African Studies*, 25, (4).

Parfitt, T. W., (1989) 'Tested to Destruction? An evaluation of aid effectiveness in Sierra Leone's agricultural sector' in *Sustainable Agriculture in Africa: Workshop proceedings and selected papers from the CAAS meeting*, University of Alberta, 1987, Vol. 2 (Africa World Press).

Parfitt, T. W., and S. P. Riley, (1989) *The African Debt Crisis* (London and New York: Routledge).

Parfitt, T. W., (1990) 'Lies, Damned Lies and Statistics: The ECA – World Bank Debate on Structural Adjustment', *Review of African Political Economy*, 47.

Ravenhill, J., (1985) *Collective Clientelism; the Lomé Conventions and North-South Relations*, (New York: Columbia University Press).

Stevens, C., (1988) 'The Lessons from Lomé 3', *Lomé Briefing*, 2.

Stevens, C., (1989) 'Commodity Prices in the 1980s; a decade of decline for the ACP's *The Courier*, 116.

UNCTAD, (1989) *Trade and Development Report* (New York: United Nations).

World Bank (with UNDP), (1989a) *Africa's Adjustment and Growth in the 1980s*, (Washington: World Bank).

World Bank, (1989b) *Sub-Saharan Africa: From Crisis to Sustainable Growth* (Washington: World Bank).

3 African Debt Crisis and the IMF Adjustment Programmes: the Experiences of Ghana, Nigeria and Zambia

Razaq A. Adefulu

INTRODUCTION

The recent crises in Africa's political economy, and the uneasy relationship between the bulk of these countries and the Bretton Woods financial institutions, backed by the Group of Seven (G7) industrialised countries have spawned interesting debates over the linkage between the G7-dominated capitalist world economy (CWE) and the development process in the 'peripheral' African countries.

There are three interrelated issues currently confronting the political economy of the fifty odd independent states of Sub-Saharan Africa (SSA). The first is the external debt issue. This has assumed crisis proportions because Africa's external debt has been rising rapidly in recent years. While there are variations in statistics depicting the stock of Africa's debt, a report in the *Africa Recovery* (December 1989, p. 16) has suggested that SSA debt 'rose to an estimated $143.2 billion in 1989'. In the same year, North Africa's debt was $101.4 billion, implying a total debt for Africa of some $245 billion in 1989 compared with $241 billion in 1988.

At the OAU-organised African debt seminar held in Cairo in August 1989, it was revealed that the continent's debt and debt burden will continue to rise in the 1990s. Figures released at the end of the seminar showed that Africa's total debt in 1987 was $203.1 billion. Debt servicing as a percentage of exports was 40.6 per cent in that year. By 1995, Africa's debt is expected to have risen to some $605.2 billion, while its debt servicing as a percentage of exports would have risen to 89.5 per cent (see Table 3.1).

The second issue facing Africa is related to the ongoing structural adjustment programmes (SAP). These programmes, which have already been adopted by some thirty African countries, were in most cases initiated with the support/approval of the Bretton Woods institutions, viz: the

TABLE 3.1   *Africa's rising debt burden**

	Debt ($ bn)	Debt service ($ bn)	Debt as % of GNP	Debt servicing % of exports
1987	203.1	20.2	82.4	40.6
1995	605.2	65.1	167.5	89.5
2005	1 496.8	168.7	293.9	163.3

* 22 countries.

SOURCE: *Africa Recovery*, Vol. 3, No. 3 (December 1989), p. 17.

International Monetary Fund (IMF) and the World Bank. They have entailed macro economic policy reforms including, *inter alia*: adjustment of the currency exchange rates of most African countries; freezing of public sector wages; reduction or total removal of subsidies; privatisation of public enterprises; and trade liberalisation (Umanna, 1987, p. 45). Few analysts would disagree with the view that Africa's 'disarticulated' economies are overdue for fundamental restructuring, and that SAP would probably accelerate the process of rational allocation of productive resources in the short term. But many would dispute the supposedly beneficial impacts of current programmes on standards of living, long term growth and development in Africa, south of the Sahara.

The third issue which flows from the above is the question of economic and political developments in Africa in an era of declining growth, poverty, and quasi-authoritarianism pervading the length and breadth of the continent. On the economic front, Africa is 'still struggling' to reduce its rising population, provide food security, increase the growth of its overall GDP, and increase the per capita income of its peoples (World Bank, 1989, pp. xi–xii; UN, 1990, p. 69). At the political level, there are demands for reforms to enhance the establishment of representative governments and institutions accountable to the people. Hence, in Africa, the crucial political issue for the 1990s is that of establishing 'good governance' defined in terms of 'a public service that is efficient, a judicial system that is reliable, and an administration that is accountable to the public' (World Bank, 1989, p. xii).

These three problematic issues of development have been variously analysed, and competing development scenarios have been advanced from two distinct political economy perspectives which we prefer to label as the *liberal* and *Marxian* perspectives.[2] It is against this background that this chapter analyses the current crises in Africa's political economy. The chapter begins with a brief outline of the presumed causes of African debt crisis, proceeding to examine the controversial SAP. A review of the competing analyses of the effects of SAP leads us to a comparative analysis of the structural adjustment experiences of three SSA countries, namely Ghana, Nigeria and Zambia. The overall objective here is to highlight the market-orientated development philosophy underpinning the IMF/World Bank policies in Africa, and the peoples' reactions to them.

PERSPECTIVES ON THE AFRICAN DEBT CRISIS

There have been competing analyses of the causal factors responsible for African debt. From the liberal analytical standpoint, which sees the goal of orderly development as the 'promotion and protection of negative free-dom',[3] (McKinlay and Little, 1986, p. 24) and the structural arrangements for achieving this goal as being necessarily based on private enterprise and the individual's freedom to enter voluntarily into exchange transactions, the root of African debt crisis has been traced to the negative effects of massive state involvement in the development process.

The sub-Saharan economy, according to liberal analyses,[4] was buoyant in the first decade of independence with a 3.8 per cent average annual growth rate of GDP being recorded in the period 1960–70 (World Bank, 1984, p. 58). External debt service as a percentage of GDP was 1.2 per cent in 1970, while in the same year (1970), external debt as a percentage of exports of sub-Saharan goods and services stood at 5.1 per cent (World Bank, 1984, p. 69). These trends continued well into the early 1970s.

Between 1974 and 1984, however, the African economy was plagued with a number of internal problems which contributed to the debt crisis of the 1980s. First, the commodity boom of the 1970s created a false sense of security. With increased revenues from oil and non-oil primary exports, Sub-Saharan Africa, in the liberals' view, embarked on ambitious development programmes involving high public expenditures, often on non-viable projects such as 'large conference centres, administrative buildings, university centres, hotels, highways' which are known to have little or no economic return (World Bank, 1984, p. 24). Some of these projects, according to the World Bank study, were undertaken purely 'on the basis of political prestige or on the basis of inadequate regard for their likely economic and financial rates of return' (World Bank, 1984, p. 24). Indeed, 'pure' liberals have argued that foreign economic aid to the poor countries of Africa (and particularly those in debt) is unnecessary because 'much aid goes to support projects and programmes which do not promote development' (Bauer and Yamey, 1983, p. 10). With the burst of the commodity boom, most African governments, reluctant to reduce public expenditure, resorted to borrowing from external sources, especially from commercial banks in Europe and North America, and also from the Eurodollar markets where financial transactions are unregulated.

Secondly, natural disasters, especially the prolonged drought, frustrated the production of Africa's main export commodities – cocoa, coffee, sisal, and lumber – between 1977 and 1983. Export volumes declined and this meant a substantial fall in export receipts. However, import volumes continued to grow, creating trade imbalances for most African countries in the 1980s. In Cote d'Ivoire, for example, one study reveals that the period 1978–80 was 'characterised by a slow-down in exports [while] the continuation of investment necessitated massive external borrowing, resulting in the sharp rise of outstanding debt from $2423 million in 1978 to $4986 million in 1980, an increase of more than 100 per cent' (Quattara, 1986, p. 1096).

Thirdly, the decline in per capita food production between 1981 and 1983 created the need for food imports which added to Africa's debt burden. Thus, 'the accelerated pace of food imports in 1980–82 suggests that agricultural growth may have been over-estimated. Cereal imports totalled 9.24 million tons in 1982, implying that one in five people in sub-Saharan Africa (an equivalent of its entire urban population) is now fed by imports' (World Bank, 1984, p. 10).

Finally, the decline in investment returns due to 'poor climate, soil, rapid population growth and poor standards of health, education and institutional development' (World Bank, 1984, p. 24), coupled with ill-informed macro economic policies, aggravated the decline in the growth of per capita GDP. This, in the face of accelerating consumption, created balance-of-payments deficits largely financed with external borrowing. As the World Bank (1988a, p. xix) put it:

> Slow growth, as a result of extremely difficult natural circumstances, often compounded by poor economic policies and depressed commodity prices, played a major role in the early emergence of debt problems in Africa.

Such are the liberals' descriptions of the causes of SSA's debt. To the extent that post-colonial African states and their public sectors have played major roles in the economy, liberal scholars and institutions argue that the current debt problems are a direct consequence of inflexible state intervention in economic management. In order to solve these problems and revive Africa's ailing economies, they have prescribed rigorous adjustment policies aimed at minimising the role of the state.

Still on the origins of African debt crisis, there is also an alternative explanation offered by neo-Marxian and non-Marxian scholars and institutions.[5] From this alternative standpoint, the organising goal of a coherent development strategy for Africa is conceived in terms of 'equality', and the structural arrangements for achieving such a goal must be based on the 'reconstitution of the economic base of the society' (McKinlay and Little, 1986, p. 57). Thus, the root of African debt crisis has been traced to the malfunctioning capitalist world economic system (George, 1988).[7] Since the bulk of Africa is in the 'periphery' of this system, and insofar as there are: unequal trade exchange; unregulated operations of, and the scramble for profits by, monopoly capital; and the expropriation of Africa's economic surplus by the metropolitan capitalist countries,[8] it is not surprising that these 'peripheral' African countries are riddled with debt problems traceable to the international economic system because of the following factors.

First, the recession in the OECD countries negatively affected the demand for African commodities, and ensured the decline in dollar prices of African exports. All these led to massive borrowing to finance development projects in SSA. As ECA (1988, p. 16) recently put it:

the recession in the OECD countries – Africa's major trading partners – affected commodity demand and prices. Instead of pursuing traditional Keynesian policies, governments in those countries opted for anti-inflationary policies which prolonged the recession, further depressed import demand and raised interest rates. Between 1980 and 1987 the unit value of African exports fell by 24 per cent while their volume contracted by 35 per cent.

Secondly, the fall in Africa's export earnings created a foreign exchange gap. In the face of declining net inflows of external resources this had to be filled with loans from commercial banks in Europe and official and officially guaranteed export credits (ECA, 1988, pp. 11–12).

Thirdly, successive oil price hikes since 1973 prompted low income, and non-oil exporting African countries borrowed from commercial and official sources in industrialised countries simply to pay for their energy imports. (UNCTAD, 1988, pp. 91–4). Paradoxically, oil-exporting African states benefitted from the oil price increases of the 1970s. With increased income from oil exports, these states resorted to profligacy evidenced by a massive importation of 'luxury' goods, the implementation of non-viable projects – all of which consumed their oil incomes and a significant proportion of their external reserves, thus prompting massive borrowing by 1980–1 and the subsequent 'debt explosion' of 1982 to date.

Finally, overzealous commercial banks in Europe and North America, according to critical analysts, encouraged Sub-Saharan oil exporters (Nigeria, Gabon, Cameroon) to borrow in spite of declining commodity exports and usually at variable interest rates. These banks helped to sow the seed for the African, and indeed, the Third World debt crisis. As ECA has recently argued:

The fact that a considerable proportion of the external debt was contracted at high and sometimes variable interest rates added a new and growing dimension of cost to the debt portfolio. (ECA, 1988b, p. 16)

This alternative view on the origins of the African debt crisis, while not discounting internal factors entirely, places the main burden of explanation on external causes. Nor surprisingly, therefore, a debt moratorium is seen as an important part of any solution. In addition, these analysts emphasise intra-African co-operation as a means of enhancing economic growth and self-reliant development on the continent.

As Jean Labbens (1987, p. 97) has argued, public indebtedness is not a new phenomenon. What seems to be new on the subject is the way in which competing ideological solutions have been proffered to solve the debt problems. The basic question being raised in the SAP debate centres on whether or not these programmes can solve African debt problems, redress balance-of-payments deficits, and engineer long-term growth and development in the continent without destroying its productive base.

THE INTERNATIONAL POLITICS OF RESTRUCTURING AFRICAN ECONOMIES FOR DEVELOPMENT

The idea of restructuring African economies for self-reliant development is not new. In the past, there have been the United Nations' (UN) 'decades of development', and Brandt's 'programme for survival',[9] both of which identified the problems facing Africa and the remedial measures to combat them. Prominent among these measures is the idea of continuous foreign economic aid to Africa, defined in terms of net financial flows and the transfer of technology to the continent.

From 1960–80, development assistance was sought for Africa by various international agencies. But in the same period, African governments and peoples were urged to increase agricultural output, promote industrialisation schemes and provide incentives to private entrepreneurs. These development strategies of the past have been re-emphasised in recent years in the IMF/World Bank package of policies for restructuring African economies. The next section outlines the main characteristics of these policies and their implications for Africa.

The IMF and the politics of adjustment in Sub-Saharan Africa

Following the debt crisis and the inability of African states to finance their imports, the Washington institutions – IMF and the World Bank – have argued the case for comprehensive programmes aimed at fundamentally restructuring African economies. Although it is dangerous to generalise about these programmes, there is sufficient evidence to suggest that the main components of SAP include:

   (i) exchange rate reforms or currency devaluation;
  (ii) trade liberalisation;
 (iii) export promotion;
  (iv) rationalisation of public expenditure, capital investment and employ-
       ment in the public sector;
   (v) privatisation and commercialisation of public enterprises;
  (vi) producer price adjustment;
 (vii) wage restraints;
(viii) withdrawal/reduction of subsidies;
  (ix) reform of the tax structure; and
   (x) financial/administrative reforms. (Umanna, 1987, p. 45)

Meticulous implementation of these policies, it is argued, would lead to the removal of structural rigidities, efficient allocation of productive resources, sustainable growth and balance-of-payments equilibria, all of which would solve sub-Saharan debt problems in the long run. In return for their commitments to the implementation of SAP packages, sub-Saharan African countries are expected to derive benefit from increased financial aid especially from multilateral sources (IMF/World Bank), and from bilateral donors.

While African countries appear to have fulfilled their part of the bargain, it is worth noting that the promised resource flows (particularly from multilateral sources) to the continent has diminished in recent years. As the UN (1990, p. 15) has noted:

Between 1980 and 1983, IMF credits to Sub-Saharan Africa grew by 1 per cent annually in real terms. This fell to 0.5 per cent in 1984, 0.1 per cent in 1985 and then turned negative. In both 1986 and 1987, Sub-Saharan Africa paid the IMF $500 million more than the continent received in new credits, and in 1988 it paid $250 million.

While the 'pains and gains' of SAP obviously vary and are, in any case, dependent on the 'specific conditions under which the adjustment programme is adopted, including the strength and the political orientation of the country in question', (ECA, 1988a, p. 2) it is helpful for our purpose here to profile the experiences of Ghana, Nigeria and Zambia which have adopted the IMF/World Bank adjustment policies.

Ghana

Ghana launched an Economic Recovery Programme (ERP) in April 1983. Prior to the launching of this programme, there had been a decade of unprecedented decline in Ghana's economic performance. Dr Kwesi

Botchwey, Ghana's Secretary (i.e. Minister) for Finance and Economic Planning, justifying the IMF/World Bank sponsored ERP, argued that the programme was necessary because, as he put it:

> Between 1970 and 1980, the domestic savings rate fell from 12 per cent to 3 per cent of GDP, the rate of investment fell from 14 per cent to 2 per cent of GDP, per capita income fell by 30 per cent, export earnings by 52 per cent, while inflation measured on an annual basis by the consumer price index averaged about 44 per cent per annum.
>
> On the balance of payments side, gross official reserves were all but depleted, and very large payments arrears had accumulated, amounting to well over $500 million at the end of 1982. (Botchwey, 1988, p. 85)

The ERP was intended to create an environment for sustainable growth, and to attain external payments viability over the medium term. According to Botchwey (ibid), it was designed to achieve four main objectives, namely:

(a) the realignment of relative prices in favour on productive activity and the progressive relaxation of administrative controls on prices;
(b) the restoration of monetary and fiscal discipline to reduce inflation;
(c) the promotion of private investments through improved incentives and better financial intermediation; and
(d) the rehabilitation of economic and social infrastructures through increased public investment.

The policy instruments designed to achieve these objectives include: some 90 per cent devaluation of the Ghanaian cedi; massive cuts of imports and public expenditure; and a wage freeze. These policies were secretly conceived and gradually put in place by the Provisional National Defence Council (PNDC) with the support of the IMF and the World Bank, both of which promised and indeed made available substantial credits. As noted in *West Africa* (13 January 1986, p. 67):

> Unknown to most people, talks between the government and the IMF had begun in July 1982. An understanding was reached by February 1983. In April, the World Bank installed a resident representative after a three-year absence. In May, Ghana and the IMF agreed on a one-year standby credit of $252.3 million. In Paris that November, the World Bank held a donors' conference for Ghana, the first since 1970, and over $150 million was pledged. A second IMF standby credit for $183 million was arranged to run from July 1984 to December 1984.

This revelation gives rise to two important observations. First, as ECA

(1988, p. 2) has pointed out, the nature of SAP in Ghana and indeed in Sub-Saharan Africa is such that most countries implementing the programmes are heavily dependent 'on external financial flows'. One implication of this dependence is that the domestic human and material resources of these countries are not often sufficiently mobilised in the process of implementing SAP; another is that the countries concerned are 'obliged to surrender control over critical elements of national economic policy to external determination with serious political implications' (ECA, 1988, p. 2).

Secondly, the idea of secretly negotiating a SAP package with the IMF without public knowledge obviously makes a mockery of democracy in Africa. With the exception of Nigeria (where there was a major debate in 1985), SAP measures in Sub-Saharan Africa are usually handed down to the people from the top. But to avert social unrest, which the implementation of SAP is likely to engender, it is desirable – at least in political terms – to ensure that African peoples are adequately informed about the 'social costs' of the programme. Moreover, people at the grassroots level must be actively involved in its implementation and this implies that SAP measures must be aimed at empowering ordinary people, and especially women, to take greater responsibility for improving their lives; must foster grassroots organisation; nurture rather than obstruct informal sector enterprises; and promote nongovernmental and intermediary organisations (World Bank, 1988, p. xii).

The undemocratic nature of SAP conceptualisation and implementation aside, it has to be mentioned that Ghana's ERP yielded some fruitful results. In the first three years (1983–6) of its application, real GDP growth averaged 6.3 per cent per annum, while there was a 'robust growth' in per capita income during the same period. Externally, there was a substantial reduction in the balance-of-payments deficit from $243 million in 1983 to $57 million in 1986 (ibid).

The remarkable success of Ghana's ERP was achieved at considerable social and economic costs. At the social level, there was a large-scale retrenchment of 'civil servants, teachers, office workers and, in general terms, the myriad of people employed by the State' (*West Africa*, 25 July 1983, p. 1710). Sacked workers who were hungry, and the employed Ghanaians who suddenly became poor had to 'resort to plain begging, to doing manual work for which they were never trained or, worse, to practices which cannot see the light of the day' (ibid).

At the economic level, a number of problems surfaced. A report in *West Africa* (22 October 1984, p. 2119) has revealed that a substantial decline in major sectors of the economy was recorded in 1984. The cedi costs of imports rose; inflation rose from 32.5 per cent in January to 174.1 per cent in June 1984; agricultural and industrial production declined substantially; and most importantly, there was food shortage.

These negative effects of ERP – some of them unanticipated – led to a review of the programme in 1987. The idea was to consolidate what Dr Botchwey described as the 'important gains made under ERP 1 and, to begin to build on this foundation a dynamic, increasingly self-reliant and nationally integrated economy . . .' (Botchwey 1988, p. 85). New priorities were set for the adjustment efforts which would cover the period 1988–90.

Accordingly, less ambitious objectives were set and realistic strategies adopted for the second phase of Ghana's ERP. The real GDP growth rate projected for 1988–91 was put at 5 per cent per annum; inflation would be reduced from 39 per cent in 1987 to 5 per cent in 1991; and an overall balance-of-payments surplus of $120 million was projected for the period (ibid). The policy instruments for achieving these objectives of ERP II were the standard SAP package. They included: (ibid, pp. 85–6)

(i)   the improvement of the incentive structure to enhance efficient production;
(ii) the reform of the state owned enterprises;
(iii) financial sector reform designed to strengthen the banking sector; and
(iv) new legal regimes to govern private investment.

In order to address the social problems of the ERP, the PNDC introduced the *Programme of Actions to Mitigate the Social Costs of Adjustment (PAMSCAD)*. Aimed at alleviating the hardships suffered by the most vulnerable groups – the rural households in the Northern and Upper Regions; the unemployed and the under-employed rural dwellers; and the retrenched public and private sector workers – PAMSCAD was favourably received by the international community, particularly the aid donors.

An international donors' conference held in Geneva on 16–17 February 1988 in support of PAMSCAD yielded some money. From the World Bank came a pledge of $10 million; USAID ($22.7 million); World Food Programme ($15 million); Austria ($10 million); and Japan ($15 million) (Bing, 1988, p. 4). These pledges of financial support for Ghana's PAMSCAD, though encouraging, are illustrative of the extent to which that country is dependent on multilateral and bilateral donors who have recognised that there are 'social consequences of the economic reform programmes they have urged upon Africa' (ibid).

Nigeria

Nigeria's SAP package was introduced in July 1986 amid great controversy. The 'kleptocracy' of Nigeria's Second Republic, the decline in export earnings (due to the collapse of the price of crude petroleum on which Nigeria depends) and the seemingly insatiable demand for foreign goods and services had plunged the country into burdensome debt of some $22 billion in 1986 (World Bank, 1988, p. 256).

It was against this background that Babangida's administration introduced a SAP in 1986 with the following objectives:

(i) restructure and diversify the productive base of the economy in order to reduce dependence on the oil sector and on imports;
(ii) lay the foundation for sustainable non-inflationary growth;
(iii) achieve fiscal and balance-of-payments viability;
(iv) reduce unproductive investments in the public sector, improve the sector's efficiency and enhance the growth potential of the private sector. (*Nigerian Economist*, 1988, p. 10)

The policy instruments for achieving these objectives include, inter alia:

(a) measures to stimulate domestic production and broaden the supply base of the economy;
(b) adoption of a realistic exchange rate policy through the establishment of a Second Tier Foreign Exchange Market (SFEM);
(c) rationalisation and restructuring of tariffs to promote industrial diversification;
(d) trade and payments liberalisation;
(e) appropriate pricing policies for petroleum products and
(f) rationalisation and privatisation of public enterprises.

With the rejection of the IMF standby loan in 1985, it is generally believed that the IMF and the World Bank were not involved in the formulation of Nigeria's SAP. But as the programmes were being implemented, it became clear that the Washington institutions have been actively involved. In an interview granted to *West Africa* magazine, Nigeria's former Finance Minister Dr Chu Okongwu belatedly admitted that:

the IMF has a role to play; the World Bank has a role to play . . . [Both] the World Bank and the Fund have worked with us collaboratively on the Structural Adjustment Programme (SAP) and its elements, and they have reviewed and approved SAP. The monitoring process will begin, but we shall monitor it in collaboration with the Fund (*West Africa*, 1986, p. 2145).

With this revelation, it is clear that Nigerians were not sufficiently informed about the Fund's involvement in SAP formulation until its implementation began in 1986.

The SAP programme has attracted widespread criticism. It is argued that it has had strong negative effects on the most vulnerable sections of the society. One survey in the *Nigerian Sunday Times* (12 February 1989, p. 10) reports that:

With regard to the young ones, many of them suffer from kwashiokor [malnutrition] while the adults are getting leaner by the day. In terms of nutritional and medical well-being, the people are worse off.

The indigenous manufacturing industries have not escaped from the negative impacts of SAP. A report on the Nigerian economy compiled by the Manufacturers Association of Nigeria (MAN) has pointed out, inter alia, that: (a) local sourcing of raw materials has surprisingly declined by 6 per cent; (b) turn-over is up by 33 per cent but sales are down because incomes are stagnant and demand is weak while prices are leaping; (c) the cost of imported raw materials rose by 111 per cent; (d) the cost of local raw materials rose by 98 per cent partly due to the growing cost of credit which led to an 81 per cent rise in ex-factory prices and (e) poor infrastructure continues to constitute a major barrier to capital in-flow (Ogundele, 1989, pp. 1–2).

Since the introduction of SAP, consumer goods prices have risen by 150 per cent. But the most worrying aspect of the programme is its apparently eroding effect on Nigeria's sovereignty. The Nigerian government spent \$5 billion on the Ajaokuta Steel Complex, but the World Bank recently 'recommended that the project be revised with the argument that it is cheaper to import the nation's steel needs' (*Sunday Concord*, 24 September 1989, p. 8).

These are some of the lacunae in SAP which critics have argued would hinder long term development in Nigeria. Yet the Babangida regime is firmly convinced that there is 'no viable alternative to SAP'. (*National Concord*, 6 June 1989). Indeed, the Nigerian military government is fond of cataloguing – in a propagandist fashion – the 'impressive gains' of the programme. These, according to the official view, are (*Guardian*, 18 August 1989, p. 7):

   (i) increased production in all areas of the agricultural sector and remarkable reduction in food imports, thus bringing [Nigeria] nearer self sufficiency in food production;

  (ii) more employment opportunities at all levels through NDE [National Directorate of Employment] and DFRRI [Directorate for Food, Roads and Rural Infrastructure];

 (iii) higher capacity utilisation in industry with most factories back in production;

 (iv) expansive rural development of water supply, electrification, sanitation, housing and feeder roads;

  (v) increased local sourcing of industrial materials;

 (vi) positive primary health care facilities, resulting in a reduction in the mortality rate and a healthier nation;

(vii) liberalisation of the external trade and payments system;

(viii) building up of external reserves and achieving a realistic exchange rate for the Naira [the Nigerian currency].

The official account of the gains from SAP is contestable on several grounds. First, while it is true that agricultural production has increased, the increase has been mainly in the cash crop sector. As Ojo (1989, p. 44) has instructively pointed out:

Of the various components of agricultural production, cash crop sub-sector recorded the most consistent performance. In 1986–1988, the component increased by 2.9 per cent a year in comparison with 3.3 per cent in 1981–1985 . . . The major cash crops contributing to the improvement were groundnut, palm kernels, rubber and cocoa whose output increased by 7.5, 15.0, 10.0 and 35.0 per cent respectively . . . There is evidence that a good portion of total agricultural production was diverted to exports during the period because of new price incentives arising from improved marketing conditions and currency depreciation which boosted local earnings.

While the production of food crops recorded an average annual growth of 5.9 per cent between 1986 and 1988, this was not enough to meet the country's food requirements because of 'diversion to export', and also because of growth in demand from the food processing industries and the teeming Nigerian population (Ojo, 1989, p. 44). Thus, there is a scarcity of basic foodstuffs such as rice (the importation of which is banned), yams, eggs, palm oil, plantain, and milk. This in turn has meant that the 'prices of our staple foods have gone beyond the reach of the common man' (Offor, 1989, p. 7).

Secondly, the scarcity of foreign exchange has meant that only a few indigenous manufacturing industries can afford to meet the cost of indispensable imported raw materials. Many manufacturers have resorted to securing foreign exchange from unofficial sources (the black market), and usually at extraordinary rates, which invariably push up production costs. A case in point is the Nigerian newsprint industry where the Naira cost of production of local newsprint has risen from N965 in 1986 to N5850 in 1989 – an increase of 506 per cent in three years (*National Concord*, 3 February 1989, p. 3). Given this, it is not surprising that there has been capacity under-utilisation in the manufacturing industry. Although the index of manufacturing production increased at an annual average rate of 14.5 per cent between 1986 and 1988, compared with 1.4 per cent in the pre-adjustment 1981–85 period, evidence suggests that this growth was not an indication of full capacity utilisation. In 1981, the average capacity utilisation reached a peak of 73.3 per cent, but it declined to 37.1 per cent in

1985. However, it rose gradually from 38.2 per cent in 1986 to 44.5 per cent in 1988 (Ojo, 1989, p. 45).

High unemployment is one of the social consequences of capacity under-utilisation in the manufacturing sector. While unemployment statistics in the country are unreliable because many unemployed persons do not bother to register, documented evidence suggests that 'unemployment rates since the Adjustment Programme was launched have risen generally. The average national unemployment rate between 1983 and 1985 was 4.9 per cent, while it increased to 5.7 per cent between 1986 and 1988' (Ojo, 1989, p. 48).

Finally, the official argument that water supply, electrification, housing and feeder roads in the rural areas have been 'expanded' cannot be supported with empirical facts. Indeed, Ojo (1989, p. 49) has revealed that:

> Since 1981, only few transportation, water supply, health and educational facilities have been provided due to the cutback in government revenue. A new situation developed in 1986 when the prohibitive costs of providing such facilities restrained the installation of many new facilities . . . The rural areas have traditionally lacked social services and other amenities when compared with urban areas.

From the above observations, one conclusion to be drawn from the government's pronouncements about the 'gains' of SAP is that the benefits of adjustment have not filtered to the 'grassroots' level; another is that the costs of the programme have been borne largely by the rural population and low income classes defined in terms of the 'urban poor and the physically disadvantaged'. One study shows that, except in 1986, the rural price index has increased more than the urban index. For the critical year of 1988, rural prices increased by 39.9 per cent compared with the 27.1 per cent in urban areas (Ojo, 1989, p. 49). On the other hand, low income urban groups have been more affected by increased costs of food, medical care, education and transportation (ibid).

The negative fallouts of SAP – depreciation of the Naira by nearly 80 per cent; low capacity utilisation; rising inflation and unemployment – contributed to the riot of May 1989. That riot led to the introduction of SAP relief measures on 8 June 1989.

The relief measures involved the provision of N100 million ($13.4 million at the rate of N7.4683 = $1) extra budgetary grant to finance food and employment boosting programmes. Thus, the National Directorate of Employment (NDE) is to recruit about 62 000 graduates and semi-skilled job seekers; all vacancies in the primary and secondary schools are to be filled; the Federal Ministry of Works is to offer employment to engineers and surveyors; all schools are to establish farms to improve the nation's food production capacity; motor spare parts are to be imported duty free; pharmaceutical companies are to be encouraged to import drugs; whilst the government transport network – the Mass Transit network – will be given special attention (*Guardian*, 9 June 1989; *National Concord*, 9 June 1989).

The May 1989 SAP riot in Nigeria simply confirms the unpopularity of the IMF stabilisation programmes in Africa, particularly among the 'various influential sectors of the population (notably the urban groups) whose discontent can lead to political instability' (Haynes *et al.*, 1987, p. 344). Furthermore, while the Nigerian public is being urged by government officials to abide with the short-term pains of SAP in the interest of long-term development, evidence suggests that 'the lifestyles of many of those urging the public to put up with their deepening privations continue to be characterised by unabashed opulence' (*Guardian*, 9 June 1989).

Zambia

With a population of 6.9 million, and a per capita GNP of some $300 in 1986, landlocked Zambia is largely dependent on copper, which accounts for about 90 per cent of her export earnings, and tobacco, which provides some 2 per cent of foreign exchange (*Eurostat*, 1986, p. 154).

The profit-oriented multinationals operating in pre-independence Zambia concentrated mainly on copper and tobacco production for export to Europe, while little attention was given to food production. The neglect of subsistence agriculture meant that at independence in 1964, Zambia had to import basic food items ranging from vegetables, bread, milk, beef and sugar, to coffee and tea. The social infra-structure was undeveloped and thus post-colonial Zambia inherited 'a few kilometres of tarred roads, just over 1000 secondary school graduates, 100 university graduates, foreign police and army, no Zambian pilots, and a single indigenous medical doctor' (Nsingo, 1988, p. 78).

With this under-development, Zambia began its 'reforms and structural adjustment programmes' right from 1964. The first decade (1964–74) of Zambia's adjustment programmes was less painful because high copper prices ensured that Kaunda's government had sufficient revenue to enable it to finance its development programmes. The manufacturing sector was transformed; commercial agriculture was improved to broaden the export base; tarmac roads were built; free (that is, non-fee paying) education from primary school to the university level was provided; teacher training colleges and district hospitals were built and free medical services were provided (ibid, p. 79).

With the 1973 oil price increase and the gradual decline of copper prices which eventually collapsed in 1975, Zambia began to run trade deficits from the mid-1970s. The decline in export earnings fostered a gradual reduction of imports and the elimination of subsidies. In 1976, the IMF was

invited in and since then, there have been 'successive devaluations' of the
Zambian currency (the kwacha) as well as restructuring of the government's expenditure and deregulation of the economy.

As the economy moved from bad to worse – with a current account
surplus of $108 million of 1970 turning to a deficit of some $302 million
(World Bank, 1988, p. 250), and an external debt of $5.63 billion in 1986
(*Africa Recovery*, October 1987, p. 26–7), Zambia had to conclude an
agreement with the IMF for a standby loan of SDR100 million (about £76
million) (*Financial Times*, 19 September 1985, p. 3) subject to the adoption
of a package of economic policy reforms which comprised (*Africa Newsfile*,
17 July 1989):

   (i) the introduction of a foreign exchange auctioning system which gra-
        dually fostered massive devaluation of the Kwacha;
  (ii) the removal of all food subsidies;
 (iii) a reduction in public expenditure;
  (iv) retrenchment of civil servants;
   (v) the 'rationalisation of personnel structures in the mines and other
        sectors of the economy'; and
  (vi) trade liberalisation.

The adoption of these policies, particularly the withdrawal of subsidies, led
to high prices of consumer goods and especially of maize (the staple food).
The result was the violent food riots in the copper-belt in December 1986,
and Kaunda's government had to make 'a quick climb-down by reducing
prices of all essential commodities' (ibid).

In May 1987, Zambia suspended its dealings with the IMF and insisted
that only 10 per cent of its export earnings could be used to pay its
creditors. Furthermore, the government announced in May 1987 its own
economic recovery programme – *the Interim National Development Plan
(INDP)*. Its objectives were to (Nsingo, 1988, p. 83–4):

(a) increase real GDP by 2.2 per cent in 1987–8;
(b) reduce inflation from 60 per cent to 15 per cent by the end of 1988;
(c) reduce the government's deficit financing from 18 per cent of GDP in
    1986 to 5 per cent in 1988;
(d) improve the state's capacity to manage the economy; and
(e) improve the performance of state-owned institutions.

Since, contrary to the IMF prescription, the achievement of the INDP
objectives involve increased government expenditure, it is not surprising
that the Zambian Plan 'has suffered from the suspension of IMF support'
(ECA, 1988b, p. 20). Meanwhile, the economic situation in Zambia
continues to deteriorate. There is a severe foreign exchange shortage

which implies that Zambia cannot, at present, pay for its imports of capital goods and essential commodities. Consequently, the country is being forced to seek a 'rapprochement' with the IMF (*Africa Newsfile*, 17 July 1989, p. 8–9). But unless there a:₂ 'human dimensions' to the imminent IMF-Zambia adjustment policies, another round of violent riots may be expected to erupt in a country which has been politically stable since independence.

Adjustment programmes in Sub-Saharan Africa: an overview

The experiences of the three countries profiled above point to two shortcomings in the conceptualisation and implementation of SAP in Sub-Saharan Africa. First, SAP in its current form ignores the fact that the production base of post-colonial African states is narrow, and that the bulk of these states rely on one or two export products whose prices are often unstable in the international market for their foreign exchange earnings. Faced with unpredictable export earnings, most African states find it difficult to service debt and at the same time pay for desirable imports to cushion the effects of SAP. As Killick and Martin (1989, p. 7) have instructively observed, Africa is in a 'vicious circle' because:

> Import strangulation holds back export growth, thus perpetuating import shortages. The uncertainties created by the debt situation – and the rescheduling process – further depress investment which, in turn, holds back the restructuring necessary if the economies are to recover. Depressed export earnings and import capacities reduce government revenues, increasing budget deficits and weakening government's abilities to improve the balance of the economy. It will take a huge effort if these vicious circles are to be broken.

Secondly, the standard SAP package with its emphasis on devaluation and domestic credit squeeze tends to ignore the inflationary effect of the former, while underestimating the social cost of the latter in terms of its effects on living standards in Africa. However, the World Bank (1988b, p. 88) has admitted that:

> Increases in consumer prices, reforms in the public sector that lead to reduction in public employment and expenditures in the social sectors, and reforms in trade and exchange rates that change the relative prices can all cause transitory unemployment and declines in real income for some. While the costs of not adjusting are heavy, the hardships that groups adversely affected by adjustment undergo are very real.

African leaders are, of course, aware of the high cost of non-reform and are certainly in favour of adjustment policies that will address the current economic problems given their commitments to the *African Priority Programme for Economic Recovery, 1986–1990 (APPER)* adopted by the OAU Heads of State in July 1985, and the *United Nations Programme of Action for African Economic Recovery and Development, 1986–1990 (UN – PAAERD)* adopted by the General Assembly in May 1986. Their objections to the current SAP are based on their observations that some of its policies tend to exacerbate Africa's dependence on external financial flows, while its huge internal resources are not fully mobilised in 'the drive for true development' (ECA, 1988a, p. 2).

These understandable criticisms of SAP by African leaders have informed their acceptance of ECA's *African Alternative Framework to Structural Adjustment Programmes for Socio-Economic Recovery and Transformation (AAF-SAP)* (1989).[10] The AAF-SAP in its approach to the current crises facing Africa's political economy has called for some modifications of the IMF adjustment policies, and has argued the case for alternative policies that would enable African states to strengthen and diversify their production capacities. Some of the measures proposed in the AAF-SAP include (ibid, p. 38–40):

(1) Land reforms;
(2) Devotion of at least 20–25 per cent of total public investment to agriculture;
(3) Allocation of an increasing share of foreign exchange for imports of vital inputs for agriculture and manufacturing sectors;
(4) Sectoral allocation of credit using credit guidelines that would favour the food subsector and manufacture of essential goods;
(5) Adoption of investment codes and procedures tailored to the promotion and development of small-scale industries;
(6) Use of selective nominal interest rates in such a way that interest rates on loans for speculative activities would be greater than the rates on loans for productive activities;
(7) Creation and strengthening of rural financial institutions;
(8) Rehabilitation and rationalisation of installed productive and infrastructural capacities, and setting up of an effective national maintenance system;
(9) Utilising the existence of *de-facto* multiple exchange rates systems in a rationalised manner and/or creating and streamlining such a system for purpose of resource transfer, resource mobilisation and reversal of capital flight and ensuring availability of essential goods;
(10) Creation of special funds for loans at subsidised interest rates to certain groups of economic operators.

The AAF-SAP package is essentially reflationary and its implementation would require substantial amounts of money which could be raised from external and internal sources. The goal of ECA's 'structural transformation' is an integrated, self-reliant and sustainable economic development in Africa. But given Africa's current poverty, this goal cannot be achieved without external financial support.[11]

CONCLUSION

The enormous issues raised by the African debt crisis, economic recovery programmes and the roles of the Washington institutions, though complex, have been modestly discussed in this chapter. From the foregoing analysis, three conclusions emerge. First, the origins of the debt crisis in Africa are traceable to both internal and external factors. But the surest way to find solution(s) to this crisis is through consistent policy dialogue between creditors and debtors and certainly not through competing ideological debates (UN, 1990, pp. 47–8).

Secondly, Sub-Saharan African economies are certainly in need of structural reforms. But care must be taken to ensure that the processes of adjustment do not paralyse the productive base of African countries. The peculiar nature of African economies and the constraints they impose must be taken into account in the adjustment programmes (ECA, 1989, p. 8).

Finally, to make SAP a politically acceptable strategy in Sub-Saharan Africa, its social costs must be evenly distributed. The flamboyant lifestyles of state officials must be curbed, and more efforts directed towards reducing the inflation which has brought hardship to millions of Africans. Programmes such as the PAMSCAD in Ghana and the SAP relief measures in Nigeria must be taken seriously to cushion the negative side-effects of adjustment programmes in Sub-Saharan Africa.

NOTES

1. This is a revised version of a paper presented at the 1989 Annual Conference of the Development Studies Association held at the Queen's University of Belfast. The author is grateful to the editors of this compendium for their useful comments, and to Trevor Parfitt for his constructive suggestions on the draft.
2. For more on this see R. A. Adefulu (1988).
3. For an extensive discussion of this idea, see Friedman (1962, Chapter 1).
4. There are variants of the liberals' analyses of the African and, indeed, Third World debt crisis, but see, Serageldin (1989) especially p. 23; World Bank, *World Debt Tables 1987–88*, pp. xix–xxiii and World Bank (1984).
5. Again there are variants of the Marxists' analyses of the African debt crisis; see George (1988); Onimode (1988); and at institutional level, UNCTAD (1988),

Chapter IV; UN-ECA (1988a) pp. 3–4.
6. It is not suggested that these authors are 'Marxists'; they are cited here for their succinct discussion of the 'socialist' viewpoint on the goal of an orderly development.
7. For extensive discussion of the capitalist world economy, see Wallerstein (1979).
8. For theoretical expositions of these points, see Emmanuel (1972), Amin (1976) and Ake (1981).
9. The period 1960–70 was the first UN development decade; the second development decade covered the period 1970–80. For more on this, see UN Department of Public Information (1981); on the 'Programme of Survival', see Brandt (1980).
10. ECA, *African Alternative Framework to Structural Adjustment Programmes for Socio-Economic Recovery and Transformation* (AAF-SAP) was adopted by African Ministers for Economic Development, and the OAU Finance Ministers on 10 April 1989 at Addis Ababa. On 17 November 1989, the UN General Assembly held a 'special plenary' meeting on the AAF-SAP document which was adopted by an 'overwhelming vote'. The US was the only country that voted against it because, as James Wilkinson, the US Ambassador at the UN, put it, 'the document overlooks that progress which has occurred over the past several years, largely as a result of internationally supported adjustment programmes'. See Harsch (1989, p. 2) for details.
11. This is one of the views expressed at the African Leadership Forum meeting held in September, 1989 at Washington. For details see *Africa Recovery* (October 1989, pp. 1, 2 and 24–8).

REFERENCES

Adefulu, R. A., (1988) 'The Lomé Convention and the NIEO: A Study in the Political Economy of North-South Relations', unpublished PhD thesis, Lancaster University.
Africa Newsfile, 1989 40 (17 July).
Africa Recovery, 3 (1989a: October; 1989b: December).
Ake, C., (1981 *A Political Economy of Africa* (London: Longman).
Amin, S., (1976) *Unequal Development: An Essay on the Social Formations of Peripheral Capitalism* (New York: Monthly Review Press).
Bauer, P. T., and B. S. Yamey, (1983) 'Why we Should Close our Purse to the Third World', *The Times* (11 April).
Bing, A., (1988) 'Ghana: Adjusting the Social Conscience', *Africa Recovery*, 2 (2).
Botchwey, K., (1988) 'The Recovery "Involved a Major Orientation of Economic and Financial Policies"', *The Courier*, 111 (September–October).
Brandt, W., (1980) *North/South: A Programme for Survival* (London: Pan Books).
ECA (1988), *Issues for the Joint Statement of African Governors in IMF and World Bank* (Addis Abbaba: ECA).
ECA (1989), *Survey of Economic and Social Conditions in Africa 1986–7* (Addis Abbaba: ECA).
Emmanuel, A., (1972) *Unequal Exchange: A Study of the Imperialism of Trade* (New York: Monthly Review Press, 1972).
EuroStat (1986), *ACP Basic Statistics 1986* (Luxembourg: Statistical Office of the EC).

Financial Times (1985) (19 September).

Friedman, M. (1962) *Capitalism and Freedom* (Chicago: Chicago University Press).

George, S., (1988) *A Fate Worse than Debt: A Radical Analysis of the Third World Debt Crisis* (London: Penguin).

Guardian (1989), 'After the Anti-SAP Riot' (Lagos) (9 June).

Harsch, E., (1989) 'UN Votes AAF-SAP "A Basis for Dialogue"', *Africa Recovery* (December).

Haynes, J., T. Parfitt and S. Riley, (1987) 'Debt Crisis in Sub-Saharan Africa: The Local Politics of Stabilisation', *African Affairs*, 86.

Killick, T., and M. Martin, (1989) 'African Debt: The Search for Solutions', *Africa Recovery*, 3.

Labbens, J., (1987) 'The Public Debt as Seen by the Classical Economists', *International Social Science Journal*, 111.

McKinlay, R. D., and R. Little, (1986) *Global Problems and World Order* (London: Francis Pinter).

National Concord, (1989) 'President Babangida's Address to the Armed Forces Consultative Assembly', (6 June).

Nigerian Economist, (1988) 1 (7–20 June).

Nsingo, K., (1988) 'Problems and Prospects of Economic Structural Adjustment in Zambia', *The Courier*, 111 (September–October).

Offor, H., (1989) 'Food Prices Rise to Unbearable Level', *Daily Times* (2 February).

Ogundele, J., (1989) Manufacturers Raise Alarm on the Economy', *The Guardian* (Lagos) (24 September) 1–2.

Ojo, M. O., (1989) 'An Appraisal of the Socio-Economic Impact of Structural Adjustment Policies in Nigeria', *CBN Economic and Financial Review*, 27 (March).

Onimode, B., (1988) *A Political Economy of the African Crisis* (London: Zed Books).

Quatarra, A. D., (1986) 'The Balance of Payments Adjustment Process in Developing Countries: The Experience of the Ivory Coast', *World Development*, 14.

Serageldin, I., (1989) *Poverty, Adjustment and Growth in Africa* (Washington: IBRD/The World Bank).

Sunday Concord, (1989) 'Massive Frauds Becloud Steel Dream', (24 September).

Umanna, O. J., (1987) 'A General Survey of the Experiences of Some Less Developed Countries under the Structural Adjustment Programme', *Central Bank of Nigeria Economic and Financial Review*, 25 (December).

UNCTAD, (1988) *Trade and Development Report 1988* (New York: UN).

UN Department of Public Information (1981), *International Development Strategy for the Third United Nations Development Decade* (New York: UN).

UN Department of Public Information (1990), *Debt: A Crisis for Development* (New York: UN).

Wallerstein, I., (1989) *The Capitalist World Economy* (Cambridge: Cambridge University Press).

West Africa, No 3441 (25 July 1983); No 3606 (13 October 1986).

World Bank, (1988) *World Development Report 1988* (New York: World Bank).

4 Negative 'Dutch Disease': 'the Zambian Disease'[1]

Desmond Norton

THE PROBLEM

Consider a labour-abundant, capital-scarce, developing economy producing two composite goods, tradeables (T) and non-tradeables (NT). Unless otherwise indicated, it is assumed that all production and imports are for final demand: domestic primary factors are the only inputs. Within each composite category, goods prices are assumed constant until further notice. Those in T are determined by given world levels and the structure of protection, while those in NT are endogenous. Tradeables consist of a resource-based subsector such as mining (R), plus agriculture and manufacturing (AM). It is supposed that the economy is initially heavily dependent on a booming R sector, the entire output of which is exported, but that the relevant minerals approach depletion; in comparative statics analysis only the extreme case of actual depletion is considered. That is the direction in which the key (copper) resource sector of Zambia has been moving. How the structure of the economy is likely to react to such depletion, the difficulties it is likely to face, and some policy implications, are examined. Consideration is also given to a problem in many ways similar to resource depletion – that in which there is substantial permanent shift in the terms of international trade against a resource upon which the economy had earlier been heavily dependent. Zambia has also had to face that dilemma in recent decades. Unless otherwise indicated, it is assumed that both before and after the resource sector shocks, some of each good is produced.

The past fifteen years have seen much research into the structural problems which the emergence of a booming resource sector can create. The London *Economist* (1977) seems to have been the first to have termed these as aspects of 'the Dutch Disease', in view of the structural difficulties of the Dutch economy following major offshore gas finds. Given the experiences of Zambia in recent years, it seems appropriate to label the problems associated with depletion or price-collapse of a previously crucial resource as symptoms of 'the Zambian Disease'.

Much of the Dutch Disease literature employs neoclassical trade theory methods, assuming factor price flexibility and full employment, as well as current account balance of payments equilibrium. Such assumptions should be relaxed for a developing economy in the face of a key resource

59

collapse. In that context Dutch Disease models can be thrown into reverse to a limited extent only. Perhaps that is why what has above been termed the Zambian Disease has attracted little attention in the journals; see, however, Daniel and Evans (1986), Pinto (1987) and Edwards (1988).

Unless otherwise indicated, it is assumed that each good is produced under (industry) constant returns to scale, with strictly diminishing, but positive, marginal products to each variable input. Assuming that each sector uses only two factors, the discussion below (pp. 61–5) concerns mainly the short-run, defined as a period in which each sector competes for a common pool of intersectorally mobile labour (which moves to equate wages between sectors), but is constrained by a fixed amount of a sector-specific factor. The specific factor is capital in the case of NT, ore-bearing deposits in the case of R and capital in the case of AM. As in Neary (1978), the medium-run is a period of disequilibrium, during which the economy is adjusting capital as well as labour from short-run to long-run equilibrium. Comparative statics analysis of the long-run, when both capital and labour are fully mobile between sectors, is deferred (see pp. 65–8). For tractability, the aggregate capital stock is assumed constant. For the most part, population is also assumed constant in the post-boom (or crisis) era. The likelihood of inequalities emerging between absorption and output following resource sector shocks is virtually ignored in both these sections. However, thereafter (pp. 68–70) we turn to an important question in longer-run dynamics. This involves consideration of longer-run transfer effects of current account international payments deficits which a developing country is likely to incur following depletion of R or permanent adverse movement in its terms of trade. The key question is: If a lower-bound constraint is imposed on national (as distinct from domestic) product, under what circumstances will the country be unable to meet its obligations in regard to interest payments? If it cannot do so, it is said that there is no feasible solution to the model. Finally, the concluding section (pp. 70–3) briefly reviews the Zambian experience in recent decades. The question of the optimal rate of resource depletion is not addressed.

Many labour-abundant developing economies, such as Zambia, have pursued policies biased against agriculture (A). Nevertheless, it will be concluded that in such economies, A will be a key growth sector in the long-run following resource depletion or permanent terms of trade collapse against R. Technical change is for the most part ignored. However, it will become apparent that if labour-augmenting technical change is introduced, and if its rate of change is no lower in agriculture than in the other sectors, then A will remain a key long-run growth prospect following depletion of R or collapse in its price.

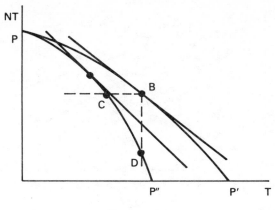

FIGURE 4.1

THE SHORT-RUN

Short-run response to resource depletion

Given the allocation of capital between sectors, start with the economy initially in short-run equilibrium during the boom era, before depletion of R, at point B on the production frontier PP′ in Figure 4.1. It is assumed that point B is also a position of long-run equilibrium, which implies that PP′ is nested in, and tangent to, a long-run transformation locus at B (Mayer, 1974). If wages were fully flexible, the economy after resource depletion would move to the full-employment short-run locus PP″, the exact point depending on the pattern of demand. With a large share of NT output being accounted for by services, it is reasonable to assume that neither composite good is inferior: normality is therefore assumed. Hence, due to the fall in aggregate demand, the price of NT must fall following resource depletion.[2]

Reversing the argument of Snape (1977), non-inferiority implies that the new short-run equilibrium must be to the left of point D in Figure 4.1. So output of T will contract. The diagram also indicates that output of NT could increase after resource depletion, since the absolute value of the slope of PP″ at C exceeds that of PP′ at B. If NT output is increased, that of T will be reduced all the more so. Thus, assuming factor price flexibility, the short-run effect of resource depletion on NT output is *a priori* indeterminate: while reduced income discourages demand for NT, its reduced price increases quantity demanded while its lower marginal cost encourages increased production of NT.[3] However, as will be shown in Figure 4.2, AM must expand.

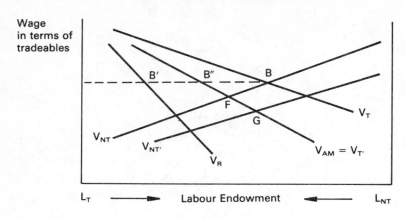

FIGURE 4.2

In summary, assuming wage flexibility, the market's short-run response to depletion in R will be: (i) P_{NT} will fall relative to P_T. (ii) Production of T will fall. (iii) The effect of NT is *a priori* indeterminate: NT production could rise or fall. (iv) AM production will increase.

Consider next the short-run impact of resource depletion on factor returns. One reason for interest in this question is because, if the short-run return on capital rises in one sector relative to the others, then that sector will expand in the medium-run until returns on capital are again equated across sectors. With tradeables as the numeraire for prices, continue to assume flexible wages. The direction of response in the other endogenous variables after the fall in P_{NT}, induced by the collapse in R, is determined by the value marginal product of labour in NT, V_{NT}. The response of the factor market in the case in which the decline in P_{NT} induces increased NT production is shown in Figure 4.2.

The locus of the value marginal product of labour tradeables, V_T in the diagram, is the horizontal sum of V_R and V_{AM}. V_{NT} (drawn for the initial price of NT) is measured in terms of tradeables. Start with full employment at point B with returns to labour (and to capital) being equated across markets. Employment in NT, T, R and AM can be read from points B, B' and B''. After resource depletion V_R is irrelevant, so V_T goes to $V_{AM} = V_{T'}$. If P_{NT} did not change, the new equilibrium would be at point F. However, because resource depletion reduces P_{NT}, the V_{NT} locus shifts downwards by a constant proportionate amount to, say, $V_{NT'}$. The new equilibrium is therefore at point G in the diagram. The increased employment in AM and NT means that output in those sectors rises.

Following depletion, all labour previously in R has moved to the NT and AM sectors. In the NT sector, because production becomes more labour-intensive, the return on capital has increased in terms of NT; however, it could have increased or decreased in terms of AM, due to AM's higher relative price. In the AM sector, because production there is also more labour-intensive, the return on capital has increased in terms of AM and, given the improved internal terms of trade of that sector, in terms of NT also. Figure 4.2 also shows that in terms of AM, the wage common to all sectors falls. Furthermore, the diagram shows that since the output of NT increases, the wage in terms of NT falls. The real wage, therefore, unambiguously falls. Thus, if (as in Figure 4.2) the output of NT expands in short-run response to resource depletion, and assuming wage flexibility: (i) the real return on capital in NT could rise or fall; (ii) the return on capital in the AM sector unambiguously increases; (iii) real wages fall.

The case in which NT output contracts in response to the fall in P_{NT} can be similarly shown. Starting at point B, R goes to zero as before. However, in this case P_{NT} falls by more than in Figure 4.2. For labour market clearance, $V_{NT'}$ and V_{AM} must now intersect to the southeast of point B. The effects on factor returns could be read from the diagram, indicating that: (i) the real return on capital in NT falls; (ii) the return on capital in AM unambiguously increases; (iii) the effect on the real wage is ambiguous – in terms of NT it increases; but it falls in terms of AM.

Suppose that we start as before at point B in Figure 4.2, but that real wages, in terms of AM, are completely rigid downwards. That might be because real wages are at a (possibly conventional) subsistence level to begin with, and because nobody is willing or able to work at a lower wage. After depletion, employment in the AM sector stays at B″. If P_{NT} stayed unchanged, unemployment would go to BB″. But P_{NT} would fall, the reduction in P_{NT} now being accentuated by the spending effect of unemployment. Hence, unemployment will rise to a level greater than BB″, and output and employment in NT could go close to zero.

An extreme case of wage rigidity has just been considered. It is more likely that wages will be rigid at levels above the post-resource-depletion full employment level, but generally below the initial pre-depletion level. Then, in the medium-run, and under the experience of unemployment, the ratchet effect of what was initially a relatively high real wage is likely to erode, and the level at which wages are rigid, as well as the unemployment level, will tend to decrease over time. But if, as in some developing countries, there is an absolute floor to the real wage, and if (due to subsistence needs) that floor is higher than the new market-clearing level, then some unemployment will be sustained. In the absence of famine, the population must continue to consume at or above subsistence. It may do so for many years if the economy runs current account balance of payments deficits. Such deficits, along with readjustment of capital between AM and NT, may prevail in the medium-run for decades. For long-run development, the economy will have to restructure its capital stock, so that (as shown later) AM output is further increased.

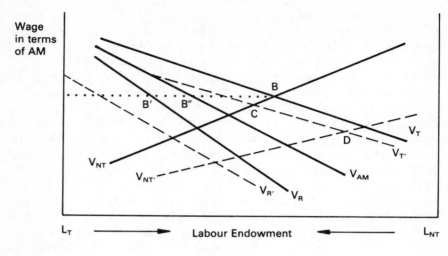

FIGURE 4.3

Short-run response to terms of trade collapse

Resource depletion for the moment aside, consider now the effects of a permanent adverse movement in the terms of international trade against the resource-based activity. Following the approach up to now, examine first the effects over a period in which the specific-factor endowments of each sector stay fixed. Because relative prices within tradeable goods have changed, prices will now be expressed in terms of only the AM subset of T.

Assume, because of a permanent collapse in world demand (due, say, to development of substitutes), that the price of R falls by x per cent. Consequences can be read from Figure 4.3. The initial short-run and long-run equilibrium is at B in the diagram. Employment in tradeables and non-tradeables, and in the AM and R subsectors, can be read from points B, B″ and B′. After the collapse in P_R, V_R (measured in terms of AM) falls by x per cent to $V_{R'}$. The value marginal product of labour in tradeables is now given by V_{AM} for relatively low L_T, but goes to the dashed locus $V_{T'}$ for higher L_T. If P_{NT} did not change, the new full employment equilibrium (with factor price flexibility) would be at point C in the diagram. Output of both AM and NT would then increase, while that of R would contract. There will, however, be an income effect operating against NT. On the plausible assumption of non-inferiority, the price of non-tradeables will fall. Thus V_{NT} will shift downwards to, say, $V_{NT'}$. The intersection of $V_{NT'}$ and $V_{T'}$ will be located to the south-east of point C, at, say, D in the diagram. Note, however, that if the reduction in P_{NT} is sufficiently small, the new short-run equilibrium, D, could lie to the south-west of point B. Comparing the initial equilibrium at B with the new short-run equilibrium,

D, it can be seen that (a) while moving in opposite directions, the output of tradeables and that of non-tradeables could increase or decrease; and (b) the output of AM expands while the R sector contracts.

Short-run distributional effects of the adverse terms of trade change are similar to those applying in the case of depletion. In regard to factor returns in terms of AM (the key determinant of living standards in a developing country), and still referring to Figure 4.3: (i) The return to labour falls from that at B to that at D; and (ii) with lower employment in R, that sector's specific-factor intensity increases. For this reason, and also because the price of R has fallen, the specific factor rental in terms of AM falls in R. Also, (iii) because production in NT could become more, or less, capital-intensive, that sector's return on capital, in terms of NT, could rise or fall. However, the decline in P_{NT} will tend to reduce the return on capital in terms of AM in the NT sector. (iv) The only gainers in the short-run are capitalists in the AM sector, who get the same prices as earlier for their outputs, but who now hire labour more cheaply.

It is easy to see from Figure 4.3 that if wages are rigid at any level above that at D (which lies somewhere to the south-east of C), then unemployment will prevail. Such unemployment would be higher than that suggested by the $V_{NT'}$ locus, as drawn, for with workers then idle, spending on non-tradeables would fall by more than that implicit in the diagram, causing V_{NT} to shift further to the right. Note that capitalists in AM would still gain if wages were rigid at levels between those implied by points B and D.

The economy is likely to react to an adverse terms of trade change against the resource sector in a manner similar to its response to depletion. Thus, current account payments deficits may prevail in the medium-run for decades, and for long-run development, the capital stock will have to be restructured so that AM output is further expanded.

LONG-RUN COMPARATIVE STATICS

A common error with regard to the 'Zambian Disease' is in estimating its duration, which is often assumed to be transitory (Daniel, 1986, pp. 1, 7). Efforts are made to ease the symptoms rather than resolve the illness directly. The situation is then compounded as side-effects of prescribed cures become problems in themselves. If the economy is approaching total depletion of a resource, then recognition of the problem as one of a permanent nature is likely to be fast. If, however, the problem is caused by a lasting movement in the terms of trade against the R sector, recognition and adaption may be slow. Terms of trade deterioration has often been thought to be a temporary phenomenon and so policymakers' 'cures' may also be temporary. Typically, deficits will be run in the current account balance of payments, and attempts will be made to hold an overvalued exchange rate in the hope of avoiding inflationary effects of devaluation.

Resource depletion: long-run comparative statics

Still ignoring long-run transfer effects of current account payments deficits incurred in response to the loss of R, consider now the medium-run and long-run restructuring of the capital stock between sectors following depletion of R and subsequent to the reallocation of labour in the short-run. Factor prices are assumed flexible until further notice. In the long-run there will generally be some restructuring of the capital stock between the NT and AM sectors, and between the agricultural (A) and manufacturing (M) subsectors. It is assumed that M is highest, NT is intermediate, and A is lowest, in capital intensity, and because A is likely to be large relative to M in developing countries, it is also assumed that AM as a whole is labour-intensive relative to NT. There is empirical support for these crucial assumptions.[4]

In the long-run, after resource depletion, the economy can be viewed as one of the Heckscher-Ohlin type with two sectors, NT and AM. With the capital stock given but mobile between these sectors, the release of labour from R, at given output prices, will cause the labour-intensive sector, AM, to expand absolutely, while NT will contract in absolute terms (Rybczynski, 1955). Given the plausible assumption of normality, the contraction of NT will be accentuated by the fall in demand for that good.

In regard to changes in the composition of AM, it has just been seen that AM expands for two reasons: (i) at given output prices, because AM is labour-intensive; also, (ii) because the demand for NT falls. It follows from (i) that the more labour-intensive subsector, A, will expand, while the highly capital-intensive subsector, M, will contract. But due to (ii), NT releases more of the productive factors to the AM sector than would have otherwise been the case. Taken in isolation, release of extra labour causes A to expand, whereas release of extra capital, taken in isolation, causes M to expand. However, given that the economy is abundant in labour relative to capital, a net effect will be to cause expansion in A because, following depletion in R, the economy will have moved from a position of comparative advantage in R to one of dominant comparative advantage in the labour-intensive commodity, A. Furthermore, we can be sure that A will have expanded relative to M provided that the share of the labour force initially employed in R is sufficiently large. It follows that after depletion, agriculture must be a key long-run growth sector, and that policies which impede agriculture during the resource boom and in the medium-run following depletion will impede long-run growth.

Interference by the policymaker might be desirable when growth in A is impeded. Harmful government intervention aside, there are two reasons why growth in A might be retarded. Firstly, the AM sector in general, and A in particular, could miss out on technical change in the form of learning by doing while the boom prevails in R. Suppose that such learning by doing is external to the firm, and, in the spirit of the Neary-van Wijnbergen (1985) model, the question which arises is whether an existing subsidy to the AM sector (introduced to correct the existing market failure) should be increased during the boom. Secondly, the wage rate after the boom is over may be rigid at too high a level, thereby preventing A from acquiring additional labour necessary for expansion.

The policymaker faced with a boom which is expected to be temporary can interfere with market forces by further taxing resource-based profits which can then be distributed to AM, or a policy of wage restraint, which would assist AM in hiring enough labour to continue production, could be adopted. Correctly administered, the policy of increasing subsidies during the boom could maximise the present value of output; for a two-period exposition, see Neary and van Wijnbergen (1985).

Alternatively, a policy of wage restraint would also reduce incentives for labour to move from AM to R during the boom, so that AM could continue to operate on a moderate scale (and therefore need not greatly miss learning by doing). An advantage of wage restraint is that it sets living standards during the boom at levels from which downward flexibility might be easier. During the boom period, living standards, in the presence of a free labour market, might have increased substantially. In consequence, workers' expectations may cause wages to become rigid at high levels as their conception of subsistence is revised upwards. As Corden (1984, p. 359, note) suggests, 'it might be argued that the true Dutch Disease in the Netherlands was not the adverse effects on manufacturing of real appreciation but rather the use of Booming Sector revenues for social service levels which are not sustainable, but which it has been politically difficult to reduce'. Restraining the wage at a lower level could prevent this kind of situation. The A component of AM would be the principal beneficiary from this action, since it is labour-intensive.

Terms of trade collapse: long-run comparative statics

Consider next the long-run effects of permanent terms of trade deterioration against R. Take A as the numeraire in terms of which prices are measured, and at first ignore real wage rigidity.

The decline in the terms of trade increases the labour endowment of the economy outside sector R. Given the capital stock, it follows that the labour intensity of the non-R economy increases. Suppose for the moment that the price of NT, like that of M, is exogenously given. One could then aggregate NT and M into a single commodity sector, NTM, and deal with a Heckscher-Ohlin sub-economy of two sectors, NTM and A, A being labour-intensive and NTM capital-intensive. Given the prices of M and NT, A would then expand absolutely in the long-run following terms of trade deterioration, while NTM would contract absolutely. So, recognising that the demand for NT would in fact fall, it follows that A would expand in absolute terms.[5] Hence, because it is labour-intensive, A would be a key growth sector. Policies unfavourable to A in response to the terms of trade deterioration are therefore likely to suppress long-run growth. Wage rigidities, which impede the mechanisms just outlined, operate to the same effect.

LONG-RUN DYNAMICS: DOES A FEASIBLE SOLUTION EXIST?

It has been noted, in response to resource-sector depletion and/or permanent adverse movement in the terms of trade, that the authorities might deliberately operate current account balance of payments deficits so as to keep living standards at or above some floor level. Consequential borrowing abroad might reflect failure in recognition of the fundamental problem, myopic policies during the boom era (as in Zambia) including failure to accumulate adequate foreign assets, or, if the permanence of the resource sector shock is recognised, the intent might be to repay, after restructuring the economy, the debts incurred. The question arises as to whether there would then be a feasible solution for the model: If a constraint floor is imposed on national (as distinct from domestic) product, what are the implications for borrowing, interest rates, long-run growth and other variables, if the country is not ultimately to be forced into repudiating its debts, or if lending countries do not waive interest payments or transform loans into grants?

In order to highlight the issues involved, consider a situation in which population stays at its immediate pre-crisis level, and suppose that domestic product gradually decays following the beginning of the depletion and/or terms of trade crisis, at a constant rate γ, over the period $0 \leqslant t \leqslant \tau$. It is assumed that the economy gradually and simultaneously is restructuring output. Hence, over the period $0 \leqslant t \leqslant \tau$,

(1) $Y(t) = Y(0)e^{-\gamma t} \quad \gamma > 0$

where $Y(0)$ is the immediate pre-crisis (end of boom era) level of domestic product, initially assumed to equal national product; thus it is assumed for simplicity that net foreign assets are initially zero and that there are no net factor payments to/from abroad to begin with. Setting $Y(0) = 1$,

(2) $Y(t) = e^{-\gamma t} \quad 0 \leqslant t \leqslant \tau$

National product is

(3) $\check{Y}(t) = Y(t) - iD(t)$

where the interest rate on debt, i, is a positive constant and D is external debt outstanding. It is assumed that in an attempt to maintain living standards, the country operates a current account payments deficit equal to a constant proportion, ß, of the difference between the pre-crisis (end of boom era) level of national (and domestic) product and its current national product. Thus

(4) $D(t) = \int_0^t \beta\{1 - \check{Y}(t')\}dt'$ $0 < \beta < 1$

Hence, for $0 < t < \tau$,

(5) $\check{Y}(t) = e^{-\gamma t} - i\beta \int_0^t \{1 - \check{Y}(t')\}dt'$

As shown in the appendix, manipulating (5), and setting $\check{Y}(0) = Y(0) = 1$, implies

(6) $\check{Y}(\tau) = 1 + \{\gamma/(\gamma + i\beta)\}[e^{\gamma t - e^{\,i\beta\tau}}]$

It is assumed that following the decline and ultimate restructuring, domestic product reaches a low-level equilibrium at $t = \tau$, and that thereafter it either stays constant or grows at rate α. Hence, for $t > \tau$,

(7) $Y(t) = Y(\tau)e^{\alpha(t-\tau)}$ $\alpha \geqslant 0$

So, observing equations (2) and (7), and letting the parameter A denote

$e^{-\gamma t}\, e^{-\alpha\tau}$, for $t > \tau$:

(8) $Y(t) = Ae^{\alpha t}$

Hence

(9) $\check{Y}(t) = Ae^{\alpha t} - i\beta \int_0^t \{1 - \check{Y}(t')\}dt'$

where, from equation (3), the carry-forward interest burden of debt incurred before $t = \tau$ is embodied in the $\check{Y}$ term on the right hand side. Proceeding as with equation (5), it is shown in the appendix that, for $t > \tau$, (9) implies

(10) $\tilde{Y}(t) = \alpha A(e^{\alpha t} - e^{\alpha \tau} e^{-i\beta \tau} e^{-i\beta \tau})/(\alpha - i\beta) + 1$
$$+ [\gamma/(\gamma + i\beta)]\{e^{-\gamma \tau} - e^{i\beta \tau}\}e^{i\beta(t-\tau)}$$

Clearly, if $\alpha = 0$ (the case of no growth in domestic product from its low-level equilibrium at $t = \tau$), equation (10), which applies for $t > \tau$, indicates that

(11) $\tilde{Y}(t) = 1 + \text{Constant}[e^{-\gamma \tau} - e^{i\beta \tau}]e^{i\beta(t-\tau)}$ Constant > 0

Because γ, τ, i and β are positive, $-\gamma \tau < i\beta \tau$, implying that [. . . .] in (11) is negative. Thus $\tilde{Y}(t)$ will more rapidly fall below any floor constraint level the higher the values of those parameters, and will ultimately become negative. In this case the model has no feasible longer-run solution, meaning that lenders will have to write off debt, or that the country will be forced to repudiate it, or that a continuously shrinking population due to Malthusian catastrophe and/or mass exodus, are the only alternatives.

It should also be clear, if the country does borrow abroad during the years of decay and restructuring, if ensuing debts are not waived or repudiated, and if its population is not continuously to shrink in the longer-run, then domestic product must grow after $t = \tau$. Even then (with $\alpha > 0$) there is no guarantee that continued collapse in living standards (as represented by national product) can be averted. Given the debt overhang and the interest thereon, inspection of (10) indicates that, for any particular γ and τ, the ultimate longer-run rate of growth in output, α, must be sufficiently high relative to $i\beta$, if continuous decline in living standards (with national product ultimately becoming negative) is to be averted. These considerations strongly suggest that lenders will indeed have to forget about much of their past loans to countries severely affected by the 'Zambian Disease'.

THE EXPERIENCE OF ZAMBIA: AN OVERVIEW

At independence in 1964, Zambia enjoyed one of the highest living standards in Sub-Saharan Africa. Directly and indirectly, it depended fundamentally on copper. The economy remained in relative boom until 1975, when the price of copper collapsed. In real terms, that price has stayed low since then. At the same time the prices of imports continued to rise. Hence, the terms of trade after 1974 moved very much against Zambia, forcing the country into an unprecedented crisis. With the advent of substitution away from copper due to modern technology, it seems that the unfavourable terms of trade movement is permanent. Long-term prospects for the economy are rendered more gloomy when it is noted that its main ore beds are likely to be depleted by around the year 2000. The details which follow are drawn from Ndulo and Norton (1987).

Zambia at first responded to the terms of trade collapse as though it were temporary. Furthermore, by maintaining overvalued exchange rates, and by extending a maze of administrative controls (including cumbersome systems of import licensing and foreign exchange allocation), initial policy responses in many ways only deepened the crisis. The imperative of fundamental reform, aimed at restructuring the economy away from copper dependence, came to be widely recognised in Zambia only from around 1983.

Compared to an index of 100 in 1974, the terms of trade index had fallen from 49 in 1980 to a low of 28 in 1982. By the early eighties, real per capita incomes had declined by more than 50 per cent of their levels a decade earlier. With copper making up about 90 per cent of merchandise exports, the collapse in its price was mirrored in the balance of payments. Foreign exchange reserves became negligible and the country resorted to heavy external borrowing. In spite of that, external trade payments arrears accumulated. Between 1974 and 1982, and in current dollars, Zambia's import prices increased faster than can be explained by world inflation and oil price movements. This reflected increasing mark-ups by exporters to Zambia to cover costs of delays in payment. Thus, by 1982 trade payments arrears imposed indirect strains on Zambia's payments balance.

In 1982, significant arrears on debt service emerged for the first time; yet debt service paid absorbed 38 per cent of export earnings. In 1983, debt service due, including IMF repurchases and charges, came to almost 50 per cent of export earnings. To those obligations should be added accumulated external trade payments arrears, which summed to almost 100 per cent of export earnings.

It was assumed in the preceding sections that all production and imports were for final demand. We must now relax that assumption, and rectify the conclusion (pp. 64–5) that the only certain gainers in the short-run from terms of trade collapse in R are capitalists in the AM sector. In fact, the huge terms of trade deterioration had pronounced effects on Zambia's capacity to import. The continued sharp fall in real copper prices, combined with failure to restructure the economy fast, had resulted in a situation in which by mid-1985 the volume of imports (including essential inputs) was about 50 per cent below the 1980 level, and 75 per cent below the 1974 level. Scheduled debt service obligations now came to over 70 per cent of export earnings, and further trade payments arrears were accumulating.

By 1985, the chronic shortage of foreign exchange, through its impact on spare parts and materials, had led to massive excess capacity. Most companies were operating well below 50 per cent of capacity. The rate of capacity utilisation had declined, from about 65 per cent in 1981, in tandem with the decline in foreign exchange allocations. A 1985 policy document noted that out of a total fleet of 6000 tractors in the country only 38 per cent were in working condition. Out of 1700 serviceable trucks in the private sector, only about 800 were in running order. Because of the low level of transport capacity available, it was difficult to get crops to market, thereby indirectly accentuating the foreign exchange crisis. Some 50 per cent of the fleet of the United Bus Company of Zambia was grounded, thereby impeding access by workers to their places of employment.

Largely in reflection of (misguided) policy responses to the terms of trade collapse, the economy, by the early 1980s, was dominated by a regime of controls that distorted relative prices, in the sense that the signals they conveyed led to inefficient resource allocation. *First,* price control of goods, and the structure of protection, meant that goods prices were out of line with domestic resource costs. Price control, combined with the protective structure, meant that some goods got negative effective protection. A relatively high (low) effective rate of protection in a sector means that there are strong incentives for resources to be drawn into (away from) that sector. According to a 1984 World Bank study of Zambia, effective rates of protection escalated from low positive rates on capital goods to high rates on import-competing consumeables. The study also found that some foods had negative effective rates of protection, and agricultural machinery had low or negative effective rates of protection. This penalised the flow of resources into those sectors. (Recall the earlier conclusions regarding agriculture as a key growth sector in a labour-abundant economy following decay of the R sector.) *Second,* the currency was overvalued, which meant that imports were artificially cheap in terms of Zambian kwachas, while exporting was less profitable than otherwise. *Third,* interest rates were administratively controlled, leading to a situation in which real interest rates were negative. By making import-intensive capital goods more attractive than they would otherwise have been, this further accentuated the foreign exchange crisis.

Realisation that the problems of the copper sector were long-term, and that policy by way of short-run stabilisation was inappropriate, took some years. If markets had been free, the economy would automatically have shown some tendencies toward restructuring away from copper dependence. But much of the intervention in the agriculture and industry sectors, as well as general macroeconomic, exchange rate and commercial policies, was suppressing such tendencies. Fundamental reforms, aimed at supporting market forces toward restructuring, were forced on the system toward the mid-eighties. As initially implemented in 1983–6, these involved goods price liberalisation and attempts to neutralise the structure of effective protection between sectors, interest rate decontrol, and exchange rate liberalisation through an auction system for foreign exchange. (However, see Colclough, 1988, for policy reversals in 1987.) The extent of currency overvaluation is hinted by noting that just before the introduction of the auction system (in October 1985) the exchange rate was 2.35 kwacha to the US dollar; under the auction, it quickly depreciated, reaching k8.07 = $1 in mid-July 1986, and k15 to the dollar in December.

Restructuring the economy away from copper dependence will take decades. In the meantime, living standards will have to be maintained at or above subsistence levels. Thus, foreign borrowing will have to continue. Some of the problems this entails were discussed above (pp. 68–70). However, in the 1983–6 period several bilateral lenders made funds available to Zambia on easy terms, and some countries waived the originally negotiated interest payments – as, it seems, must inevitably be the case in the absence of outright debt repudiation by Zambia.

ALGEBRAIC APPENDIX

Differentiation of equation (5) in the text gives

$$d\check{Y}/dt = -\gamma e^{-\gamma t} - i\beta + i\beta\check{Y}$$

Hence, $d\check{Y}/dt - i\beta\check{Y} = -\gamma e^{-\gamma t} - i\beta$

Multiplying both sides by the integrating factor $e^{-i\beta t}$ implies:

$$d\check{Y}e^{-i\beta t}/dt = -\gamma e^{-(\gamma + i\beta)t} - i\beta e^{-i\beta t}$$

Integrating,

$$\check{Y}(t) = \gamma e^{-\gamma t}/(\gamma + i\beta) + 1 - Ke^{i\beta t}$$

where K is a constant. Setting $\check{Y}(0) = Y(0) = 1$ determines $K = \gamma/(\gamma + i\beta)$, which implies equation (6).

The derivation of equation (10) is similar to that of (6). Using the integrating factor $e^{-i\beta t}$ as before, (9) implies

(*) $\check{Y}(t) = \alpha Ae^{\alpha t}/(\alpha - i\beta) + 1 + Be^{i\beta t}$

The parameter B in (*) can be identified by equating equation (6) and (*) for $t = \tau$, yielding

$$B = \{\gamma/(\gamma + 1\beta)\}[e^{-(\gamma + i\beta)\tau} - 1] - \alpha Ae^{(\alpha - i\beta)\tau}/(\alpha - i\beta)$$

Substituting this value for B into (*), and re-arranging terms, yields equation (10).

74   *Development Perspectives for the 1990s*

NOTES

1. For help and comment I thank Frank Barry, Fergus Gaines, Patrick Honohan, Dermot McAleese, Alistair MacBean, Mary O'Dea, Renee Prendergast, Louis Smith and Richard Snape.
2. The argument that P_{NT} must fall implicitly assumes that, following changes in income distribution induced by the collapse in R, the marginal propensities to spend on NT of the various factor owners are not such as to cause the demand curve for NT to shift to the right beyond a certain distance. See Corden (1984), note 5. It is plausible to assume that this will not occur.
3. General equilibrium effects of resource depletion or terms of trade collapse can be decomposed into factor movement (supply side) effects and spending effects (Corden and Neary, 1982). In the present case, it is probable that production of NT will fall because: (a) The spending effect on NT depends on the marginal propensity to consume NT, which will be large since 'in mineral-exporting LDCs where increased government spending on construction and public services is likely to be the main channel for use of mineral rents, the marginal propensity will be high' (Daniel, 1986, p. 4). (b) The factor movement effect on NT depends on the relative use in each sector of the mobile factor, labour. If (because of the predominance of a very labour-intensive subsector A in AM) NT is capital-intensive relative to AM, then this effect will be small.
4. According to Henry's input–output tables for Ireland (Henry, 1980, Appendix 1), the direct requirements capital/labour ratio – measured as capital per man-year in thousands of pounds – was: agriculture, 4.1; trade margin and services, 11.0; economy-wide average, 10.7. Given the importance of agriculture in Ireland, these figures imply that industry was more capital-intensive than services (the bulk of non-tradeables), and that it was much more capital-intensive than agriculture. The relative capital intensity of agriculture in developing countries is presumably even lower. Hence the assumption that AM is more labour-intensive than NT in developing countries.
5. It is conceivable that M could expand relative to A (though A itself would expand). Thus, suppose that R is very intensive in its specific factor and that it employs very little labour, that the marginal propensity of specific-factor owners in R to spend on NT is very high, that NT is relatively capital-intensive and that M is even more capital-intensive. Contraction of R would then release little labour, and the main direct effect would be reduced spending on NT. NT would then release plenty of capital, but little labour, to the AM sector, thereby inducing M to expand relative to A.

REFERENCES

Colclough, C., (1988) 'Zambian Adjustment Strategy – With and Without the IMF', *IDS Bulletin*, 19 (1) 51–60.
Corden, W. M., (1984) 'Booming Sector and Dutch Disease Economics: Survey and Consolidation', *Oxford Economic Papers*, 36, 359–80.
Corden, W. M., and J. P. Neary, (1982) 'Booming Sector and De-Industrialisation in a Small Open Economy', *Economic Journal*, 92, 825–48.
Daniel, P., (1986) 'Editorial', *IDS Bulletin*, 17 (4) 1–9.
Edwards, S., (1988) 'Terms of Trade, Tariffs, and Labour Market Adjustment in Developing Countries', *World Bank Economic Review*, 2, 165–86.

Evans, D., (1986) 'Reverse Dutch Disease and Mineral Exporting Developing Countries', *IDS Bulletin*, 17 (4) 10–13.

Henry, E. W., (1980) *Irish Input-Output Structures, 1976*, (Dublin: The Economic and Social Research Institute).

Mayer, W., (1974) 'Short-Run and Long-Run Equilibrium for a Small Open Economy', *Journal of Political Economy*, 82, 955–67.

Ndulo, M., and D. Norton, (1987) 'Macroeconomic Policy Issues', in H. O'Neill and Others, *Transforming a Single-Product Economy: An Examination of the First Stage of Zambia's Economic Reform Program, 1982–86*, (Washington: Economic Development Institute of the World Bank, 1987).

Neary, J. P., (1978) 'Short-Run Capital Specificity and the Pure Theory of International Trade', *Economic Journal*, 88, 488–510.

Neary, J. P., and S. van Wijnbergen, (1985), 'Natural Resources and the Macroeconomy: A Theoretical Framework', in J. P. Neary and S. van Wijnbergen (eds), *Natural Resources and the Macroeconomy*, (Oxford: Blackwell).

Pinto, B., (1987) 'Nigeria During and After the Oil Boom: A Policy Comparison with Indonesia', *World Bank Economic Review*, 1, 419–45.

Rybczynski, T. M., (1955) 'Factor Endowment and Relative Commodity Prices', *Economica*, N.S. 22, 336–41.

Snape, R. H., (1977) 'Effects of Mineral Development on the Economy', *Australian Journal of Agricultural Economics*, 21, 147–56.

The Economist, (1977) 26 November, 82–3.

5 Trade Policies and Economic Performance of Developing Countries in the 1980s[1]

S. M. Shafaeddin

INTRODUCTION

It has been argued that developing countries should liberalise their trade regimes in order to expand production and exports of manufactured goods and consequently enhance their economic development.[2] While there is no general agreement on the details of trade liberalisation measures, their main elements can be identified as: the removal or conversion to tariffs of import quotas, import licensing and other quantitative restrictions; the reduction of the level and the variability of import tariffs rates and compensatory devaluation of the local currency.

The proponents of trade liberalisation argue that, generally speaking, these measures would tend to reduce government intervention in foreign trade and remedy the bias against exports *vis-à-vis* sale in the domestic market. They also claim that quota and other quantitative restrictions interfere with the price mechanism, that high and prolonged tariff protection involves allocative and X-inefficiencies and that discriminatory tariffs create distortions and impede the progress of competitive firms and industries. Devaluation is seen as being necessary to change the incentive structure in favour of tradeable goods *vis-à-vis* non-tradeable goods, and to increase competitiveness of exports in international markets. A further advantage of devaluation is that it would compensate for the reduction in relative prices of importables caused by tariff reductions (Weiss, 1988, ch. 7). The example of Asian NICs, particularly South Korea, is often cited as countries with liberal trade regimes by proponents of this school of thought.

The 1980s provide us with a unique opportunity to examine the performance of developing countries in the light of the above-mentioned argument. Over this period a large number of developing countries have undertaken trade liberalisation measures and exchange rate adjustments. The experience of a sample of these countries is examined in this chapter. In the second section, the export and general economic performance of the

77

sample countries is reviewed. It is shown that, while their export and economic performance vary, only a few newcomers have joined the list of sucessful exporters of manufactured goods (henceforth exports). Otherwise, countries with a higher level of development, previous industrial base and manufacturing export capabilities continued to show high export growth. It is also shown that rapid expansion of supply capability is a necessary condition for rapid export expansion, but not a sufficient one; that rapid (slow) export expansion may not necessarily lead to good (sluggish) general economic performance; and that good economic performance could be achieved without rapid export expansion. In addition, it is argued that rapid growth of exports of manufactured goods has been at the cost of some deterioration in the terms of trade and in some cases at the cost of availability of supply to the domestic market and of de-industrialisation. Many low-income countries have suffered from both de-industrialisation and negative or sluggish export growth.

In the third section it is argued that there is no clear association between trade liberalisation and exchange rate policies, on the one hand, and export and economic performance, on the other. The impact of trade liberalisation and devaluation on those performances tends to be mixed, depending on the supply capabilities of the countries concerned and on the nature of the policies adopted. In low-income countries, the implementation of liberalisation measures and devaluation may not only fail to stimulate exports of manufactured products, but may also be accompanied by de-industrialisation and even heavier dependence on exports of primary commodities. It is also argued that Asian NICs, far from pursuing a liberal trade regime, applied a mixture of input-substitution and export promotion, the precise nature of which changed over time. The final section of the chapter presents some conclusions.

COUNTRY PERFORMANCES

The analysis of the performance of developing countries is based on a sample of thirty-two countries and draws on data and information available in UNCTAD. The sample is chosen from countries in different regions, with different levels of development, industrial bases,[3] debt burdens and also with different initial trade policy stance and varied attempts at trade liberalisation and exchange rate adjustment. The data used are derived from World Bank sources (the most up-to-date ones available in UNCTAD) and are based on the UNIDO definition of manufactured goods. Accordingly, manufacturing includes processed and semi-processed commodities. Such inclusions may inflate growth of exports of manufactured goods in cases where value added in processing is small and the relative importance of exports of these products has increased. For the purpose of calculating exports in real terms and the terms of trade, the World Bank unit value indices for exports are employed. These indices appear to be based on guessed estimates and hence should be regarded with a certain degree of caution. For countries where exports from export processing zones (EPZ) constitute a significant proportion of total exports of manu- factured goods, e.g. Mauritius, Malaysia and to some extent Mexico, the figures on growth of exports may be inflated. This could happen where the import-intensity of EPZ exports (which are usually highly import- intensive) increases over time. For example, in the case of Mauritius the import-intensity (excluding imports of capital goods) of EPZ's exports rose from 56 per cent in 1982 to 68 per cent in 1986.[4]

Various indicators of relative export performance are employed in the literature. These include indices of revealed comparative advantage, com- petitiveness, diversification and so on. Here, growth rates of exports in real terms (henceforth export volume), net barter terms of trade and income terms of trade have been examined.

The data on export volume provide some indication of the relative abilities of countries to export (but not necessarily the capacity to produce) irrespective of the gains attained, costs involved and the impact of exports on their general economic performance. When expansion of export volume is accompanied by the expansion of output, it is likely to have a positive impact on real variables such as employment. Changes in the net barter terms of trade are an indication of the distribution of gains from trade between the exporter and the importers. The income terms of trade measure the results of efforts in exportation in terms of the capacity to purchase relevant import items.

As far as the inter-relations between exports of manufactured goods, supply capabilities and general economic performance are concerned, three main indicators have been chosen: growth of manufacturing value added (MVA) and GDP, and changes in consumer price indices. Figures on growth of MVA and GDP in particular can also be used to show whether or not export expansion has been accompanied by growth of production in relevant cases.

The necessary data for the analysis of countries' performance are shown in Table 5.1. The countries are classified into three main categories according to their rate of growth of export volume: high (A), low or negative (B) and moderate (C). Within each category countries are grouped according to their growth of MVA and rate of consumer price inflation. Within each group countries are ranked according to their rate of growth of volume of exports of manufactured goods.

Export volume and terms of trade

According to Table 5.1, eleven out of thirty-two countries enjoyed a high

TABLE 5.1 *Average annual growth rates of exports, output, terms of trade, purchasing power and consumer prices of sample countries (1980–7)**

Countries	Export volume^a		Net barter terms of trade^e		purchasing power		Value added^a		Consumer price index
	Manufactures	Total	Manufactures	Total	Manufactures	Total	Manufactures	GDP	
A. High export growth:									
a. High output^f growth and low or moderate inflation									
Indonesia	43.7	2.4	-3.8	-4.4	39.9	-2.2	7.5	3.8	10.3
Malaysia	16.9	9.0	-2.1	-4.0	14.9	5.0	6.7	4.7	4.0
Korea	14.8	14.8	-2.1	0.8	12.7	14.0	10.9	8.7	8.9
Sri Lanka	14.0	5.7	-1.8	-2.5	12.2	3.2	6.2	3.9	12.8
Mauritius	13.7	11.1	-0.5	-7.7	13.2	3.4	11.2	6.2	11.3
Thailand	13.6	11.4	-2.9	-2.0	10.7	9.4	6.1	5.7	6.1
Pakistan	12.8	9.0	-2.2	0.0	10.6	9.0	9.1	6.8	7.0
Average^a	*18.5*	*9.1*	*-2.2*	*-2.8*	*16.3*	*6.0*	*8.2*	*5.7*	*8.6*
b. High output growth and very high inflation									
Turkey	42.9	22.5	-1.7	0.4	41.2	22.1	8.4	5.6	47.2
c. Moderate output growth and moderate inflation									
Venezuela	19.1	-1.4	-2.5	-6.5	16.6	-7.9	2.7	0.6	14.6
d. Low output growth and low inflation									
Morocco	15.2	3.2	-2.6	1.1	12.6	2.1	1.6	2.8	8.8
e. Low output growth and very high inflation									
Mexico	23.8	8.7	1.4	-4.0	25.2	4.7	0.5	1.1	69.5
Average for A	*21.0*	*8.1*	*-1.9*	*-2.6*	*19.1*	*5.7*	*6.4*	*4.6*	*18.2*
B. Low or negative export growth:									
f. High output growth and low or moderate inflation									
India	2.6	4.0	2.4	2.0	0.2	2.0	8.3	4.9	10.3

81

g. Moderate output growth and low or moderate inflation									
Bangladesh	4.9	5.5	-1.6	0.7	3.3	4.8	3.1	4.0	11.7
Singapore	4.2	6.9	1.3	0.4	2.9	6.5	4.9	6.0	3.0
Kenya	1.4	-2.2	-3.3	-1.0	-1.9	-3.2	4.4	3.5	11.2
Average	*3.5*	*3.4*	*-1.2*	*-0.3*	*1.4*	*2.7*	*4.1*	*4.5*	*8.6*
h. Moderate output growth and high inflation									
Columbia	-3.1	8.1	2.8	-4.2	-0.3	3.9	3.1	3.2	22.6
i. Low or negative output growth and high or very high inflation[h]									
Ghana[d]	2.9	-0.9	-1.2	-1.7	1.7	-2.2	1.0	1.2	53.3
Yugoslavia	2.6	1.7	0.8	3.5	1.8	5.2	2.7[b]	0.9	60.0
Costa Rica	2.2	3.4	-0.5	-2.1	1.7	1.3	–	1.4	29.2
Chile	1.4	4.2	-1.1	-2.2	0.3	2.0	1.3	1.5	22.8
Nigeria[c]	1.1	-7.1	-0.8	-7.1	0.3	0.0	1.0	-2.0	15.3
Bolivia[c, d]	-0.3	-0.5	-2.6	-8.6	-5.6	-9.1	-5.5	-1.6	1725.0
Côte d'Ivoire	-1.5	2.1	-0.5	-0.8	-2.0	-1.4	-2.0[i]	2.4	6.9
Uruguay	-2.2	3.0	1.1	-0.3	-1.1	2.7	-0.6	-0.5	55.0
Peru	-2.5	-1.0	-2.2	-5.0	-4.7	-6.0	3.0	2.3	93.4
Argentina	-3.8	-0.8	1.2	-2.8	-2.6	-3.6	-0.7	-0.6	279.3
Jamaica	-4.1	-3.1	-0.5	0.2	-4.6	-2.9	2.2	1.0	16.7
Ecuador[c, d]	-6.9	3.1	4.4	-5.7	-2.5	-2.6	0.8	1.1	25.7
Sierra Leon[c, d]	-6.7	-5.5	-0.5	-0.9	-7.2	-6.4	2.1	0.3	66.8
Average	*-1.7*	*-0.1*	*-0.2*	*-2.6*	*-1.9*	*-0.6*	*0.28*	*0.5*	*188.4*
Average for B	*-0.4*	*1.1*	*-0.04*	*-2.1*	*-1.2*	*0.4*	*1.1*	*1.6*	*139.3*
C. Moderate export growth:									
j. High output growth and low inflation									
Senegal	7.2	6.8	-0.5	-0.7	6.7	6.1	5.2	3.7	8.8
k. Low output growth and high inflation									
Philippines	5.3	-0.9	0.6	-0.02	4.7	-0.9	0.1	0.5	16.2

82

1. *Low output growth and very high inflation*

Brazil	6.4	6.2	-0.2	0.1	6.2	6.3	1.5	2.9	153.4
Average for C	*6.3*	*4.0*	*-0.03*	*-0.2*	*5.9*	*3.8*	*2.3*	*2.4*	*59.5*

Notes:

a In constant 1980 prices.
b 1980–86.
c Exports of manufactured goods constitute less than 5 per cent of total exports.
d Exports of manufactured goods are less than $75 million.
e The export unit value deflated by the unit value of exports of manufactured goods from developed market economy countries.
f Manufactured value added (MVA) only.
g All averages are simple ones.
h Côte d'Ivoire is also included despite its low inflation because of other common characteristics.
i The industrial sector.

* The notations for percentage growth rates are as follows:

Exports : high: more than 10; moderate: between 10 and 5; low: less than 5;
MVA   : high: more than 5; moderate: between 5 and 3; low: less than 3;
Consumer prices: very high: more than 30; high: between 30 and 15; moderate: between 15 and 10; low: less than 10.

SOURCES: Based on World Bank's Data Bank and *World Tables*, except for the consumer price indices and the unit value indices of manufactured goods which are based on IMF, *IFS*, various issues and on UN *Monthly Statistical Bulletin*, various issues, respectively.

rate of growth of exports of manufactured goods (Category A) and three countries showed moderate growth rates (Category C). Of the remaining countries (Category B), half suffered from negative growth rates and the other half showed positive but low rates of growth of manufactured exports.

With the exception of Pakistan, countries in Category A were also among the successful exporters of 1970s. If anything, the growth rate of exports of the majority of them decelerated in the 1980s presumably because of the slow-down in international trade. Indonesia, Turkey, Mexico, Pakistan and Venezuela are the only ones which accelerated their exports of manufactured goods.

The majority of countries in Category A are located in South and South-East Asia. They enjoyed relatively high levels of development and had a substantial industrial base at the beginning of the period. By contrast, the majority of countries in Category B began the period with a lower level of development and a smaller industrial base. These are mainly located in Africa and Latin America and including many heavily-indebted countries.

The rapid expansion of export volume in the case of Category A countries has not been without costs. On balance, these countries have suffered more than those in Category B from deterioration in the net barter terms of trade of their manufacturing exports. The simple average annual rate of decline in the terms of trade has been 1.9 and 0.04 for Categories A and B respectively. Moreover, except for Mexico, no country in Category A shows positive change in the terms of trade. By contrast, seven out of eighteen countries in Category B enjoyed improvement in their terms of trade for manufactured goods.[5]

As a result of significant deterioration in their net barter terms of trade, performance of Category A countries in terms of purchasing power of exports of manufactured goods is not as impressive as their performance in terms of export volume. Nonetheless they still stand out, except for Venezuela and Indonesia, both of which suffered severely from the fall in petroleum prices, the combination of fast growth rate and large share of exports of manufactured goods in total exports contributed to significant improvement in their overall income terms of trade. Such performances are in sharp contrast with those of certain countries in Category B, mostly group i, which suffered from both falling volume and declining net barter terms of trade of both manufactured goods and total exports.

Hence, on balance, countries in Category A enjoyed significantly better export performance despite their higher loss in net barter terms of trade. Most of them are Asian countries which displayed impressive export performances in the 1970s as well.

Exports and general economic performance

With regard to the association between exports of manufactured goods and total exports and general economic performance, it appears first of all that good (sluggish) export performance is not necessarily associated with good (sluggish) economic performance. It is of course true that for the majority of countries in Category A high export performance was accompanied by rapid expansion of manufacturing and total output as well as price stability. Nevertheless, one cannot identify any direction of causation. If anything, one could claim that supply capabilities have contributed to the sustainability of export growth in these countries in the 1970s and 1980s. In some countries, e.g. Mexico, rather than being an engine of growth, exports of manufactured goods have been accompanied by little growth of output and by rising inflation. Morocco and Brazil also display a similar pattern to a varying degree.

Secondly, in the case of India and other countries in Category B, rapid or moderate growth of MVA and GDP and reasonable price stability have been achieved without fast export expansion.

Thirdly, comparison of groups (f), (a) and (i) indicates that rapid supply expansion is not necessarily accompanied by rapid export growth, implying that other conditions are also required for export expansion.

Fourthly, twelve out of thirty-two countries, mostly in Group B.i (but Mexico and Morocco are two notable examples from Category A) have shown a degree of de-industrialisation in the 1980s in the sense that the share of MVA in GDP has fallen. In some countries, such decline has been accompanied by negative rates of growth of both MVA and GDP (Bolivia, Uruguay, Argentina); in some others MVA expanded at a very slow rates (Mexico, Morocco, Bangladesh, Colombia, Philippines, Brazil, Ghana, Chile, and Ecuador).[6]

Finally, in thirteen out of eighteen countries in Category B, the dependence on exports of primary commodities increased in the 1980s due to slow growth of exports of manufactures. In seven of these countries (Chile, Uruguay, Argentina, Jamaica, Ecuador, Colombia and Bangladesh) the share of MVA in GDP also fell (see also Table 5.A1 for the relevant ratios).

To sum up, good economic performance has been achieved both with and without fast export expansion. Supply capabilities have played an important role in successful exportation and there has been a significant association between the initial level of industrialisation and export expansion. In a number of countries, particularly low-income ones, slow export growth has been accompanied by de-industrialisation.

The inter-country and inter-regional differences in export and general economic performance lead us to the following questions. Why have countries with a higher initial level of development and industrial base, and the Asian countries, continued to perform better than others? Why have countries with a small industrial base, particularly in Africa, failed in both export and general economic performance? While *a priori* one may list a number of external and internal factors which have influenced such divergence, in this paper the focus will be on the role of trade policies and exchange rate adjustments. The impact of two other important factors – investment and imports – have been analysed in Shafaeddin (1989).

TRADE POLICIES AND EXCHANGE RATE ADJUSTMENTS

Have trade liberalisation and a tendency towards uniform import duties and exchange rate adjustment resulted in better economic performance? In particular, has exchange rate devaluation stimulated exports of manufactured goods? Have countries, which have shown relatively better economic and export performance, particularly South Korea, followed a liberal trade regime? This section will shed some light on these questions while discussing trade and exchange rate policies of the sample countries.

General tendencies

A number of unresolved conceptual, methodological and practical problems make a precise judgement on the impact of trade policies on trade and economic performance very difficult. The most important conceptual problems are related to the definition of the orientation of trade strategy,[7] the distinction between trade liberalisation and trade policy reform, and the relations between trade orientation and market orientation. For example, if by outward orientation is meant neutralising the bias in the incentive structure against exports, two different approaches to the issue are available. One is to liberalise both imports and export regimes leaving trade absolutely to the operation of market forces. The other is to equalise the incentives to exports and imports regardless of the level of import barriers and export incentives.[8]

The main practical problems are related to difficulties in separating the impact of trade policies from those of industrial and macro-economic policies and the interactions between internal policies and external conditions. Another problem is the lack of comprehensive data. To analyse the impact of import regimes on exports and output performance, one needs the effective rate of protection. Up-to-date calculations are not available for all countries and even where they are available they suffer from differences in the methodology of calculation. Above all, there is sometimes a confusion in the literature between the uniformity in nominal and effective tariff rates.[9] Nevertheless, since in practice many developing countries have been advised in the current decade to aim towards more uniform nominal tariff rates, the use of nominal rates would not be irrelevant for our purpose.

Apart from the tendency towards uniformity in tariff rates, the distinctive feature of the 1980s, as far as trade policies of developing countries are concerned, is that most of them have taken one, or a combination, of the following measures in response to changes in the external situation: conversion of non-tariff measures to tariffs, reductions in tariff rates, expenditure switching (devaluation) and expenditure reduction.

For the reasons mentioned above, in-depth research on the impact of trade and exchange rate policies on export performance is required. Nevertheless, some preliminary inferences may be made based on the main features of changes in the trade and exchange rate policies of the sample countries. Figure 5.1 provides some qualitative information, mainly on two extreme cases from the sample countries: high and low export and economic performers, i.e. group a in Category A and group i in Category B (see Table 5.1). Mauritius was excluded from the first group because trade and exchange rate policies have hardly any relevance to EPZs which are responsible for almost its entire export of manufactured goods. (EPZ is also important in Malaysia, although to a lesser extent, and should be born in mind in the interpretation of data.) In the case of low performers we included countries with both low and higher incomes and industrial bases. India and Singapore from Category B (groups f and g) are included as well because of their high general economic performance despite low export growth. The Philippines represents Category C. The chart depicts the relative, rather than the absolute position of the countries in their tendencies on various policies. For measuring selectivity (i.e. disparity) in tariff and non-tariff measures, a particular index developed for the purpose was employed as explained at the bottom of Table 5.A2.

Accordingly, one obtains mixed results. Among both high and low performers one finds countries which followed similar import and exchange rate policies. Within each category one could find countries with similar exchange rate policies but different import regimes. For example, low-performing nations such as Argentina, Peru, the Philippines, and high performers like Indonesia and Pakistan, undertook significant real exchange rate devaluation, and in all these countries the import regime remained highly restrictive despite some changes. Bolivia, Uruguay and Chile, like Argentina, Peru and the Philippines, show significant real exchange rate devaluation, but unlike the latter countries they had low levels of import barriers at the beginning of the 1980s and, in the case of Bolivia and Uruguay, undertook further significant liberalisation during the 1980s. In many low-income countries trade liberalisation and exchange rate devaluation not only did not stimulate exports but were also accompanied by de-industrialisation. India was neither active in its exchange rate policies, nor in liberalising its import regime, yet it showed a significant degree of success in GDP growth and price stability, despite its relatively low export growth.[10] Some higher performers, e.g. Malaysia, Thailand and South Korea, devalued their currency moderately and intensified liberalisation of their import regime. Nevertheless, their high performance should not be attributed solely to liberalisation of their import regimes. These countries at the same time exhibited high supply capabilities and investment performance and are among countries which enjoyed high growth rates of imports (Shafaeddin, 1989). Moreover, their low average tariff rates should not imply that they have followed a liberal trade regime, as will be explained shortly.

Before doing so, it will be useful to examine in some detail the interrelation between the level of development and initial industrial base on the one hand, and trade strategies and devaluation on the other.

The level of development and the initial industrial base

Import regime

The number of sample countries is small and does not include many low-income countries. Nevertheless, it appears that most of the low performers of Figure 5.1 which significantly reduced their import barriers, whether from a low or high level of protection, were countries with low levels of development and a particularly small industrial base. By contrast, high export performers who have either relatively low import barriers or reduced their import restrictions, were countries with relatively high levels of development, a substantial industrial base and, thus, significant supply capabilities.

These results are not surprising. Trade policies play different roles for the two groups concerned. For the low-income group, the main issue is establishing an industrial base, i.e. industrial supply capability. Before developing such capacity, import liberalisation would lock them in primary production. For the countries which have already gone through long years of import-substitution and developed an industrial base, the main issue is the transition of their mature, or nearly mature, industries into a competitive one in both domestic and external markets. In some of these countries, the capacity to produce capital goods has facilitated adjustment to changes in the external situation and reduced the negative impact of import compression on investment. South Korea is once again a good example. The relative success of Brazil, as compared with Mexico, in its 1984–5 policy reform is another example (Ros, 1986, p. 335–61).

Devaluation and the stability of the exchange rate

The literature on devaluation is inconclusive and often fails to differentiate between developed and developing countries and among various developing countries.[11]

The results of this study show that for most low-income countries (in

FIGURE 5.1 Typology of selected sample countries according to their growth in absorption and relative position in trade and exchange rate policies in the 1980s

Countries	Real effective exchange rate devaluation[a]			Growth in absorption (annual average)		Trade regime — Imports (all charges, NTMS)				Indices of selectivity of import barriers[b] — changes				changes		NTMs
	S	M	L	Negative	Positive but less than GDP_g	Low and reduced significantly	Low and maintained or reduced	High but reduced (S)	High but reduced (L)	S	L	H	M	H	M	L
Low Performers: Group B.i																
Bolivia	X			X		X				X				X		X
Chile, Uruguay	X				X	X				X				X		X
Jamaica	X				X	X						X		X		X
Ghana	X				X			X								
Costa Rica	X				X			X		X				X		X
Argentina		X[c]		X					X	X						X
Nigeria	X			X					X	X				X		
Group C																
Philippines	X			X			X			X						X
High Performers: Group A.a																

Korea, Rep. of	x						x		x
Sri Lanka	x^c						x		x
Thailand	x			x		x			x
Malaysia	x			x		x	x		
Indonesia	x^c		x		x			x	
Pakistan	x		x	x		x			x
Group B.f									
India	x^c				x	x	x		
Singapore	x^d	x		x		x	x		x

Notes:
S = significant; M = medium; L = little; GDP_g = annual average growth rate in GDP.30; [a] S = more than 20 per cent;
M = between 20 and 5 per cent; L = less than 5 per cent;
[b] High = higher than the average sum plus °0 per cent of the average.
 Medium = the range of average ± °0 per cent of the average.
 Low = less than the sum average minus °0 per cent of the average.
[c] Real exchange rates.

SOURCE: Based on tables A.2 and A.3 and UNCTAD's Data bank on Trade Control Measures of Developing Countries.

Category B) with a small industrial base and underdeveloped supply capabilities, large devaluations of real exchange rates not only did not stimulate exports, but were also accompanied by high inflation (see Table 5.1). For countries with higher incomes and a substantial industrial base the results vary. In some cases, for example Korea and Thailand, a small depreciation of the real exchange rate is associated with high export performance. By contrast, for certain others devaluation seems not to have stimulated exports (e.g. Argentina, Costa Rica, etc.). Yet, in some other higher income countries (e.g. Mexico and Turkey) a large devaluation is accompanied by a high rate of growth of exports and a high rate of inflation. Nevertheless, for the majority of countries in Category A, where devaluation is associated with high export performance, higher export performance is also associated with higher terms of trade losses (see also Table 5.1 and pp. 79, 83).

In such low-income countries of Category B as Ghana, Nigeria, Bolivia, Sierra-Leone, etc., to achieve a certain rate of real exchange devaluation, a large devaluation of the nominal exchange rate is necessary (see Table 5.A3) because devaluation leads to inflation. In these countries, short-run import price elasticities of demand and export price elasticities of supply are low. Exports consist mainly of primary commodities whose international prices are demand-determined and denominated in foreign currency. These prices are not altered by devaluation by an individual (small producer) country, and hence, devaluation does not stimulate external demand unless a number of countries producing the same commodity devalue in the same period, as was the case in the 1980s. To produce even small volume expansions, such devaluations have to be large since the price elasticity of demand for primary commodities is low.[12] In these circumstances, the impact of the volume expansion is partially offset by the decline in international prices with the result that yet larger devaluations would be required to increase export value. Large devaluations, however, tend to lead more to inflation than output expansion, not only in the primary sector but also in the manufacturing sector.[13] While normally short-run supply elasticities are higher in the manufacturing sector, this is not necessarily the case in countries with a small industrial base and low levels of production capability.

In those South-East Asian countries with higher levels of development, a substantial industrial base and/or excess capacity, skilled manpower and developed infra-structure, particularly those with an important capital goods sector and with manufacturing export capabilities, a small change in the nominal exchange rate is sufficient to obtain real exchange devaluation (see Table 5.A3). In these countries, the manufacturing exports usually show higher supply and demand elasticities. Moreover, prices of manufactured goods are cost-determined; and devaluation by an individual producer also *does* alter those prices, in terms of foreign currency, and stimulates their external demand. The export price elasticities of demand for many manufactured goods being more than unity,[14] the terms of trade losses (caused by individual or collective devaluation) would not be as high as in the case of primary products, and a small devaluation would usually be enough to stimulate demand for exports. It should be noted, however, that the terms of trade losses may not always be less in the case of manufactured goods. For the 1980s, in a number of new exporting countries, e.g. Turkey, Pakistan, Thailand, Bangladesh, Kenya and Jamaica, terms of trade losses in the manufacturing sector have been greater than those in the primary sector.

Even in countries with an important industrial base, the supply (production) elasticities of tradeable goods depend, to some extent, on the availability of foreign exchange. When, as in the case of Korea and other South-East Asian countries, the availability of foreign exchange is relatively buoyant, the manufacturing sector responds positively to relative price changes (Shafaeddin, 1989). Import compression, by contrast, reduces supply and import demand elasticities,[15] limiting the responsiveness of production of tradeable goods to devaluation. In these circumstances, devaluation may lead only to inflation, particularly, as in the case of Brazil, where wage indexation prevails or it stimulates exports without stimulating production. It may also lead to inflation as happened, for example, in Mexico (Shafaeddin, 1989).

It is sometimes argued that in the medium- or long-term, by giving appropriate signals to decision-makers, devaluation serves as an instrument for re-allocation of resources and stimulates production and exports of non-traditional goods leading to diversification.[16] However, as far as the 1980s are concerned, the results of the analysis for the medium-term would not be much different from those of the short-term with one qualification. For low-income primary producing countries and higher income countries which suffer from import compression, the production capacity tended to increase in the primary rather than in the secondary sector, even in the medium-term. In fact, as noted earlier, the manufacturing sector suffered from de-industrialisation. Moreover, as Bhaskar (1989) indicates, devaluation by a number of producers of the same commodity (tea) may lead to the expansion of output of primary commodities and to terms of trade losses (Bhaskar, 1989).

The impact of devaluation on exports of manufactured goods in the long-run could be exemplified by the case of Chile which started employing liberal exchange rate policies in the early 1970s. There, percentage share of the manufacturing sector in GNP declined from 27.4 in 1970 to 22.1 in 1980 and to 21.8 in 1987.[17] The share of exports of manufactures in total exports increased from about 4 to nearly 9 per cent over the period of

1970s, but declined again to 7 per cent in 1986.[18] Meanwhile, the share of exports of non-traditional primary-goods such as fruits, vegetables and some other food items, expanded.

In the case of higher-income countries which have suffered from import compression, e.g. Brazil and Argentina, the import-intensity of the modern manufacturing sector is far greater than those of primary commodities.

In conclusion, the devaluation and 'trade liberalisation' of the 1980s in primary producing countries and those countries which suffered from import compression, has led to an absolutely contrary result to what had been intended in terms of resource allocation.

Trade regimes of Asian NICs and other main exporters of manufactures

The record of trade policies of Asian NICs and other main exporters of manufactured goods does not indicate that they have followed a liberal trade regime either in the 1980s or in the previous period. Since South Korea is often cited as an example of a country with a liberal trade regime, in the following pages we refer mainly to this country. Most of Asian NICs have started their industrialisation with import-substitution, but after they reached a certain level of development they applied a mixture of import-substitution and export promotion with selectivity and a discriminatory incentive structure.

Mixed policies of import substitution and export promotion

While, at present, most Asian NICs have relatively low import barriers, this does not imply that they do not provide incentives for production for the home market. In these countries, as in Japan, the shift to export orientation did not mean the end of import-substitution. First, in all these countries the effective rate of protection has been higher, and still is higher, than the nominal rate; hence domestic industries in most of these countries still enjoy some protection.[19] In fact, even in nominal terms some of them appear more protective than many other developing countries. For example, in the mid-1980s South Korea ranked eighth in the sample countries of this study, in terms of the combination of mean tariffs, 'all charges' and frequency of Non-Tariff Measures (NTMs), thirteenth in terms of mean tariffs alone, twelfth in terms of all charges and eleventh in terms of frequency of NTMs.[20]

Secondly, the exporters of manufactured goods have been provided with incentives and concessions of one kind or another in the countries concerned. For example, in the case of South Korea, the value to exporters of the concessions is estimated to have been around 10 per cent of gross export receipts in the late 1960s.[21] Even in the 1980s exports were provided with various incentives including favourable interest rate, tax concessions and subsidies by the governments of most of these countries. Malaysia intensified its import-substitution policies in the late 1960s and in 1970s, but at the same time introduced important incentives for exports in 1968. Thailand has also followed mixed policies since 1972 after intensive import-substitutions in 1960s.[22]

Hence, one distinctive feature of most Asian NICs in both 1970s and 1980s is that they have followed a mixed trade policy.

Selectivity

Figure 5.1 indicates that most countries with good export and economic performances seem to have followed more than others the selectivity principle in their nominal tariff structure, and to some extent in the structure of non-tariff measures. By contrast, most low export performers, Jamaica being one notable exception, have followed, relatively speaking, a uniform import incentive structure (both tariff and NTMs) in their import liberalisation efforts (also see Table 5.A2). The method of calculation of the selectivity index used here is very preliminary, as mentioned earlier, due to data constraints. To check these results a more satisfactory index (coefficient of variation) was used for calculation of dispersion of tariff rates for which the calculation was feasible. On balance, the results confirm those attained here.

In South Korea, Malaysia, and Thailand as well as most other South-East Asian countries the tariff system has been geared at any particular period to protection of certain industries on a selective basis. The bias however depended on the state of industrialisation and has changed over time. For example, in the 1950s South Korea provided selected light industries with duty-free status for imports of non-competitive capital goods and raw materials while imposing high tariffs on finished goods, and very high tariffs on luxury items (Hong, 1979, pp. 45–53). In late 1970s the bias in discriminatory tariff rates were changed in such a way that the effective rate of protection favoured consumer durables and machinery which enjoyed effective rates of up to 135 per cent (Arndt, 1987).

A comparison of import liberalisation efforts of Sri Lanka and Colombia in the late 1970s is instructive as far as the issue of selectivity is concerned. Sri Lanka liberalised its import regime on a discriminatory basis. The effective protection coefficient varied from −5 to 3.[23] By contrast, Colombia liberalised its import regime on a uniform basis.[24] In the case of Colombia import liberalisation led to a severe decline in output and exports of the manufacturing sector mainly in the 'late industries'. These industries still required infant industry protection and depended on imports more than the traditional industries which enjoyed a certain degree of maturity. By contrast, in the case of Sri Lanka output and exports expanded fast, particularly during the first couple of years before the country faced problems caused by sluggish external demand.[25]

In most successful Asian countries, particularly in South Korea, the discriminatory incentive structure was not confined to the import regime alone. It was also applied to the export regime and the industrial and investment incentive structures in terms of availability and price of imported capital goods and in terms of interest charges and other investment costs.[26]

The theoretical argument against and in favour of selectivity is an extension of the argument against and in favour of protection and other forms of government intervention in international trade. The proponents of free trade would argue that selectivity contributes to price distortion and as a result to misallocation of resources. The main arguments in favour of selectivity include: 'infant industry protection', scarcity and externalities. The infant industry argument is well known. One should add, however, that a country cannot by definition, develop dynamic comparative advantage in all production lines at the same time.

The scarcity argument is complementary to the infant industry argument. Real and financial resources, particularly foreign exchange and skilled labour are scarce in developing countries. Hence to spread resources in an excessively diversified manner, without being able to accumulate in any sector the level necessary to start a process of cumulative causation, is sub-optimal (OCampo, 1986, p. 158).

The externality argument[27] is related to the diseconomies created for infant (and other) industries caused by consumption of imported luxury goods. Each dollar spent on these goods denies availability of that amount of scarce foreign exchange to industries where the need for it may be very great.[28]

Finally, if the intention is to provide a uniform incentive structure to various industries, the introduction of a uniform nominal tariff would not serve the purpose since a uniform effective rate of protection requires non-uniform nominal tariff rates because various industries do not use the same inputs. Even if they do, the input-output coefficients are different and the share of imports in total inputs may vary in each case.

It should be emphasised that as the arguments in favour or against protectionism and liberalisation cannot be generalised, 'selectivity' also ought to be considered within a particular context and be related to the level of development and the state of industrialisation of a country.

CONCLUSIONS

Our analysis of the sample countries for 1980–7 in this study indicates that their export and economic performance varied in the 1980s. On balance, a number of Asian countries with higher levels of development, an initial industrial base and supply capabilities, continued relatively rapid manufacturing export and output growth together with a reasonable degree of price stability. Higher rates of growth of export volume in these countries as well as a number of others was significant enough to achieve high rates of growth of purchasing power of exports of manufactures. This was so despite the fact that their higher export volume growth was achieved at the cost of loss in their net barter terms of trade in excess of the terms of trade losses of other countries studied. Most low-income countries of Africa and heavily indebted countries in Latin America showed poor performance in all respects. While supply capability seems to have been an important determinant of export performance, in the majority of cases policies to stimulate exports have been partially at the expense of availability of supply to the domestic market. Consequently, some of the countries which have managed to expand their exports may not be able to sustain their export growth in the future.

The impact of trade liberalisation measures and devaluation on export performance has also been mixed depending on the level of development, supply capabilities, availability of imports and the nature of policies adopted. In low-income countries these measures did not stimulate exports of manufactured goods and led to inflation, output failure and in many cases to de-industrialisation. By contrast, their dependence on primary commodities increased. In other words, in terms of resource allocation, exchange rate devaluation and trade liberalisation led to results contrary to those intended. It appears that, for countries with a small industrial base, development of supply capabilities is the first step towards industrialisation and this cannot be achieved through trade liberalisation and exchange rate devaluation. Until a certain stage in the process of industrialisation is reached, infant industry protection is required.

In countries with higher levels of development and a significant industrial base, without severe import compression, which pursued a mixture of import substitution and export promotion policies and followed 'selectivity' in their policies, the result has been, on balance, more favourable. These countries could rely more than others on exchange rate adjustments to stimulate exports of manufactured goods. Otherwise countries which suffered from import compression failed to stimulate exports. Moreover, they suffered from inflation and slow, or negative output growth. Most Asian countries of the sample are among the former group, and the record of their trade policies does not indicate that they have followed a 'liberalized trade regime'.

One implication of these findings is that no general prescription on trade and industrialisation policies can be provided. Individual countries should be allowed to gear their trade policies to their industrialisation and development objectives according to their need, level of development and particular characteristics. Within such a framework, however, trade policy

reform, not necessarily liberalisation, could be necessary. Another implication is that the acceleration of exports for debt repayment seems to have
reached its limit. Unless debt relief is obtained, many developing countries
will be facing irreversible socio-economic problems.

Before ending this paper, it should be mentioned that a large number of
other factors have also contributed to export and economic performance of
countries concerned, some of which have been considered elsewhere by
the present author.

NOTES

1. The author is a member of UNCTAD Secretariat. The views expressed in this
   article are those of the author and do not necessarily reflect the views of the
   UNCTAD Secretariat. The author has benefited from substantial ideas and
   comments provided by B. L. Das and from comments by Professor H. W.
   Singer, D. Evans and T. Ganiatsos. The author is, however, responsible for
   any remaining errors. This article is a part of a longer study being prepared by
   UNCTAD.
2. See, for example, Little, Scitovsky and Scott (1970), Balassa (1982). For a
   critical survey of the issues see Weiss (1988), ch. 7.
3. For the ranking of the sample countries according to the level of income and
   their level of industrialisation, see Table 5.A4. In this study the cut-off point
   for low income (and development) is per capita GDP of around $600 in 1986.
   Countries with a manufacturing value added (MVA)/GDP ratio of less than 15
   per cent are considered as having with a low level of industrialisation. Thus
   except for the Philippines, Sri Lanka, Pakistan, India and Indonesia (in the last
   case MVA/GDP is deflated because of the importance of petroleum in GDP),
   low income countries of Table 5.A4 also show a low level of industrialisation.
4. E. Ghani (1989), mimeo, Table 9, based on national statistics.
5. If one excludes Ecuador in the list of group B countries because of its small
   exports and somewhat sceptically significant improvement in its terms of trade,
   the disparity between the figures for the two categories will change significantly
   (the average rate of growth of the net barter terms of trade for group B will rise
   to 0.2).
6. Singapore has been excluded from the list because it is very likely that the share
   of MVA in GDP declined because the country has reached a level of development beyond which the service sector expands more rapidly. Moreover,
   Singapore is a service port.
7. Some scholars use trade share (export and/or import ratio in GDP) as an
   indicator of trade orientation. Others employ the incentive structure (and
   compare, e.g. real effective exchange rate for exportables and importables), or
   they classify the countries according to the type of policy instruments employed
   (see Helleiner, 1988).
8. In practice, however, to reach neutrality, in many countries the import barriers
   are reduced, and at the same time, export incentives are increased (see
   Preusse, 1988, pp. 883–97).
9. Moreover, there are some confusions and contradictions. If it is the nominal
   rate which is being recommended, it is irrelevant since industrial activities are

affected by the effective rate; if it is the effective rate reaching, and keeping a uniform rate is not practical. This is not only because of difficulties in calculations, but also because any change in the uniform rate could change the effective tariff structure.

10. Although its growth rate of exports was modest, since the country is following, an import-substitution strategy, by definition, it is not a high export performer.

11. See Bond (1985, pp. 56–77) for empirical evidence on the importance of devaluation. The IMF (1988, p. 731), in one of its recent publication, has stated that 'It is clear that there is no simple relation between developments in real exchange rates and in current account balance' (cited in Stewart, 1989, pp. 1–43). Mitchell Kellman and Peter C. Y. Chow (1989) showed that exports of the East Asian NICs were insensitive to changes in real exchange rate, but highly sensitive to changes in external demand (see their article 'The Comparative Homogeneity of the East Asian NICs Exports of Similar Manufactures'. N. Kaldor has shown that even in developed countries the relations between devaluation and export performance is weak (see his article: 'The effects of devaluations on trade in manufactures' in Kaldor, 1978). F. Stewart, op. cit., has argued that devaluation is not always effective in developing countries. The present author has benefitted from this study in formulation of the argument contained in the following pages.

12. According to a recent study the price elasticities of exports of developing countries to OECD countries for the period 1974–84 varies from −0.61 to 0.08 for SITC $(0 + 1)$, and −0.42 to 0.04 for SITC $(2 + 4)$ (see Marquez and McNeilly, 1988, pp. 306–14).

13. Obviously, they could lead to the expansion of volume of *exports* of primary products when there is already excess supply.

14. For exports to OECD, the estimated elasticities vary from −1.85 to −1.03 for the period 1974–81 (see Marquez and McNeilly, op. cit., Table 5).

15. There would be a shift towards a more inelastic part of the demand curve on the left hand side. After imports are cut beyond a limit, it would be very difficult to do without essential items. Further problems may also be caused by devaluations when accompanied by removal of quantitative restrictions, because the available foreign exchange might not necessarily be allocated rationally to the industries on priority bases (see Stewart, op. cit., p. 27).

16. See, for example, Wattleworth (1988, pp. 166–80). Wattleworth, op. cit., refers to the potential for adverse terms of trade effect of devaluation on primary commodities. He adds, however: 'The funding is not an argument against devaluation, since the beneficial effect of such a policy in other areas, e.g. non-traditional exports, might outweigh the short-run effect in major commodity exports'.

17. Based on World Bank, World Tables (1988–9, pp. 184–7).

18. Based on UNCTAD, op. cit., Table 4.3. See also Weiss (1988), ch. 7.

19. See Arndt, op. cit., p. 38, Table 4. Even in Singapore and Hong Kong, invisible barriers of one kind or another remained at least up to very recently (ibid, p. 37).

20. Based on UNCTAD, Computer *Data Bank in Trade Control Measures of Developing Countries*, Geneva.

21. See Arndt, op. cit.; for 1960s and 1970s see also Hong (1979), ch. 3.

22. See Arndt, op. cit.. See also Singer and Gray (1988, pp. 395–403).

23. A tariff structure of six bounds was employed to give reasonable 'effective protection to local industries and a range of zero per cent to 500 per cent tariff rates were used for essential and luxury goods, respectively'. (See Rajapatrirana

98 Development Perspective for the 1990s

(1988, pp. 1143–57), particularly p. 1150).
24. Tariffs were reduced by 50 per cent across the board (see J. Antonio OCampo (1988)).
25. See OCampo, op. cit., see also Singer and Gray (1988, pp. 395–403).
26. See Bradford, op. cit., particularly pp. 305–14; for South Korea also see Hong, op. cit., particularly ch. 3 and pp. 269–70.
27. The effects of production externalities are a part of the infant industry argument; here the argument is on the externalities created by consumption for production of other goods.
28. The 'revenue raising' is another argument in favour of taxing imports of luxury goods.

REFERENCES

Arndt, H. W., (1987) 'Industrial Policy in East Asia', *Industry and Development*, 22, 1–66.
Balassa, B., (1982) *Development Strategies in Semi-Industrial Economies*, (Baltimore: Johns Hopkins University Press).
Bhaskar, V., (1989) *Export Incentives, Exchange Rates and Commodity Prices: The Implication of Interdependence*, (London: Commonwealth Secretariat).
Bond, M. E., (1985) *Export Demand and Supply For Groups of Non-Oil Developing Countries*, IFS Papers (March) 56–77.
Bradford, C. I., Jr, (1987) 'Trade and Structural Change: NICs and Next Tier NICs as Transitional Economies', *World Development*, 15, 299–316.
Ghani, E., (1989) *Trade Regime and Trade Performance of Mauritius in the 1980s*, mimeo (Geneva: UNCTAD).
Helleiner, G. K., (1988) 'Trade Strategy in Medium-Term Adjustment', Paper presented to the World Institute for Development Economics Research (Copenhagen) Conference on International Trade, Helsinki, August.
Hong, W., (1979) *Trade Distortions and Employment Growth in Korea*, (Seoul: Korea Development Institute).
IMF (1988), *World Economic Outlook* (Washington, DC: IMF).
Kaldor, N., (1978) *Further Essays on Applied Economics*, (London: Duckworth).
Kellman, M., and P. C. Y. Chow (1989), 'The Comparative Homogeneity of East Asian NICs Exports of Similar Manufactures', *World Development*, 2 267–73.
Little, I. M. D., T. Scitovsky and M. Scott (1970), *Industry and Trade in Some Developing Countries*, (London: Oxford University Press).
Marquez, J., and K. McNeilly, (1988) 'Income and Price Elasticities for Exports of Developed Countries', *Review of Economics and Statistics*, May, 306–14.
OCampo, J. Antonio, (1986) 'New Developments in Trade Theory and LDCs', *Journal of Development Economics*, 22, 129–70.
OCampo, J. Antonio, (1988) 'The Effects of Liberalisation and Direct Import Control on Colombian Manufacturing, 1976–1986', Paper Presented to WIDER Conference on International Trade, Helsinki, August (1988).
Preusse, H. G., (1988) 'The Indirect Approach to Trade Liberalisation: Dynamic Consideration on Liberalisation-Cum-Stabilisation Policies in Latin America', *World Development*, 8, 883–97.
Rajapatrirana, S., (1988) 'Foreign Trade and Economic Development: Sri Lanka's Experience', *World Development*, 10, 1143–57.

Ros, J., (1986) 'Mexico's Stabilisation and Adjustment Policies (1982–1985)', *Labour and Society*, 335–61.

Shafaeddin, S. M., (1989) *Trade Policies, Investment and Economic Performance of Developing Countries in the 1980s* (Geneva: UNCTAD).

Singer, H., and P. Gray, (1988) 'Trade Policy and Growth of Developing Countries: Some New Data', *World Development*, 3, 395–403.

Stewart, F., (1989) 'Proposals for a Review of GATT, Article XVIII: An Assessment', 1–43 in United Nations, *Uruguay Round, Papers on Selected Issues* (New York: United Nations).

UNCTAD, *Data Bank in Trade Control Measures of Developing Countries* (Geneva: UNCTAD).

Wattleworth, M. (1988) 'The Effects of Collective Devaluations on Commodity Price and Exports', *IMF Staff Papers*, March, 166–88.

Weiss, J., (1988) *Industry in Developing Countries*, (London: Croom Helm).

World Bank (1988–9), *World Tables* (Washington, DC: World Bank) 184–7.

APPENDIX

TABLE 5.A1 *Countries with declining share of manufacturing sector[a] in GDP and/or exports (1980–1)*

Country	Percentage share in GDP		Percentage share in exports	
	1980	1987	1980	1987
Category A				
Mexico	22.1	21.2		
Morocco	17.1	15.8		
Category B				
Bangladesh	9.9	9.2	67.2	63.2
Singapore	22.2	26.7	54.0	44.8
Côte d'Ivoire			9.4	7.1
Colombia	17.0	16.8	20.4	9.7
Ghana	7.8	7.1	3.2	2.6
Costa Rica			24.3	30.9
Chile	21.4	20.7	9.5	7.4
Bolivia	14.6	10.8	3.0	1.5
Uruguay	22.4	21.7	38.2	27.0
Peru			17.1	14.7
Argentina	22.1	21.4	23.2	18.2
Ecuador	17.7	17.3	3.0	1.5
Sierra Leone			56.1	47.6
Category C				
Philippines	24.4	23.7		
Brazil	28.4	27.0	38.6	38.1

Note:
[a] In cases where the ratio has increased, the space is left blank.

SOURCE: As Table 5.1.

TABLE 5.A2   *Index of 'selectivity'ª of the import barriers for manufactured products of the sample countries (mid-1980s)*

Groups	Countries	Year of reporting	Tariffs	Total charges	Non-tariff measures
	Category A				
a	Indonesia	1987	299.0	276.0	36.4
	Malaysia	1987	320.1	245.6	418.8
	Korea	1987	62.4	55.6	203.6
	Sri Lanka	1988	198.0	139.0	248.2
	Thailand	1986	175.7	127.3	1,067.9
	Pakistan	1986	153.5	161.1	34.1
b	Turkey	1987	284.0	280.0	45.0
c	Venezuela	1988	298.8	229.9	189.7
d	Morocco	1988	175.8	115.4	346.3
e	Mexico	1988	157.9	140.4	371.3
	Category B				
f	India	1987	122.4	64.5	115.3
g	Singapore	1988	900.0	600.0	673.8
	Kenya	1987	185.6	178.3	145.6
h	Colombia	1986	167.2	73.7	93.0
i	Ghana	1987	38.9	64.6	238.1
	Yugoslavia	1987	114.7	105.8	256.8
	Costa Rica	1987	352.6	350.2	209.0
	Chile	1988	25.2	56.4	465.8
	Nigeria	1987	210.9	203.0	552.9
	Bolivia	1986	3.5	3.5	378.9
	Côte d'Ivoire	1987	134.8	134.7	1,404.5
	Uruguay	1988	113.5	79.8	363.0
	Peru	1987	123.5	97.3	213.8
	Argentina	1988	153.0	112.7	240.3
	Jamaica	1986	210.9	209.8	1,654.2
	Ecuador	1986	240.0	194.2	163.1
	Category C				
j	Senegal	1987	323.2	323.2	1,591.8
k	Philippines	1987	131.6	103.3	188.3
l	Brazil	1986	159.6	98.6	230.1

Note:
ª Range divided by means; for tariffs range is derived from the highest figure in the maximum column and the lowest figure in the minimum column of various product groups; for 'total charges' and NTMs it is derived from maximum and minimum for various product groups.

SOURCE: Calculated by the author, based on UNCTAD, *Handbook of trade measures of developing countries, supplement*, 1987.9

TABLE 5.A3   *Percentage change in the national currency vis-a-vis US dollar between 1980 and 1987*

Groups	Countries	Exchange rates nominal	real	effective
	Category A			
a	Indonesia	−62.0	−39.0	n.a.
	Malaysia	−13.6	−4.0	−12.0
	Korea	−26.0	−3.0	--20.0
	Sri Lanka	−44.0	8.7	n.a.
	Mauritius	−40.0	−18.0	n.a.
	Thailand	−20.4	−8.0	−20.0
	Pakistan	−43.0	−14.0	−30.0
b	Turkey	−91.0	−26.0	−38.0
c	Venezuela	−70.0	−37.0	−46.0
d	Morocco	−53.0	−26.0	−32.0
e	Mexico	−98.0	−32.0	−44.0
	Category B			
f	India	−39.0	−2.0	n.a.
g	Bangladesh	−50.0	−7.1	n.a.
	Singapore	2.0	3.0	n.a.
	Kenya	−55.0	−19.0	−21.0
h	Colombia	−80.0	−32.0	−39.0
i	Ghana	−98.0	−75.0	−77.0
	Yugoslavia	−97.0	−15.5	n.a.
	Costa Rica	−86.0	−31.0	−34.0
	Chile	−82.0	−42.0	−46.0
	Nigeria	−86.0	−67.0	−71.0
	Bolivia	a	−7.0	−21.0
	Cote d'Iv.	−30.0	−9.0	−8.0
	Uruguay	−96.0	−35.0	−36.0
	Peru	−98.0[b]	−65.0	n.a.
	Argentina	−51.0[b]	−64.0	n.a.
	Jamaica	−68.0	−25.0	−32.0
	Ecuador	−85.0	−31.0	−45.0
	Sier. Leone	−97.0	5.0	8.0
	Category C			
j	Senegal	−30.0	9.6	n.a.
k	Philipp.	−73.0	−15.0	−30.0
l	Brazil	−99.0	−4.0	−5.0

Note:
[a] Difficult to measure, but extremely high.
[b] 1980–86.

SOURCES: UNCTAD Secretariat based on IMF sources.

TABLE 5.A4 *GDP per capita and the ratio of manufacture value added (MVA) to GDP of the sample countries (1986)*

Countries	per capita GDP $ USA	$\frac{MVA}{GDP}$	Countries	per capita GDP $ USA	$\frac{MVA}{GDP}$
Singapore	6773	35	Jamaica	1024	20
Venezuela	3423	23	Ivory Coast	920	13
Yugoslavia	2648	34[a]	Thailand	799	21
Argentina	2540	30	Morocco	687	17
Republic of Korea	2342	30	Bolivia	637	14
Uruguay	2166	24	Senegal	564	17
Brazil	2023	26[b]	The Philippines	557	25
Malaysia	1733	22	Nigeria	473	8
Costa Rica	1627	19[b]	Indonesia	441	14
Mexico	1601	26	Ghana	409	11
Mauritius	1365	19	Sri Lanka	389	17
Peru	1351	20	Kenya	333	11
Chile	1381	21[b]	Pakistan	312	16
Colombia	1167	22	Sierra Leone	309	6
Turkey	1157	26	India	269	15[a]
Ecuador	1165	20	Bangladesh	153	8

Notes:
[a] 1985.
[b] 1984.

SOURCES: Based on UNCTAD Data Bank.

6 Upstream Foreign Direct Investment by Korean Manufacturers

Wang-Taek Jun and Renee Prendergast

INTRODUCTION

Since the launching of its first five-year development plan in 1962, the Korean economy has grown rapidly. Between 1962 and 1987, per capita GNP in current prices rose from $81 to $2690. During the period, real GNP grew at the rate of over 8 per cent per annum and per capita real GNP at 6.4 per cent. Rapid growth was accompanied by deep structural change. In 1965, agriculture accounted for 38 per cent of GDP, industry for 25 per cent and services 37 per cent. By 1987, the share of agriculture had fallen to 11 per cent, that of industry had risen to 43 per cent and services to 46 per cent. In the same period, the share of manufacturing in GDP rose from 18 to 30 per cent.

There can be no doubt that the fast export growth was a major factor in Korea's economic takeoff. Exports accounted for 9 per cent of total demand in 1965. By 1987, they accounted for 45 per cent. Between 1965 and 1980, the annual average growth rate of exports was 27.2 per cent. Between 1980 and 1987, it was 9.6 per cent. Korea's export growth began in the early sixties when the government's strategy shifted to export promotion. A major element of the strategy involved devaluation of the exchange rate and a commitment to prevent its real appreciation. Exchange rate policy was reinforced by other elements designed to directly benefit exporters. These included access to subsidised credit, access to inputs at world prices as well as tax concessions and input subsidies (Petri, 1988). Initial export success was in line with Korea's comparative advantage and came in industries such as clothing, textiles and wigs. These were industries in which Korea had or could easily acquire technological capability. They were also relatively labour-intensive and hence appropriate to Korea's factor endowment (Westphal et al., 1984).

Korea's export success was accompanied by a heavy dependence on imports and, from the early sixties, export-promoting strategies were implemented in the context of widespread import barriers. Part of the intention behind *The Heavy and Chemical Industries Development Plan*, published in 1973, seems to have been to reduce Korea's dependence on imported capital and intermediate goods. Competition from other emerging nations such as China in labour-intensive exports may also have been a factor. While the plan initially focused on import substitution (Westphal *et al.*, 1984), it soon became apparent that export activity had to be an integral part of the new strategy, since the industries concerned were characterised by very substantial economies of scale. Following initial difficulties and some major revisions, the plan eventually succeeded in transforming the structure of the Korean economy. This change was reflected in the composition of exports with increases in the proportion of machinery and intermediate goods such as chemicals, fertilizers and steel.

Since 1980, there have been a number of major changes in Korea's policy environment. These have involved the removal of export incentives, a reduction in the number of import categories subject to quantitative restrictions, and systematic tariff reductions. According to Petri (1988), the switch to a more neutral industrial policy was associated with an accelerated expansion of machinery – particularly consumer electronics – and more limited growth in heavy intermediate goods.

Destination and structure of Korean exports

Table 6.1, which presents information on the destination of Korea's exports between 1968 and 1987, shows that throughout most of the period North America was the principal market for Korean exports. While the relative importance of the North American market declined during the seventies, it revived again in the early eighties. Other notable features of the table are the rise and fall of the Middle Eastern market and the substantial importance of the European market since the mid-1970s.

Table 6.2 shows that the composition of Korean exports changed substantially in the period 1970–85. Sectors such as iron and steel, metal manufactures and transport equipment, which were only of slight significance in 1970, had become major export sectors by 1985. The change is particularly marked in the case of transport equipment which in 1970 accounted for only 1 per cent of exports, compared to 20.7 per cent in 1985. Other notable changes are: the increasing importance of electrical machinery, whose share in total exports rose from 5.3 to 11.9 per cent during the period; of footwear, whose share rose from 2.1 to 5.0 per cent and of non-electrical machinery, whose share rose from 1 to 3.7 per cent. The declining importance of clothing and textile yarn and fabric is also reflected in the table.

Table 6.3 further amplifies the picture and shows the significance of the US market for several of Korea's major exports. The table shows that, in 1985, the United States was Korea's main market for iron and steel, metal manufactures, non-electrical machinery, electrical machinery, clothing, footwear and miscellaneous manufactured goods. In addition, it shows that

TABLE 6.1   *Korea's exports by principal district (percentage of total)*

	Asia	Middle East	North America	Latin America	Europe	Others
1968	27.2	6.3	54.8	0	7.9	3.5
1973	41.9	6.8	33.4	3.8	11.8	2.1
1978	26.3	13.0	34.5	1.9	18.7	3.9
1983	19.6	17.5	36.3	2.2	15.5	4.8
1987	24.1	9.0	41.7	2.6	16.6	3.6

SOURCE: *Major Statistics of the Korean Economy* (1989) (Seoul: Economic Planning Board).

TABLE 6.2   *Major Korean export sectors, 1970 and 1985 (percentage of total exports)*

Sector (SITC)	1970	1985
Textile, yarn and fabric (65)	10.2	7.1
Iron and steel (67)	1.6	6.0
Metal manufactures (69)	1.0	5.0
Non-electrical machinery (71)	1.0	3.7
Electrical machinery (72)	5.3	11.9
Transportation equipment (73)	1.0	20.7
Clothing (84)	25.7	14.7
Footwear (85)	2.1	5.0
Misc manufactured goods	13.7	5.9
All other goods	38.4	20.0
	100.0	100.0

SOURCE: Based on data from P. F. Allgeier (1988), 'Korean Trade Policy in the Next Decade: Dealing with Reciprocity', *World Development*, 16, 85–97.

in all of these sectors, with the exception of iron and steel and metal manufactures, the US market accounted for over 50 per cent of Korea's total exports. At the four digit level, the pattern is still more marked. In all the major subsectors of the electrical and non-electrical machinery industries, Korea depends heavily on the US market. By contrast, Japan is Korea's leading market only in the case of iron and steel.

Petri (1988) constructed an index of revealed comparative advantage (RCA) for Korean exports and compared it with indices for the US, Japan, other developed countries, East Asian NICs and East Asian LDCs. Using the correlation coefficient between RCAs in the manufacturing subsectors of the different countries as a measure of export similarity, Petri concluded that in 1985, Korea export patterns were clearly like those of the Asian NICs and Japan and unlike those of the United States. It is thus not

TABLE 6.3 *Markets for Korea's leading exports, 1985*

Sector (SITC)	Share (%) to US	Share (%) to Japan	Share (%) to other Asian and Pacific nations
Textile yarn and fabric (65)	15.24	13.12	27.51
Iron and steel (67)	34.07	24.08	19.17
– Primary forms (672)	14.65	58.73	18.73
– Pipes and tubes (678)	69.87	3.62	6.60
Metal manufacture (69)	40.09	2.39	15.53
Non-electric machinery (71)	51.32	7.45	11.63
– Aircraft engines (7114)	71.03	11.15	12.92
– Computers (7142)	89.71	1.01	3.55
– Statistical machinery (7143)	64.11	0.36	2.36
– Office machinery (7149)	62.64	14.46	14.56
– Mech handling equip (7193)	52.82	0.62	18.84
Electrical machinery (72)	52.91	10.09	14.87
– TV receivers (7241)	57.95	0.50	15.97
– Radios (7242)	50.03	2.42	5.91
– Telecom equip (7249)	65.30	11.13	5.95
– Domes elec equip (7250)	72.33	3.01	8.78
– Semicondtrs, compts (7293)	54.07	12.22	23.01
Transp equip (73)	15.04	5.47	16.94
– Passenger cars (7321)	0.39	0.13	0.85
– Ships (7353)	13.07	1.86	20.10
Clothing (84)	51.21	13.65	1.42
Footwear (85)	74.30	7.50	1.46
Misc mnftrd goods (89)	59.32	10.76	6.59

SOURCE: P. F. Allgeier (1988), 'Korean Trade Policy in the Next Decade: Dealing with Reciprocity', *World Development*, 16, 85–97.

unreasonable to expect that the US would be a more important export market for Korea than either Japan or the Asian NICs. Korea's imports from the US have been and remain substantial, but they have not grown in line with Korean exports to the US. Since 1982, Korea's trade balance with the US has been in surplus. The surplus rose steadily from $0.29 billion in 1982 to $9.55 billion in 1987. This in turn gave rise to increased protectionist pressure on Korean imports to the US.

Protectionism and the Korean economy

Many of Korea's major exports to developed countries are in product categories with high levels of non-tariff barriers (NTBs), measured as the percentage of all imports by value subject to NTBs. Paradoxically, this was often to Korea's advantage in the past and enabled it to enter markets where earlier Japanese gains had triggered a protectionist response. As long as this protection was directed specifically against Japan, it opened up opportunities for Korean exporters and accelerated rather than retarded export growth (Petri, 1988). This seems to happened in the case of some of Korea's newer industries: colour television sets, steel, automobiles and semi-conductors. However, once Korean exports accounted for a substantial market share, they in turn have tended to become subject to restrictions. In the case of older industries such as clothing, where Korea's competitive position is being eroded by other developing countries, barriers such as multifibre arrangement (MFA) quotas have sharply restrained exports of some items but have helped to maintain the export quantities in others.

The importance of the US market for Korean exports and the deteriorating US trade balance with Korea have already been noted. It is widely accepted that given the protection proneness of Korea's major exports, protectionist pressure, especially in the United States, is likely to increase. One option for Korea is to seek to diversify its export markets, especially by increasing sales to Japan with which Korea has a substantial trade deficit. Some developments in this direction took place during 1988. Another option is to attempt to forestall protectionist pressure by locating production facilities in major markets. As the next section will show, this option is being increasingly pursued by Korean firms. Some of the problems associated with this option are also explored in this paper.

FOREIGN DIRECT INVESTMENT

Inward investment

In the period following the war, the Korean economy was in an extremely weak condition and offered few attractions to foreign investors. In 1961, the Korean government took legislative steps to encourage inward investment. The first foreign affiliate was set up in 1962 by the American textile firm Chentex to produce nylon filament. During the period, per capita real GNP grew at the rate of 6.4 per cent per annum. However, in the late sixties and early seventies, substantial amounts of investment came from small Japanese companies seeking cheap labour to produce household appliances and consumer goods for the Japanese market.

Following the switch to a selective industrial policy targeted on the development of the heavy and chemical industries in the mid-1970s, the Korean government's FDI policy sought to encourage foreign investment in large-scale, high-technology, export-oriented industries and to discourage foreign investment in low-skill, labour-intensive industries that competed with Korea's domestic enterprises in overseas markets. As a result, by 1980, basic chemicals accounted for 11.3 per cent of cumulative FDI, petroleum products 12.4 per cent, metals 12.1 per cent and electrics and electronics 14.4 per cent.

TABLE 6.4   *Inward investment by year for selected years, 1963–87*
(approval basis)

Year	No. of Projects	Amount (US $1,000)
1963	1	304
1968	20	8,361
1973	194	156,606
1978	41	128,438
1983	75	267,753
1984	103	419,049
1985	127	531,720
1986	203	356,000
1987	284	1,202,000

SOURCE: *Investment Guide to Korea* (1988) (Seoul: Ministry of Finance).

In the early 1980s, the Korean government eased the restrictions and allowed foreign investment in all industries except those on a negative list. Investors became free to retain 100 per cent ownership and procedures for the approval of new ventures and the remission of dividends were simplified. These changes (which came into effect in July 1984) were accompanied by rapid increases in foreign direct investment (Table 6.4).

Outward investment

Korean overseas investment started in 1968 with an investment in forest development in Indonesia. Much early foreign investment by Korean firms was directed towards the acquisition of raw materials which were shipped to Korea for processing and export. A good deal of the remainder was in trade-related, on-site servicing or processing facilities designed to facilitate the continued expansion of industrial exports and overseas construction. In the early period, manufacturing was not significant. Up to 1984, it accounted for 16.3 per cent of total FDI compared with 78 per cent for raw materials and export servicing (Table 6.5).

Total foreign investment by Korean firms increased substantially during the 1980s, especially from 1986 onwards. The composition of investment also changed with manufacturing accounting for between 35 and 40 per cent of the annual outflow in the years 1986–8. The increase in FDI in the latter half of the 1980s was facilitated by the movement of the Korean current account into surplus in 1986 and by a switch in government policy from restricting to encouraging investment abroad. Other factors contributing to the increase in foreign investment particularly by the manufacturing sector were increasing protectionism in major markets, labour unrest and rising labour costs in Korea, and the appreciation of the Won.

As in the case of exports, North America is the main destination of

109

TABLE 6.5 *Outward investment by industrial sectors*

Sectors	1968–1984	%	1985	%	Amounts 1986	%	1987	%	1988	%	Accumulated amounts as of 1988	%
Mining	173,742	34.2	70,835	60.4	73,678	42.8	202,153	50.9	64,965	30.5	410,588	36.7
Forestry	71,680	14.1	3,211	2.9	419	0.3	247	0.1	450	0.2	52,509	4.7
Fishery	10,930	2.1	2,089	2.0	3,831	2.2	2,329	0.6	13,618	6.4	25,592	2.3
Manufacturing	82,782	16.3	20,105	17.3	70,104	40.8	157,746	39.8	74,500	35.1	386,853	34.7
Construction	46,535	9.1	2,898	2.7	1,910	1.1	2,768	0.7	5,165	2.4	36,214	3.1
Transportation & warehousing	3,714	0.7	58	0.1	74	0.1	1,010	0.3	496	0.2	3,175	0.3
Trading	68,009	13.4	12,138	10.5	14,343	8.3	20,273	5.1	40,545	19.0	133,093	11.9
Real estate	21,425	4.3	2,785	2.6	2,897	1.7	800	0.2	7,473	3.5	34,062	3.0
Others	29,455	5.8	3,703	3.3	4,693	2.7	9,919	2.5	5,707	2.7	37,076	3.3
Total	508,545	100.0	117,822	100.0	171,999	100.0	397,235	100.0	212,919	100.0	1,119,162	100.0

SOURCE: *Weekly Information on Foreign Direct Investment*, 28 October 1989 (Seoul: The Export-Import Bank of Korea).

Korean foreign direct investment and its share of the total has increased in recent years. South East Asia and the Middle East are also important destinations and, in 1988, foreign direct investment in Europe grew significantly (Table 6.6). By 1988, the two most important sectors were mining and manufacturing. 45 per cent of all mining investment went to the Middle East and the remainder to South East Asia and North America. 58 per cent of all manufacturing investment went to North America and a further 22 per cent to South East Asia. Investment related to trading was the most important of the remaining sectors. Of this, 64 per cent went to North America, 16 per cent to South East Asia and just under 16 per cent to Europe.

ECONOMIC THEORIES OF FOREIGN DIRECT INVESTMENT

The Hymer–Kindleberger approach

Foreign direct investment on a large scale is a phenomenon of the post-war period. Early writers on the subject took the view that firms would set up operations abroad if by doing so they could earn rates of return higher than those achievable at home. Hymer (1960) argued that such explanations were not sufficient to account for the existence of multinational enterprises (MNEs). If it were simply a matter of a higher rate of return being achievable abroad, capital would move through organised capital markets rather than through firms that specialise in the production and distribution of goods since, compared to local firms, such firms have to overcome the costs of operating in a different political and legal environment. According to Hymer, it was, therefore, necessary that MNEs should be able to earn a higher rate of return than existing or potential local firms. They could do this if they possessed some advantage which was more than sufficient to compensate for the costs of doing business in an alien environment. The advantages would have to be such that they could be transferred from one country to another and not be acquired by local firms. Such advantages might include differentiated products and patented technology or inventions. Exploitation of such advantages through FDI would also have to be more profitable than the alternatives of exporting or licensing. Exporting was often excluded by tariff, non-tariff or transport cost barriers. Furthermore, local production might allow better adaption to local market conditions and have demand-stimulating effects. The reasons why FDI might be preferred to licensing were: the imperfect nature of the market for knowledge, the desire to maintain control over advantages, the dangers of creating new competitors and the costs of transferring knowledge and of policing contracts.

The Hymer-Kindleberger approach was extremely influential and the

TABLE 6.6 *Korean overseas investment by sector and region (1988)*

Sector	South East Asia	Middle East	North America	Latin America	Europe	Africa	Oceania	Total
Mining	165,690	292,469	133,035				53,924	645,118
Forestry	30,645		1,050				22,314	54,009
Fishery	2,995		17,684	16,628	40	242		39,751
Manufacturing	111,831	23,022	299,851	27,400	36,179	9,066	8,803	516,152
Construction	4,476	19,782	29,282			1,690	610	55,840
Transport and warehousing	2,142	147	1,520	200	220			4,229
Trading	25,430	98	99,529	2,550	24,190	2,110	1,166	155,073
Real estate	20,405		8,951	155	4,090		461	34,062
Others	965	2,389	35,105	2,787	920	56,902	4,145	103,213
TOTAL	384,579	337,907	626,007	49,720	65,639	70,010	91,585	1,605,447

SOURCE: *Weekly Information on Foreign Direct Investment*, 2 September 1989 (Seoul: The Export-Import Bank of Korea).

TABLE 6.7   *Ratio of R & D to total sales*

Sector	1970	Korea 1980	1984	USA 1983	Japan 1984	W. Germany 1981	France 1982
Manufacturing	0.34	0.5	1.3	3.8	2.3	3.3	5.4
Machinery industry	1.2	0.97	2.22	5.8	2.6	3.1	2.5
Electronics and electrical industry	1.2	1.73	3.88	8.6	4.6	7.3	8.9

SOURCE: *Electronics, Electrics* (in Korean), vol. 8, 1987 (Seoul: Korean Institute of Economics and Technology).

possession of internally transferrable advantages continues to be regarded by many scholars as a necessary, though not sufficient, condition for foreign direct investment. The types of ownership advantages emphasised by Hymer and others involve barriers to entry and imply a degree of monopoly power. Lecraw (1977) and Wells (1981), in pioneering studies of multinationals from developing countries, regarded ownership advantages as an important factor in explaining why firms from one LDC invested in another, but they emphasised that the forms of ownership advantage involved were of a different nature. Among the ownership advantages identified by them were the experience of LDC firms in using mature standardised technologies and in adapting these technologies for operation at relatively small scales using relatively labour-intensive techniques. Similarly, Giddy and Young (1982), in their study of non-conventional MNEs, concluded that foreign direct investment by these firms could be explained by their possession of firm-specific advantages provided this was taken to include production engineering skills and marketing adaptability.

While Korean manufacturing firms investing in South-East Asia might be regarded as possessing firm specific advantages compared to host country counterparts, it is more difficult to imagine what advantages Korean firms investing in the United States might possess *vis à vis* US firms. The competitiveness of Korean electronics products in the world market does not stem from product differentiation or technological superiority. Korean firms serve the lower end of the market and compete on price. Their cost competitiveness depends on the exploitation of economies of scale and, above all, on the country-specific advantage of relatively cheap labour. In the past most of Korea's technological effort went into the building up of production capability and indigenous R&D effort was not substantial. While R&D expenditure as a percentage of total sales has increased substantially in recent years, especially in electronics, it is still below that of Japan and substantially below that of USA, West Germany and France (Table 6.7). Korean enterprises are still heavily reliant on the

US and Japan for the introduction of high technology. In 1987, royalty payments amounted to $523.7 million or about 1 per cent of the value of manufactured exports (Table 6.8). In 1988 they rose to $676.3 million. In that year 39.2 per cent of total payments were made by the electric-electronics industry and 18.7 per cent by the machinery sector. Table 6.9 provides comparative assessments of Korea's electric and electronics technology. The table shows that Korean technology is inferior to that of developed countries on all of the criteria listed, but especially so in the case of design and testing.

All of the above would seem to indicate that Korean firms cannot be regarded as possessing technological advantages compared to domestic firms in advanced industrial countries. Neither does it seem likely that they possess marketing advantages compared with those firms. As noted earlier Korean exports tend to be directed towards the lower end of the market where they compete on price. Furthermore, a high proportion are sold on an OEM basis (i.e. under the buyer's brand name). Consequently, Korean trade marks and brand names are not well-recognised, although an effort is now being made to establish them.

The product life cycle model

This model (first set out by Vernon (1971)) hypothesises three stages in the life cycle of a product: the new product stage, the maturing product stage and the standardised product stage. Unstandardised new products are first produced on an experimental basis in high-income technologically-advanced countries (e.g. the US). As the product matures, standardisation occurs and the presence of economies of scale leads to an expansion of production which is matched by an expansion of demand as the price of the product falls. Markets for the product appearing in other advanced countries are initially served by exports from the US, but eventually a combination of cost factors and the emergence of indigenous producers causes US firms to begin to service these markets by means of local production. In the third stage, a fully standardised product emerges and price competition intensifies. In order to reduce costs, firms break up the production process and locate its labour-intensive stages in low-wage LDCs.

The product life cycle model seemed to offer useful insights into the timing and location of FDI by advanced country firms. A later version of the model (Vernon, 1974) emphasised the oligopolistic nature of MNE firms and the three stages of the product cycle were replaced by three stages of oligopolistic competitive behaviour. From our point of view, the model might offer some insight into Korean manufacturing investment in South East Asia but it can be of little help in explaining upstream investment by Korean firms in countries such as the US.

TABLE 6.8 *Korea's royalty payments ($ million, current prices)*

Country	1962–76	1977–81	1982	1983	1984	1985	1986	1987	1988	Total
US	29.7	159.2	59.5	80.7	116.1	154.8	191.6	239.9	330.0	1,361.5
Japan	63.7	139.8	29.3	37.1	53.2	74.6	129.5	181.4	214.7	923.3
W Germany	8.2	14.0	2.9	3.8	11.6	11.6	19.1	18.6	22.1	111.9
France	1.6	14.3	3.6	2.7	3.6	7.6	19.2	25.1	47.9	123.6
Others	10.4	124.1	20.4	25.2	28.7	46.9	53.6	58.7	61.6	429.6
Total	113.6	451.4	115.7	149.5	213.2	295.5	411.0	523.7	676.3	2,949.9

SOURCE: *The Korea Herald*, 7.6.1989.

TABLE 6.9   *Comparative assessment of Korea's electronics and electrical technology with other developed countries*

	Electronics and electrical industries	Machinery industry
Design technology	50	60
Precision engineering technology	70	88
Die manufacturing technology	60	60
Assembly technology	90	90
Testing equipment	55	60

SOURCE: *Electronics, Electrics* (in Korean), vol. 8, 1987 (Seoul: Korean Institute of Economics and Technology).

Internalisation theory

As Marx was the first to point out, markets and firms are alternative forms of the division of labour. This insight, which was re-discovered by Coase (1937) has become an important analytical tool in the analysis of MNEs. Internalisation takes place when the internal market of the firm replaces the external market to avoid the disadvantages or to capitalise on the advantages of market imperfections. The advantages of internalisation may lie in the reduction of costs associated with the co-ordination of particular sets of activities, in securing control over crucial intermediate goods, in the ability to price discriminate and in the avoidance of the consequences of certain forms of government intervention. It is argued in the literature on MNEs that an important cause of internalisation (i.e. FDI instead of licencing) is market failure in the technology markets. This is due to the public good nature of knowledge itself and the costs of negotiating and policing technological contracts. Another empirically important instance of internalisation (FDI instead of importing) is vertically integrated raw material based investment to insure continuity of supply. A third important cause of internalisation (FDI instead of exporting) is trade restrictions in the form of import controls of various kinds.

The upstream investment behaviour of Korean firms is unlikely to be explained by market failure in the technology markets for reasons stated earlier. A more promising avenue for exploration might be government induced market failure in the form of protectionism. Korean firms might be led to invest in US markets because the option of servicing these markets through exports was no longer available to them. The problem that then has to be confronted is that of the ability of Korean firms to do this given their lack of ownership advantages *vis á vis* US firms. While some authors, notably Buckley and Casson, have argued that market failure is both a necessary and sufficient condition for FDI to occur, it remains the case that a specific group of firms cannot engage in FDI unless they have the competitive advantages enabling them to do so.

Evidence seems to indicate that the ability of Korean firms to invest in the US depends on their access to low cost intermediate goods from Korea. According to a recent report in *Korean Business World*, Korean investors in the United States source up to 80 per cent of their inputs from Korea and further evidence from interviews suggests that, for some products, this could be as much as 90 per cent. Why, it might be asked, does this give Korean companies a competitive edge? Could not US companies also benefit from the import of intermediate goods from Korea? One reason why they do not do so is because of the quasi-internalisation of intermediate goods production in Korea.

Like Japan, Korea possesses a dual industrial structure, consisting on the one hand of large diversified conglomorates engaged primarily in final assembly and marketing and on the other of sub-contractors who supply components and sub-assemblies to the large enterprises. The large contractors have preferred to source their intermediate goods through the external market for the following reasons. First, the production costs of the large enterprises are substantially higher than those of sub-contractors because their overhead costs and labour costs are higher – the latter owing to the development of dual labour markets in the 1960s and 1970s. Secondly, while the large firms do not own the subcontracting firms, they exercise considerable control over them since they supply them with raw materials, technology, designs and even financial support. Thirdly, while the large firms maintain a close supportive relationship with their sub-contractors, at the same time they insure the competitiveness of supply by sourcing from more than one sub-contractor. Fourthly, the use of sub-contractors simplifies the internal coordination problems of the large firms while the long term contractual relationships simplify the problems of external coordination and minimise the transactions costs associated with external markets.

Thus, while large enterprises do not fully internalise their operations by means of ownership of intermediate goods production, the unique relationship between them and their sub-contractors means that they can achieve the benefits of internalisation at a lower cost. This pattern of operations is extended to the international production operations of Korean firms. Korean subsidiaries abroad import a major proportion of their inputs from their Korean sub-contractors and their foreign operations consist mainly of assembly. In short, Korean firms convert country-specific advantages into internationally transferable advantages. These advantages are not licenceable, and they are not directly exportable because of market failure in the intermediate goods market.

While the internalisation or quasi-internalisation of country-specific advantages based on low labour costs assists the competitiveness of Korean manufacturers engaging in foreign manufacturing operations, it remains the case that Korean manufacturers source their most highly sophisticated components from Japan or the US. The Japanese and US suppliers of these parts may have closer relationships with domestic manufacturers in the same line of business as the Korean companies. Given that Japanese companies, in particular, are often operating in the upper end of the same broad market as Korean enterprises, they will be wary of Korean encroachment on their market share. Our preliminary survey of Korean enterprises suggested that there was some evidence of irregular supply of key inputs. In the view of the companies concerned, these threats to their input supply were part of the competitive armoury of rival Japanese firms. In a recent interview in *Korea Business World*, the Director of Korea Overseas Investment Institute was cited as claiming that one of the difficulties which Korean firms met in attempting to meet EC localisation ratios was the unwillingness of local producers to supply them with key inputs.

While their reliance on advanced country producers for certain key inputs limits the extent to which Korean subsidiaries can benefit from the internalisation of country-specific advantages, even greater limits are being placed on this by the parts localisation programmes of the countries in which their plants are located. It is unlikely that Korean manufacturing plants in advanced countries can continue to produce competitively if they are forced to increase the local content of their products. For this reason, Korean firms have begun to set up assembly and component production plants in countries such as Mexico, which have free access to the US market and where labour is cheap. Here again, however, there is a need to meet localisation requirements and Korean plants which are basically final assemblers may have difficulty meeting these unless they can bring some of their sub-contractors with them and reproduce abroad the industrial structure which exists in Korea.

The eclectic paradigm

The eclectic paradigm of international production was first put forward by Dunning in 1976. Its main hypothesis is that a firm will engage in foreign production if three conditions are satisfied. The first condition is that the firm possesses net ownership advantages *vis à vis* firms of other nationalities in serving particular markets. Assuming the firm does posess net ownership advantages, the second condition is that it must be more beneficial to the firm to use them (or their output) itself rather than sell or lease them to foreign firms. Assuming the first and second conditions are satisfied, it must be in the global interest of the firm to utilise its advantages in conjunction with at least some factor inputs outside its home country; otherwise the foreign market would be served entirely by exports (Dunning, 1988).

An important aspect of Dunning's theory is its incorporation of elements of location theory in the explanation of foreign investment by multi-national enterprises (MNEs). The MNE can be seen as a vehicle for transferring mobile resources (technology, capital, marketing skills) to areas with immobile complementary inputs such as markets, raw materials and labour. Dunning (1986; 1988) briefly discusses investment by Third World MNEs in advanced industrial countries. Such investments, he argues are made 'either to gain access to export markets or to acquire particular skills and/or technologies and sometimes to make their international presence known'. This seems to suggest that, contrary to Dunning's own hypothesis, MNEs from developing countries invest in developed countries solely in order to gain the benefits of locational advantages. According to the eclectic paradigm outlined above, location advantages only come into play when the first two conditions are satisfied. Thus, insofar as he explains upstream FDI by developing country MNEs by locational advantages alone, Dunning seems to admit that his theory does not have the explanatory power claimed for it.

In arguing against Kojima's hypothesis that MNEs invest abroad in sectors which require intermediate products that the home country is comparatively well suited to supply, Dunning (1988) claimed that any alleged dichotomy between the patterns of US and Japanese direct investment was a false one. Any differences that existed reflected different stages of evolution as much as anything else. As firms became more multinational and took a more global perspective, their ownership advantages would become less based on particular assets which were country specific in origin and more on firm-specific advantages, such as their ability to successfully coordinate and manage a network of geographical activities. All of this seems to amount to a tacit admission that firm-specific advantages are not necessary for foreign direct investment and certainly do not explain it at a particular stage in a country's economic development. While Dunning seemed to take the view that Japanese firms would eventually follow the pattern of US and European MNEs, we would suggest that there a considerable body of evidence that at least part of Japanese competitiveness depends on a unique relationship with subcontracting firms which they are now attempting to reproduce in those countries in which they are engaged in foreign direct investment.

EVIDENCE FROM CASE STUDIES

The preceding section suggested that the major theories of foreign direct investment shed only limited light on the phenomenon of upstream foreign investment by less developed country firms. In this section, we examine the experience of two industrial sectors – electronics and textiles – which between them account for a major share of Korean FDI. In discussing the motivation of FDI in these two sectors, we classify investments as defensive or offensive.

Defensive investments

Defensive investments occur when the value of sales or market share is perceived to be in danger and a company attempts to preserve a market position already established through export. The threat to market share or sales may be due to protectionist measures and/or pre-emptive moves by competitors in an oligopolistic market.

In order to protect its domestic television industry, the US government established an Orderly Market Agreement (OMA) with Korean, Taiwanese and Japanese exporters in 1979 and imposed a quota on their imports. The quota was imposed for three years and was later extended to 1983 when it was replaced by an anti-dumping measure. As a result of the quota, colour TV (CTV) exports from Korea were restricted to 333 000 units compared with 435 000 units exported in the previous year. Those from Taiwan were restricted to 376 000 units compared with previous sales of 625 000 units. As a result, the Taiwanese companies Tatung and Sampo set up production operations in the US in 1980 and 1981 (Table 6.10). The Korean company Goldstar followed suit in 1982. Prior to the imposition of the quota, Goldstar's exports to the US were 167 000 units. Its quota of 91 000 units was significantly lower than that of its main Korean competitor, Samsung. While the quota was undoubtably important in motivating FDI by Korean firms, it seems likely that oligopolistic competition (Vernon, 1966; Knickerbocker, 1973) also played a role. The competition we refer to does not derive from ownership advantages *vis à vis* US firms but has to do with rivalry between Korean and Taiwanese firms in a particular market niche.

In the American TV market, the majority of advanced country producers cater for the upper end of the market, whereas Korean and Taiwanese firms sell in the lower end. In the up-market niche, quality and design are important, price elasticity of demand is low and income elasticity high. In the lower end of the market, price elasticity of demand is high and income elasticity of demand is low or even negative. While there is some overlap between these market segments, the overlap is partial. With one or two exceptions (e.g. Funai and Orion), Japanese firms operating in the US market do not directly compete with Korean firms because they serve a different market segment. Taiwanese firms operating in the US market compete directly with Korean firms and, in the market segment in which they operate, Korean and Taiwanese firms can be regarded as oligopolistic competitors. Consequently, they react sensitively to each other's behaviour.

TABLE 6.10   *Foreign-owned colour TV manufacturers in US*

Company	Location	Year of investment	Production capacity in 1983 ('000)	Brand
Japanese				
Sony	San Diego, California	1972	650	Sony
Matsushita	Franklin Park, Illinois	1974	600	Quasar Panasonic
Sanyo	Forest City, Arkansas	1976	800	Sanyo
Mitsubishi	Santa Ana, California	1977	150	M G A
Toshiba	Lebanon, Tennessee	1977	300	Toshiba
Sharp	Memphis, Tennessee	1979	300	Sharp
Hitachi	Anaheim, California	1979	150	Hitachi
J V C	Elmwood Park, New Jersey	1982	200	J V C
Dutch				
North American Phillips	Tenessee California	1974	1,000	Magnavox Sylvania Philco
Taiwanese				
Tatung	Longbeach, California	1980	100	Tatung
Sampo	Georgia	1981	240	Sampo
Korean				
Goldstar	Huntsville, Alabama	1982	300	Goldstar
Samsung	Roxbury, New Jersey	1984	400	Samsung

SOURCE: United States International Trade Commission (1984) *Colour Television Receivers from the Republic of Korea and Taiwan*, Publication No. 1514 (Washington: USITC).

When the US government suspended the quota imposed in 1979 and replaced it with anti-dumping duties, the duty applicable to Korean TV imports was 14.64 per cent, compared with 5.46 per cent on Taiwanese imports. The higher duties imposed on imports from Korea made the Korean market share vulnerable to competition both from Taiwanese imports and Taiwanese production located in the US. This combination of anti-dumping duties and competition from firms already located in the market caused another Korean firm (Samsung) to set up production facilities in the US in 1984. Thus, although the FDI of Korean firms in the US was motivated by protectionism, there was also evidence of a 'follow-the-leader' pattern of behaviour.

Acquisition of technology

Korea's export activity played an important role in the development of its technological capability in new industries set up from the late sixties onwards. Export by Korean companies was carried out mainly on an OEM basis. Buyers contributed product designs and helped install or improve methods of quality control. They also suggested changes in production processes, improvements in management techniques and production organisation (Westphal et al., 1981, 1984). Furthermore, by enabling Korean manufacturing plants to gain access to economies of scale, export activity played a role in increasing total factor productivity to unusually high levels (Nishimizu and Page, 1987). Any loss of export activity would damage Korean firms in two ways: first, by depriving them of the economies of scale which are necessary for their competiveness in the down-market niche and, secondly, by depriving them of a means of acquiring further technological capability.

While economies of scale are all-important for competitiveness at the lower end of the market, in the up-market niche competitiveness derives more from product differentiation. In order to move up-market, it is necessary for Korean firms to improve the design and quality of their products. Foreign direct investment in developed market economies is seen by some Korean firms as a means of facilitating the acquisition of higher levels of technological capability. For example, Goldstar's first European investment was made in West Germany despite the fact that its labour costs are among the highest in Europe. The reason given for this choice was that Germany possesses advanced technologies in consumer electronics. Similarly, in the field of industrial electronics, Samsung Electro-Mechanics has invested in Japan. The purpose of some of the investments by Samsung Electronics and Daewoo in the United States seem also to have been the acquisition of technological capability.

Offensive investments

Market opportunities

The product life-cycle theory predicts that, in the standardised stage of the cycle, developed country markets will be served through foreign production in LDCs whose country-specific advantages are more appropriate to the production of the good in question. The consumer electronics industry in the United States has been in decline since the mid-seventies due to the rapid inroads made by Asian manufacturers. In 1972, there were eighteen American-owned TV manufacturers in the United States. By the 1980s, only five remained. Some firms left the industry altogether, while others ceased their manufacturing operations and became the major buyers of Korean and Taiwanese exports. As a result, Japanese, Korean and Taiwanese manufacturers in Asia and Phillips in Europe became leaders in the consumer electronics field. They were able to build on their existing expertise and expand into new product areas, e.g. microwave ovens and video tape recorders. Since American-owned electronics firms are not involved in the manufacture of these items, imports into the United States are not subject to trade barriers. Nevertheless, foreign firms locate production facilities for these products in the US. Possible explanations for this are as follows:

(i) firms can achieve economies of scope by producing these products in conjunction with others such as TVs which are subject to strong protectionist measures.

(ii) the fact that these products are not subject to trade restrictions means that it is possible for firms to import components freely.

(iii) by manufacturing various products in the local production base, companies can appease the US government and also help to ease US pressure on their government.

A different form of market opportunity was seen in the textile industry. Because of trade barriers imposed by the US government on major exporters since 1961, some exporters moved into high-value-added market segments. US manufacturers were also involved in the high-value-added market niche. Although a number of countries producing for the lower end of the market were not subject to trade-barriers, they did not exhaust demand in that niche. This provided a market opportunity for some Korean firms to enter the US market through FDI. Using mass production techniques, they were able to compete in the lower end of the market despite the disadvantage of the high US labour costs. The firms in question were engaging in FDI not because protectionism cut off an export market which they previously served but because general protection of the market created a market opportunity which they were able to exploit.

Improvement of international market image

LDC firms may invest in an advanced industrial country in order to improve their international market image or to make their presence known in the international market. For this purpose, the LDC firm chooses the biggest, most attractive market and, for Korean firms, this is normally the

US. This form of investment is undertaken to increase market share not just in the host country, but also in other markets. A company may thus engage in foreign investment even if its market share in the host country is not very substantial. Such investments may themselves initially make a loss but they may be profitable in the context of the firms total operations at least in the longer run. The market image and recognisability of their brand is improved, as also is their bargaining strength with buyers. The improved image which a firm acquires as a result of investment in a developed country not only benefits it on the international market but also in the domestic market. Paradoxical though it may seem, the latter is important to Korean firms because, although they export a major proportion of their output, their domestic market operations are often the main source of their profits.

CONCLUSIONS

This paper has concentrated mainly on the issue of upstream investment by Korean MNEs. Our argument has been that the phenomenon of upstream investment is not well explained by any of the conventional theories and that this form of FDI is mainly motivated by factors external to the firm rather than factors internal to it.

The defensive motivators of upstream investment derive mainly from protectionist pressures in advanced industrial country markets. Such investments are possible in so far as firms are able to internalise home country advantages through the import of intermediate goods. Defensive investment may also be motivated by the decision of a rival oligopoly to gain market advantages through FDI. Investment motivated by the need to acquire access to higher levels of technology can also be regarded as defensive, though such investments have an offensive content as well.

According to the conventional view, FDI has offensive motivators when a firm invests to exploit a market through internally-created monopolistic firm-specific advantages such as unique technology or market skills. In the case of Korean upstream investment, however, the offensive motivator does not derive from the internal capability of the firm but from external factors such as market opportunities, often in a low-value-added market niche. Opportunities may arise in such niches because they are not of interest to producers serving the upper end of the market and/or because protection means that they cannot be supplied through imports. It thus seems that LDC MNEs engaging in upstream FDI share a common feature with LDC MNEs engaged in downstream or cross-market investment. This is that they do not in the main compete directly with the advanced country MNEs (or in our case domestic firms). In the cases examined by Lecraw and Wells, LDC MNEs were distinguished by their skill in small-scale manufacture. In the cases we examine, the distinctive feature of LDC MNEs was that they produced standardised products for the lower end of the market.

The upstream FDI of Korean firms is thus motivated by locational advantages offered by the host country. Many of the locational advantages we have identified can be changed through policy intervention in the host country and this may present difficulties in the future. The ability of Korean MNEs to invest in DCs in many cases depends on access to low-cost intermediate goods from Korea. To the extent that this is threatened by local content requirements the viability of these firms may also be in question.

REFERENCES

Allgeier, P. F., (1988) 'Korean Trade Policy in the Next Decade: Dealing with Reciprocity', *World Development*, 16, 85–97.
Buckley, P. J., (1981) 'A Critical Review of Theories of Multinational Enterprise', *Aussenwirtschaft*, 36, 70–78.
Buckley, P. J., (1983) 'New Theories of International Business: Some Unresolved Issues', in Casson, op. cit.
Business Korea, (1987), 5 (4).
Casson, M. C., (1983) *The Growth of International Business* (London: Allen and Unwin).
Coase, R. H., (1937) 'The Nature of the Firm', *Economica*, IV, 386–405.
Dunning, J. H., (1972) (ed.), *International Investment* (Harmondsworth: Penguin).
Dunning, J. H., (1981) *International Production and the Multinational Enterprise* (London: Allen and Unwin).
Dunning, J. H., (1988) *Explaining International Production* (London: Unwin Hyman).
Giddy, I. H. and Young, S., (1982) 'Conventional Theory and Unconventional Multinationals: Do New Forms of Multinational Enterprise Require New Theories?' in A. M. Rugman (ed.) *New Theories of the Multinational Enterprise* (New York: St. Martin's Press).
Hymer, S., (1960) '*The International Operations of National Firms: A Study of Direct Investment*', (MIT, unpublished Ph.D thesis).
Jun, Y. W., (1987) 'Reverse Direct Investment: The Case of Korean Consumer Electronics Industry', *International Economic Journal* 1.
Kim, K., (1988) 'Korea in the 1990s: Making the Transition to a Developed Economy', *World Development*, 16, 7–18.
Korean Institute of Economics and Technology (1987), *Electronics, Electrics*, 5 (Seoul; KIET)
Kindleberger, C. P., (1969) *American Business Abroad* (New Haven, Conn., and London: Yale University Press).
Kindleberger, C. P., and D. Audretsch, (1983) *The Multinational Corporation in the 1980s* (Cambridge, Mass.: MIT Press).
Knickerbocker, F. T., (1973) *Oligopolistic Reaction and the Multinational Enterprise* (Cambridge, Mass.: Harvard University Press).

Kojima, K., and T. Ozawa, (1985) 'Towards a Theory of Industrial Restructuring and Dynamic Comparative Advantage', *Hitosubashi Journal of Economics*, 26, 135–45.

Korea Business World (1988), 4 (10).

Korea Journal (1986), 26 (10).

Korea Electronics Show News (1987), October.

Korea Trade Promotion Centre, *Korea Trade and Business* (1988), 6 (5).

Korean Export-Import Bank (1989), *Weekly News of Foreign Direct Investment*, 606, September.

Lecraw, D. (1981) 'Internationalization of Firms from LDCs: Evidence from the Asian Region' in K. Kumar and M. G. McLeod (eds) *Multinationals from Developing Countries* (Lexington, Mass.: Lexington Books).

Major Statistics of the Korean Economy (1988) (Seoul: Economic Planning Board).

Marx, K., (1977) *Capital*, vol. 1 (London: Lawrence and Wishart).

Nishimizu, M., and Page Jr., J. M., (1987) 'Economic policies and productivity change in industry: an international comparison', mimeo (Washington, DC: World Bank).

Petri, P. A., (1988) 'Korea's Export Niche: Origins and Prospects', *World Development*, 16, 47–63.

Vernon, R., (1971) *Sovereignty at Bay* (London: Longman).

Vernon, R., (1974) 'The Location of Economic Activity', in J. H. Dunning (ed.), *Economic Analysis and the Multinational Enterprise* (London: Allen and Unwin).

Wells, L. T., (1983) *Third World Multinationals* (Cambridge, Mass.: MIT Press).

Westphal, L. E., Y. W. Rhee and G. Pursell, (1981) *Korean Industrial Competence: Where it Came From*, World Bank Staff Working Paper No. 469, (Washington, DC: The World Bank).

Westphal, L. E., Y. W. Rhee, L. Kim and A. H. Amsden, (1984) 'Republic of Korea', *World Development*, 12, 505–33.

World Bank, *World Development Report*, (1985, 1986, 1987, 1988) (New York: Oxford University Press).

7 Food Aid and Agricultural Disincentives

Jim Fitzpatrick and Andy Storey

INTRODUCTION

The principle of distributing food aid in disaster or famine situations is largely uncontroversial. Most people agree that when starvation is a reality or a threat there is a moral imperative to act, whatever the costs or side effects. However, in practice most food aid is not used in emergencies. It is used to support projects or for commercial sale in non-famine situations. In such uses food aid has for long been controversial and strong negative views about it still persist.

One of the most persistent objections to non-emergency food aid is the view that it acts as an obstacle to local agricultural production in the recipient country, thereby perversely worsening the very problem which necessitated the food aid in the first place. This 'disincentive' effect could operate in a number of different ways:

(i) availability of food aid may allow a government to neglect its own agricultural sector (policy disincentive);
(ii) if the food aid introduces exotic food tastes not supplied locally, the potential for self-sufficiency will be damaged (dietary disincentive and import dependency effect);
(iii) in the case of ill-conceived food-for-work, farmers might be drawn away from cultivation of their own crops, or where food aid is distributed freely (perhaps in a post-famine situation) farmers might be discouraged from working at all (a labour disincentive);
(iv) food aid, by causing local market prices to be depressed, reduces the incentive to local farmers to produce (price disincentive).

The price disincentive argument is the most fundamental and perennial criticism of food aid, and the present article concentrates primarily on this largely unresolved aspect of the disincentive issue.

Underlying this chapter is the view that one reason for the apparent stalemate on the price disincentives argument is a 'communications gap'. This exists between food aid 'experts' (researchers, economists, etc) on the one hand, and two other groups: namely on-the-ground practitioners, and the wider interested public. The 'experts' feel that their arguments for or

against disincentive effects are largely self-evident and require little explanation, while practitioners listen in bewilderment and conclude that
what the former group has to say is largely irrelevant or incoherent. The
purpose here is not therefore to break any new ground but rather to
present the basic issues regarding price disincentive effects in a manner
which is intelligible to the food aid practitioners and to other interested
parties. The article addresses three questions:

– how do price disincentives occur?
– will food aid always cause such effects?
– are price disincentive effects always bad?

HOW DO PRICE DISINCENTIVES OCCUR?

The operation of the traditional market model of economists can be clearly
seen in the case of food markets in developing countries. Ignoring for the
moment any imports, exports, or food aid, a sudden bumper harvest
results in a glut unless the population can be persuaded to buy more food.
Such 'persuasion' will probably involve farmers having to accept lower
prices in order to dispose of extra production, with the eventual compromise market clearing price probably being lower than the pre-harvest one.
This lower-price outcome can only be avoided if the behaviour pattern of
consumers is changed, i.e. if they are prepared to buy more food at any
given price than they would have done previously, so that a lower price is
not necessary to persuade them to consume more. The effect of the arrival
of external food aid can be similar to that of a bumper harvest. If people's
demand for food is unaltered at the prevailing price, then the additional
food supply will only be consumed if the average price is reduced.

The description above demonstrates that in a market economy, new
additional food aid will reduce average food prices unless consumer
demand is also altered. The potential price disincentive effect arises
because the lower market price will apply to all food, and not just to food
aid. Farmers will receive a lower price for their crops. Given the usual link
between price and production, this means that over time farmers may
reduce the amount of crops they grow or sell. This is what is known as the
'price disincentive effect' of food aid. It means that food aid, if it depresses
local market prices, may lead to reduced local food production and
self-sufficiency. While generally couched in national 'macroeconomic'
terms for a country as a whole, a similar mechanism may operate at
regional or local level. If an area is relatively isolated, and is not well linked
into national markets, food aid could have a negative price effect even if
this were not occurring at the national level.

WILL FOOD AID ALWAYS CAUSE PRICE DISINCENTIVES?

The fundamental chain of causation underlying price disincentive effects is that food aid increases food supply, causes market prices to be lower than they would otherwise be, and therefore lowers agricultural production. A key issue is thus whether food aid will always reduce market prices or whether there are exceptions to this. There are three situations in which food aid need not cause prices to fall: one relating to the 'supply', and one to the 'demand' side of the market model; and one relating to the nature of the food markets in less developed countries (LDC).

Commercial market displacement

On the supply side, food aid will not reduce market prices if it does not increase the total available food supply. The net amount of food available will not increase if the food aid merely replaces commercial imports that the recipient country would otherwise have purchased, ie. its 'usual market requirement' (UMR). When this occurs it is known as 'commercial market displacement', but would be better described as 'import replacement'.

Commercial market or import displacement is officially frowned upon by some donors for a number of reasons:

(i) When the objective of food aid is to increase the food consumption in the country beyond existing levels, this will not be achieved if the aid simply substitutes for commercially imported food.

(ii) Ensuring that commercial imports are not displaced reduces potential losses to exporting countries, which might otherwise see their export markets eroded by the availability of food aid. Politically, the agricultural producers in the donor country would also be less supportive of food aid if they saw it as a substitute for, rather than an addition to, world food trade.

For these reasons, an agreed international mechanism was put in place by the Food and Agriculture Organisation (FAO) in the mid-1950s to ensure that food aid recipient countries continue to import their 'usual market requirements' (UMRs) simultaneously with any food aid. However, UMRs are not always strictly enforced for the poorest countries. This is so for two reasons: first, because LDC import needs often fluctuate widely from year to year so there is a wide margin of error in UMR calculations; and second, in recent years many observers have argued that 'commercial market displacement' may be desirable – it provides poor LDCs with a form of aid which is equivalent to free foreign exchange, a potential development resource of which many LDCs are desperately short. Also, food aid now accounts for a much smaller proportion of the international food trade than before, so its potential for significant displacement of commercial trade has been reduced (although this aid is now more concentrated in the poorest countries of Africa where the potential for 'commercial market displacement' is relatively greater).

The 'commercial market displacement' issue highlights a frequent inconsistency in food aid objectives. Frequent objectives are:

(i) additional food supply for nutritional reasons;
(ii) foreign exchange and budgetary support;
(iii) avoidance of price disincentives.

Objectives (i) and (ii) cannot in principle be achieved simultaneously because exchange/budgetary savings can only arise when food aid displaces commercial imports. Achievement of objective (iii) can also be fully guaranteed only with objective (ii), but not with objective (i).

Another practical implication of this issue arises in relation to the conventional view that food aid should be supplied only to food deficit countries. One reason for this view is that there is a need for additional food in such countries. A second reason is that these countries import food anyway, so why not supply it free, ie. replace commercial imports. However, it is not possible to make both arguments simultaneously since they may involve mutually exclusive objectives.

Assessing the extent to which food aid displaces commercial food imports in practice is a difficult problem – one needs to know what imports would have been without the aid. Most studies of the issue agree that over half of all food aid has tended to displace commercial imports (Maxwell and Singer, 1979). This proportion may well have been higher for major recipient countries such as Egypt, Sri Lanka and South Korea; however, the figure for India, for over twenty years the largest recipient of food aid, was probably less than one quarter (Clay and Singer, 1985, p. 16). Displacement is also taking place in African countries which account for a growing proportion of all food aid (Maxwell, 1986a).

It would be simplistic to argue that 'commercial market displacement' is invariably a good thing and that food aid is best when it is not additional. In such cases, food aid cannot achieve nutritional objectives requiring a larger total supply at the national level (although it could do so at the local level through redistribution of supply). A further consideration must be the use made by the government of the foreign exchange and budgetary savings. If devoted to armaments or placed in Swiss bank accounts, the developmental impact is clearly limited (or negative). This possibility is sometimes used as an argument for donor influence over the use of 'counterpart funds'.

Creating additional demand

The view that food aid, when additional to normal commercial supplies, lowers prices, assumes that demand is unaffected. However, if the arrival of food aid can cause more food to be utilised at any given price level, then the depressing effect on prices may be offset or the automatic price fall avoided, i.e. although food aid does indeed increase food supply, prices may not be lowered. Such increased demand can be brought about in two main ways.

Direct targeting

The first of these is by directly targeting the food aid to those most likely to consume it on top of their existing consumption, and without requiring the incentive of lower prices. In this way most of the new supply will lead to a corresponding increase in food consumption without affecting prices. Such targeting can be achieved through: direct distribution to the poor via institutional feeding, food for work, and other development projects; a system of food stamps or fair price shops which allows the poor to obtain the food aid at zero or subsidised prices; distribution of 'self-targeting' commodities which tend to be consumed chiefly or exclusively by lower-income groups.

It is unlikely that food aid will directly create new food consumption on a full one-to-one basis. Even the poorest families usually have some non-food needs and will probably sell some of the food they receive to help meet these needs. However, it is a virtually universal phenomenon that out of any additional income available, the poor will spend a higher proportion on food than will the better-off. Similarly, the poor are the most likely to eat any additional food directly, rather than use it to replace food they would have bought on the local market.

Evidence suggests that free or subsidised food distribution can be successful in directly raising the overall demand for food, and hence limiting price disincentive effects. Subsidised distribution of food aid through fair price shops was one factor offsetting the expected detrimental price impact of food aid on Indian agriculture in the 1960s and 1970s (Isenman and Singer, 1977, p. 237). Two-thirds of the World Food Programme (WFP) project food aid to Peru was directed specifically to hungry and malnourished people for whom it was estimated to represent entirely additional consumption (Griffin, 1979, p. 50).

Indirect additional demand

This can be generated through the wider economic impact of food aid in a number of ways: firstly, food aid, eg. food-for-work, can be used in development projects which raise the incomes and living standards of the poor, and hence their ability to purchase food. Similarly, counterpart funds arising from the sale of monetised food aid can be used for developmental purposes to raise the incomes and food demand of the poor. Also, even when the better-off benefit from non-targeted food aid, their increased disposable incomes may be devoted to products produced by the poor, which could in turn indirectly allow the poor to buy more food. When food availability is a general constraint on development, reflected in rapidly rising food prices, food aid can free up this bottleneck and allow average real incomes to rise in the medium to long run.

It should, in principle, be possible to ensure that project (more so than programme) food aid generates genuinely additional food demand. However, the potential advantages of project food aid may be difficult and expensive to obtain in practice. For example, the administrative mechanisms designed to ensure that the food reaches specified target groups may prove too costly or too weak: $160m of cereals food aid, distributed through a food subsidy scheme in Bangladesh in 1982–3, benefited better-off consumers at least as much as poorer ones (World Bank, 1986, p. 147). There are also domestic political factors involved. As Huddleston (1983, p. 26) has noted: 'governments find it difficult to offer [subsidies] to the voiceless poor while denying them to the more vocal and politically powerful middle classes'. The experience of project food aid in practice has probably been more encouraging than these reservations would suggest. As Clay and Singer (1985) show food-for-work programs do not appear to have depressed local food production in the large food-for-work programs of Bangladesh and Ethiopia; so some degree of additional demand creation was, presumably, taking place.

The nature of LDC food markets

An underlying assumption in the foregoing discussion is that LDC food systems operate on a free-market basis. However, this is seldom so. When it is not, the potential price disincentive effect may not operate. For instance, many LDCs operate a system of *administered agricultural prices*. These frequently involve a buffer stock for price stabilisation purposes. When prices tend to fall, surplus stocks are bought in, to be sold later when prices are tending to rise. If such a system is operating successfully, the price disincentive effects of food aid can be dampened in the same way as those of a good harvest. Indeed, the food aid can itself be used to help establish a buffer stock system.

Market segmentation is another means by which disincentive effects on domestic farmers could be eliminated. In this situation the price of food to the consumers is allowed to fall, but producer prices are maintained at higher levels by some form of market intervention. This sort of market segmentation is possible in LDCs which regulate their agricultural sectors through parastatal marketing bodies. A budget deficit will, of course, be necessary to finance the 'wedge' between consumer and producer prices, but this could be financed by the sales of food aid.

Clay and Singer (1985) suggest that a dual-price system was one factor in the successful management of food aid in Colombia, Brazil and Tunisia. The results of this approach were higher levels of both food production and consumption in the countries concerned. Differentiated markets also operated in India, and are concluded to have been an appropriate policy tool in the avoidance of price disincentive effects (Isenman and Singer, 1977, pp. 230–3). Maxwell (1986a, 1986b) argues that such two-tier pricing systems could play a similarly positive role in Senegal and Ethiopia.

The record is not, however, entirely one of success. Despite stated policy goals to the contrary, severe disincentives to wheat production occurred in Egypt when cheap bread policies (financed at least partly by food aid) had positive income and nutritional effects for poor consumers (Clay, 1986, pp. 65–6). The barriers to successful market management in Africa in general are large, due to transport, communication and other problems: not only will the 'official' price probably diverge from the actual prices faced by rural producers and consumers, but prices between different rural areas often diverge considerably also (Lele and Candler, 1983, p. 216). As Ahmed and Rustagi (1985) show, these problems are much more serious in Africa than in Asia.

The temptation for many African governments is to utilise food aid to keep urban retail prices down, but without any measures to support producer prices. Indeed, as Matthews (1985, pp. 30–1) has noted:

> the deliberate intention of food aid distribution may be to lower food prices and thus transfer income away from the agricultural sector, perhaps as part of an industrialisation strategy based upon the extraction of an agricultural 'surplus'.

A possible response to this 'urban bias' issue is that food aid may also be used as a lever by donors to push recipient governments towards the adoption of more efficient and equitable policies towards their agricultural sectors. However, this response in turn raises questions about the efficiency and motivations of donor policies. An apparently successful example of such leverage comes from Mali, where the proceeds from food aid sales were switched gradually away from the subsidisation of consumer prices and towards the support of producer prices, under pressure from several donors (UN, 1987, p. 13).

ARE LOWER FOOD PRICES ALWAYS A BAD THING?

There are three foundation stones to the price disincentive criticism of food aid. The first is that food aid automatically increases food supplies. The second is that such increased supplies lead to lower market prices. The circumstances in which these assumptions might fall down were discussed in the previous section. The third element, discussed here, is that lower food prices are a 'bad thing' because they are a disincentive to local agriculture in LDCs.

The supply response

If all the measures discussed so far – commercial market displacement, creation of additional demand, operation of buffer stocks or two-tier pricing – fail to stop agricultural producer prices falling as food aid arrives, then will this necessarily lead to lower levels of domestic agricultural output?

It is unclear what the size of the output response to changes in price tends to be. Economists measure this by the 'price elasticity of supply' (PES). This refers to the amount by which agricultural output changes in response to a price change, e.g. if a 2 per cent fall in price causes a 1 per cent fall in output, the PES is 0.5. The higher the price elasticity of supply, therefore, the greater will be the price disincentive effect. At its simplest, a high PES is bad for food aid and a low PES is good for food aid.

There is a body of opinion which maintains that the PES is positive but rather small, perhaps of the order of 0.2 (Isenman and Singer, 1977, p. 230). These findings of a low PES are strongly challenged by the World Bank (1986, pp. 68–71): the Bank claims that if measured over a sufficiently long period the PES is highly significant, tending to be at least three times higher than the short-run response. To support this claim, the Bank quotes studies which indicate that 10 per cent higher agricultural prices in Argentina between 1950 and 1972 would have led to 9 per cent higher farm output; in Chile, for the 1960–82 period, the output response to similarly higher than actual prices could have been up to 20 per cent. (The magnitude of the PES effect is generally assumed to be the same for both price rises and falls, although the sign will obviously differ.)

There is some evidence that the PES for all crops taken together is lower than the PES for each individual crop. This is because the resources which are pulled out of the production of one crop as its price falls may be switched into the production of other crops; thus, a food aid-induced fall in the price of domestic foodcrops might lower the production of those particular crops, but not of total farm produce to the same extent, e.g. more non-food crops may be grown instead. For this reason studies which focus only on a single crop must be treated with caution (Barnum and Squire, 1980, p. 294). Evidence from India suggests that if food aid did lower domestic cereal prices then one consequence was a switch away from cereal production and towards oilseed and pulse production, so overall agricultural production may have been raised (Clay and Singer, 1985; Clay,

1986). The World Bank (1986, pp. 68–9) accepts the validity of this point but argues that unless the average price of all agricultural commodities is at least sustained, then resources will be withdrawn from agriculture entirely in the long-run, although one short-run response to lower prices will be some substitution between crops.

There is one additional aspect of this issue which should be spelled out. If the PES is low because of shortages of inputs, or because of poor infrastructure, then the immediate implication appears to be that food aid will not have major disincentive effects on domestic agriculture. But what if the input shortages and infrastructural failings are due to government neglect or discrimination? And what if these government policies have been encouraged by the availability of food aid? This brings us back to the 'policy disincentive' argument mentioned in the introduction. In such circumstances a policy disincentive effect could make it appear that there is no significant 'price disincentive' effect.

Income distribution issues

As stated at the outset, the main purpose of this paper is to examine whether food aid tends to reduce food prices, and whether lower food prices mean lower levels of domestic food production. Its main conclusion so far is that these effects can operate, but that they can also be avoided under certain conditions. However, it is also necessary to raise the question of how seriously any negative production effects which occur should be considered relative to potential benefits resulting from lower food prices and increased total supply. In other words, are there cases when food aid-induced lower agricultural prices and production are acceptable due to other benefits, which can arise in the form of improved income distribution? When food prices fall, some producers may suffer and output will be lower, but the poor could still be better off, and this latter effect might be regarded as of greater importance. In low income areas, such as South Asia, not only landless labourers but also a large percentage of small farmers are net purchasers of food, using cash incomes to supplement their own production.

That lower food prices may benefit the rural as well as the urban poor is confirmed by several studies. In Bangladesh a large number (in some years a majority) of farm households are net purchasers of rice (Nelson, 1983, p. 46). Similar results pertain for Kenya (Colclough, 1985, p. 39) and Senegal (Maxwell, 1986). So a policy of promoting lower food prices need not necessarily be a manifestation of 'urban bias'.

What the distribution issue emphasises is that food aid should not be judged solely on its incentive or disincentive impact. A proper assessment can only take place in the context of a broad view of the recipient economy, a view which includes distribution, output and other effects and which recognises the linkages between agriculture and other sectors. As has been seen, to even assess the price disincentive effect alone, it is necessary to extend the analysis beyond the agricultural sector. To formally weigh the price disincentive effect against other benefits and costs of food aid requires an even more encompassing framework. The data needed to construct such a model is simply not available in most LDCs (Deaton and Siaway, 1988, p. 84); furthermore, many of the effects are inherently difficult to quantify (e.g. impact on the status of women). It therefore seems inevitable that only partial and inadequate assessments can be made, and that available evidence can only be suggestive rather than conclusive.

CONCLUSIONS

Objections to food aid on the grounds that it causes price disincentive effects to LDC agriculture rest on the arguments that: food aid increases food supplies; increased food supplies depress local food prices; lower local food prices reduce local food production. What emerges from this review of the issue is that the matter is not a clear-cut one either for or against food aid. It is, nevertheless, possible to draw a number of conclusions:

(i) Price disincentive effects can arise through the two-stage mechanisms referred to above, i.e. lower market prices leading to lower food production. However, under a variety of circumstances these effects can be avoided. This means that the proper use of food aid, and the avoidance of negative side effects, will depend heavily on proper planning and management.

(ii) Even when some disincentives do occur, these may not be such that food aid can be rejected out of hand on that account. No more than any other form of aid, food aid cannot be judged by reference to one criterion alone, namely its effects on local prices or production. After all, an excess of aid-supported teachers, trucks, tents or training programs can also be a disincentive to local initiative. Few would suggest that they should therefore be stopped entirely.

Decisions about the desirability or otherwise of food aid should therefore involve a rounded judgment taking account of a range of considerations about local production and prices, but also about income distribution, nutrition, cost effectiveness and other issues. When food aid is deemed desirable on balance, the task facing project planners and implementors is to devise ways by which potential disincentive effects can be minimised.

NOTE

1. This chapter is based on research carried out for CARE, New York, but the views expressed are those of the authors only. Helpful comments on earlier drafts were received from Ed Clay, Brady Deaton, Raymond Hopkins, Alan Matthews, Emily Moore and Hans Singer. The usual disclaimer applies.

REFERENCES

Ahmed, F. G., and N. Rustagi, (1985) 'Agricultural Marketing and Price Incentives: A Comparative Study of African and Asian Countries', paper prepared for FAO, International Food Policy Research Institute.

Barnum, H. N., and L. Squire, (1980) 'Predicting Agricultural Output Response', *Oxford Economic Papers*, 32 (2).

Clay, E. J., (1986) 'European Food Aid and Africa's Food Needs', in J. Fitzpatrick (ed.) *Can Europe's Food Surplus Solve Africa's Famine?* (Dublin: Irish Council for the European Movement Conference Papers).

Clay, E. J., and H. W. Singer, (1979) 'Food Aid to Developing Countries: A Survey', *World Development*, 7, 225–247.

Colclough, C., (1985) 'Competing Paradigms in the Debate about Agricultural Pricing Policy', *IDS Bulletin*, 16.

Deaton, B. J., and A. Siaway, (1988) 'A Food Aid Strategy for Haiti', draft paper prepared under the Technical Support to Mission (TSM) Contract of Virginia Polytechnic Institute and State University and Tusregee University.

Griffin, P., (1979) 'The Impact of Food Aid – Peru, A Case Study', *Food Policy*.

Huddleston, B., (1983) 'The Case for Increasing Food Aid: How Much and To Whom?', *IDS Bulletin*, 14.

Isenman, P. J., and H. W. Singer, (1977) 'Food Aid – Disincentive Effects and Their Policy Implications', *Economic Development and Cultural Change*, 25.

Lele, U., and W. Candler, (1983) 'Food Security in Developing Countries: National Issues' in C. K. Eicher and J. M. Staatz (eds), *Agricultural Development in the Third World* (Baltimore: John Hopkins).

Matthews, A., (1985) *The Common Agricultural Policy and the Less Developed Countries* (Dublin: Trocaire/Gill and MacMillan).

Maxwell, S. J., (1986a) 'Food Aid to Senegal: Disincentive Effects and Commercial Displacement', *IDS Discussion Papers*, 225.

Maxwell, S. J., (1986b) 'Food Aid to Ethopia: Disincentive Effects and Commercial Displacement', *IDS Discussion Papers*, 226.

Nelson, G. O., (1983) 'Food Aid and Agricultural Production in Bangladesh', *IDS Bulletin*, 14.

United Nations (1987), 'World Food Programme Policy Paper on Food Aid, Food Self-Reliance and Development in Africa', UN Programme of Action for African Economic Recovery and Development.

World Bank, (1986) *World Development Report* (Washington, DC: Oxford University Press).

8 Food Aid and Structural Adjustment in Sub-Saharan Africa

H. W. Singer

CONVERGING CONSENSUS

The role of food aid in structural and sectoral adjustment support (SAL) for Sub-Saharan Africa (SSA) will be a matter of greatly increased importance over the last decade of this century. This is the result of a convergence of three factors:

(i) A consensus that the problems of Sub-Saharan Africa are of such exceptional severity and of such unique nature as to require and justify new approaches and to impose an obligation to leave no potentially useful resources unused. This consensus includes agreement on special treatment for SSA in respect of debt reduction and special facilities for SSA have been readily accepted.

(ii) A consensus that adjustment and sectoral support, in the case of SSA must be more 'growth-oriented', have a more 'human face' and require both a longer term horizon and increased resources.

(iii) A consensus that there is both need and potential absorptive as well as financing capacity for additional food aid, subject to assurance that food aid helps to provide incentives for increased local food production and physical and human investment in recipient countries.

Standing as it does at the crossroads of such increasingly accepted policy orientations, the subject clearly deserves new thinking preparatory to constructive action.

QUANTITATIVE DIMENSIONS

As a starting point for visualising the quantitative scope of such constructive action over the next decade, we take the IFPRI estimate of cereal food aid needs for SSA low-income countries in 1990 of 11.36 million metric tons.[1] Compared with a present annual flow of 4–5 million tons (varying with the acuteness of emergencies and international response), this would

139

require an expansion by some 7 million tons per annum, an expansion of the current total flow of food aid from 10 million tons to 17 million tons.[2] There is no doubt that such additional supply capacity exists (some of this additional 7 million tons could come from within SSA by way of triangular transactions). Given the proposed link with SAL, much of this additional 7 million tons would take the place of present commercial food imports, freeing foreign exchange for developmental imports (targeted towards stimulating domestic food production) hopefully reducing food aid needs towards the end of the decade. The problem is not one of supply capacity but of aid capacity: even a doubling of food aid would leave total aid flows at 0.39 per cent of donor GNP (instead of the present 0.35 per cent), still a long way below the 0.7 per cent UN target; it would do little more than restore food aid to the levels of twenty-five years ago, and would also bring it to the level of one-sixth of total aid flows proposed at that time by expert analysis (UN and FAO, 1962; Chakravarty and Rosenstein-Rodan, 1965). It would also do no more than to maintain the present share of food aid (about 20 per cent) in the rising cereal import requirements projected on present trends for SSA in the 1990s. It would represent 4 per cent of present stocks, or 6 per cent of cereal world trade, or 0.02 per cent of donors' GNP.

The real limit is not aid capacity but absorptive capacity, in the positive sense of making this useful as an efficient instrument for bringing SSA back towards renewed growth and development. It is here that its integration with the present SAL effort becomes vital. In the rest of the paper we will explore ways of doing this. It will emerge that such possibilities exist, to the mutual benefit of SAL and food aid, making both into better instruments of support for SSA.

Any action would, of course, start on a smaller and more experimental scale than the estimates of the ultimate limit of 7 million tons annually given above. It would also be largely on a country-by-country and trial basis, without necessarily any quantitative target. A more modest proposal for immediate action involves the creation of a new international facility of $1 billion a year; the 50 per cent of this proposed as food aid (and this not all for SSA) would represent at present prices about 1.5 million tons of cereals, one-fifth of the potential scope estimated above (Reutlinger, 1988). This proposal is rightly described as 'obviously only a beginning, though a respectable one' (ibid, p. 64). At this stage, clarity about objectives and methods of integration of food aid and financial aid and the achievement of efficient income transfer seem more important than discussion of quantitative magnitudes.

A MENU OF POTENTIALITIES

Food aid can contribute to structural adjustment in nine different ways:[3] contributing to overall available resources, to cushion the austerity of the adjustment process; setting free foreign exchange, helping with the stabilisation of the balance of payments as a necessary preliminary to resumed economic growth; sustaining incomes and employment of the poor, essential during the difficult transition period from retrenchment to resumed growth; protecting vulnerable groups from the harsh short-run impact of stabilisation and adjustment policies; maintaining essential economic and social services during the transition period; reduce budget deficits and inflation – an important element in stabilisation and adjustment; help to provide domestic food stability and food security in SSA – an essential political precondition for acceptability and viability of adjustment; support essential reforms measures and sectoral programmes often related to food production; through counterpart funds help to provide local finance for projects or programmes within a structural adjustment context.

With such a multitude of possible objectives and effects, it becomes important to be clear about intentions, and to choose the forms of food and financial aid, and other methods of combination, in the light of the main objectives. It will be useful to look briefly at these objectives in turn.

Increase overall resources – cushion austerity

It is increasingly recognised that the SSA countries must be given a greater incentive as a *quid pro quo* for the dangers, risks and uncertainties that are involved in the short-term (stabilisation) part of the adjustment process. Experience has shown that many programmes fail at this first hurdle. Most SSA countries are so poor, and in some of them the political, social and economic structure is so fragile, that the promise of better things to come may be heavily discounted. 'In the long run we are all dead' and the run may be shorter in SSA than elsewhere. So any increase in the *quid pro quo* would be welcome, particularly if front-loaded to come during the difficult initial period. To be front-loaded, the additional food aid would normally have to be on a quick-disbursing programme basis; or else given to countries where an infrastructure and absorptive capacity for additional food aid already exists. As an increase in overall resources, 70 per cent additional food aid would represent $2 billion per annum; the same order of magnitude as some of the other provisions and facilities, but the more realistic suggestion of $500 million per annum would clearly be a subsidiary factor taken as a simple resource flow. To take account of the minority of food-exporting SSA countries, this flow would have to be mixed with fungible financial resources and/or partly on the basis of triangular transactions; although theoretically food-exporting countries could also benefit from increased exports made possible by switching resources into increased exports, either by way of increased investment or by switching production out of food-aid commodities. (If they are genuinely and viably food-exporting, this need not endanger their own food security.) From this angle, food aid and related financial aid should be targeted to countries in the greatest danger from initial austerity, or to those where scarcity of overall resources is the main bottleneck preventing growth, i.e. countries with unutilised production capacities, unemployment, unused land or where inputs and investments do not require foreign exchange. This particular purpose is frustrated if current food aid is merely switched into financial aid associated with SAL (although it could increase the efficiency of the resource transfer).

Freeing foreign exchange – balance of payments support

This will generally be the more important contribution of additional food aid. Practically all SSA countries are in a foreign exchange constraint more binding than the savings/investment constraint. To satisfy this purpose, the food aid would have to displace commercial imports and in general be on a programme basis. Food-exporting countries would not directly benefit. The associated financial aid and conditionality would be designed to make certain that good developmental use is made of the foreign exchange set free, and in particular that it helps with sectoral programmes and projects which are part of the overall adjustment process. If the foreign exchange thus set free is added to reserves or used for debt repayment, this will not directly help to make adjustment easier or more growth-oriented, but it may help indirectly by increasing credit-worthiness and making it easier to restore capital flows or obtain import credits. But this can hardly be a direct objective.

To the extent that it replaces commercial imports, food aid is fully equivalent in value to financial aid for the recipients, but for the donors the cost of transporting and delivering the food aid (itself requiring associated financial aid) has to be treated as an extra cost factor. In so far as the displaced commercial imports come from other SSA (or other developing) countries, this would call for triangular transactions or additional financial aid for food-exporting SSA countries – not just for reasons of equity as in the preceding case, but in direct compensation for actual loss suffered. For the donors, the aid given would be at the cost of reduced commercial exports, but this would be compensated by other exports paid for with the foreign exchange set free, e.g. for agricultural inputs or for inputs needed to utilise capacity made idle for lack of foreign exchange – a widespread fact of life in SSA today.

Sustaining income and employment of the poor

Two related criticisms of present SAL approaches are that (a) they are unduly restrictive in the initial period, imposing sacrifices well before any benefits can be expected; and (b) that these sacrifices tend to fall most severely on poorer sections of society, increasing inequality of income distribution. Increasingly, these worries are accepted as matters of legitimate concern. Food aid is particularly well suited to respond to such concerns. Food aid is aid with built-in targeting towards the poor who spend a larger part of their incomes on food; as the classical 'wage good' or 'subsistence fund' it also has a built-in tendency to favour labour-intensive activities; it is well suited to relieve urban poverty directly – it is the urban poor who are most affected by the necessary higher priorities to agriculture and exports and other SAL conditions; through monetisation and use of counterpart funds food aid can finance rural public works projects which create demand for local food and help to provide the infrastructure needed to support higher prices as an incentive to food producers, such as improved rural roads. In many developing countries, including SSA ones, there is experience and an established administrative structure for such food-for-work or food-aid financed cash-for-work projects.

   With such multiple advantages, and complementarities with what are increasingly recognised as problems in SAL procedures, this potential for fruitful combination of food aid and SAL is crying out to be more systematically exploited. In SSA, the threat to incomes and employment during the transitional stabilisation period is superimposed upon a long-run decline, in some countries dating back up to twenty years. Moreover, there is a danger that declines in income and employment in the initial period may become cumulative and create downward 'vicious circles', frustrating the objective of structural adjustment intended 'to lay the foundations for subsequent viable growth'. Timely maintenance of employment and incomes can prevent such vicious circles; for this purpose it would be essential for food aid to be included at an early stage, i.e. as part of the stabilisation as well as the adjustment package, rather than being added later as a compensatory afterthought. In this case also, prevention is better than cure. But the compensatory function of food aid has a justification of its own, discussed in the next section.

Protecting vulnerable groups

Apart from the recognised need for 'protecting the poor during periods of adjustment'[4] in general, there is a further need for protecting specially vulnerable groups among the poor. The best-known exposition of this case for children is UNICEF's plea for 'Adjustment with a Human Face' (Cornia et al., 1987). The destruction of human capital in SSA as a result of the economic and debt crises, often reinforced by the initial austerity of the adjustment process, is not only unacceptable on humanitarian grounds; it is also incompatible with the objective of adjustment of laying the foundations for viable growth. In addition to sound policies, this objective will certainly require a well-fed, healthy, educated and skilled future labour force. It is now known that malnutrition and the associated ill-health of young children can have permanent effects on their intelligence and future productivity. Between birth and the age of five a child does most of its learning and develops practically all its brain potential. While it is one of the declared objectives of adjustment to improve the efficiency of social expenditures such as education, malnutrition among children reduces school attendance, increases drop-out rates and makes children less capable of benefiting from education. Food-aided child/mother health clinics, provision of school meals, nutrition education and direct nutritional supplements can all have high direct benefit/cost ratios (as the Bank's own research has established) and even higher indirect, not easily measurable, benefits. Here food aid has a well-established tradition and infrastructure with a strong multilateral basis in WFP and UNICEF. Its association with the adjustment process will not only give adjustment 'a human face' and be politically more acceptable; it will also make it more efficient and logically consistent. Destruction of human capital as part of the adjustment process defeats its own purposes.

Protection of vulnerable groups, with the help of food aid, is also a traditional and suitable field for NGOs who may be better equipped for close targeting. Involvement of NGOs is a declared objective of providers of both adjustment assistance and food aid.

Maintain essential services

SAL programmes often emphasise increased cost efficiency of public services, usually in the context of reduced overall expenditure and increased taxation, often involving direct user fees. Governments may interpret the mandate of increased cost-efficiency as requiring the cutting-down of services in rural areas, especially remote rural areas (where they may be most costly to deliver), and concentrating on economic 'directly productive' services, to the detriment of essential social services (endangering human capital), by indiscriminate user fees (making access to public services less equal), by cutting down on essential current and maintenance expenditure (clinics without drugs, schools without blackboards, agricultural marketing boards without spare parts for broken-down lorries or without fuel to run them, etc.). Short-run cost efficiency in the accounting sense is not necessarily true long-run developmental cost efficiency.

Such interpretations of cost efficiency may not be in line with the preferences of those providing adjustment support, but the alternative would be increased interference with the right of sovereign governments to have their own priorities. The declared principle of adjustment is to limit conditionality to macro-economic quantities, but to leave distribution within these quantities to the judgement of the government. Food aid provides a means of preserving this principle while giving governments both incentives and the means to avoid sacrificing true long-term cost efficiency.

Reduce budget deficit and inflation

Programme food aid results in government revenue and represents an important source in some SSA countries. At the same time, by drawing money out of the private sector it reduces inflationary pressure, which is an objective of many SAL agreements. Higher food prices are one of the most potent sources of inflationary spirals which frustrates many SAL measures such as devaluation and other measures designed to improve the balance of payments and outward orientation. The revenue from food aid sales can also be used to promote local food production by paying higher prices in a segmented food market, or spending on rural infrastructure and agricultural research and extension, subsidising inputs or increasing the supply of incentive goods in rural areas. All this will make the general SAL policy of higher prices for farmers more effective. Food aid fills a budgetary gap created by selective food subsidies, and prevents diversion of government revenue from essentials for production growth.

The contrary fear that the lowering of food prices acts as a disincentive for local farmers should be ruled out if the food aid is given in the framework of a SAL programme which shifts incentives in favour of the rural sector. In any case, both historical experience, from the Marshall Plan to India, as well as economic analysis, contradict the necessity of such a disincentive effect. An analysis of sixteen developing countries which achieved particularly high growth rates in food production during 1961–76 shows that they received 80 per cent more food aid per capita than the average food-aid recipient country (Bachman and Paulino, 1979). Much of the fear of such a disincentive effect is due to a mistargetting of criticism on food aid instead of surplus-creating agricultural and protectionist agricultural policies in the industrial countries and neglect of the agricultural sector in developing countries. (Structural adjustment ought to deal with the first as well as the second factor.) Another reason is simplistic market analysis to the neglect of the dual market structure in nearly all developing countries.

Provide domestic food security

Food riots as a result of food insecurity are one of the main political obstacles to the acceptance and even more to the implementation of structural adjustment programmes. Food aid flexibly and fungibly mixed with financial aid and help with the establishment of stabilisation stocks can fulfil this function. The World Bank/WFP co-operation in setting up a food-aided rice price stabilisation stock as part of a Bank-supported programme of agricultural reforms in Madagascar provides an example which should be capable of multiplication in other SSA countries (Nicholas, 1988, p. 88). Such arrangements require multi-annual planning of both the food aid and financial aid components of the support package, with fungibility between the two, in the sense that at a time of sufficient stocks aid assumes more financial forms, and *vice versa*. Food security will often require the maintenance of selective and targetted food subsidies; the gradual reduction in and phasing out of food subsidies is greatly preferable to abrupt abolition; and there is already an African precedent for using food aid in a Bank sectoral adjustment loan package to fund at least half of a targetted food subsidy scheme.[5] (Nicholas, 1988, p. 89).The EEC has pioneered the fungible substitution of financial and food aid when in 1984 it introduced its 'substitution accounts', replacing food aid with financial aid or technical assistance when the supply of food is not necessary or desirable (Franco, 1988, p. 96). Another contribution to food stability could be provided by flexible commodity aid when aid can be switched between food, fertilizer, seeds, pesticides, livestock feed, etc. The use of the IMF Compensatory Financing Facility could also be a flexible alternative to food aid; it now provides for a temporary excess in the cost of cereal imports, but its use has been restricted by tighter conditionality.

Support essential reforms

SALs typically include measures such as liberalising food trade (abolition or reform of parastatal marketing boards), reduction of food subsidies, land reform, resettlement, and civil service reform (often involving reduction in numbers employed). All these measures involve some initial disruption and costs before the benefits come forth. In this they reflect the general feature of the stabilisation/adjustment process, i.e. that the bad news (retrenchment) comes first while the good news (better-founded growth) comes later. Just as food aid can help to resolve the stresses resulting from this unfortunate sequencing, so it is also the case for specific reforms such as those mentioned. The use of food aid to help in the initial stages of such reforms as land reform, resettlement and food subsidies is well-established, and much experience exists in the WFP and elsewhere for SSA and other areas. In other cases such as civil service reform or liberalising food trade, the use of food aid would require new approaches – at first probably different approaches on a pilot or experimental basis. This application of food aid may apply specifically to the sectoral rather than overall adjustment programmes (which, in fact, represent the bulk of SAL). As an example, food aid seems well designed to maintain government workers laid off as a result of public sector reform and to help in their retraining and, where it applies, their rural resettlement.

Using counterpart funds

Counterpart funds from the sale of food aid provide an opportunity for that continued dialogue with the recipient government which is so essential to a harmonious adjustment process. They can be used to help finance rural public works projects to increase the income transfer efficiency of food aid, increase demand for local food and offset any 'urban bias' or disincentive effect – in other words, counterpart funds can be considered as a normal form of monetisation of food aid. Conversely, counterpart funds arising from financial aid can provide the local finance for food-aided projects, especially if this also serves as a catalyst for the (often very modest) foreign exchange required. The disposition of counterpart funds would also be a natural basis for continued dialogue, not only with the government, but among all the sources of financial and food aid giving rise to counterpart funds. The best arrangement would clearly be on a multilateral basis through the World Bank (directly or through the Consortia and Consultative Groups) and the WFP (directly or through the UNDP Round Tables). Such multilaterally co-ordinated administration, already shaping up in a number of SSA countries, could make an important contribution to successful adjustment, helping SSA back to the path of development.

CONCLUDING REMARKS

This paper is limited to the use of extended developmental food aid in adjustment. Unhappily, much of the food aid to SSA in the next few years will still have to be labelled as 'emergency'. This is not to say that a broadened and more effective system of emergency food aid cannot also make an important, indeed indispensable, contribution to adjustment (which is itself a form of rehabilitation from Africa's 'chronic emergency'). But even with this limitation it has become apparent that there are many promising openings. No doubt their realisation will bring to light problems and difficulties, but the potential difficulties seem too great to be ignored. Multilateral and multilaterally co-ordinated food aid in the service of growth-oriented adjustment would also remove food aid from its unwanted link with surpluses and agricultural export wars.

NOTES

1. IFPRI Policy Briefs 2 'Third World Food Markets'. The figure appears in the section on 'Food Aid Trends and Projections' by Hannan Ezekiel. Estimates of food aid needs prepared by the US Department of Agriculture and by FAO broadly agree that even on a 'status quo' basis food aid needs to exceed current availabilities by some 50–80 per cent. On a basis of nutritional needs, the required extension would be vastly larger but neither the authors of these projections nor of this paper assume that the task of eliminating hunger should be solely assigned to food aid.
2. This figure also is close to results obtained by the USDA and FAO.
3. This list is based on similar enumeration of functions of food aid from Shaw and Singer (1988) and Hope E. Sukin (1988) with some additions.
4. The title of a paper presented by the World Bank at a meeting of the Development Committee in April, 1987.
5. The reference is to Morocco, which is not part of SSA.

REFERENCES

Bachman, K., and L. Paulino, (1979) *Rapid Food Production Growth In Developing Countries*, Research Report 11 (Washington, DC: IFPRI).
Chakravarty, S., and P. N. Rosenstein-Rodan, (1965) *The Linking of Food Aid With Other Aid* (Rome: UN and FAO).
Cornia, G. A., R. Jolly and F. Stewart, (1987) *Adjustment With a Human Face* (Oxford: Oxford University Press).
Franco, M., (1988) 'Food Security and Adjustment – the EC contribution', *Food Policy*, 13 (1) February.
Nicholas, P., (1988) 'Adjustment and the Poor – the Role of the World Bank', *Food Policy*, 13 (1) February.
Reutlinger, S., (1988) 'Efficient Alleviation of Poverty and Hunger – A New International Assistance Facility', *Food Policy*, 13 (1) February.
Shaw J., and H. W. Singer, (1988) 'Food Policy, Food Aid and Economic Adjustment', *Food Policy*, 13 (1) February.
Sukin, H. E., (1988) 'US Food Aid For Countries Implementing Structural Adjustment', *Food Policy*, 13 (1) February.
UN and FAO (1962), *Development Through Food* (Rome: UN and FAO).

9 Peasants, Participation and Productivity: an Evaluation of Sandinista Agrarian Reform 1979–90

Andy Thorpe and Deborah McGurk

The final triumph of the Sandinista uprising in July 1979 led to radical changes in Nicaragua. Agrarian reform has been central to this revolution and so an understanding of it is central to an appreciation of the development strategy followed by the FSLN (Frente Sandinista Liberacion Nacional). This chapter seeks to provide such an understanding for the first post-Somoza decade in Nicaragua.

Most commentators agree the Sandinistas' agrarian strategy to have been both flexible and pragmatic (Deere *et al.*, 1985; Austin *et al.*, 1985; Collins *et al.*, 1985; Kaimovitz, 1986). Such a conclusion is perhaps understandable given the ongoing commitment to 'national unity' over a time period when external political, military and economic pressures were paramount. The need to switch resource allocation between various sectors of the rural population has been recognised as essential to retain plurality of support. It would be incorrect, however, as will be argued here, to view such shifts as ad-hoc measures introduced to cure a temporary ailment. Instead they should be explicable in the context of the model of accumulation dominant at the time for, as Lehmann (1978, p. 345) reminds us:

> The formulation of a model of accumulation is prior to the design of forms of organisation of work or even the distribution of property at a particular moment in time. A successful revolution creates its own models, unsuccessful ones are failed imitations.

Formulation of such a model preceded the eventual overthrow of Somoza (Palmer, 1985, Kaimovitz, 1986) and initial post-triumph policy culminated in the institutionalisation of this model, which we have termed the 'statist' model. This model resulted from the inherited agro-export agriculture of the Somoza era and reigned until the 'bottom-up' developmental approach necessitated a shift towards a decentralised peasant-based accumulation. This chapter proceeds by first recognising the historical specificities of Nicaraguan agriculture before examining the 'statist' model (1979–84) and its successor, the 'peasant' model (1984–present) in terms of performance and popular participation.

THE INHERITED ECONOMY

The development of an indigenous feudal economy was truncated by the arrival of the Spanish conquistadores in the early sixteenth century, although major dislocations did not materialise until coffee cultivation was introduced in the middle of the nineteenth century. Coffee production began the process of peasant displacement, proletarianisation and trade dependence so characteristic of many of today's 'Third World' economies. In Nicaragua's case this was exacerbated by the introduction of cotton cultivation in the early 1950s which saw export earnings from just this single crop rise to $5.2 million by 1963 (Wheelock, 1980). Similar expansion also took place in coffee production and the creation of large beef cattle ranches and capital-intensive sugar plantations resulted in a particularly distorted economy such that

> From the early 1950's to the mid-seventies, the agricultural land used to produce luxury crops expanded almost 40%. By the 1970's 90% of all agricultural credit was earmarked for export crops with virtually none for local food production. In 1955, Nicaragua imported 21,000 tons of grains, by 1978 this country was importing over ten times that amount. (Collins *et al.*, 1985, p. 107).

The marginalisation of the peasantry from the fertile Pacific Plains caused the land frontier to be rolled-back into the mountains as the peasants sought and found new, albeit less productive, land to cultivate. This rapid change accelerated the process of proletarianisation within the countryside whilst creating an agrarian capitalist class affiliated to Somoza.

By 1978, the year preceding Somoza's downfall, the concentration of landholding was extremely skewed with just 0.4 per cent of the economically active population (EAP) possessing almost half the cultivated area. At the other extreme, 37.1 per cent of the EAP were now divorced from the land whilst a further 36.4 per cent had become sufficiently marginalised to have become reliant upon seasonal work or off-farm activity to supplement their consumption needs. These marginalised sectors shared little of the benefits of an average 7.8 per cent annual increase of agricultural GDP during the 1960s and 1970s (World Bank, 1983) given their limited entitlements. Instead, their lack of entitlements (direct or trade) consign them to the poorest 50 per cent of the Nicaraguan population, a proportion that was only consuming 68 per cent of the UN basic calorific requirements in 1971 (Reinhardt, 1987). These individuals also suffered in health terms from the increasing technical intensity of production in the agro-export sector,[1] a production bias which served to heighten the need for recourse to external financing flows during the last years of Somoza.

Nicaragua's external balance was fluctuating but generally deteriorating from the mid-to-late 1970s. The surge in international commodity prices which allowed an impressive swing from trade deficit to surplus in 1976 proved to be only a temporary respite for the stricken economy as the deterioration in the military situation caused a serious capital flight in the closing Somocismo years.

The Nicaraguan economy in 1979, then, was neither predominantly feudal nor plantation-orientated (Wheelock, 1980) but, as in a number of other cases (Deere, 1982; Ruhl, 1985; Mason, 1986), a dualistic legacy. There existed both a modern agro-export sector and a traditional peasant sector producing food crops for domestic consumption. This was the Sandinistas' inheritance.

1979–84: THE STATIST ACCUMULATION MODEL

The underlying reality of the Nicaraguan situation dictated a number of questions which would need resolution if the permanency of the people's revolution was to be established. Should emphasis be placed upon social or individualistic organisational forms? Should the emphasis on export-orientated agriculture be maintained or instead should production for domestic consumption prevail? Should policies be orientated towards large-scale capital-intensive production methods or were there other, more appropriate, policies in the Nicaraguan context?

In a sense events pre-empted such discussion for, with the flight of Somoza and his affiliates, the FSLN found themselves in possession of monopoly powers in the banking and foreign trade sectors, along with access to vast tracts of ex-Somozista land. Such an inheritance, allied to FSLN commitments to spread the surplus generated through production as widely as possible, led to the adoption of a 'statist' model of accumulation whereby

> [the state would]. . . . 'lead' the accumulation process by undertaking productive (as opposed to infrastructural) investment and restructuring existing capital along lines consistent with a new structure of income distribution and consumption. To act as a centre of accumulation the state must ensure the availability of adequate real and financial resources, relying on surpluses from productive state enterprises and not merely its ability to tax away private surplus or borrow abroad. Thus the economy will be mixed in the sense that the state will have a decisive presence in modern production and will control key areas of trade and

finance; but in the private production sphere, peasant food production and supporting activity will be given priority. (Coraggio and Irvin, 1985, p. 31)

Evidence provided by agrarian policies adopted by the FSLN over the period 1979–84 is wholly consistent with the thesis of a state-led accumulation model, as we shall now demonstrate.

The Somoza lands were formally taken into FSLN hands by Decree no. 3 on 20 July 1979, effecting one of the most simple and costless land reforms in history. The subsequent decision to incorporate these farms into Area de Propriedad del Pueblo (APPs) or state farms is justified by many commentators on a variety of grounds. Some felt productivity would decline if such confiscated lands were turned over to an as yet unorganised peasantry (Kaimovitz and Stanfield, 1985); while yet others refer to the infeasibility of such a transfer (Reinhardt, 1987). Others saw the need to ensure a secure source of foreign exchange and thus prevent the emergence of a rural elite or the endangerment of economies of scale (Deere et al., 1985). Such reasons may well be valid but they tend to obscure the main motive for the formation of APPs, namely the accumulation process (Kleiterp, 1988; Ruccio, 1988).

The capital-intensity of the predominantly agro-export confiscated Somozista lands provided the greater potential for surplus that was necessary to fulfill both long-term investment programmes and FSLN welfare pledges. Consolidation of control over the designated APPs was not quite so simple however, for in many areas an insurrectional form of worker self-management had been installed in the latter stages of the uprising.[2] It is perhaps a measure of the belief in, and commitment to, the revolution by the agricultural proletariat and peasantry that the embryonic workerist communes were relinquished to the state with little objection. It was to these APPs, the area of which seems to have initially been over-estimated by the FSLN (Banmeister and Niera, 1984), that the FSLN attached priority given the need to re-activate production as quickly as possible, as Wheelock made clear in 1984:

In the first years, we had as the focus of attention the Area of Peoples property. We dedicated ourselves to consolidating production units and the production complexes; we dedicated ourselves to the organisation of the enterprises. . . . (in Kaimovitz and Stanfield, 1985)

Of the land confiscated, which totalled between 1.1 and 1.6 million manzanas (MZ)[3] (depending on data source), over 90 per cent was in the large farm category (500 MZ and above); only 0.3 per cent was of farms of less than 50 MZ (Peek, 1982). This land transfer placed about 20 per cent of the agricultural land into state hands, giving it control over 15 per cent of cotton, 12 per cent of coffee and 8 per cent of beef cattle production (Reinhardt, 1987).

Direct state control of surplus production is not, then, as extensive as might be thought, and is explicable in terms of the FSLN commitment to the mixed economy. This commitment should not be thought sufficient to allow dismissal of the notion of state-led accumulation, for it ignores indirect controls over private production through the levers of trade, finance and constitutional proclamation. This control is best exemplified by reference to the private sector immediately after the FSLN's assumption of power on 19 July 1979.

The implementation of Decree 3 did not eliminate the agrarian capitalist classes, for over 20 per cent of land still remained in larger, private farms, but it understandably caused consternation within this sector. Similarly, the smaller peasants and landless workers had high expectations of bene-fitting from Somoza's overthrow. The initial prioritisation of the APP sector provided insufficient employment to appease the rural masses, and by late 1979 takeovers of non-Somoza farmland were increasing. Whilst restitution of a number of these farms did occur, in a number of other instances the take-overs were legitimised. This, allied to the decrees in April and May creating tenancy rights while reducing rentals by 85 per cent, went some way to ameliorating the demands of the agricultural workers and poor peasantry.

Such a policy, favouring as it did the rural poor, caused increased tensions within the large private farm sector, provoking decapitalisation and hence a reduction of marketable surplus. Thus in order to stimulate the production of a surplus in this sector, various indirect incentives were introduced. These included guaranteed export prices, low personal and corporate tax-rates, low-cost government financing for replanting coffee trees, along with credit at negative real interest rates to cover all working costs (SUAS, 1987). The credit policy was not just targetted at large farmers, but reflected a recognition by the FSLN of the role credit control plays in raising agricultural output.

The FSLN sought to transform rural social structures through the Asociacion de Trabajadores del Campo (ATC). This organisation grouped both petty producers and wage-labourers into one entity, due to their perceived similarity of interest. In point of fact, it was envisaged that APP prioritisation *vis-à-vis* resource allocation would lead to the growth of this sector and the eventual subsumption of individualistic forms of production. The incorporation of all agrarian semi-proletarians into one mass organis-ation was thus consistent with the chosen developmental path. Indeed, the support offered by the ATC in the formation of Cooperatives de Credito y Servicio (CCS) in 1979/80 suggests the ATC leadership itself was prepared to press on towards more collective forms of production.

The same idea is reflected in the decision to create a National Foodstuffs

Enterprise (ENABAS) immediately after Somoza's downfall. ENABAS, as well as providing a state monopoly in the international basic grain trade, also allowed the FSLN to introduce a national grain procurement policy. The influence of ENABAS over the private grain producing sector was limited by the inaccessibility of much of the principal grain producing areas, and by inadequate storage and drying facilities. Nevertheless, the role foreseen for ENABAS was large – witness the intent to purchase 40 per cent of the maize and bean crops in the first post-revolutionary crop cycle.[4]

Land consolidation into APPs, FSLN credit and trade controls, and the creation of a single mass organisation responsible for articulating rural worker demands, support the view that initial FSLN policies favoured a statist model of accumulation, as do the further FSLN agrarian programmes initiated over the period to 1984. At the same time however, the FSLN commitment to a 'trickle-up' development philosophy based upon the 'logic of the majority' would begin to undermine the model, thereby paving the way for a switch to a peasant-based accumulation process.

The need to continue the process of reactivitating the economy was of prime importance, underlined by the introduction in 1980 of the Programa de Reactivacion Economica en Beneficio del Pueblo (Plan 80). In order to finance the social welfare policies of Plan 80, increasing production in the agricultural sector was viewed as a matter of urgency. Response to initial land tenure policies had proved of some success and served to focus further attention on land distribution and production organisation. Again the ATC was in the forefront, arguing for greater land access (Deere *et al*, 1985). In response the FSLN introduced the 'law of fixed rental' (March 1981) by which the private sector was compelled to make idle or under-utilised land available for rental at FSLN-set rates and, following its minimal success, then introduced the Ley de Reform Agraria in August 1981. This reform (Decree No. 782) allowed the expropriation in the Pacific coast region[5] of either inefficiently farmed land in holdings of over 500 MZ or lands over 50 MZ if they were being farmed under pre-capitalist production relations. While these expropriations provided compensation to the former landowners on the basis of how efficiently they had been farmed, like a number of other Latin American reforms (Kay, 1981/2) it was a distinctive reform insofar as it placed no maximum ceiling upon landholdings, as long as they were being efficiently farmed. The objectives of the plan were: to resolve agrarian capitalists' fears over the likelihood of land expropriation; to increase land utilisation thereby increasing grain output; and to consolidate support amongst the semi-proletarian classes (Deere *et al*, 1985). Expropriation of this land from the private sector is not enough to vindicate our 'statist' thesis: we must rather look to see how this land was redistributed.

The obvious solution would have been to consolidate expropriated land into the recently established state sector. However, the size of the APP had provoked some indigestion: problems included insufficient technical and administrative staff; inexperienced management; a commitment to offer permanent employment to previously seasonally-unemployed workers; less repressive management procedures leading to reduced per capita productivity; a lack of operating budgets; ill-defined FSLN statements regarding worker participation in decision-making; and excessive overcentralisation. As a consequence of this, state farms incurred large losses in 1980 (Kaimovitz, 1986), although merger of the Agricultural Ministry (MIDI) and the Agrarian Reform Ministry (INRA) to form MIDINRA, and subsequent reorganisation of the state farm sector was beginning to ameliorate the situation by August 1981. Transfer of the newly expropriated land to the APPs was not then a viable proposition at this time.

Instead, after a great deal of internal debate (Deere *et al.*, 1985), the decision was taken to distribute this land to those willing to join together in a cooperative. Whilst direct distribution to individual peasant producers was not ruled out, the emphasis was firmly on developing the cooperative aspects of production in a voluntaristic manner. Indeed, in the eyes of MIDINRA (1983, quoted in Zalkin, 1987, p. 969) the CAS production cooperatives (Cooperativas Agricolas Sandinstas) were seen as a 'higher form of organisation of work that generates solidarity and cooperation, going beyond the relations of competition and exploitation among men'. Cooperative formation appears easily reconciliable then with a statist model, cooperatives representing a 'half-way house' towards fully collectivised production.

Progress, however, would be slow, as the FSLN recognised the need for such cooperatives to be grounded on solid organisational principles to avoid the errors which had beset a number of earlier established cooperatives. For this reason, only 40 per cent of the approximately 238 000 MZ which were expropriated in the law's first year of operation (Collins, 1985) were immediately redistributed. Beneficiaries totalled 6236 members in 372 new cooperatives (Deere *et al.*, 1985). In 1982, the process speeded up, resulting in nearly 70 000 cooperative members controlling a production area of over 1.2 million MZ. Of this, over two-thirds was farmed by Cooperativas de Credito y Servicio, with around two-thirds of total cooperative membership.

Control over this expanding cooperative sector was still retained through ENABAS operations, credit provision facilities and the formation of new parastatals (PROAGRO, AGROMEC) responsible for input provision to APPs and the peasantry alike. ENABAS' role as a grain procurement agency had grown significantly by 1982; its storage capacity was 16 per cent higher than 1980 and it had built up a network of 1158 rural reception centres, coupled to over 250 intermediate centres. More crucially, however, ENABAS producer price policy was corrected, providing more attractive producer prices. Percentage rises in prices for the basic grains between 1978 and 1982 were: maize 162 per cent, rice 193 per cent, beans 144 per cent and sorghum 86 per cent. (CIERA, 1982 in SUAS 1987).

These price changes were linked to the goals of the National Food Program (PAN), a self-sufficiency strategy precipitated by the US cut-off of wheat shipments in March 1981 (Zalkin, 1987). PAN involved a redefinition of priorities, with highest priority given to ensuring consumer food security alongside national food security, with aspirations towards a future role as a grain exporter.[6] The most important aspect of PAN, however, was the direct incentive it provided to producers, causing production to rise so dramatically in just two years that self-sufficiency was realised in the case of beans, rice and chicken, while both wheat and maize imports were reduced (SUAS, 1987).

These guaranteed prices compared favourably with those offered by private purchasers, enabling ENABAS to procure 59 per cent of the total marketed production in 1982, although this figure conceals wide differences by crop-type.[7] The dominant role of ENABAS in the procurement sphere re-emphasises for us the centrality of the state in the accumulation process. It did not, however, lead to the surplus extraction that might have been expected, for as part of its welfare strategy, the FSLN subsidised urban food distribution to the extent that prices paid by urban consumers were below that paid to producers. This effective consumer subsidy was to grow to represent 6 per cent of the national budget by 1982 (Austin *et al.*, 1985).

Similarly, statist control continued to be exercised in the sphere of credit and input provision. Although credit volumes were reduced due to poor past repayment levels (SUAS, 1987, Collins, 1985), the credit that was made available encouraged the further socialisation of production through the more favourable rates advanced to cooperative applicants.

With inputs, the principal supplier of fertilisers, handtools, pesticides and seed was PROAGRO, a state agency with forty-nine sales outlets and 850 employees by 1982. In the same year, 903 tractors, 201 harvesters and 2415 farm implements were distributed through the state agency for agricultural machinery provision (AGROMEC), albeit largely in a manner favouring the APP sector, and technical assistance was given in the form of state-provided agricultural technicians, numbering 723 in 1982.

However, at the same time the state was seeking to consolidate its control over the accumulation process as detailed above, other factors were at work which began to negate centralistic control. These in turn provoked ministerial discussion, and would eventually undermine the statist model.

CONTRADICTIONS WITHIN THE STATIST MODEL

As we have previously indicated, the perceived motor' of accumulation, the APP, suffered from low productivity for a variety of reasons. The restructuring of January 1981 proved to be only a moderate success. While production levels soared in subsequent years, costs of production remained somewhat higher than in the private sector causing a number of state farms to default on loan repayment (Kaimovitz, 1986). Indeed, explicit recognition of this failure is found in the MIDINRA Annual Plan of 1985 (p. 227). 'We have to say that we are not yet organisationally or ideologically able to substitute for the private producer from the point of view of his efficiency.'

The role of peasant cooperatives as a step towards the collectivisation of production also began to be questioned, but this was less to do with problems of internal productivity than with acts of external aggression. Beginning in late 1982, counter-revolutionary attacks by the US-backed Contras concentrated on the disruption of the export harvest in general and the destruction of state farms and cooperatives in particular. In response a new type of cooperative formation arose; these Cooperativas de Autodefensa (CAD) sprang up mainly (70 per cent) in the war-zones and numbered 224 by June 1984 (SUAS, 1987). Cooperatives still remained in the front-line of Contra attacks however, with an average of ten per month being destroyed according to MIDINRA estimates in September 1984. In order to generate necessary levels of food production, it thus became increasingly imperative to re-consider private peasant production potential.

Further attention was directed to both self-sufficiency needs and productivity levels by the external financing problems experienced in 1983. While the trade deficit of $351 million was comparable to previous years, US pressure within the international banking arena reduced the flow of long-term capital to a trickle of just $17 million from $283.3 million and $253.4 million for 1981 and 1982 respectively (*International Financial Statistics*, 1983). Consequently the centrality of investment plans necessitating high levels of imported capital inputs again appeared on the agenda, with stress being placed on the relative efficiency of the small private producer per dollar invested.

Similarly, the 'trickle-up' process of mass expression was beginning to gain momentum, principally through the articulation of the Union Nacional de Agricultores y Ganderos (UNAG). UNAG was a comparatively new mass organisation established in 1981 to represent the interests of small- and medium-size producers. Prior to this date the FSLN-perceived identicality of interests between peasant producers and wage labourers had seen both incorporated into the ATC. While the ATC initially spoke with one voice this was in large part due to the majority of its members being wage-labourers (79 per cent out of a total membership of 58 000 in November 1979) (Kaimovitz, 1986), a situation which changed as the cooperative movement gained strength in 1980. By June 1980 ATC membership had soared to 120 000 but small and medium producers felt increasingly alienated by the 'workerist' orientation of the ATC. The alternative, membership of the Union de Productores Agricolas de Nicaragua (UPANIC), was also unsatisfactory, as UPANIC was primarily orientated to the needs of the agrarian capitalist classes. The incorporation of UNAG was a consequence of this alienation and led to a rapid decline in ATC membership, down to 42 000 within a year, while UNAG came to represent over 100 000 members (Luciak 1987). More importantly however, the FSLN,

> by organisationally separating the peasant capitalist and small independent producer from both the rural workers and the agrarian bourgeoisie, . . . [set the stage] . . . for creating policies favourable to small and medium commercial producers (Kaimovitz 1986, p. 110).

These fundamental factors all contributed to the ongoing discussion within MIDINRA from 1982 onwards over whether a statist accumulation strategy was indeed the most desirable one (Kleiterp, 1988, Collins, *et al.*, 1985). Within a wider framework the question of modern vs traditional agriculture also arose, although the question is largely a subordinate one given the state/modern and private/traditional dichotomy that existed.

It transpires, then, that theoretical discussion, as well as underlying economic realities, were leading to a deep questioning of the statist accumulation model. But which factors were decisive in causing a switch to a peasant-based accumulation strategy, if indeed a switch did occur?

THE PEASANT MODEL (1984–)

It would be naive to suggest just one single event was the causal factor for a shift in the orientation of FSLN strategy. Nevertheless, one factor does appear to stand out. The nature of the FSLN revolution has been heavily reliant upon and receptive to initiatives from 'below', whether it be to do with questions of Atlantic Coast autonomy (Freeland, 1988; Rooper and Smith, 1986) or agrarian development strategy (Luciak, 1987; Ortega, 1985). Consequently an analysis of the voting patterns in the 1984 national election (see for example, Kaimovitz and Stanfield, 1985) confirmed local FSLN worries over the then present emphasis on state-led accumulation. Support had been lost even in Masaya, historically a FSLN stronghold. Desire to reincorporate these unsatisfied individuals into the transformation process led to further deliberations at the national level.

The electoral results, when combined with the increasingly vocal demands of UNAG which had by now 'become an effective champion of the interests of peasants as agricultural producers and has taken the lead in creating economic and political structures that will ensure peasant participation in national life' (Luciak, 1987) and the continuing effect of the war, would succeed in replacing the statist model of accumulation.

That such a shift in accumulation strategy has occurred can be substantiated on three grounds, namely the reorganisation of production, procurement and distribution within the agricultural sector since 1984, all of which have increased the peasant's role at the expense of the state. The reorganisation of production shifted cultivation away from state farms and towards individual producers. The state sector, which controlled production on 23 per cent of Nicaragua's cultivable land area in 1982, did decline slightly in the subsequent two years, but its decline was much more marked after 1984 as attempts were made to strengthen its management structures. Changes in 1988, the '*compactation*', once again reorganised the APPs, reduced Empresa de Reform Agraria sizes and turned further land over to either cooperatives or private farmers, leaving the state sector responsible for just 13 per cent of farming land (Nicaraguan Special Report, Summer 1988).

Consequent to this, the titling of land to private individuals or cooperative groups (as initiated by the 1981 Agrarian Reform Law) accelerated. This rapid increase in titling was due in no small respect to legitimising squatter claims upon lands they already occupied. Nevertheless, at a disaggregated level peasant pressure, particularly in Masaya, allied to comprehensive localised MIDINRA productivity studies, led to designation and thence expropriation of large landholdings in areas defined as 'special agrarian reform zones'. Extensions to the agrarian reform legislation in January 1986 added further impetus to the 'peasantisation' of the agrarian economy.

Concurrently with this reorganisation of production, the role of the state in output procurement was also reduced. While the majority of export crops still allowed statist surplus appropriation due to FSLN international trade monopolies, the position regarding domestic grain procurement became increasingly flexible. In 1985 all official marketing restrictions were dropped for corn and beef producers in the war zones and the government began negotiating (rather than setting) prices with producers in direct competition with private intermediaries.

Inroads were also made into the state's dominance of agricultural input provision, with UNAG setting up a cooperative to provide necessary inputs (along with consumer goods) directly to its members in 1985. At the same time the benefits of artificial prices for imported inputs which favoured the APP and large private farmer were erased by the currency reform of February 1988.

It transpires then that, on a number of fronts, circumstantial evidence points to a shift in accumulation strategy in Nicaragua as 'Nicaraguan policymakers have come to see peasant producers in an increasingly favourable light' (Reinhardt, 1987, p. 955).

THE SECOND DECADE

The evolution of agrarian policy in Nicaragua's first decade of revolution has been shown here not to be merely a series of ad-hoc measures, but to constitute an accumulation model – first state-led then peasant-based. Any clear model for economic development in Nicaragua became buried after 1988, however, by the severity of its macroeconomic crisis, requiring drastic measures to stabilise the economy. While their relative importance is disputed, the US trade embargo, the Contra war with its military expense and economic losses, economic mis-management and over-bureaucratisation are seen as contributing to this.

The adjustment programme saw a series of devaluations of the cordoba, beginning in February 1988 with a fall of 5000 per cent. The abolition of price and wage controls, higher interest rates and moves to reduce the state deficit (such as cutting state employment by 10 per cent in February 1988) followed. In 1988 production fell by 9 per cent but the most dramatic impact of the devaluations was an inflation of over 30 000 per cent (126.6 per cent per month in December 1988) (*Barricada Internacional*, 19 August 1989).

Policies in 1989 brought inflation down sharply by 1990, but the whole programme has had considerable social cost. The economic situation and possible escapes from it undoubtedly helped the US-backed UNO coalition to electoral victory in February 1990. With the FSLN still the largest single political force in Nicaragua and the UNO-majority insufficient to reform the revolution's constitution, the future development strategy of the country will be watched with interest.

NOTES

1. Such as increases in aerial DDT application on cotton (Pfeiffer, 1986) and coffee residues polluting water supplies.
2. These properties, known as Communas Agrarias Sandinistas, were run through general assemblies composed of workers, peasant inhabitants and local guerilla leaders, with decisions taken on the basis of a simple majority.
3. 1 Manzana = 0.7 hectares = 1.68 acres.
4. In the event only 12 per cent of maize and 24 per cent of beans passed through ENABAS' hands for a variety of reasons: these included staff and transportation shortages, producer payment methods and low guaranteed prices (Austin *et al.*, 1985).
5. In all other regions the figures were 1000 MZ and 100 MZ respectively.
6. US intervention aimed at curtailing Nicaragua's export outlets added impetus to PAN: Standard Fruit, for example, cancelled its Nicaraguan banana contract in October 1982 (Thompson, 1988) and the following year the US reduced Nicaragua's sugar quota by 90 per cent (Conroy, 1985).
7. While 95 per cent of rice and 92 per cent of sorghum passed through ENABAS hands only 25 per cent of the marketed corn did (Zalkin, 1987).

REFERENCES

Austin, J., F. Fox and W. Kruger, (1985) 'The Role of the Revolutionary State in the Nicaraguan Food System', *World Development*, 13, 15–40.

Barricada Internacional (1989), 19 August.

Banmeister, E., and O. Niera, (1984) 'Economia y Politica en las Relaciones entre el Estado y el Sector Privado en el Proceso Nicaraguense', (Managua: Conference Paper).

Collins, J., F. M. Lappe, N. Allen and P. Rice, (1985) 'Nicaragua: What Difference Could A Revolution Make?' *Food First*, 2nd ed. (London: Food First, 1985).

Corragio, J. L., and G. Irvin, (1985) 'Revolution and Democracy in Nicaragua', *Latin American Perspectives*, 12, 23–37.

Conroy, M. E., (1985) 'External Dependence, External Assistance and Economic Aggression against Nicaragua', *Latin American Perspectives*, 12, 39–67.

Deere, C. D., (1982) 'A Comprehensive Analysis of Agrarian Reform in El Salvador and Nicaragua, 1979–81', *Development and Change*, 13, 1–41.

Deere, C. D., P. S. Marchetti and N. Reinhardt, (1985) 'The Peasantry and the Development of Sandinista Agrarian Policy 1979–84', *Latin American Research Review*, 20, 75–109.

Freeland, J., (1986) *A Special Place in History* (London: Macmillan).

International Financial Statistics, 1978–88 (Washington, DC: IMF).

Kaimovitz, D., and D. Stanfield, (1985) 'The Organisation of Production Units in the Nicaraguan Agrarian Reform', *Inter-American Economic Affairs*, 12, 51–77.

Kaimovitz, D., (1986) 'Nicaraguan Debates in Agrarian Structure and their Implications for Agricultural Policy and the Rural Poor', *Journal of Peasant Studies*, 14, 100–17.

Kay, C., (1982) 'Achievements and Contradictions of the Peruvian Agrarian Reforms', *Journal of Development Studies*, 18, 2, 141–70.

Kleiterp, N., (1988) 'Implementing a New Model of Accumulation', Working Paper 22, sub-series on Money, Finance and Development (The Hague: Institute of Social Studies).

Lehmann, D., (1978) 'The Death of Land Reform: A Polemic', *World Development*, 6, 339–45.

Luciak, I. A., (1987) 'Popular Democracy in the New Nicaragua: The Case of a Rural Mass Organisation', *Comparative Politics*, 20, 35–57.

Mason, T. D., (1986) 'Land Reform and the Breakdown of Clientelist Politics in El Salvador', *Comparative Political Studies*, 18, 437–516.

MIDINRA (1985), *Plan de Trabajo* (Managua).

Nicaragua: Special Reports on the Economy, Bulletin issued 1979–89 (London: Nicaragua Solidarity Campaign).

Ortega, M., (1985) 'Workers' Participation in the Management of Agro-Enterprises of the APP', *Latin American Perspectives*, 12, 69–81.

Palmer, S., (1985) 'Carlos Fonseca and the Construction of Sandinismo in Nicaragua', *Latin American Research Review*, 20, 91–109.

Peek, P., (1982) 'Agrarian Reforms and Rural Development in Nicaragua 1979–81', Rural Employment Policy Research Programme, (Geneva: ILO).

Reinhardt, N., (1987) 'Agro-exports and the Peasantry in the Agrarian Reforms of El Salvador and Nicaragua', *World Development*, 15, 941–59.

Rooper, A., and H. Smith, (1986) 'From Nationalism to Autonomy: the Ethnic Question in the Nicaraguan Revolution', *Race and Class*, 17(4), 1–20.

Ruccio, D. F., (1988) 'State, Class and Transition in Nicaragua', *Latin American Perspectives*, 15, 50–71.

Ruhl, J. M., (1985) 'The Honduran Agrarian Reform under Suazo Cordova 1982–5: An Assessment', *Latin American Economic Affairs*, 63–80.
Swedish University of Agricultural Sciences (SUAS) (1987), 'The Nicaraguan Food and Agricultural Sector', *Rural Development Studies*, 22.
Thompson, C. B., (1988) 'War by another Name: Destabilisation in Nicaragua and Mozambique', *Race and Class*, 29(4) 21–44.
Wheelock, R. J., (1980) *Imperialismo y Dictadura* (Havana: La Habana).
World Bank Development Report (1977) (New York: Oxford University Press).
Zalkin, M., (1987) 'Food Policy and Class Transformation in Revolutionary Nicaragua 1979–86', *World Development*, 15, 961–84.

10 Food Crop Storage and Marketing in Haiti

Robert E. Maguire

INTRODUCTION

In Haiti, as export crop production has deteriorated and the population continues to expand, particularly into urban centres, 'the marketing system of food has become the backbone of this poor nation, and of paramount importance for its survival' (Girault, 1984, p. 177). Essential foodcrops such as corn, sorghum, cassava and beans are almost exclusively the product of a peasantry that continues to encompass the overwhelming majority of the country's producers and that is 'squarely planted in a cash economy' (Murray and Alvarez, 1973, p. 15).

The literature on Haiti's food crop marketing system tends to analyse it only superficially from the perspective of the peasant producers. It has focused on the established marketing system as it relates to export crops, marketing intermediaries (particularly cash crop speculators and the women – *madanm sara* – who market food crops), and urban distribution. Peasant producers are portrayed as participants in the system only insofar as they sell their crop to a middleman (or woman) at, or before harvest, or engage a female partner to sell their crop at local or regional markets. In general, the system is viewed as benign toward small producers, with its characteristic openness and competition between intermediaries ensuring 'that the risk of exploitation of the peasants remains low' (Lundahl, 1984, p. 191).[1]

In growing numbers, small farmers are challenging the experts, not through written analysis, but rather by their actions. Throughout the late 1970s and the 1980s, hundreds of democratic, community groups and associations of peasant producers and their families, ranging from a dozen to over a thousand members, have formed all over Haiti. For the most part they have come into existence through grassroots organising efforts undertaken by church-sponsored leadership training centers and programs. In their quest to confront and solve problems that give rise to their persistent poverty, these groups and associations often identify a need to gain greater control of food crop harvests as a top priority.

Small farmer efforts, referred to generically as *estokaj* or food storage programmes, are built around grain storage, marketing, and credit activities. They also often include components of education and training in

TABLE 10.1   *New or expanded small farmer* estokaj *programmes funded since 1986 by the Inter-American Foundation*

Organization type	Department	No. of small farmers participating
Cooperative	North	1650
Cooperative	Northwest	1100
Cooperative	Central Plateau	3800
Gwoupman Assoc.	Central Plateau	500
Gwoupman Assoc.	Artibonite	1900
Gwoupman Assoc.	Artibonite	315
Gwoupman Assoc.	Central Plateau	625
Gwoupman Assoc.	Northeast	250
Gwoupman Assoc.	Southeast	350
Community Groups	West	700
Community Groups	West	500
Community Groups	Central Plateau	350
Community Groups	Artibonite	1900
Community Groups	Central Plateau	540
	Total participants:	14 480

SOURCE: Inter-American Foundation data.

management, administration, grain storage and marketing. These programmes have become common throughout Haiti. One small grassroots development agency, the Inter-American Foundation, has made grants in the past three years to fourteen new or expanded small farmer-initiated *estokaj* programmes that have a total participation of approximately 15 000 small farm families (see Table 10.1). Other international funders, such as Oxfam (UK), Catholic Relief Services (USA), Misereor (Germany), and Caritas (Switzerland), also support grassroots-initiated *estokaj* programs in Haiti.

Little has been written about attempts of small farmers to challenge the established food crop marketing system. That is not surprising since it is only recently that Haitian peasants have organised to try to gain greater control over their farm economy. Most grassroots *estokaj* programs are still in their early stages. This essay, based upon the author's ongoing involvement with Haitian grassroots development and peasant organisations begun in the late 1970s, attempts to provide new insights into the marketing of peasant produced food crops in Haiti as related to this new and growing phenomenon among that country's small farmers.

The topic under consideration is particularly compelling since it helps to expose how a corrupt and authoritarian political structure reaches into every peasant garden and directly thwarts grassroots development efforts linked to ideals of distributive justice. As such, this essay offers considerations for development planners, funders, and researchers when weighing priorities and actions to support the poor in their quest for social and economic change.

This constituency of experts, including scholars called upon as consultants, has been criticised for 'applying technocratic solutions to socio-economic problems [and] disregarding major social, political, and cultural constraints to improving the standard living of the "poor"' (Plotkin, 1988, p. 14). Haitian grassroots groups are focusing on social, political and cultural constraints as an *a priori* need in a development process that includes attention to problems such as soil conservation, cropping techniques and erosion control. Groups and organisations involved in bottom-up development programmes view these problems as solvable only in the context of overcoming the aforementioned socio-political constraints.

Hence, it follows that development planners, funders and researchers are obliged to understand and consider not only technical and environmental issues, or the relationship of people with the land, but also the relationships among people and groups as they occupy the land. This prerequisite prepares us to deal genuinely with concrete, and elusive, problems of human development – and underdevelopment – from the perspective of the poor.

A GRAIN SILO BRINGS HOPE

In August 1987, in a small village in Haiti's Artibonite Valley, the 315 small farmers of the Organisation of Agricultural Development Groups – OGAD in Haitian Creole – celebrated the completion of the construction of their grain storage silo. The four-chambered block building with a capacity of 20 000 *marmites* (approximately 50 tons) had been built by OGAD's members using their own resources, complemented by those granted by an international development agency. It was the centerpiece of a food storage and marketing programme for members' harvests of corn, sorghum, rice and beans. With the construction of the silo and creation of a $1 200 revolving credit fund OGAD would be able to begin a programme to allow it, in effect, to purchase members' grains at depressed, harvest period prices and store them in the silo for later use or sale as prices increase.

OGAD's farmer-members, all of whom cultivate fewer than 1.5 *carreaux* (just over four acres) have annual net incomes of about $100. They expected to derive several important benefits from the possibility of increasing control of their crops beyond the farm gate. Broadly, their initiative would bring them increased revenue through the sale of their grain in local and regional markets, as prices typically begin their post-harvest climb when supplies begin to dwindle. Net profits from sales would be returned to members as share profit according to the degree of each farmer's participation in the programme. They would also achieve heightened measures of food security, since the silo would render it possible for members to reserve grain supplies for household consumption between harvest periods and for use as seed stock for the next planting.

Fundamentally, participation in the OGAD *estokaj* programme would increase the range of choices of the organisation's members. By so doing it would enable them to begin to lessen their dependence on *speculateurs* and others (mainly women) to whom they are linked for credit, markets and supplies.[2]

HOPE IS SETBACK

At 11:00 p.m. on 24 November 1987, about two months after OGAD's silo began receiving members' corn harvest and five days prior to the scheduled elections sanctioned by Haiti's popularly-approved 29 March 1987 Constitution, a group of between thirty and forty armed masked men swept out of the darkness and attacked the structure. An unarmed group of OGAD members guarding the silo, in response to the rumours of imminent attack that had begun to circulate several weeks before the actual assault, fled into the night as bursts of weapon fire pierced the air around them. Hiding at a distance, they could only watch as the marauders swiftly hauled away some of the corn and then spread gasoline inside and around the building and torched it. As quickly as they had appeared, the criminals left the glow of the billowing smoke and flames and plunged back into the night, shouting and firing their weapons in the air.

Word of the attack spread quickly throughout the valley and into the foothills. By dawn, most of OGAD's members had assembled before the still smouldering ruin of the precious asset designed to bring them a better future. The destruction had been devastating. Lost in addition to the building were approximately 6000 *marmites* (around 10.5 tons) of corn, with a current market value of about $4800. Tragically, the destroyed corn stock included not only that destined for eventual sale, but that set aside by these poor families to help feed themselves between harvests and to provide seed stock for the next planting. Adding insult to injury was the fact that with the destruction of its saleable asset, OGAD's revolving credit fund, which included each member's hard-earned $1.00 share in the association, was completely decapitalised. The only good news was that no lives were lost.

On 25 November 1987, the morning following the attack, OGAD's treasurer, during an interview with a radio reporter, stated, 'Since we are motivated and hopeful, we cannot abandon the silo project. During coming meetings we will study how we can go ahead with our grain storage activity which is crucial to our survival as peasants'.

Even eighteen months after the attack of the night raiders, no renewed implementation of the OGAD silo programme had occurred. Thanks to a supplemental grant from the international funder, OGAD was able to replace both the seed stock that burned in the fire and members' share investment in the revolving fund. Since the fire, however, members have been forced to sell their crops through the traditional channels they hoped the *estokaj* program would enable them to bypass. Intimidated by the assault, some farmers have left the small groups of which the association is composed. Even the core membership of about 250 has been reluctant to take any concrete steps to revitalise the programme, largely because of the fear of harsher reprisals from their attackers, who continue to circulate throughout the valley with impunity, making threats and making known their dissatisfaction with OGAD and its objectives.

Believing that it could salvage some of the materials from the silo's shell for eventual use in a renewed effort, OGAD's Administrative Council recommended in mid-1988 that the structure be taken apart, block by block. Members balked, however. Their reason was hauntingly simple. As one expressed it, 'We have to leave our silo there so our children will never forget what THEY have done to us'.

THE NIGHT RAIDERS

Who are THEY, and why did they so viciously loathe the aspirations of this group of poor farmers? In the valley the identity of the masked marauders of that dark night could not remain a secret. Easiest to identify were the ringleaders, particularly since rumours of an impending attack could be attributed to them. In the twisted reality of Haitian justice, however, no charges can be brought against any of them because, essentially, they are the same people who mete out 'justice' in the valley. Indeed, the only arrests made following the incident were of several OGAD Administrative Council members, arrested for 'troublemaking' by the local sheriff, or *chef de section*, two days after the attack when they returned home from reporting the incident over the radio. Only the rapid intervention of several Haitian and international human rights and private voluntary organisations saved these men from torture and possible death. Ironically, the sheriff who arrested them is one of the key figures implicated in the silo attack. For the sake of understanding the link between local and national power structures, it should be noted that the *chefs de section* are members of the Haitian army.

Six others have been identified as ringleaders, including another rural sheriff. The other five, several of whom made their vehicles available to transport the marauders from the town to within a mile of the silo that dark night, are *gwo neg* (big shots) from the closest regional market town. These men, at the top of the local power structure, were all officials of the

Duvalier regime and have maintained close contact with the army. They are also founding members of the *gwoup sans maman* (the motherless ones), a paramilitary terrorist gang created after the fall of the dictatorship and allegedly supported by the Haitian military.

Among these ringleaders, significantly, is one of the area's largest moneylenders and grain speculators. He rules over a network of men called *sekrèté*, whose job is to scour the countryside buying grain from peasants at the lowest possible prices. The moneylender also makes usurious loans to peasants at interest rates of at least 20 per cent per month.

EVOLUTION AND SUDDEN CHANGE

Why did the valley's 'leading citizens' feel it necessary to mobilise themselves to destroy this small silo? To answer this question it helps to try to understand precisely why peasant food crop storage and marketing programs have become increasingly common in Haiti.

The apparent surge in 'nitiatives such as OGAD's is the outcome of two developments. First is the evolution of peasant groups. These eight- to fifteen-member groups (*gwoupman*), the existence of which is a prerequisite for a broad-based, participatory food storage and marketing programme, have grown out of more than a decade of work in leadership training and community organisation. That work has been undertaken quietly and persistently primarily by Catholic church-affiliated leadership training centers. By mid-decade, the number of well-organised, stable peasant groups in various parts of Haiti had climbed into the hundreds. Many had reached the point where their meagre resources could no longer even begin to address their needs or their newly-acquired capacity to act. Hence even before the fall of the Duvalier dictatorship on 7 February 1986, several well-stablished peasant associations had taken tentative steps toward launching *estokaj* programs.

The sudden fall of the house of Duvalier after twenty-nine years of authoritarian rule opened the door to increased *gwoupman* confidence to initiate action programmes. Critical to that surge was the fact that the uprooting, or *dechoukaj*, of the family dictatorship exposed weaknesses in the complex web of violence, control and exploitation that had dominated the countryside for the purpose of extracting peasant resources.[3] The politics of violence, lead throughout Haiti by individuals such as those who attacked the OGAD silo, had discouraged peasant farmers not only from initiating economic activities, but, more fundamentally, from joining or maintaining membership in a development group in the first place.[4]

Uncertain of their position after their patron left Haiti, these henchmen of the regime, particularly the now-infamous *ton-ton macoutes*, momentarily hesitated, leaving a power vacuum. Evidenced by the aforementioned surge of requests for funding support, community groups and associations throughout the country immediately and anxiously moved to initiate action programs geared to confront obstacles blocking their socio-economic advancement. Simultaneously, other peasants, previously fearful of the *macoutes*, began to join existing groups or form new ones.

GRAIN STORAGE AS A PEASANT PRIORITY

In April 1987, in the midst of the post-Duvalier surge of peasant-initiated *estokaj* programs, thirty-five Haitian silo managers gathered for a workshop to discuss their programmes and the challenges facing them. Workshop findings provide a source of information on why small farmers have identified the need to control food crop harvests beyond the farm gate as a top priority.[5]

Of primary importance is the assurance of increased food security. Simply, grain storage programmes help to ensure that farm families and, more generally, entire communities, have adequate supplies of basic grains from harvest to harvest. Even when adequate grain is available for post-harvest storage, harvest to harvest shortfalls can occur. Traditional Haitian grain storage techniques such as *gwan-n*, *makon sou do tol*, *mayi pike*, *kalbas*, *barik*, *diakout-sak* and *kolonbye* are oriented toward individual families and have limited capacities for storage. It is not unusual for a farm family to use up its supplies before the next harvest replenishes them.[6]

Exacerbating this constraint to food security is the fact that small farmers, facing cash flow problems or emergency cash needs in between harvests, might chose to sell stored supplies rather than to seek a loan from a private money lender. Such loans, often in the range of $50 to $300, carry short-term interest rates of from 10 per cent daily to 40 per cent monthly.

Estokaj programs also confront a related food security issue: the frequent necessity to purchase grain supplies between harvests or seed stock for planting the next crop. Workshop participants indicated that peasants are sometimes forced, in effect, to buy back their own harvests for food or seed from the intermediaries to whom they previously sold them at low harvest prices. Price fluctuations between harvests can range upwards to 400 per cent, depending on factors of supply, location, and crop type. For example, in two areas, the price of corn varied from 7 to 15 gourdes ($1.40 – $3.00) and 12 to 15 gourdes ($2.40 – $3.00) over a recent post-harvest period. It is surmised that the fluctuation was less in the latter market because of greater accessibility to supplies from a variety of producing areas.

A well-managed and capitalised *estokaj* programme can help small producers avoid these dilemmas, argued workshop participants. Given their larger capacities for collective storage, silos enable farmers to store a higher percentage of their individual harvests. Without access to capital at fair market rates, however, poor farmers cannot take advantage of this improvement. It is of the utmost importance, therefore, that grain storage programmes have a revolving credit fund that will enable them, in effect, to purchase each member's crop, at current harvest prices. Not only does this help to alleviate the cashflow problems of participating producers, but it should result in enhanced revenue through the cash return received by producers when their surplus grain is subsequently sold in open markets.

Hence *estokaj* programs go beyond food security objectives to include those of value added and higher return, linking them directly to marketing. By putting primary food crop marketing under their control, farmers stand to benefit from profits generated by the sale of grain at prices higher than those offered by the *speculateurs*, *madanm sara*, and *sekrèté* when local markets are flooded. In addition, workshop participants pointed out, grain storage programs can help to stabilise the price of grain at local markets.

The managers refuted concerns that small farmer silo programmes create another class of *speculateurs* by citing the primary food security objectives of the initiatives. They also argued that the ethical and moral orientation of the education and training processes that are integral to the formation of groups, and the broad, grassroots participation engendered by these programmes mitigate any tendency in this direction.

The managers concluded that silo programmes are integral to helping peasants begin to liberate themselves from persistent poverty. With increased storage capacity and their working capital fund, they offer the prospect of a greater return *and* of the liberation of the farmer from the necessity of usurious loans between harvests.

THREATS AND OBSTACLES

It is perhaps this last point that was behind the attack on the OGAD silo. *Estokaj* programmes are a vehicle for small farmers to organise and obtain access to resources that will enable them to challenge the status quo of the food crop marketing system. This is a fundamental threat to those who control that system and who unceasingly use their position and resources to extract from the poor. A US Congressional critic of the Haitian *gwo neg* has observed that they see a threat in anything which will prevent them living in luxury through the sufferings and hard work of the poor.[7]

As the silo managers were meeting to share information, those threatened by these programmes were organising to reclaim the terrain they had momentarily yielded following the ousting of Duvalier. By mid-1987, silo programmes and, generally, participants in peasant groups, particularly managers and administrative council members, began receiving threats from local officials and adherents of the *ancien regime*.

Those same persecutors of the peasant groups, sometimes actively supported by military officials, circulated rumours that *gwoupman* programs are 'communist' and advised that any revolving loan funds should not be repaid. It was made crystal clear that peasant participants in these programmes, particularly if they repaid their loans, would be viewed as supporting 'communists'. This invidious assault was particularly strong in the Northwest, North, and Central Plateau, where peasant organisation is at its strongest.

These local skirmishes formed part of a wider pattern, however, being only one aspect of the overall struggle in Haiti for political power and democratic process. In late March 1987, the Haitian people overwhelmingly ratified a constitution that set forth clear and unalterable guidelines for democratic elections. It also mandated the exclusion of those with clear links to the former dictatorship from running for office. Following that national referendum, *macoute* or reactionary elements, feeling their backs increasingly to the wall, began to lash out at democratic forces and institutions all over the country. Among those on the offensive were paramilitary organisations like the aforementioned *gwoup sans maman*.

Estokaj programmes were particularly vulnerable to threats and violence. By mid-1987, in response to the confrontational situation, many groups had formed vigilance teams to guard grain silos round-the-clock. Armed with only their farm tools, these groups, as the OGAD case demonstrates, were ineffective against armed arsonists ready to resort to unrestrained violence to meet their goals.

To date, among the myriad menacing actions taken against grassroots groups by *macoutist* elements, only three peasant grain storage silos have been actually attacked and destroyed. Not coincidentally, all three are located in the Artibonite Valley axis, a stronghold of *macoutes* under Duvalier and a key area for food crop production in Haiti. While a few groups have been able to continue their programmes relatively unaffected in the past two years, the majority, even if not actually attacked, have been negatively affected in some way by the threats and violence. Decreased group participation by frightened members, transport boycotts orchestrated against groups by truck owners in collusion with *gwo neg*, and the flight to the city of the beleaguered manager of at least one silo programme are among the concrete manifestations of those negative effects.

That grain storage programmes in particular have received these threats reaffirms their crucial place in enabling the rural poor to begin to break the status quo that keeps them poor. By aiming to control their crops beyond the farm gate, small farmers have clearly touched a nerve amongst those at the top of the food crop marketing system.

Another vignette sheds a bright light on what is at stake in the ongoing struggle to control the backbone of the Haitian economy. In this instance the issue boils down to a fundamental human concern: education of one's children.

Sometime in mid-1988, a moneylender in the Central Plateau, who also happens to be a military official and, as such, had been involved in speading rumours of the 'communist' nature of *gwoupman*, confided his reasons for opposing the efforts of the poor to improve their situation.

> Look, I have nine kids to send to school in Port-au-Prince. It costs me a lot to pay their tuition and lodging in the city, and I can't afford it on my military salary. I make loans to peasants, and I depend on the high interest from those loans to have the cash I need to be able to send and keep my kids in school.

When asked if perhaps peasants have the right to try to organise themselves so they might, in turn, be able someday to send their kids to school, his response was direct. 'No. It is my right to send my kids to school before the peasants can send theirs. If I can't send my kids, their kids have no right in school, either.'[8]

UNANSWERED QUESTIONS

This paper examines a series of relatively new developments at the Haitian grassroots, about which little is known. Assuming that the peasant organisations undertaking them will be able to survive ongoing political crises and continue their efforts, much more will be discovered about their nature and impact. From what is already understood, we can clearly conclude at this point that the localised programmes undertaken by small farmers to improve their lives by increasing their control over harvests cannot be divorced from wider problems of man-to-man relationships and the Haitian political economy.

Many questions still must be addressed in order to understand fully both producer perception of the established food crop marketing system and the full impact of their efforts to gain greater control beyond the farm gate. While some of these questions introduce points beyond the immediate scope of this paper, they are presented below since the full range indicates areas for further research on the broad topic of food crop marketing in Haiti. Greater knowledge of the impact of ongoing programmes is particularly important to those responsible for providing resources that enable them to exist.

– What effect will successful *estokaj* programmes have on the traditional role of women in food crop marketing in Haiti?

– Will poor participants in the traditional grain marketing structures become displaced by *estokaj* programmes without finding a place in the altered system?

- Will silo programmes create a new class of speculators?
- How can the poorest of the rural poor, such as those who are forced to sell their crops to intermediaries while still 'in flower', participate effectively in these programmes?
- What is an appropriate scale for grassroots silo programmes? Can large programmes succeed without a corresponding ability to control transport?
- Can silo programmes become self-sustaining, or will they depend on continual inputs of 'free money' to be able to provide what is, essentially, a service to group members?
- Without greater control of transportation and markets, do *estokaj* programmes actually benefit traditional speculators and the truckers by creating a situation where the producers, and not they, absorb losses due to spoilage, insects and rodents?
- Can community silo programmes stabilise both the local food supply and market prices?
- How will producers invest the increased revenue brought through the silos, providing there actually is some?
- What impact will *estokaj* programmes have on farmer incentive to produce more through increased investment in labour and capital improvements?
- To what extent might increased producer control over harvests and, by extension, increased income, act as a catalyst for them to begin to tackle other, technical and environmental problems confronting them?
- To what extent are producers and managers of stored grain programmes making sound, wise use of insecticides? Are there practical alternatives to chemically-derived insecticides?

While conclusions on the economic, social, political and environmental impact and effectiveness of *estokaj* programmes cannot yet be drawn, it is quite clear that Haitian small farmers are not satisfied with the traditional food crop marketing practices. Further investigation of evolving *estokaj* programs will enable scholars, policy-makers, programme administrators and other experts not only to answer the questions posed, but to understand more clearly the causes and characteristics of grassroots poverty and underdevelopment. As such, it will allow experts to use their talents more effectively to help alleviate this tremendous burden of human suffering.

POSTSCRIPT

By late 1989, OGAD had decided to reinstitute its *estokaj* program. With external financial support, it began to construct four, smaller, decentralised silos. Concurrently, it reinitiated its membership education programme in silo administration and management, in anticipation of receipt of members' grain by mid-1990.

Despite cosmetic changes at the top of the national political structure, OGAD continues to confront a hostile environment, particularly as evidenced by recent actions orchestrated by local *gwo negs*. In March and again in April, before the new silos were even built, the homes of two of OGAD's leaders were burned by thugs affiliated with a *chef de section*. As in 1987, it appears that OGAD, however strongly motivated, will face debilitating obstacles until the broader political economy is reformed.

NOTES

1. Literature on Haitian agricultural marketing systems includes: Girault, C. (1981), Locher, U. (1975), Lundahl, M. (1979), Mintz, S. (1960), Mintz, S. (1971), Moral, P. (1959), Murray, G. F. and M. D. Alvarez (1973).
2. 'Konstriksyon silo ak fomasyon manb yo', proposal presented to the Inter-American Foundation by Organizayson Gwoupman Agrikol Pou Devlopman (OGAD), March 1986.
3. For an excellent historical analysis of peasant resource extraction in Haiti see Trouillot, M. R. (1990).
4. See also Maguire, R. (1986).
5. See Institut de Consultation, d'Evaluation et de Formation du Personnel (ICEF) (1987), and Maguire, R. (1987).
6. These diverse food crop storage techniques are described in the report on the workshop, cited above. Essentially, they store dried grains in a container or small depot raised off the ground. In the case of the *gwan-n*, braided ears of corn are hung from a tree or pole.
7. See Fauntroy, W. E. (1987).
8. Personal communication from the representative of a voluntary organisation with whom the conversation reported took place. Haitian informants cite the salary of a corporal in the Haitian army at $200 a month. The salary of enlisted men is cited as $160 a month.

REFERENCES

Fauntroy, W. E., (1987) 'Testimony of the Honorable Walter E. Fauntroy, Chairman of the Congressional Task Force on Haiti before the Subcommittee on Western Hemisphere Affairs/Committee on Foreign Affairs', *Congressional Record*, 18 November.
Girault, C., (1981) *Le Commerce du Cafe en Haiti* (Paris: Editions du Centre National de la Recherche Scientifique).
Girault, C., (1984) 'Commerce in the Haitian Economy', in C. Foster and A. Valdman (eds), *Haiti – Today and Tomorrow*, (Lanham, Maryland: University Press of America) pp. 173–80.
Institut de Consultation, d'Evaluation et de Formation du Personnel (ICEF)

(1987), 'Atelye Travay Sou Estokaj', (Port-au-Prince, Haiti: mimeographed document, May).

Locher, U., (1975) 'The Market Systems of Port-au-Prince', *Working Papers in Haitian Society and Culture* (New Haven: Antilles Research Center).

Lundahl, M., (1979) *Peasants and Poverty: a Study of Haiti* (New York: St Martin's Press).

Lundahl, M., (1984) 'The Roots of Haitian Underdevelopment', in C. Foster and A Valdman (eds), *Haiti – Today and Tomorrow* (Lanham, Maryland: University Press of America) pp. 181–204.

Maguire, R., (1986) 'Standing Tall: Balanced Development in Haiti', *Grassroots Development*, 10(2) 8–12.

Maguire, R., (1987) 'Development Notes: Leading the Way', *Grassroots Development*, 11(2) 44–5.

Mintz, S., (1960) 'Peasant Markets', *Scientific American*, 203, 112–18, 120, 122.

Mintz, S., (1971) 'Men, women and trade', *Comparative Studies in Society and History*, 13, 247–69.

Moral, P., (1959) *L'economie haitienne* (Port-au-Prince, Haiti: Imprimerie de l'Etat).

Murray, G. F., and M. D. Alvarez, (1973) *The Marketing of Beans in Haiti: An Explanatory Study*, (Port-au-Prince, Haiti: Institut Interamericain des Sciences Agricoles).

Plotkin, D., (1988) 'Women, Trade, and Transportation: Obstacles to Economic Development Among Haitian Market Women In Spite of Rural Road Improvement', unpublished paper presented at the XIV International Congress of the Latin American Studies Association, New Orleans, Louisiana (March).

Trouillot, M. R., (1990) *Haiti, State Against Nation: The Origins and Legacy of Duvalierism* (New York: Monthly Review Press).

11 Underdeveloping the Arctic: Dependency, Development, and Environmental Control

Michael Pretes

INTRODUCTION

The Canadian Arctic is an underdeveloped region within a developed nation. In many respects – economic dependence, a resource-based economy, limited political power, and ecological damage, among others – the Arctic shares common characteristics with other underdeveloped, often 'Third World', regions. The causes of arctic underdevelopment are complex, but have traditionally been analysed solely in economic or political terms. This paper considers this underdevelopment in economic, political and ecological terms, aspects which have been combined in the emerging theoretical framework of 'sustainable development'.

The Canadian Arctic is not alone in facing economic, political and ecological development problems. That the Arctic is an underdeveloped region is often obscured because is it part of a developed, industrial nation. The developmental dilemma of such underdeveloped regions is often adumbrated by the position of these regions within developed countries. The Brazilian Amazon, the Australian Outback and Soviet Siberia are examples of peripheral regions that are more underdeveloped than metropolitan regions within the same country. The developmental conditions within the Canadian Arctic and the Brazilian Amazon are particularly striking, and will be noted further in this paper.

Developed and underdeveloped regions are defined here in terms of their relationship to natural resources and the environment. Six aspects of this relationship can be noted:

(1) Developed regions are economic 'centres' and are able to control the disposition, development rate and selling price of resources; underdeveloped regions are unable to do this.

(2) Developed regions are able to retain revenues and economic rents from the sale of resources; underdeveloped regions lose much of their resource revenues to resource corporations based in developed regions.

177

(3) Developed regions have diversified economies that emphasise secondary and tertiary sectors. Underdeveloped regions depend almost entirely on the export of a few raw materials.

(4) Developed regions are able to exert political control over their own affairs. Underdeveloped regions are not able to control their own political affairs, or are in no position to challenge political decisions emanating from central authorities. The small, sparse population in underdeveloped regions further inhibits political control and authority.

(5) Developed regions exert social and cultural control over their own affairs. Underdeveloped regions rely on borrowed social and cultural institutions such as land tenure systems, dispute resolution mechanisms, cultural tastes, etc.

(6) Control of natural resources is fundamental to control of the ecological process. Because developed regions have control over their resources, they are able to control their own economic ecology, that is, they control the environmental foundations of the economic system and thus the system itself. Resources are a part of the environment, thus *control of resources leads to control over the environment*. In this sense underdeveloped regions are unable to control their own environments; they are environmental colonies of developed regions.

Developed and underdeveloped regions are defined by their relationship to the environment. Political and economic structures in developed regions can control and manipulate resources and resource production within the region, and thus can control and manipulate the environment. The environment in underdeveloped regions is controlled and manipulated by *external* entities: colonial or neo-colonial governments and resource corporations, among others. Developed regions are able to manipulate the environment in underdeveloped regions, inhibiting local initiatives for environmental protection, for example. This situation is present at both the national and regional level. An underdeveloped nation in Latin America, Asia or Africa will have its environment and resources controlled by external factors. An underdeveloped *region* within a developed nation will also face a similar situation. Development in the Canadian Arctic and the Brazilian Amazon, for example, is controlled by the southern metropolitan regions of these countries. Control over the patterns of resource exploitation in northern Canada is vested politically in the national capital and economically in private companies based in the south.

The dependency school of development has pointed out the exploitative relationship between developed and underdeveloped regions. The developed regions, or metropolises, are able to control development in the underdeveloped regions, or satellites, hence, development is affected by external factors. The closer the ties between metropolis and satellite, the quicker the pace of underdevelopment in the satellite. Underdevelopment is viewed as a *process* in which metropolitan regions are able to exploit and control the satellites. Natural resources are derived from the satellites, processed in the metropolis where most of the surplus value accrues, and then marketed to the satellites in the form of manufactured goods. More sinister implications of this process are the manufacture of metropolitan styles and tastes which, touted in the guise of 'modernity', are sold to the satellites in the form of superfluous consumer goods. This interpretation of development would be enhanced by a consideration of the environmental aspects of resource dependency and control.

The Canadian Arctic and the Brazilian Amazon have both witnessed extensive manipulation of their environments for the benefit of metropolitan regions within the same country. The historical process of this intervention is sketched briefly below. A more complete discussion of development in the Arctic and Amazon can be found in Pretes (1988), and in the citations given in the text.

UNDERDEVELOPMENT IN THE ARCTIC

The process of underdevelopment in all circumpolar regions is in many ways similar, but this paper will focus only on the underdevelopment process in Canada. The area under discussion is the Canadian Arctic and sub-Arctic, collectively termed the North. While definitions of the North vary, the term is used here to refer to the Yukon and Northwest Territories, which, as territories, are under the direct control of the Canadian federal government, and do not share in the division of powers given to the provinces. In this discussion, the term 'Arctic' should be understood to include sub-Arctic regions as well.

The Canadian North was explored, settled and exploited primarily for economic reasons, with little concern for the environment. Economic incursions were periodic, generally to extract a particular resource that was in current demand. The northern environment was manipulated for the benefit of metropolitan interests. Little consideration was given to the interests of the original inhabitants and environmental managers, the Native people. In pre-contact times the North could well be considered a developed region: resources and the environment were under the control of the Native residents. The environment was managed in accordance with local wishes and needs; indeed, a thriving and sustainable economy was present throughout much of North America. As environmental control was gradually lost to external entities the northern economy became highly unstable and was characterised by periods of boom and bust. The Native traditional economy was eroded and replaced by a wage economy. During bust periods the wage economy was not sufficient to support the population and a welfare economy developed. Native people became dependent on government and private enterprises to provide for many of their needs. Missionaries exacerbated this situation by restricting nomadic lifestyles and encouraging permanent settlements.

Government now accounts for 29 per cent of total jobs and 35 per cent of total wages in the Northwest Territories, for example, compared to only 9 per cent of total jobs and 12 per cent of total wages in Canada (Special Committee on the Northern Economy, 1988). The large government presence dominates the economy: the public sector accounts for 55 per cent of the territorial domestic product (Patterson, 1988). There is a substantial literature on the transformation from traditional to wage and welfare economies in the North; see, among others, Brody (1975), Watkins (1977), Berger (1977, 1985), Grant (1988), Irwin (1988), and Zaslow (1988).

With the loss of environmental control the traditional economy could not sustain itself, and the region underdeveloped. Private corporations played a role in the underdevelopment process. The Hudson's Bay Company obtained a royal charter in 1670 and was given monopolistic control over much of northern Canada. The firm generated substantial profits that accrued to investors in Great Britain and Canada. The company harvested furs from the shores of Hudson Bay, and traded for furs harvested inland. Furs were harvested indiscriminately, without regard for maximum sustainable yield. Eventually the firm expanded its harvest area into the Mackenzie Valley and Yukon region. This expansion was viewed benignly by the British and Canadian authorities, as the presence of expansionist-minded Americans and Russians in Alaska was considered a threat to British territorial interests. This alliance of corporation and state served both economic and political interests: the Hudson's Bay Company was concerned with profiting from its northern territories, while the British government wanted to protect territorial claims in North America. This alliance effectively brought control of the environment into the hands of the state and private investors.

In 1896 gold was discovered in the Klondike River, a tributary of the Yukon River. The boom was sudden and short. For the next few years prospective miners and businessmen poured into the Yukon boomtowns of Whitehorse and Dawson City. The population swelled; people came from Canada, the United States, Great Britain, and elsewhere, most with the intention of striking it rich and then returning home. Little of the revenue generated in the Yukon remained in the territory; most of it went to southern mining companies or was brought back by private individuals. Minerals replaced renewable resources as the principal economic activity in the Yukon.

The most recent northern boom was connected to the extraction of petroleum and natural gas. This boom stimulated the northern economy during the 1970s, but – like past booms – was short-lived. Oil prices collapsed towards the end of the decade, and much of the North's transient population was left without employment. Long-range planning has been lacking. Much of the northern population lives in small (population 500–1500) communities with poor infrastructure, high birth rates, low income levels, high unemployment, and limited secondary and tertiary economic sectors. The implementation of large-scale 'mega-projects' such as petroleum drilling or pipelines has done little to affect the situation in small northern communities. These mega-projects depend on outside financing, and tend to be capital-intensive. They provide short-term jobs but no long-term training; there is little benefit to small communities as most of the jobs are in the larger centres.

Plans for a Mackenzie Valley pipeline were scotched in the late 1970s, but have currently been revived. This pipeline would cost an estimated $5 billion and would provide about 5000 temporary construction jobs. Northerners would receive only about 140 permanent positions, which would last for the life of the pipeline, about thirty years (Pretes and Robinson, 1990).

The promise of employment is a weak argument in the face of the considerable environmental damage that would result from mega-projects. The James Bay hydroelectric project in northern Quebec, for example, flooded Native villages and led to environmental degradation, and expected economic prosperity has not reached all Native residents. The government of Quebec profited from the energy transferred out of the North. Bunker (1985) has argued that an unbalanced energy flow is evidence of underdevelopment. Energy is exported from one region to benefit another. Katzman (1987) has criticised Bunker's position with respect to the Amazon, noting that ecosystems are open and receive vast inputs of solar energy. Conditions in the Arctic, however, lead to other conclusions. Most solar energy is reflected by snow and ice cover, and the carrying capacity of the arctic environment is extremely limited. Hence projects like James Bay or northern pipelines entrench the North's position as a net energy exporter without concomitant inputs.

Mega-projects will not provide the sustained levels of employment needed for northern residents, nor do they give environmental control to local people. Mega-projects may give some short-term benefits, but over a longer period they will intensify the external control over the northern environment. This will prolong the underdevelopment of arctic Canada. The resource booms in the Canadian Arctic – furs, whales, minerals, petroleum and natural gas and hydroelectric power – have all been accompanied by extensive intervention in the northern environment. The extraction and exploitation of arctic resources has been controlled and dictated by southern economic and political interests, for reasons of sovereignty or fiscal gain. This process has removed control over the environment from the hands of local residents, leading to underdevelopment.

UNDERDEVELOPMENT IN THE AMAZON

Financial gain was the motivating factor behind exploration and exploitation of Brazil's Amazon region or Amazonia – defined as the states and territories of Amazonas, Pará, Roraima, Rondônia, Amapá and Acre. As in the Canadian Arctic, Native people in Amazonia had established their own economic systems that relied upon the use of forest and river resources. The local environment was the basis of this traditional economy. After contact with Europeans this economy gradually eroded. The present Amazonian economy is unstable, relying on the export of primary resources to metropolitan regions. Environmental control has shifted from local to external hands.

The process of underdevelopment has been in place for many years. Land grants were used to attract Portuguese settlers to Brazil (Frank, 1969). Most of the early settlements were in coastal areas, but penetration of the interior became necessary to explore for resources and to protect Portuguese sovereignty claims through occupation. In the sixteenth century, brazilwood and sugar brought prosperity to Amazonia and north-eastern Brazil. The boom periods for these resources, along with rice, cotton and cocoa, gradually turned to bust as Brazil faced increased competition from other nations with plantation economies.

Amazonia's greatest boom period was the rubber boom of the late nineteenth century. Amazonian cities such as Manaus and Belém doubled in size within several decades. In the period 1901–10 Brazil exported 345 079 tons of rubber (Burns, 1980). Ironically, Brazil now *imports* two-thirds of its rubber (Guppy, 1984), due to deforestation and a shift away from rubber production (and towards non-renewable resources).

The rubber boom soon ended. A plantation economy was developed in Malaya and soon displaced Brazilian production. The remaining population became more dependent on a wage and welfare economy fostered by the government itself. Government land policy hurt small farmers and aided large ones. As Guppy (1984) has noted, there is enough land in Brazil outside Amazonia to give each Brazilian family 10 hectares. Much of the rich farmland in southern Brazil is under-utilised. Land distribution is unequal: 50 per cent of farmers own only 3 per cent of farmland, while 43 per cent of farmland is owned by only 1 per cent of farmers (Guppy, 1984).

Current resources exploited in Amazonia include petroleum, gold, ranching and hydroelectric power. The state oil company, Petrobrás, has found sizable petroleum deposits in the Amazon basin. Although the petroleum would be extracted from Amazonia, the revenues would accrue to a state corporation and the benefits would be felt primarily by residents of southern Brazil. Brazil's large foreign debt has also prompted the federal government to develop all possible foreign currency-earning resources. Gold production in Amazonia is almost 40 per cent controlled by foreign companies (Vanvolsem and Crevels, 1988). Both petroleum and mineral resources are largely controlled by external entities.

Ranching is responsible for most deforestation. 60 per cent of land clearance was done by large-scale developers and ranchers, while only 17.6 per cent was done by peasant farmers (Guppy, 1984). Massive deforestation leads to nutrient loss, rather than nutrient recycling. Saleti and Vose (1984) conclude that 'large-scale clearance for cattle pasture . . . [would] be the worst type of Amazon development, leading to major water runoff, erosion, and soil degradation, and the greatest possibility of induced climatic change'. Colonisation schemes attracted new settlers, but many farmers were unsuccessful and now constitute a cheap labour pool supporting the ranching economy.

The pursuit of hydroelectric power is an even more blatant colonial venture. Hydroelectric projects serve two purposes: they provide energy for industry in southern Brazil, and they encourage settlement and continued resource extraction in Amazonia. In the late 1970s the Tucurui Dam flooded 800 square miles, destroyed the local environment, and harmed Native groups (Hay, 1988). Brazil is now examining as many as forty-seven potential dam sites in Amazonia, many of them on the Xingú River or its tributaries (Chernela, 1988). According to this source, the construction of only five of these dams would flood an area of 18 000 square kilometres, and could displace as many as twenty-four different Native groups. This project – the Altamira-Xingú dam complex – is estimated to cost over $10 billion and to produce over 17 000 MW of electricity (Chernela, 1988). The Brazilian state expects that enhanced availability of electric power will prompt increased settlement in the interior. Clearly environmental decisions are being made by federal, and not local authorities.

These mega-projects are likely to have similar consequences to those in northern Canada: increased short-term employment, long-term unemployment and welfare dependence, an economy distorted towards primary resource production, environmental degradation, and the destruction of indigenous populations. As in northern Canada, an alliance of state and private industry has gradually wrested control of the Amazonian environment away from the inhabitants, both Native and non-Native.

DEPENDENCY AND SUSTAINABLE DEVELOPMENT

Dependency theorists, most notably A. G. Frank, have argued that underdevelopment is a process of regional exploitation. Developed, metropolitan regions are able to exploit underdeveloped, satellite regions, locking them into a state of dependence (see Frank, 1969). The satellite produces primary raw materials that are sent to the metropolis for processing. The metropolis in turn is able to use the satellite as a market, disposing of manufactured goods there. This relationship is favourable to the metropolis, which augments its economic exploitation through political, social and cultural dominance.

An additional form of dominance is environmental. Metropolitan regions dominate the environment of their satellites. Through control of resources and especially the ability to generate resource markets, the metropolis gains control over the natural resources of the satellite. In order to acquire finished products, the satellite must sell its resources. Since all aspects of the resource trade are controlled by the metropolis, often including ownership of the resources themselves, the metropolis can control and manipulate the environment of the satellite. The short outlines of resource extraction in the Canadian Arctic and the Brazilian Amazon have indicated the ability of developed, metropolitan regions to control the environments of their hinterlands.

More attention must be given to environmental factors in development. Dependency theory has provided a useful explanation for the problems of underdevelopment in peripheral regions. When coupled with an understanding of underdevelopment as environmental control, the theory fits well within the emerging literature on sustainable development.

Sustainable development is a loose theoretical framework that recognises the importance of economy-environment integration. It gives a more comprehensive ecological understanding of the role that economics plays in man's relationship with nature. Sustainable development policies are those that include an environmental component in the development process. They often advocate reduced dependence on non-renewable resources, and greater local decision-making (see, for example, Schumacher, 1974, Higgins and Higgins, 1979, and the World Commission on Environment and Development, 1987).

Definitions of sustainable development are numerous, but generally share the following characteristics:

(1) Emphasis on compatibility between economic activity and the environment.

(2) Emphasis on compatibility between economic activity and indigenous social groups.

(3) A move away from non-renewable resource use, substituting instead a greater use of renewable resources; this is analogous to living on interest, not principal.

(4) A shift to greater local control over resources and their use. This will include more decentralisation and more local decision-making. Environmental control will be localised.

(5) A move to a more equitable distribution of wealth and resources.

(6) A multisectoral approach to economic change, including diversification of the economy and avoiding dependence on one commodity.

(7) An emphasis on economic *activity*, rather than on economic *growth*.

These characteristics indicate a possible 'greening' of dependency theory. For regions such as the Arctic and Amazonia, adoption of policies oriented towards the above are essential.

Northern Canada is underdeveloped because its environment is controlled externally. The two territories in northern Canada, the Yukon and the Northwest Territories, are politically dependent on the federal government. Canada is a federal state, with political power divided between federal and provincial governments. But because the two northern territories are not provinces, they do not participate in the division of powers guaranteed in the Canadian constitution. Although territorial governments exist, they have no constitutional protection, and devolved powers can be revoked at any time by the federal government. Federal administration of the territories is directed through the Department of Indian Affairs and Northern Development (DIAND). This and other agencies has supported developmental programmes that often go against the interests of northern residents, including Native people. Developmental agendas are set by federal, and not territorial, authorities.

On a practical basis the North has little input into national politics. The territories together have only three seats in the House of Commons, and only two senate seats. Heads of northern governments are not guaranteed participation in First Ministers' Conferences, an important Canadian political institution. Northern representatives attend only by invitation and only as observers.

Since the Yukon and NWT are territories, they have no control over their own resources. Under the Canadian constitution, resources in the provinces are held by the Crown in right of the province. In the territories they are held in right of Canada. Hence all aspects of resource development are directed by the federal government. The federal government also retains the revenues from all northern resources. As in Brazil, the Canadian government views the North's resources as the property of all Canadians, to be used for the benefit of the nation. Through control of resources and all economic and political institutions the Canadian government is able to control the environment of the North, and to continue exploiting the region as a colony.

CONCLUSION

The Canadian Arctic, along with Amazonia, is an underdeveloped region within a developed nation (in the case of Amazonia this distinction is relative). Underdevelopment is defined as failure to control and manipulate the environment. In the Canadian Arctic, the environment is controlled and manipulated by external factors, viz. the federal government of Canada and external resource corporations.

Dependency theory partially explains the nature of underdevelopment, which is described in terms of political and economic relationships. But dependency theory does not emphasise the environment as a factor in the relationship between developed and underdeveloped regions. By combining dependency theory with an environmental interpretation of development, we move closer to the tenets of sustainable development.

Sustainable development is not so much a theory as a series of guidelines for economic and environmental policy. Implementation of these guidelines in the Canadian Arctic would reduce the dependent relationship and develop the region. Practical steps include the diversification of the northern economy and the devolution of political powers and resource control to northern governments and Native groups. Until environmental control is restored to northerners, the Canadian Arctic will remain an underdeveloped colony.

REFERENCES

Berger, T. R., (1978) *Northern Frontier, Northern Homeland: The Report of the Mackenzie Valley Pipeline Inquiry* (Ottawa: Supply and Services Canada).
Berger, T. R., (1985) *Village Journey: The Report of the Alaska Native Review Commission* (New York: Hill and Wang).
Brody, H., (1975) *The People's Land: Eskimos and Whites in the Eastern Arctic* (Harmondsworth: Penguin).
Bunker, S. G., (1985) *Underdeveloping the Amazon: Extraction, Unequal Exchange, and the Failure of the Modern State* (Urbana, Illinois: University of Illinois Press).
Burns, E. B., (1980) *A History of Brazil* (New York: Columbia University Press).
Chernela, J. M., (1988) 'Potential Impacts of a Proposed Amazon Hydropower Plant', *CS Quarterly*, 12, 20–4.
Frank, A. G., (1969) *Capitalism and Underdevelopment in Latin America: Historical Studies of Chile and Brazil* (New York: Monthly Review Press).
Grant, S. D., (1988) *Sovereignty or Security? Government Policy in the Canadian North 1936–1950* (Vancouver: University of British Columbia Press).
Guppy, N., (1984) 'Tropical Deforestation: A Global View', *Foreign Affairs*, 62 (Spring) 928–65.
Hay, D., (1988) 'Hydro Dams in Amazon Flood Forests and Indians', *The Canopy*, 1 (Fall) 1–2.
Higgins, G., and Higgins, J. D. (1979) *Economic Development of a Small Planet* (New York: W. W. Norton).
Irwin, C., (1988) *Lords of the Arctic: Wards of the State* (Ottawa: Health and Welfare Canada).
Katzman, M. T., (1987) 'Review Article: Ecology, Natural Resources, and Economic Growth: Underdeveloping the Amazon', *Economic Development and Cultural Change*, 35 (January) 425–36.
Patterson, D., (1988) 'Political and Economic Realities in the Northwest Territories', *Arcana Poli*, 1, 5–10.
Pretes, M., (1988) 'Underdevelopment in Two Norths: The Brazilian Amazon and the Canadian Arctic', *Arctic*, 41 (June) 109–16.

Pretes, M., and Robinson, M., (1990) 'Alaskan and Canadian Trust Funds as Instruments of Sustainable Development', in J. O. Saunders (ed.), *The Legal Challenge of Sustainable Development* (Calgary: Canadian Institute of Resource Law).

Saleti, E., and Vose, P. B., (1984) 'Amazon Basin: A System of Equilibrium', *Science*, 225 (13 July) 129–38.

Schumacher, E. F., (1974) *Small is Beautiful* (London: Sphere Books).

Special Committee on the Northern Economy, (1988) *Workshop on the Northern Economy: Summary of Presentations* (Yellowknife, Canada: Legislative Assembly of the Northwest Territories).

Vanvolsem, W., and Crevels, P., (1988) 'Canadian firms join search for Amazon gold', *Globe and Mail* [Toronto], 29 January.

Watkins, M., (1977) (ed.), *Dene Nation: The Colony Within* (Toronto: University of Toronto Press).

World Commission on Environment and Development (1987) *Our Common Future* (Oxford: Oxford University Press).

Zaslow, M., (1988) *The Northward Expansion of Canada, 1914–1967* (Toronto: McClelland and Stewart).

12 Beyond the Woodfuel Crisis: People, Land and Trees in Africa

Robin Mearns

The woodfuel 'crisis' of developing countries was 'discovered' in the mid-1970s at the time the world was gripped by the energy crisis that followed the oil price shocks of 1973–4. The scale of deforestation across the Third World was already recognised. As energy analysts and anthropologists began to pile up the evidence across the developing world about the huge scale of woodfuel use and the difficulties that millions seemed to be facing in getting enough wood as tree stocks declined, it seemed natural to regard both types of crisis as essentially similar.

HOW BIG IS THE CRISIS?

The woodfuel problem seemed to be a classic case of rising energy demand outstripping supply. Although the resources in this case were renewable – unlike oil, gas and coal – they were apparently being over-used at unsustainable rates. So a numbers game known as woodfuel 'gap theory' was conceived, which quickly came to dominate almost every attempt to measure the scale both of the woodfuel crisis and the remedies which would be needed to alleviate it.

The basic premise of gap theory, as normally practised, is that woodfuel consumption is the principal cause of deforestation and therefore of mounting woodfuel scarcities. To measure the scale of this imbalance, the first step is to estimate the consumption of woodfuels (and sometimes of timber, construction poles and other tree products) in a given region and compare it with the standing stocks and annual growth of tree resources. The latter may be scaled down to allow for controlled forest reserves, game reserves, and trees in remote places which are difficult to access.

Typically this produces a figure for consumption that greatly exceeds the annual growth of trees. Take the Sahelian countries, for example: recent studies have found that woodfuel use exceeds the growth rate of tree stocks by 70 per cent in Sudan, 75 per cent in northern Nigeria, 150 per cent in Ethiopia and 200 per cent in Niger (Anderson, 1987).

The next step involves projecting these present-day gaps. First assume that the difference – the 'gap' – is made up by cutting into tree stocks, since consumption has to be met from somewhere. Then project woodfuel consumption, usually in direct proportion to population growth, and calculate the resulting tree stock each year. As consumption rises and trees are felled, the annual growth falls, the gap grows bigger, and the tree stock is still further depleted. Inevitably, the stock of trees declines at an accelerating rate towards a final woodfuel and forestry catastrophe when the last tree is cut for fuel. One such estimation of the situation in Tanzania, published in 1984, showed that the last tree would disappear under the cooking pot by 1990 (Nkonoki and Sorensen, 1984). There are still many trees in Tanzania.

The final step is to ask what must be done to close the gaps to bring consumption and tree resources into balance. With few exceptions, the answer is afforestation on a staggering scale. For instance, the World Bank study which did much to legitimise woodfuel gap theory estimated that tree planting in sub-Saharan Africa would have to increase fifteen-fold in order to close the projected gaps by the year 2000 (Anderson and Fishwick, 1984). The vast scale of these remedies, and the calamitous consequences if they are not applied, naturally tend to combine to provide strong justifications for large, centrally-directed, plantation forestry projects focused on woodfuel provision.

This is not to deny that there are serious and growing woodfuel shortages in many parts of sub-Saharan Africa, and that woodfuel consumption does often exceed renewable supplies. Moreover, afforestation is an admirable objective for a great many reasons. Criticism of the methods of gap theory should not detract attention from these important facts. Indeed, supply-demand analysis, of which traditional gap theory is just one model, is clearly a valid tool for resource assessments at the national or regional level.

However, legitimate criticism can be levelled at the serious practical flaws in gap theory as it has been, and still is, applied. By ignoring these flaws, gap methods have done much to exaggerate the scale of the wood-fuel problem and foster inappropriate, largescale, energy-focused remedies at the expense of other actions which could have done much more to improve welfare, reduce deforestation, and generally assist the efforts of local people towards securing a livelihood on a sustainable basis.

FLAWS IN GAP THEORY

One serious flaw is that the large-scale aggregate perspectives of gap theory help to obscure the fact that woodfuel problems are location-specific and require precisely tuned and targeted interventions, usually on a scale appropriate to people's livelihoods. The second flaw is that this numbers game is played with weak numbers. While this fault is widely acknowledged, the game continues and its conclusions continue to be taken with great seriousness. A third and more fundamental flaw concerns the forecasting methodology, where consumption is usually assumed to rise in line with population, even while supplies dwindle to vanishing point. This is unrealistic: as scarcity worsens and wood prices or the labour costs of gathering fuels increases, many new coping strategies would come into play. Tree planting might increase, consumers may use fuels more economically, switch to more abundant fuels such as crop residues, or intensify efforts to encourage the natural regeneration of woody vegetation.

The net effect of these three major flaws is greatly to exaggerate the need for planned interventions. They imply that all supply-demand adjustments must be implemented by interventions whereas, in fact, many of them will be made naturally by ordinary people without any external assistance. This could be corrected by better information, thus putting gap theory on a respectable footing; but until this is done, the method must be regarded as a dangerously misleading planning tool.

SOME ASSUMPTIONS CHALLENGED

Many of the most basic assumptions on which planned, energy-focused interventions are based are false or highly misleading: for instance, that woodfuels are normally the principal cause of deforestation, or that the expanding circles of deforestation around cities inevitably force up woodfuel prices and hence provide a powerful economic rationale for all kinds of afforestation and conservation measures.

Far from being the principal cause of deforestation, woodfuels are more usually a by-product of land clearance for agriculture in sub-Saharan Africa. Although varying considerably in relative importance from place to place, the major sources of woodfuels are: surpluses arising from agricultural land clearance; dead branches and twigs; by-product wood from trees grown on farms or in woodlots; dedicated woodfuel plantations; and tree cutting directly for fuel, especially to make charcoal. Even where trees are cleared directly for charcoaling, in many places this reflects inadequacies in the agricultural system. Much commercial firewood and charcoal destined for the cities is produced by rural people to supplement their incomes, especially in the slack agricultural season, or in years when returns to farming are poor due to drought or to low agricultural producer prices.

The price-scarcity model which is so often assumed to underlie 'soaring' woodfuel prices in urban centres neither squares with what actually appears to be happening to woodfuel prices in many cities, nor begins to explain the many social and economic mechanisms which help to account for fuel prices.

A major obstacle to the analysis of woodfuel price trends is the poor reliability of the available data. The most robust, however, suggest that the considerable year-on-year and inter-seasonal price fluctuations which are frequently observed have more to do with the structure of the woodfuel markets than with the physical availability of wood. Woodfuel markets can be very complex and dynamic, with many actors and interested parties along the chain from wood harvesting and charcoaling, through transport to and in the city, to the great variety of wholesalers and retailers who sell to consumers. Although remarkably little is known about these multi-million-dollar businesses, we know enough to establish two crucial points. First, costs and margins can be extremely variable; and second, there is usually large scope for reducing costs or otherwise increasing the economic efficiency of the market, whether as a result of natural forces or designed interventions.

One of the largest cost-reducing measures, for example, is to make the switch from return transporting of woodfuels (where trucks make an empty journey from the city to the rural pick-up points, typical of present-day Kenya, Malawi, Tanzania and Zambia, for example) to back hauling (carrying other goods on the outward journey and woodfuel on the return trip to the city, characteristic of the highly organised charcoal trade in Sudan). By reducing unit costs and mark-ups, such changes can make all the difference to urban woodfuel supply, its impact on tree resources and the prospects for sustainable wood production for urban markets.

GIVING SCARCITY A HUMAN FACE

Conventional woodfuel thinking is premised on the belief that physical scarcity of wood is the key issue to address. As typified by gap theory, analysts and planners have measured the scale of woodfuel problems in terms of volumes of wood resources and consumption and distances from resources to consumers. In rural areas, the distance and time to collect woodfuels is commonly used as the yardstick of scarcity and the need for remedies. For urban areas, it is commonly assumed that woodfuel prices will rise as forest stocks are depleted and the transport distance from the city to its main woodfuel resources lengthens. Since increasing physical scarcity or distance can impose considerable costs on consumers, the basic aims of woodfuel interventions are to reduce these costs by reducing physical scarcity.

There is, of course, a good deal of truth in these assumptions. However, interventions are most unlikely to succeed if they do not recognise that physical scarcity means nothing unless it is related to the human dimension. We must ask whether these costs are the outcomes of physical scarcity itself or of much more fundamental issues such as labour shortages, land endowments, social constraints on access to wood resources, cultural practices or – as we have seen for urban areas – the structure of markets. These 'human issues' are both complex and dynamic and are frequently undergoing rapid and adaptive change which the outsider may easily miss.

Consider wood gathering, for instance. There is now compelling evidence from time budget studies for rural women that the time spent collecting firewood can vary greatly from one week or season to the next, depending on agricultural and other labour demands; it is often minor even in 'wood scarce' areas compared with time for collecting water, food preparation, cooking and other survival tasks; and it is perceived as a more or less severe problem – and is adjusted accordingly – in relation to the totality of labour needs and time available (Tinker, 1987; Cecelski, 1984).

The basic issue is therefore one of *labour* availability, not fuel availability. If spare labour is abundant it may not matter if woodfuel collecting trips are long or getting longer. If labour is very scarce, even the collection of abundant woodfuel supplies may be perceived as a serious problem. What matters is local perceptions of these questions and the coping strategies that people have evolved or are evolving to deal with them, not the outsider's simple physical measurements.

At the same time as these and other preconceptions are being challenged, it is now increasingly recognised that by narrowly addressing woodfuels and the symptoms of their scarcity, directly energy-focused approaches look only at the tip of the iceberg and ignore the much broader and deeper stresses in the environmental, social, economic and political systems of which woodfuel scarcity is only one manifestation. They obscure the fact that woodfuels are only one of many basic needs and that their provision – for example, by 'tree growing' – is only one single aspect of diverse household coping strategies and land management systems on and beyond the farm. Indeed, trees themselves can provide many other products and services besides woodfuel, which may be a relatively low priority claim on available wood resources. Top-down and over-specialised approaches have often failed to notice that in many places rural (and urban) people are already responding to woodfuel and other land use stresses in ways that are imaginative, innovative and with far lower cost than most project interventions.

In the high potential agricultural areas of Western Kenya, for example, where rural population densities are very high, land is scarce and farms have been repeatedly sub-divided, farmers have been employing complex and intensive agroforestry systems for many years. Wood is grown for sale in local markets, and many farmers have their own seedling nurseries to supply their own needs and often those of their neighbours as well.

However, despite extraordinarily high standing stocks of trees – the density of which actually increases with population density owing to planting and management – access to wood for own use as fuel may still be a problem for many households.

In the semi-arid Shinyanga region of Tanzania, farmers and pastoralists have responded to increasing pressures on local wood resources by developing ways of propagating trees and shrubs for live fences from cuttings, transplanting wild plants and direct seeding rather than using conventional nursery seedlings which are hard to obtain. Offtake from the live fences, which are designed to control grazing and allow fenced-off areas of vegetation to regenerate, is also used for fuel. Several communities have developed sophisticated rules and sanctions to regulate access to woody vegetation and traditional grazing reserves.

NEW REMEDIES

The more comprehensive and objective view of woodfuels now emerging recognises that there are no single, simple answers and that the problems surrounding them are inseparably linked to the complex, diverse, extremely dynamic and multi-sectoral issues underlying Africa's broader crisis of population, food, poverty, land and natural resource management. Successful remedies for woodfuel problems must be firmly rooted in these broader contexts. In particular, if planning, projects or other types of intervention are to create lasting successes they must recognise at least three basic factors.

First, they must take into account the need for local assessments and actions and the unhelpful nature of large-scale averages. The biophysical and cultural 'landscapes' of Africa, especially, are extremely diverse. Problems, and the opportunities to solve them, are therefore specific to place and to social groups in each place. The aim should be to reach underlying causes rather than heal the symptoms.

Second, there is a need for indirect approaches to woodfuel issues and greater participation by local people at every stage to help empower them to prioritise and solve their own problems. This follows from the first point, as does the fact that success normally depends on starting and strengthening processes rather than delivering technical packages. Concentrate on 'how' rather than 'what' things are done.

Third, there is a need for decentralised and multi-disciplinary approaches, including the use of competent and trusted 'grassroots' agencies, to facilitate the above. However, this does not exclude the need for economic, legal and political initiatives at the macro-level to improve the broad contexts for local, positive change.

Some of these needs have been accepted, but less frequently acted upon.

Although these perspectives are in tune with the broad paradigm shift which is now sweeping through governments, aid agencies and other parts of the development community, one has to bear in mind the enormous inertia and vested interests which can resist such basic changes to conventional structures of authority, responsibility and knowledge. Narrow specialism, false diagnoses of problems and top-down attitudes are found in all of the many disciplines and institutions which work, directly or indirectly, towards the better management of land and natural resources. Getting off the beaten track and heading for new territory with unfamiliar allies will not be easy for them, or for woodfuel specialists. But despite the enormity of the task of devising new and appropriate kinds of remedies, important lessons do at last seem to be being learnt; we can now point to cases where great progress is being made in practice.

For example, in the arid Turkana district of Kenya a rural development project funded by Norway has been working with local pastoral communities to help them develop their remarkable system of individual ownership and management of riverine forests. These forests provide fruits, construction materials, medicines and fuelwood, and are an extremely important source of dry season fodder and browse for livestock, as well as having tremendous cultural importance, since they are also commonly the sites of family graves. As the system has come under increasing pressure from outside development activities and the rapid growth of settlements, the project is seeking to support it by combining the best of local knowledge with the most appropriate of 'modern' forestry and management techniques. The emphasis is on a 'joint learning' approach based on seminars with local leaders and government foresters, and under the harsh, dry conditions of Turkana these efforts have led to notable successes in terms of tree growing and the natural recovery of vegetation by means of small-scale water harvesting and voluntary restrictions on the areas where livestock can graze.

This is just one example among the many innovative kinds of natural resource management interventions that are now taking place across sub-Saharan Africa. They share some common attributes, such as seeking to build on local knowledge and management practices and addressing a number of problems at the same time. At least indirectly, many of these interventions also contribute substantially to easing woodfuel constraints at the local level. There are encouraging signs that more and more outsiders are beginning to see the need to put people's livelihoods first in the search for sustainable solutions to land management problems in all their complexity.

NOTE

This paper outlines briefly the major arguments of a recent study commissioned by the Royal Norwegian Ministry for Development Cooperation. The eighteen-month study, carried out at the International Institute for Environment and Development (IIED), set out to identify the key issues and policy options in the field of biomass energy in sub-Saharan Africa. The full study is available as a book: G. Leach and R. Mearns, *Beyond the Woodfuel Crisis: People, Land and Trees in Africa* (London: Earthscan Publications, 1989).

REFERENCES

Anderson, D., (1987) *The Economics of Afforestation: a Case Study in Africa* (Baltimore and London: Johns Hopkins University Press for The World Bank).

Anderson, D., and R. Fishwick, (1984) *Fuelwood Consumption and Deforestation in African Countries* (Washington DC: The World Bank).

Cecelski, E., (1984) *The Rural Energy Crisis, Women's Work and Family Welfare: Perspectives and Approaches to Action* (Geneva: International Labour Organisation).

Nkonoki, S., and B. Sorensen, (1984) 'A Rural Energy Study in Tanzania: the Case of Bundilya Village', *Natural Resources Forum*, 8, 51–62.

Tinker, I., (1987) 'The Real Rural Energy Crisis: Women's Time', *Energy Journal*, 8, 125–46.

13 Agricultural and Fisheries Development in the Falkland Islands

J. H. McAdam

EARLY DEVELOPMENT

The Falkland Islands have only had a stable settlement since the early 1840s. Following an initial period of dependence on shipping and sealing, from the late 1860s until the mid-1980s, sheep farming for wool was the main revenue source in the islands. In 1867, sheep farming began to make headway on West Falkland and by 1874 the principal occupation of the Falkland Islands was officially described as 'sheep farming'. In 1850 there were an estimated 7650 sheep in the islands and this figure rose to 435 700 by 1880 and to a peak of 807 000 in 1898. This population was probably too large, and overgrazing of the better pastures may have led to the reduction in numbers of sheep after the turn of the century. The population declined steadily until 1923 when it reached a level of about 630 000 sheep, and approximately this number has been maintained to the present day.

At present the approximate average density of sheep is one sheep per two hectares although the density varies enormously from area to area. Gibbs (1947) stated that 'it varies from 1.09 acres (0.44 hectares) per sheep on the best estate to 7.43 acres (3.01 hectares) per sheep on the worst'. The total wool clip over the years followed the trend in population size, but when the population declined after 1900, the wool clip remained static at around 2100 tons, because improvements in individual wool yield compensated for the reduction in population size.

FARM STRUCTURE

It is only since 1980 – and particularly during 1984 to 1988 – that the farming structure in the Falkland Islands has undergone the first changes of any note in the entire history of the colony. Up until this recent change, the estates were all large, with the ownership of the land divided amongst very few people. In 1979, for example, there were thirty-six farms, seventeen on East Falkland, seven on West Falkland and twelve on the smaller islands. Of the total, nine were 'sole traders' or partnerships and another four could have been defined as owner-occupied in that the farm residents held more than 50 per cent of the company shareholding (Shackleton, 1976). The other twenty-three farms were owned by a total of fourteen companies; the Falkland Islands' Company (FIC) being the biggest landowner with eight farms.

In 1979 a total of 1 166 463 hectares (2 882 330 acres) was held on freehold and only 6611 hectares (16 336 acres) on lease from the Crown. The latter comprised three small farms near Stanley and very small portions of five other farms. Within the farming structure that existed up until the late 1970s, farms on East Falkland varied from 1 050 ha (2600 acres) to 161 000 ha (397 000 acres) in size. Those on West Falkland tended to be larger, most being in the 40 000–80 000 hectares (100 000–200 000 acres) range. The majority of island farms were small, that is, less than 2000 hectares (5000 acres) in size (Theophilus, 1972).

The only small paddocks on the farm are those adjacent to the settlement where milk cattle, young stock, stud rams and working horses are kept. Hay is sometimes cut from these paddocks where fertility is often high as a result of heavy stocking and application of artificial fertilizers. The rest of the farm is subdivided into large enclosures, over 25 per cent of which are over 2000 hectares (5000 acres) in size. The siting of these fence lines has been largely based on convenience, distribution of vegetation types and ease of gathering sheep.

Traditionally, the large farms have been self-contained, resulting in relatively high manning levels, but in the period up until 1982 a steady decline in the labour force through emigration or alternative employment led to severe labour shortage on the farms, especially during shearing. There is little movement of labour between farms, but since 1977 itinerant shearing gangs had been an important development, and more dependence was being placed on them. The recent trend of sub-dividing many of the large farms into smaller one-man units has not appreciably altered this arrangement.

Since the late 1970s there have been fundamental changes in the existing farm structure in the Falkland Islands, these changes accelerating since the conflict in 1982. The most significant change has been the 'split-up' of some of the larger farms into smaller privately-owned units. In an exhaustive economic survey of the Falkland Islands in 1976, Lord Shackleton suggested that the economy (which he presumed would continue to be based on agriculture) would only survive if farms were sub-divided and sold to the local people, that is transferred into private ownership. He also stressed the need to introduce some form of diversification into agriculture in the islands. At that time, the average farm size was 32 500 ha (80 500 acres) and only 4 per cent of the total sheep were in private ownership.

The changes recommended by Lord Shackleton, although slow to be implemented initially, had already started to come about several years before the conflict (McAdam, 1984). The scope for diversification was chiefly limited by the conditions and climate and the distance from markets. There was, however, scope for some form of diversification to meet a demand within the islands themselves, and this demand will presumably be enhanced for some time by the presence of a relatively large garrison and a small but significant tourist market. The diversified agricultural or rural-related activities include or might include:

(1) The production and supply of fresh milk for the islands' population.
(2) The production and supply of other livestock for Stanley and the garrison.
(3) The local processing of wool based products.
(4) The development of on-farm tourism related services.

However, the most significant change has been the fragmentation of the larger farms into a number of smaller 'one family' units.

The creation of small farm units gives rise to many considerations. The industry, while recognising the social benefits of creating relatively small owner-managed or tenant farms, was concerned at the effect of subdivision on unit costs and, through fragmented breeding policies, on wool quality. Some results of subdivision of sheep farms in South America have been most discouraging; in the Falkland Islands early opinion was divided.

However, despite these reservations, the Falkland Islands Company – in response to the Shackleton recommendations (1976) – offered one of its major farms to the government for subdivision on an experimental basis. The offer was accepted and the farm was sub-divided with the full co-operation of the company and on attractive financial terms arranged by the Falkland Islands Government. This encouraged two major farms on West Falkland to make themselves available for subdivision. Since then the process of subdivision has proceeded at a rapid rate. The proportion of land in overseas ownership has decreased from 76 per cent in 1980 to 27 per cent in 1988 (FIDC, 1988). There were, in 1989, eighty-four farms in the islands with the planned subdivision of Port San Carlos adding only a few more to this total (Table 13.1). It is unlikely that there will be any significant increases in this total unless the FIC relinquish their remaining holdings.

The local government (and through its agent, the FIDC) see the policy of subdivision as critical to the development of the islands in an economic, social and political context (FIDC, 1988). In economic terms; because it makes for tighter management and greater productivity; in social terms because it helps to create a new class of independent-minded citizen farmers; and in political terms because it puts land in the hands of local

TABLE 13.1　*Transfer of farms and stock to private ownership*

		Company owned	Privately owned	Total
Number of farms	1979	23	14	36
	1988	9	75*	84
% of total sheep	1979	95.7	4.3	
	1988	46.0	54.0	

* Includes five Falkland Islands Co. Ltd share farms

SOURCE: Falkland Islands Government (1989) *Agricultural Statistics* (Stanley: Government Printer).

people (FIDC, 1988). New farmers have been assisted by the provision of loans for acquisition and grants for development and improvement. Following in the wake of such development, a small wool mill was built at Fox Bay in 1984–5 to process greasy wool in a form ready for consumer use. A farmers' co-operative to supply agricultural materials has also opened.

The progress on subdivision was reviewed by Lord Shackleton (1982) in his updated report following the conflict. He concluded that overall, despite short- to medium-term adverse economic consequences resulting from the creation of smaller farm units, the longer term situation and current social benefits were encouraging. He did, however, urge more positive co-operation over resources among these small farms.

AGRICULTURAL PRODUCTIVITY

The performance of Falkland Islands' agriculture had not improved to any appreciable extent from the turn of the century up until the recent radical structural change brought about by subdivision. The size of the sheep population declined gradually from the early 1900s until the 1950s but had remained more or less static over the next twenty years. Although increases in the total wool clip occurred during 1971–6, these were not sustained and indeed there was a slight decline in the late 1970s. One of the reasons for lack of progress was that there had been little investment of profits in the farms. Also the profit margins had been less because of high costs and these had possibly contributed to the reduction in pasture improvement programmes on many farms between 1975 and 1980, and this in turn may have checked output. In addition, the decline of the labour force was detrimental, although providing some saving in wages. Grassland improvement schemes, fencing and general building and estate upkeep all suffered as a result of labour shortage.

Farm profitability is conditioned by high fixed costs (primarily shipping

TABLE 13.2   *The productivity and output of Green Patch farm before
subdivision (1979–80) and the total of the six individual units following
subdivision (1983–4 to 1986–7)*

Year	Sheep (× 1000)	Wool (tons)	% of total East Falkland sheep	% of total East Falkland wool
1979/80	14.85	56.6	4.38	4.71
Subdivided				
1983/84	20.61	84.3	5.75	7.10
1985/86	25.06	79.1	6.48	6.18
1986/87	23.22	76.7	5.96	6.22

SOURCE: Falkland Islands Government (1988) *Agricultural Statistics* (Stanley: Government Printer).

costs) and the often very variable world wool price. In the past because of the relatively low cost of labour and the scale of operations farms have generally been very profitable. However, in recent years the effect of the trend in wool prices (up only 15 per cent between 1974 and 1984), and the considerable increase in labour costs (up 126 per cent over the same period) and materials and fuel costs (up 185 per cent over the same period) has led to a sharp fall in the margin between revenue and costs over the period. In 1981 the mean margin of income over production and sales costs was only £0.04 (sterling) per kg of wool (Shackleton, 1982) or £0.06 per hectare of land (assuming a mean stocking rate of one sheep to 2.3 ha and 3.56 kg of wool per sheep). In 1987 the approximate net return on one sheep fleece was £5.

It is interesting to consider the effect of the recent period of rapid land reform on productivity and output from the farms. Some results of subdivision of sheep farms in South America have been most discouraging, rapid decline in overall output has accompanied such land reform. For example, Bowman (1984) records that in Peru following reform in the mid-1970s, sheep numbers were reduced to two-thirds the pre-reform values within three years of subdivision. In the Falkland Islands, data is now available on subdivision over a six to seven year period. Green Patch farm was the first to be subdivided (into six farm units) in 1979–80. It is interesting to note that the total output from the six individual family farms which replaced the one single unit has increased substantially (Table 13.2). The wool output had increased from under 57 tonnes up to 77 tonnes, representing a real increase (allowing for seasonal differences) from 4.7 per cent to 6.2 per cent of the wool produced from East Falkland. Figures from the 1980–85 subdivisions indicate increased stocking rates of up to 23 per cent and increased wool production of 27 per cent (FIDC, 1988).

THE FISHING INDUSTRY

The number of foreign trawlers (mainly eastern European and Far Eastern) engaged in offshore fisheries around the Falkland Islands increased rapidly during the 1970s and 1980s with little revenue being accrued to the islands over that period. However, after increased concern at the likely overfishing and the lost revenue, a Falkland Islands fisheries conservation zone (FICZ) of approximately 150 miles radius around the islands was declared in 1986. The fishery's major resources are *Illex* squid, fished principally by Far Eastern and Polish fleets. *Loligo* squid and a variety of finfish species are fished mainly by European vessels. The management system reflects the particular situation of the Falkland Islands and the short-lived and fluctuating nature of the squid species. To ensure that conservation targets are achieved, fishing effort is controlled by limiting the number of vessels licensed to fish in the FICZ. Revenue is accrued through licence sales and profits from joint venture companies formed between the various fisheries operators in the region and a wholly owned subsidiary of the Falkland Islands Government.

INCREASED REVENUE FROM FISHING

Up until the early 1980s the main source of revenue to the colony was from the farming sector. With the radical changes in agriculture resulting in initially lower profits from farming and the opportunity for external source revenue, from such enterprises as philatelic sales, tourism, construction, etc, farming gradually declined as the main revenue source. However, these sources were all overshadowed by the increases in revenue from the fishing sector. The declaration of the FICZ in 1986 took the growth process a major step further forward. GNP increased by 180 per cent in a single year and government earnings from overseas were effectively increased six-fold. The national income was approximately £41 million in 1987–8, a seven-fold increase from the 1982–3 level.

Such a change is quite remarkable in the fortunes of any country. The net result has been an increased degree of financial independence from the British government and complete funding of the colony and its development programme from within its own resources.

FUTURE DEVELOPMENT

There has been considerable debate as to the way development should proceed now that it is within the hands of the Falkland Islands Government. A development strategy involving three options was devised and put

TABLE 13.3   *The three development options (published November 1987)*
proposed for the Falkland Islands

---

(1)   Continued high levels of investment in on-shore fisheries development –
HIGH GROWTH

(2)   Investment emphasis on non-fishery sectors while maintaining fisheries as
an off-shore enclave – MEDIUM/HIGH GROWTH

(3)   Investment emphasis on infrastructure and social expenditure through
Government with surplus invested to provide and secure funds – MEDIUM
GROWTH

Following consultations with islanders, the report recommended a combination of
Options 2 and 3.

SOURCE: Environmental Resources, Ltd., 1987.

to the local population for discussion and opinion in 1987–8 (Environmental Resources Ltd., 1987). Drawing on the three scenarios (Table 13.3) –
one showing a high growth future based on maximising direct investment in
the fishing industry (e.g. through establishing a local fishing fleet, dry dock
facilities and on-shore processing); a second based on a major investment
programme in the non-fishing sector of the economy; and a third, more
conservative, based on infrastructure development and the building-up of a
nest egg of financial reserves – a broad consensus of views emerged. Local
opinion decisively rejected too great a dependence on the fishing industry,
but equally felt that the range of investment opportunities in other parts of
the economy was too narrow. The third scenario was seen as too conservative in its extreme form but had many favourable elements.

The consensus which emerged favoured investment across a wide front –
not rejecting or leaning too heavily on fisheries, rather drawing the best
from it to sustain the elements of Falkland Islands life which are important
to its people – particularly the special remote rural community (Environmental Resources Ltd., 1988).

The situation at present represents a relatively simplistic and extreme
form of 'booming sector' economics whereby the booming sector (fisheries) and the lagging sector (agriculture) produce tradeables facing given
world prices (Corden, 1984). There are many instances where sectoral
booms have occurred with adverse effects on other sectors. Those responsible for policy development in the Falkland Islands should be aware of
these and, in particular, attention should be paid to protection of the
lagging sector from the adverse effects of the boom (Corden, 1984).

However, there is no doubt that the two major changes which have
occurred in the Falkland Islands, the radical rural restructuring and the
emergence of fisheries as the major revenue source have affected the

traditional way of life. There has been an influx of development personnel associated with the developing fishing industry and a general swelling of the expatriate community. This has inevitably meant that the maintenance of a national identity and traditional way of life among the local populations has become increasingly more difficult.

The Falkland Islands have gone through a decade of tremendous upheaval and it is surely too much to expect them to rush headlong into rapid development programmes; rather they must be given time to adjust to their new-found wealth and prepare for the future.

REFERENCES

Bowman, D. L., (1984) 'Pastoralism and Development in High Andean Arid Lands', *Journal of Arid Environments*, 7, 313–28.

Corden, W. M., (1984) 'Booming Sector and Dutch disease economics: Survey and consolidation', *Oxford Economic Papers*, 36, 359–80.

Environmental Resources Ltd (1987), *Falkland Islands Long Term Economic Development Study*, Report to the Falkland Islands Development Corporation (London: Environmental Resources Ltd).

Environmental Resources Ltd (1988), *Falkland Islands Development Strategy*, Report to the Falkland Islands Development Corporation (London: Environmental Resources Limited).

F.I.D.C. (1988), *Falkland Islands Development Corporation, Annual Report 1988* (London: Falkland Islands Government Office).

Gibbs, J. G., (1947) *Abstract of report on the work and findings of the Department of Agriculture 1937–1946* (Stanley: Government Printer).

McAdam, J. H., (1984) 'Recent Changes in Falkland Islands Agriculture', *Interciencia*, 9, 307–10.

Shackleton, E. A. A. S., Chairman (1976): *The Economic Development of the Falkland Islands* (London: Her Majesty's Stationery Office).

Shackleton, E. A. A. S., Chairman (1982): *Falkland Islands Economic Study 1982* (London: Her Majesty's Stationery Office).

Theophilus, T. W. D., (1972) *The Economics of Wool Production in the Falkland Islands* (A report) (London: Foreign and Commonwealth Office, Overseas Development Administration).

14 Primary Health Care Operational Experience in Mexico City DF

Margaret Harrison

Problems associated with the provision of primary health care (PHC) in a large urban area continue to perplex health planners throughout the world. Drawing on research carried out in Mexico City DF in 1987–8,[1] this paper examines the operational difficulties and problems one Mexican health institution has experienced as it endeavours to provide a PHC system. The health institution under analysis is the *Secretaria de Saludridad y Asistencia* (SSA). Detailed statistical information is restricted to one part of the DF, comprising the four delegations (political administrative units) of Izta-calco, Iztapalapa, Tlahuac and Venustiano Carranza. These delegations formed the eastern administrative sector of the SSA until 28 February 1988. A resume of other health institutions also operating in the DF is provided by Ward (1987).

PHC is a model of health care advocating the provision of 'acceptable, accessible services based upon local initiative and maximum levels of community participation' (Unger and Killingsworth, 1986, p. 1002). Emphasis is placed on preventive medicine and treating the person in the context of his/her environment. Comprehensive PHC is broad in scope and includes programmes for immunisation, health education, family planning, nutrition, sanitation and the provision of essential drugs. PHC goes beyond the capabilities of merely a health institution alone; government partici-pation in socio-economic development is essential if PHC is to have any success. The PHC model was developed as a means of reaching and attending to the health needs of the rural poor (Werner, 1977 and 1980, pp. 91–105, and Rifkin, 1980, pp. 1–7). Later the concepts and theories of PHC were applied comprehensively and selectively in urban areas (Har-pham, Lusty and Vaughan, 1988, pp. 61–3).

In the late 1970s the Mexican government established the IMSS-Complamar scheme whereby the rural *campesinos*, a previously neglected sector in Mexican society, were given some health care provision. In 1981 the SSA initiated the programme for marginal areas in the large cities of Mexico. PHC in urban areas is not provided exclusively by the SSA; however, the SSA is the Mexican health institution working specifically with the poorer section of society: the self-employed, unemployed, and the population of marginal areas. By the end of 1981 the SSA had established numerous health centres in Mexico City DF, Guadalajara, Monterrey and Leon.

The programme for marginal areas in the large cities is not without its flaws. First, there is the difficulty of demarcating and defining such areas. Secondly, PHC requires community participation, which is critical to its success (Complamar, 1982, p. 53). This implies that medical personnel in a PHC scheme should be local, respected people with a good background knowledge of the area, who are prepared and able to serve the community. In remote, isolated rural communities such people may exist, but in urban areas, especially rapidly growing areas, like Mexico DF, they may not be available. The nature of the SSA programme for marginal areas in Mexico DF was designed to provide adequate cover though not necessarily functioning in established socially identifiable communities. PHC centres of the SSA aim to satisfy the criteria of being accessible, adequate, acceptable, and available and ready for immediate use. PHC centres should aim to cover 85 per cent of all health needs.

The SSA PHC system is hierarchical in structure, composed of health centres of various sizes. A building-block structure of modules has been applied, with one doctor, one nurse and one social worker[2] forming one module to care for 3000 people or 500 families. One module constitutes a Type 1 (T1) centre. Centres Type 2 (T2) to Type 3 (T3) and Type 3A (T3A) contain increasing numbers of modules according to status: a T2 usually has between two and six modules. Higher order centres perform administrative as well as specialist consultative treatment activities. Centres in existence before the introduction of the programme for marginal areas were incorporated into the new structure.

The problems of the SSA PHC programme fall into two distinct categories: structural and operational. Structural problems require national solutions; one potential solution will be discussed at the end of the paper. Structural problems mould and influence the daily operational problems of the system. Operational problems, the concern of the paper, illustrate the failings and inadequacies of the system. 'Relevant operational experience worldwide' (WHO, 1986, p. 3) is urgently required if advances are to be made in urban PHC provision. Operational problems within the marginal programme may be classified under three categories: people, resources and environment. All three categories are interrelated.

OPERATIONAL PROBLEMS: PEOPLE

Since a health service is people-orientated, analysis of people's difficulties should mark the starting-point of the investigation. Within a large urban area it is highly unlikely that every member of a module team will have

TABLE 14.1   *PHC centres and modules in 1987*

Delegation	Total no. of PHC centres	Number of Modules			
		Existing		Complete	
		M	% *	M	%
Iztacalco	7	45	100	22	48.9
Iztapalapa	20	97	80.8	49	50.5
Tlahuac	15	45	104.6	26	57.8
V Carranza	15	89	94.7	39	43.8
Total	57	276	91.4	136	49.3

M = module
* = % of total planned modules for the delegation

SOURCE: Fieldwork and SSA Region II Oriente, 1987.

close links with the immediate area where they work. Many workers live at some considerable distance from the health centre, some travelling over two hours to get to work. A lack of association with the area can mean the medical team is not committed to the area (the observation of medical centre directors). Medical personnel change on a regular basis: thus the centre may lose any sense of continuity. If SSA PHC centres lack staff commitment and community involvement it is hard to see how the centres and system can work efficiently and effectively. The whole issue of staff involvement and commitment brings into question whether an urban-based PHC system can or should aim to work according to the same principles as a rural-based PHC system.

Understaffing is a serious problem in the SSA PHC centres. Of the 276 modules in the fifty-seven centres of the eastern planning area in 1987, almost 50 per cent were without a full staff complement (three people per module) (Table 14.1). Of the twenty-seven T1 centres, thirteen did not have a full complement of staff. The most frequent omission was a social worker; there are however cases where there is no doctor or only a trainee doctor who fails to attend regularly.

Another issue of importance is the quality of the staff in terms of their qualifications (Table 14.2). The main feature of Table 14.2 is the great preponderance of unqualified or auxiliary nurses and social workers. The data refers to all SSA medical personnel working in PHC centres; some have direct contact with patients, while others hold administrative positions. Data for staff working in modules and consultancies, and therefore with direct contact with patients (Table 14.3) highlight a deficiency in doctors and social workers in all delegations. Tlahuac, the delegation furthest from the city centre and still rural in character, has fewer doctors than modules.

There are a number of reasons why there is a shortfall in medical

TABLE 14.2   *Staff qualifications*

| Delegation | Doctors | | Nurses | | | Social Workers | | |
	Tot.	Gen.	Tot.	Qu.	Aux.	Tot.	Qu.	Aux.
Iztacalco	85	71	101	9	92	26	6	20
Iztapalapa	126	107	164	30	132	60	3	134
Tlahuac	46	41	56	16	40	30	3	27
V Carranza	174	88	169	42	127	63	9	54
Total	431	307	490	97	393	179	21	158

Key: Tot. = Total, Gen. = General Medical Practitioner,
    Qu. = Qualified, Aux. = Auxiliary and in training.

SOURCE: SSA Region II Oriente, 1987.

TABLE 14.3   *Medical personnel*

Delegation	No. of modules and cons.	No. of modules	Doctors	Nurses	Social workers
Iztacalco	58	45	57	75	22
Iztapalapa	108	97	99	123	64
Tlahuac	47	45	38	53	29
V Carranza	100	89	90	107	61
Total	313	276	284	358	176

SOURCE: Cedula No. 1 del Diagnostica Situacional.

personnel; for example, the SSA pay levels are considerably lower than in other health institutions, and for social workers there is no satisfactory promotion scale. A lack of social workers means that much of the elementary PHC education does not take place. Some centres run clubs for the women of the area but again these are underfunded, lacking support, and leaders are not motivated to promote preventive PHC. In addition to a shortfall of staff, there is also a serious problem of absenteeism. Reasons for absenteeism range from illness, distance to travel to work, low morale, and dissatisfaction with the pay levels and the work environment.

The operating hours of the SSA health centres and the working hours of staff are revealing issues. Theoretically all health centres, except T1, are open from eight to eight every weekday excluding Saturday and Sunday. There is no emergency cover in the evenings so patients have to go to a hospital or wait until the following day. Doctors do not work on a call-out basis in the evenings either; in fact they are unlikely to make home visits, although social workers are more likely to call on patients at home. Health centre sessions are: morning (A.M.) 8 a.m. to 3 or 4 p.m., and afternoon

TABLE 14.4   *SSA PHC centre working hours*

Delegation	Doctors		Nurses		Social workers	
	a.m.	p.m.	a.m.	p.m.	a.m.	p.m.
	(All figures are as a percentage)					
Iztacalco	75.4	24.6	86.7	13.3	95.5	4.5
Iztapalapa	78.8	21.2	87.8	12.2	85.9	14.1
Tlahuac	76.3	21.2	83.0	17.0	79.3	20.7
V Carranza	84.4	15.6	79.4	20.6	77.0	23.0
Total	79.6	20.4	84.4	15.6	83.0	17.0

SOURCE: Cedula No. 1 del Diagnostico Situacional SSA.

(P.M.) 12 noon or 1 p.m. to 8 p.m. Analysis of the data in Table 14.4 indicates the very high percentage of all medical personnel working in the morning period. Doctors prefer the morning because this allows them freedom to work in a hospital or private practice in the afternoon. Obviously it means the centres operate at near full capacity in the mornings and run with a skeleton staff in the afternoon. Virtually all T1 centres operate from 8 a.m. to 3 or 4 p.m. and of the seven to eight hours the final hour is devoted to administration or possibly going out into the community. Spatially there is very little variation between the four delegations in terms of staff attendance.

The problem with the biased morning timetable is that patients will know they have a better chance of being seen in the morning; also if they come in the afternoon they are not sure if there will be a team of people who can see to their needs. Referral cases from T1 and T2 centres instructed to attend a higher order centre in the afternoon have no guarantee that the appropriate medical or paramedical staff will be on hand. Biased morning opening (a common feature of Mexican life) means that many patients may have to return to the centre another day. This makes the whole activity expensive in time and money for the patients. From an unpublished SSA study of patient attendance and demand in the eastern region, preliminary results indicated patient demand was greatest in the morning sessions. SSA pharmacies that dispense medicine at half price only exist in the higher order centres and are usually only open in the morning – yet another reason why patients are reluctant to attend in the afternoon.

A recognised problem in the SSA PHC system in the DF is the underuse of some facilities. Some doctors do not see as many as three patients per hour, the recognised norm by the SSA (Harrison, 1989, p. 219). There are again numerous reasons why this occurs. Medical teams may not be active in the community educating, encouraging and nuturing the principles of PHC, which generates patients. Also, patients attend a health centre when ill and need a cure, whereas very few patients give due regard to preventive medicine and regular checkups.

Other reasons why the SSA health centres are underutilised could relate to the availability of other health services: *Instituto Mexicano de Seguro Social* (IMSS), and *Instituto de Seguridad y Servicios de los Trabajadores al servicio del Estado* (ISSSTE). Many former SSA patients living in the neighbourhood may now be members of IMSS or ISSSTE schemes, thus reducing the workload of an SSA centre. Also, there is the likelihood that many areas where SSA centres are located have changed in socio-economic composition. As people move in and out of an area so SSA patients may have moved, and the medical team in the SSA centre has failed to reach new potential patients. Centres must look for new means of community involvement; otherwise the centre may become redundant. The PHC programme of the SSA must be dynamic and flexible to meet the altered circumstances of rapidly growing and changing urban areas; marginal areas may not always be marginal.

OPERATIONAL PROBLEMS: RESOURCES

Resource problems reflect the fluctuating position of Mexican state finances. When President J. L. Portillo initiated the drive for PHC, Mexico was fortunate to have a considerable amount of revenue from its oil wealth, especially during the bonanza period of the late 1970s. However, since 1982, Mexico has plummeted from one financial crisis to another. Over that period, SSA health centres within the marginal areas programme have received reduced funding and by 1988 were virtually starved of funds. Health centres find equipment is now old and not maintained. Staff continually find themselves forced to make do with whatever is available. One item which has had to be severely restricted is vehicle transportation between centres. The significance of this is that since most centres do not have telephones they have no other means of inter-communication apart from physically travelling to each other in an SSA vehicle. Some centres, especially the small T1s, actually complain that they do not have adequate equipment for sterilisation and refrigeration, and no medicine cabinets, let alone file cabinets for storing medical records.

Another major cause of concern in terms of operational competency is the lack of medicines. Higher order centres should in theory be equipped with a specific set of medicines plus general medical consumables, for example plasters, lint and so on, but there are cases when centres do not even have the basics. Doctors complain of being supplied with cheaper inferior quality medicines, some of which are past their 'use-by' date. Doctors also complain of insufficient vaccination serums; this is ironical when one considers the success of the various immunisation programmes in the DF (SSA, 1987, p. 363). With limited finances there are minimal funds for equipment, for social work or to help doctors attend training sessions on medical developments.

OPERATIONAL PROBLEMS: ENVIRONMENT

Environmental conditions in marginal areas can cause certain operational difficulties. Marginal areas may have an irregular supply of water and electricity, poor sewage facilities, and intermittent rubbish collection. Housing standards in marginal areas tend to be poor and roads may not be surfaced; areas may be overcrowded and there are few job opportunities. Marginal areas need not be marginal spatially, although many areas in the DF are. Within the DF there are also areas still considered rural, particularly the southern delegations.

As a government agency the SSA is funded from central taxes and does not have vast amounts of revenue for buying plots of land for new centres; there are still some areas in the DF lacking health care. The SSA in the past has tended to rely on the benevolence of the delegation, the individual and the Department of the DF to provide land. As a result the location of many centres is not ideal, not central to the community. If spatially separate from the community this can discourage patients from visiting the centre. Also, it can mean that the centre is not well known. There is also the danger that a centre in a peripheral position will not have all the basic services. Some T1 centres are not housed in SSA property, thus making their continued existence uncertain. However, the whole SSA philosophy behind the T1 centre is that it should be transitory: in theory, T1 centres at some strategic time will amalgamate with neighbouring T1 centres to create either a T2 or T3.

Research reveals T1 medical personnel uphold the principles of PHC and create good community relationships: as a result T1 centres are well used, relative to the larger centres (Harrison, 1989, p. 220). However, the medical personnel in the T1 centres do feel isolated from the rest of the system even if they have daily or weekly contact with their parent T3A centre.

Some centres are known to be in violent, dangerous areas; this may be why some only operate in the morning. To my knowledge one head of a centre changed her job because the area was considered unsuitable for a female. Centres located in marginal areas have problems with communications, since there are no telephones. The appointment system is highly disorganised and patients may wait all morning to see a doctor. In addition to environmental problems one must also remember that Mexico DF suffered two very severe earthquakes in 1985 which placed an extra burden on the SSA PHC centres.

CONCLUSION

The future for PHC in Mexico City DF is not good. In particular the SSA is saddled with a hierarchical, bureaucratic administration slow to alter and working with a reduced budget. Yet the SSA PHC centres satisfy the peoples' health needs. The SSA must serve the public and treat people equally, despite the spatial and social inequality that exists in Mexico DF (Ward, 1987, p. 56). Any plan to rationalise the service to increase efficiency could well be condemned for being socially divisive and going against the basic principles of the SSA. Theoretically a sound policy of rationalisation for the SSA is essential for the future, but current evidence shows that the SSA will not carry out such a policy since it is politically unwise.

However, if centres are underperforming then surely action must be taken to check wastage of personnel, resources and finance. SSA PHC centres suffer from two contradictory operational problems: understaffing, and underutilisation of resources. Both are major issues that need immediate attention if the SSA PHC programme is to have a future. Together understaffing and underutilisation have created a vicious circle of inactivity in some health centres. Clearly the SSA must develop an adequate staffing policy for recruitment and promotion. Also, PHC centres must work more closely with the communities in which they are located; in fact the centres need community participation.

Solutions to the structural problems of the SSA depend on national policies. In 1982 a plan for institutional amalgamation and restructuring was put forward. The aim was to remove health service duplication by the various health institutions, plus there was to be some decentralisation of services from Mexico DF. A new health law was introduced in 1984, but there has been little progress in the DF; the problems of duplication and wastage continue. Undoubtedly one of the major stumbling blocks is the fact the IMSS and ISSSTE are social security organisations and as such it would be difficult for them to join with the SSA. The political system has a vested interest in seeing the IMSS and ISSSTE maintain their health services, for both attend to the needs of the politically powerful groups in society (Ward, 1987, pp. 44–57). Thus, as long as the political system in Mexico remains unchanged the opportunities for the SSA remain limited. In addition, SSA activity is influenced by the six-year cycle of political administrative change. Every six years Mexico has a new president and new senior officials. Thus every six years the SSA experiences a reorganisation of staff, and this leads to a certain degree of instability. This reorganisation permeates to all levels of SSA activity, and therefore affects the operations of the PHC programme.

The future of the SSA PHC in the DF also depends on how the national government tackles the financial problems of the nation. As the SSA runs a budget deficit, pressure will increase to restrict expenditure, and ultimately this could lead to greater reductions in the health service. A choice will have to be made between expensive curative medicine and preventive PHC medicine. In the past both forms have been provided but curative has always been more important. To switch to comprehensive preventive PHC requires increased government commitment to improving the living standards of all members of society. However, a policy beneficial to the poorer sections of society is an expensive policy. If the SSA health service continues to suffer financial, administrative and political constraints, and is unable to work toward institutional amalgamation then the existing institutions will be forced to operate separately within their existing archaic structures and patients will suffer. If this happens Mexico City DF will not obtain Health for All by the year 2000, the WHO target.

NOTES

1. The author would like to thank the Leverhulme Trust and the Mexican National Council of Science and Technology for funding this research.
2. A Mexican social worker in the SSA system is equivalent to a health visitor in the UK.

REFERENCES

Complamar (1982), *Necesidades Esenciales en Mexico. Situacion actual y perspectives al ano 2000, Vol 4 Salud*. (Mexico DF: Siglo Ventiuno).

Harpham, T., T. Lusty and P. Vaughan, (1988) *In the Shadow of the City: Community Health and the Urban Poor*, (Oxford: Oxford University Press).

Harrison, M. E., (1989) 'Primary Health Care in Mexico City: What's the Future?', in *Proceedings of Conference on Project Rehabilitation in Developing Countries*, (Bradford: Development and Project Planning Centre) 209–24.

Rifkin, S. B., (1980) 'Community Participation in Health: A Planner's Approach', *Contact*, Special Series Number 3, 1–7.

SSA, *Anuario Estadistico 1986* (1987) (Mexico DF: Direccion General de Informacion y Estadistica) p. 363.

Unger, J. P., and J. R. Killingsworth, (1986) 'Selective Primary Health Care: A Critical Review of Methods and Results', *Social Science and Medicine* 22 (10) 1001–13.

Ward, P. M., (1987) 'Reproduction of Social Inequality: access to health services in Mexico City', *Health Policy and Planning*, 2 (1) 44–57.

WHO (1986), *Report of the Meeting of the Consultative Group on the organisation of health systems based on Primary Health Care*, (Geneva: WHO) 1–80.

Werner, D., (1977) *Where there is no Doctor. A village health care handbook*, (London: Macmillan, 1977).

Werner, D., (1980) 'Health Care and Human Dignity – A Subjective look at Community-based rural health programmes in Latin America', *Contact*, Special Series Number 3, 91–105.

15 Whither Development Finance Institutions? Evidence from Kenya and Zimbabwe

John S. Henley and John E. Maynard

INTRODUCTION

According to R. L. Kitchen (1986, p. 122), development finance institutions (DFIs) (or companies) are established in order to 'provide long-term finance for development projects'. They proliferate in the developing world, are fairly common in industrialised countries and exist supranationally. Particularly in those parts of the developing world traditionally influenced by British banking behaviour, they are deemed to fill important gaps in financial systems where commercial banks are reluctant to lend other than on short time scales and where as yet other capital market arrangements may be rudimentary.

Unfortunately the experience of DFIs in developing countries, both in promoting economic development and in maintaining internal financial viability, has been chequered. Many have foundered under mountains of bad debts, others have been kept going by open or disguised government subsidy, and yet others appear to have redirected their remits to functions that are arguably not 'developmental'. A number of questions arise, therefore, from these observations. How significant are different forms of finance, such as long term debt or equity investment, in the process of economic development? Under what circumstances can development finance institutions play a valid part in fostering successful new projects? Must development finance institutions be, in an accounting sense, viable? Should we be aware of, and give due weight to, wider political and social goals or should success in achieving, within an appropriate time period, specific economic or internal financial goals be the only valid criteria for evaluating performance?

These are all large issues, and it is impossible in one paper to do more than make a contribution to the debate. Below, we shall consider the theoretical background to finance and development, look in more depth at the case for development finance institutions, and then consider some evidence from the experiences of Zimbabwe and Kenya. These countries

215

present features which make them potent for discussion and comparison. Both inherited a British type of financial system, both – by African standards – have considerable secondary and tertiary industry and have seen a substantial influx of skilled European settlers. However, in recent years, their development finance institutions have performed differently. Finally, following the discussion on Zimbabwe and Kenya, we shall draw some conclusions.

DEVELOPMENT AND THE PROVISION OF FINANCE

Economic development in a country cannot proceed very far without the existence of a structured financial system. Although rudimentary capital accumulation may occur without the existence of any form of money, or alternatively on the basis of commodity money, possibilities are severely limited without the establishment of financial institutions that, working with deposits, seek and gather savings, expedite payments, and direct finance into investments and loans. What is at issue is not whether a financial system is necessary for development, but the nature of the institutions within that system and how they are influenced.

The great majority of DFIs established in developing countries have been set up under government auspices. This was the case before as well as after independence from colonial rule. In many cases this has meant 100 per cent government or parastatal ownership, but in other instances official participation involves a majority or, more rarely, a minority equity position. However, even in the latter situation, overall supervision will inevitably be in the hands of the finance ministry or the central bank. In general, the years subsequent to independence have seen an expansion of state involvement with DFIs, creating new ones, changing remits and/or taking over existing institutions and exercising increased supervision. However, since the onset of the debt crisis in the 1980s, and the increased role of the IMF and the World Bank in the financial management of many indebted African countries, further expansion of DFI operations has been subjected to increasingly skeptical analysis and review.

The case for government participation in development finance institutions has theoretical backing from several writers on the subject of finance and development, in particular, Gerschenkron (1962) and Patrick (1966). Gerschenkron relates the arrangements for the provision of finance at the outset of industrialisation to the 'degree of backwardness' of the country in question. Confining himself to certain historical European examples, he explains that England at the outset of industrialisation was, by the standards of the day, comparatively 'non-backward', and hence industrialists were in a position to supply their own capital funds. In Germany, initially a more 'backward' country, the banks took the initiative. In the case of Russia, the most 'backward' of the three countries considered, the state had to organise the provision of capital funds itself. According to Gerschenkron (1962, p. 19), 'The role of the state distinguishes rather clearly the type of Russian industrialisation from its German and Austrian counterparts'.

This thesis, if applied to contemporary developing countries, superficially appears to justify state intervention in the finance of development. However, developing countries today have to function in a very different world economy from that prevailing in the nineteenth century. It is also arguable whether Gerschenkron was correct about the process of development in his chosen examples. Nevertheless, his account of Russian industrialisation anticipates at an idea explored by Patrick (1966) in his 'demand-following' and 'supply-leading' hypothesis. He writes, 'We may term as *demand following* the phenomenon in which the creation of modern financial institutions, their financial assets and liabilities, and related financial services is in response to the demand for their services by investors and savers in the *real* economy' (Patrick, 1966, p. 174).

The financial system in the demand-following case plays a passive role, reacting to demand for financial services. The alternative, supply-leading scenario implies financial institutions taking a leading role in development. As Patrick explains, 'Before sustained modern industrial growth gets under way, supply-leading may be able to induce real innovation-type investment', (1966, p. 177). He goes on to discuss how a financial sector can be an engine of growth. Governments, he suggests, may assume a role in the process, ' . . . deliberate creation of the supply of financial services may have favourable allocative and incentive effects: it may well be desirable for the government to establish its own financial institutions or to subsidise private investment institutions' (1966, p. 186).

The notion of 'supply-leading' is associated with Keynesian demand theory, however paradoxical this may seem. The orthodox policy belief in the years following the Second World War that in advanced industrialised countries production could be increased – except of course in conditions of full employment – by a demand stimulus is here transferred to the context of the less-developed economy. The creation of financial institutions with money to lend and a battery of devices to induce borrowers to seek loans is meant, by bringing about demand for the goods and services that money can buy, to result in the growth of production. Since the early seventies, short-term Keynesian theory and policy prescriptions have lost their authority, and the assumptions of the 'supply-leading' approach to development finance may likewise be questioned.

Nevertheless, the model has been attractive to many governments in developing countries, not least because it appears to decorate with academic respectability the interventionist policies they have wished to adopt in pursuit of indigenous control of their economies. And though

Patrick himself does not neglect to warn of the dangers of assuming that creating new financial arrangements automatically leads to sound economic development, many governments in Africa, in the wake of the debt crisis, are only now beginning to re-evaluate the development finance institutions they have created or sponsored.

DEVELOPMENT FINANCE INSTITUTIONS

Development finance institutions appear under a number of guises, and there is little consistency in the usage of names. 'Development bank' for example, traditionally means an organisation that lends but does not invest, and 'development corporation' means the opposite, but rarely does the remit of an institution confine it to the specific function that, from its title, might be expected. For the purposes of discussion and analysis it is important to ascertain what an institution does rather than rely on what it is called.

Kane (1985, p. 19) specifies that 'a basic principle of development banking can be formulated: development banks restrict their lending to bankable projects'. However, in these circumstances it might be asked why government-created or sponsored DFIs are necessary? Why is the private sector not ready to finance projects that are deemed 'bankable'? There are, of course, several possible answers to this question.

First, the private sector may not have yet created adequate capital market facilities. Indeed, the whole concept of 'supply-leading' assumes, by definition, gaps in the financial system of a country in the early stages of economic development. Secondly, the private financial sector, typically foreign-owned and operating with norms and procedures taken from European practice, may be cautious about lending to and investing in many types of projects in Africa. Calculations of expected rates of return may seem rosier when evaluated by indigenous people familiar with local conditions in their countries. For example, Bhatia and Khatkhate (1975) believe that there are serious in-built constraints operating against local entrepreneurs, and that an imaginative financial approach toward them need not lead to losses.

Thirdly, in the 1960s and 1970s, leaders of newly independent developing countries were often sceptical about the virtues of capitalism. Multinational corporations (MNCs) were subject to particular scrutiny, especially when subsidiaries were 100 per cent owned by foreigners. Yet in many cases governments also wished to attract foreign investment. One of the ways of reconciling this contradictory position was to offer joint venture arrangements to prospective and existing investors whereby host governments took substantial, but usually less than 50 per cent, equity stakes in enterprises. Government ministries were not suited to both regulating and managing investments so DFIs were created to manage government investment portfolios in manufacturing industry, commerce and tourism.

Foreign investors were normally pleased to accept such arrangements because it reduced their financial exposure and, at the same time, created intermediaries with a vested interest in the viability of these projects. The DFIs could be expected to support the MNCs in their attempts to negotiate and, perhaps more importantly, to preserve special privileges, in particular, protection against competing imports and the provision of licences for the importation of essential inputs. Also governments were anticipated to be more susceptible to the idea of protecting industrial ventures with which they had an organic connection through their own DFIs, though this might involve some say in the appointment of employees and distributors. As Bates (1981, p. 102) notes, 'Privileged access is used by the elites in charge of the programmes for direct personal gain and to create a political following'. Needless to say, protection, even if theoretically justified by the 'infant industry' argument in the short-run, can lead to the emergence of monopolistic and inefficient firms in the long-run.

Fourthly, a perennial problem of capital development in most African countries has been the shortage of foreign exchange with which to purchase machinery and other essential inputs.[2] Governments are often able to tap concessional foreign funds on a government-to-government basis that are on-lent by agencies such as the International Bank for Reconstruction and Development (IBRD), the Commonwealth Development Corporation or the German Finanzierungsgesellschaft fur Beteiligungen in Entwicklungslandern (DEG), as loans to or equity stakes in DFIs. Although the financial reputations of many countries have been tarnished by the debt problems of the seventies and eighties, aid money is still frequently channelled through DFIs.

Although it is normal for the prospectuses and annual reports of DFIs to parade objectives that emphasise the virtue of project bankability, a variety of other aims are usually listed as well. Typical goals include the creation of employment, reduction of imports, saving of foreign exchange, the provision of funds to hitherto financially 'deprived' sectors of the economy (in particular, small businessmen and small farmers), the development of firms using local materials, the promotion of what are believed to be socially worthy arrangements, such as cooperatives, and the enhancement of indigenous ownership of industry. While these goals are not necessarily inconsistent with project viability in some instances they clearly can be.

Other devices may be brought into play to reinforce a government's predilections for the deliberate direction of capital funds along desired channels, in particular, an administered interest rate structure. MacKinnon refers to this as 'financial repression', though the term may legitimately be used to cover other forms of market distortion, such as flexible repayment schedules. Most commentators see little but trouble in interest rate management. As MacKinnon (1973, p. 170) starkly states,

> It [the typical banking system of colonial days] has been replaced by a very similar neo-colonial banking system, where private and official borrowers still absorb the limited finance available at low rates of interest which are often far below the opportunity cost of scarce capital.

Interest rate distortion and investment decisions based on particularistic criteria can put capital into the hands of the inefficient, incompetent and unprincipled, reduce saving, make credit rationing necessary and discourage further concessionary lending by bilateral and multilateral agencies. Small wonder that the management of some DFIs, faced with mounting financial losses from ill-conceived projects, increasingly restrict their lending and investment activities to safe projects that might in any case attract finance from commercial banks.

The losses suffered by a DFI might plausibly be considered acceptable if, from a cost/benefit viewpoint, net social benefit was positive. It is not practicable in one paper to go into this further, but put theoretically it is a perfectly valid idea. However, such are the problems connected with sound cost/benefit analysis in the context of African economies where statistics are often so unreliable, that it is normally impossible to come to firm conclusions about a criterion as slippery as net social benefit. It is perhaps worth noting that Killick's (1979) study of Ghana did not find that the commercially unviable were socially viable.

From the above it is clear that there is a place for DFIs in Africa as providers of long-term capital to industry and commerce. However, the efficient functioning of any financial institution is dependent on the existence of a market economy and a political system geared to supporting market institutions and efficiency criteria in evaluating business relations. Unfortunately, the state apparatus is only weakly institutionalised and governments are permeated by sectionalism or what Goran Hyden (1983) calls 'the economy of affection'. Market forces are all too often distorted by administrative regulations and political interference. DFIs as institutions mediating between government and business might be expected to occupy a rather uneasy space between politics and economics.

The next two sections will examine the experiences of selected DFIs in Zimbabwe and Kenya.

ZIMBABWE

The financial system and the provision of capital

By the standards of other Sub-Saharan African countries, Zimbabwe has a highly developed financial system. Apart from the DFIs and the Reserve Bank, there are five commercial banks, some foreign bank branches, four merchant banks, two discount houses, three building societies, five finance houses, a savings bank based on the post office, a number of insurance offices, and a stock exchange.

Within the financial system the market in equity capital is very limited. Only fifty-three companies – a fraction of the companies registered in Zimbabwe – are listed on the stock exchange, and this number is less than a few years ago. Trading in equities is sparse, as there is virtually no retail demand, and institutional investors, typically with excess liquidity, retain whatever shares they have or can obtain. At first sight, the existence of excess liquidity amongst institutions might seem to suggest that there is a pool of potential investment funds that can be tapped by enterprises through the issue of new equity. Unfortunately, bureaucratic procedures, political uncertainty and the problems of converting domestic funds into foreign exchange presently discourage local firms from raising finance through sale of equity.

With regard to loan capital, commercial banks lend in line with traditional British-type practice and so are not prepared to advance money over long periods. Merchant banks, though, package term loans for proven established companies and, significantly, do have some lines of credit from abroad. This enables them to go some way towards satisfying the foreign exchange requirements of selected clients.

Development finance institutions

The main DFIs are the Zimbabwe Tourist Development Corporation, the Zimbabwe Mining Development Corporation, the Urban Development Corporation, the Industrial Development Corporation (IDC), the Zimbabwe Development Bank and the Small Enterprise Development Corporation. Discussion is restricted to the IDC, and the Zimbabwe Development Bank, the most significant financing organisations in the secondary and tertiary sectors.

The Industrial Development Corporation

The IDC was established when Zimbabwe was still Southern Rhodesia. It was owned by a variety of banking and other interests, including the government, and channelled money to industry in both loan and equity form. From the outset, the Corporation pursued a very cautious policy, expanding its commitments carefully and leisurely, and so remained financially viable. To the extent that the IDC of colonial and UDI days had a policy of revolving capital funds, the 'development' character of the organisation was apparent. Thus, potential investments that were perceived by the market as too risky were, on occasion, financed by the Corporation which was able to take a longer view. However, the exceptionally measured approach adopted in those days meant that the IDC had little impact on development of the economy.

After independence, the government assumed greater involvement, and in 1984 bought out the other shareholders. Subsequently it was determined that the Corporation's capital should be steadily increased from Z$ 10m – the amount initially laid down in 1963 – to Z$ 100m, as investment opportunities arose. By the end of 1988, the amount of share capital actually called up had risen modestly to Z$ 15m.

The 1980 Annual Report, which still reflected the tenets of the pre-independence period, advised 'consideration of every application or proposal strictly on its economic merits, irrespective of all other considerations whatever' (p. 4). Later there was a change of direction. As the 1987 Annual Report points out, 'The Board took a decision in 1984 to change from a policy of concentrating on merchant banking activity to one of permanent long-term investment in equity in those affiliate companies in which the Corporation had an interest' (p. 6). Gestures have also been made to goals that imply a public purpose over and above purely commercial considerations. For example, the Annual Report for 1987 refers to import substitution and export promotion having become 'major areas of concern', and says that 'the Corporation looks forward to increasing its activity in new projects, particularly those that maximise the use of local raw materials' (p. 7).

As might be expected, the various statements of intent that appear in the annual reports of the IDC do not fully encompass all activities. For example, after independence there was a crisis of confidence in the private sector caused by political uncertainties and the onset of the recession in 1982. Many wished to sell up and repatriate their capital and consequently were willing to dispose of assets at a large discount. The IDC moved into the market and acquired a number of concerns. Some were run down and have remained moribund ever since, while others await rehabilitation. Thus the IDC could claim that through its intervention during the period of uncertainty, it has mitigated the worst effects of capital flight, preserved some jobs and brought key industries under state control. Even so, where it has become involved with new ventures – and there have not been many such ventures – it has always been in partnership with multinational corporations able to supply foreign capital and expertise.

Nearly all IDC investments have been in import substituting industries and where there is protection against competing imports and potential domestic competition (Table 15.1). Overall, the IDC has remained consistently profitable albeit achieving a relatively modest return on capital employed (Table 15.2). Future prospects may not be so good. Despite the fact that the former IDC chairman was in charge of official foreign exchange allocation, there were widespread complaints about foreign exchange shortages amongst the managements of IDC-associated firms in 1989. These shortages, it was claimed, were leading to short-time working and equipment failures due to lack of imported spare parts.

In summary, the IDC remains a marginal participant in the Zimbabwe capital market and investor in industry. So far it has not expanded its portfolio of investments to such an extent that it can exert a significant influence on the economy on behalf of the government and the government shows no inclination to create the policy environment or provide the resources for it to do so. Instead it operates much as an investment trust

TABLE 15.1 *IDC equity investments*

Sector	% of total
Metal products	21.15
Bottles and glass containers	20.31
Engineering	10.48
Motor assembly	9.54
Textiles	8.78
non-metallic mineral products	7.30

SOURCE: *IDC Annual Report*, 1987, p. 32.

TABLE 15.2 *IDC financial performance (Z$ 000s)*

	1981	1982	1983	1984	1985	1986	1987
Income	3 132	4 091	3 352	3 160	2 668	2 818	4 151
Expenses	490	574	635	885	1 035	1 092	1 253
Profits	2 641	3 518	2 716	2 274	1 633	1 726	2 898
Investments	26 144	32 955	36 161	37 458	36 867	52 225	47 576
(US $ m.)	36.5	35.8	32.7	24.9	22.5	31.1	28.6
Profits as % of investments	10.1	10.6	7.5	6.1	4.4	3.3	6.1
Expenses as % of income	15.6	14.0	18.9	28.0	38.8	28.8	30.2
Return on cap. employed (%)	7.9	9.4	6.7	5.6	3.7	3.7	5.3

SOURCE: *IDC Annual Report*, 1987, p. 32.

exercising considerable restraint in its lending policies. It is a matter for debate whether it ought properly to be regarded as a development finance institution.

The Zimbabwe Development Bank

The Zimbabwe Development Bank was established in 1983 with an authorised share capital of Z$ 50m, though by the end of 1988 only Z$ 20 had been called up. The shareholders are the Government and the Reserve Bank, who together hold 58 per cent of equity and a number of foreign and supranational organisations, such as the Commonwealth Development Corporation (CDC) and the European Investment Bank (EIB). Although 'the Bank was set up to be one of the main agencies to provide medium and long term loans and equity to productive enterprises' (Annual Report, 1988, p. 8), in practice, its equity holdings are minimal (Z$ 114 000). In 1988, it ventured beyond its basic remit by providing some short-term working capital.

The broad guidelines as to the types of projects the Bank should support contain no surprises, and are similar to those within which the IDC is supposed to operate. Thus it should favour projects that create employment, result in the production of import substitutes, use local materials, stimulate other economic developments and promote Zimbabwean ownership and management. The Bank also aims to provide technical assistance in the implementation of projects. Despite its ambitious constitution, the ZDB has not so far had a great impact on the Zimbabwean economy. Total ZDB loans outstanding at the end of 1988 stood at only Z$ 15m.

As with the IDC, the bulk of the ZDB's loan finance has been directed to light manufacturing, as Table 15.3 indicates. About a fifth of loans were advanced for 'new' investment, a third for 'replacement' investment, and the remainder for 'expansion of production'. The ZDB thus offers a fairly

TABLE 15.3   *ZDB loan portfolio*

Sector	% of total
Market gardening	1.1
Quarrying	2.4
Wood and paper products	5.1
Printing and publishing	5.3
Energy	7.8
Plastic products	13.0
Textiles and leather	18.2
Metal and metal products	22.2
Food and beverages	24.9

SOURCE: *ZDB Annual Report*, 1988, p. 20.

conventional medium- to long-term credit facility to established companies producing manufactures that are mostly import substitutes. At first glance, profits would seem to be buoyant, but discounting foreign exchange gains, the rate of profit for 1987 would be 3.3 per cent of shareholders' capital and for 1988 the corresponding rate would be 6 per cent.

What is very apparent about the direction of ZDB loans is the extent to which they are used by existing companies for reinvestment purposes, and the importance of the foreign exchange component. Rationing of foreign exchange by the authorities has restricted the importation of capital equipment to such an extent, the chairman of Lonrho claimed in May 1989, that major companies were obliged to engage a senior manager full time for the sole purpose of sourcing foreign exchange to meet essential requirements.[3] Not surprisingly, the ZDB's foreign funds, obtained from its non-Zimbabwean shareholders' contributions to the bank's equity and an EIB overdraft facility which are not subject to exchange control regulations, have been in high demand.

As in the case of the IDC, the performance of the ZDB hardly qualifies it as a 'development' organisation. Like the IDC it has expanded its commitments only slowly – indeed this caution has led to some comment in official circles. Effectively its business has come to mean the provision of foreign exchange funds to established companies and these firms do not necessarily need to borrow on a term loan basis.

KENYA

Introduction

In contrast to Zimbabwe, in Kenya DFIs have been locked into a downward spiral following a rapid shift in monetary policy from a period of over-valued currency and repressed interest rates to a period, beginning in 1981, of continuous devaluation and positive interest rates. In Kenya the full foreign exchange risk is carried by the borrower yet hedging is not permitted by the Central Bank. The 1988 Finance Act for the very first time permits Kenyan companies to claim tax relief for foreign exchange losses.

Currently there are twenty-three commercial banks and forty-one non-banking financial institutions in Kenya. The banking system continues to be dominated by three large retail banks who collectively account for more than 60 per cent of deposits. As in Zimbabwe, commercial banks will not extend term loans for more than three years. Such loans have to be backed by collateral whose marketable value exceeds the face value by as much as 150 per cent. Moreover, because of the time lags involved in gaining possession of land, banks are very reluctant to accept land deeds as collateral. A more important restriction for foreign-owned companies is the requirement that they can only borrow up to 20 per cent of their *initial* equity. This was relaxed in the 1986 Finance Act to the proportion of equity owned by Kenyans and the size of duties paid on imported capital equipment.

The Nairobi Stock Exchange was established in 1954. There is no formal trading floor, instead orders are taken by telephone and trades are arranged through daily call-over meetings. Fifty-five companies are listed and seventy-three issues of ordinary and preference stock. Market capitalisation as at June 1985 was estimated at KSh 4320m ($ 266m). These seemingly impressive statistics disguise the fact that as in Zimbabwe there is virtually no trading of stock, no more than 4000 trades in 1985. Not surprisingly, there are no specialised merchant bank underwriters. Basically equities and government paper are bought to hold by institutions who are primarily interested in dividend yields.

Kenya has three main DFIs involved in investment in industrial and commercial enterprises. The largest, the Industrial and Commercial Development Corporation (ICDC) had investments with a book value of KSh 1.3 billion in 1986, compared with the next largest, the Industrial Development Bank, which recorded an investment book value of KSh 699m in the same year. The third industrial DFI had investments of KSh 415m. The analysis will be concentrated exclusively on the ICDC, the only DFI to hold significant equity investments (47 per cent of its portfolio).

Industrial and Commercial Development Corporation

The ICDC was set up in 1954 for investing and lending money towards the promotion of industrial and commercial development. At present, it has eight wholly-owned subsidiaries, six majority-owned subsidiaries, and a substantial collection of associate companies where it holds a minority of the capital. A small loans scheme was introduced in 1965 to encourage small business development. According to its mandate, the ICDC is supposed to conduct its business operations prudently and logically, with due regard to suitable feasibility studies before money is invested in a project, and with appropriate monitoring once projects are under way. The ICDC is only concerned with long-term finance, except in the case – exceptionally – of those seeking money via the Small Loans Scheme, where working capital may be provided.

Sources of funds

'Total Funds Employed', as they have been built up over the years to June 1987 are summarised in Table 15.4. The majority of funds came from the Kenya government, though it is unclear how the aggregate amount is split

TABLE 15.4 *Total funds employed by the ICDC (KSh m)**

As at end of June	Government funds	Bank loans	DEG (see later)	Cap. and rev. reserves	Total
1981	581.1	26.7	1.3	83.6	692.7
1985	682.2	59.8	80.3	211.4	1033.7
1987	719.0	34.3	121.4	274.9	1149.6

* The figures do not show the 'current portion of loans'

SOURCE: *ICDC Annual Reports.*

between grants and loans. As the Auditor General states in the 1985–6 Annual Report (p. 24), 'for several years, the attention of the Corporation had been drawn to matters relating to loans and grants received from the Government and for which agreements on the total amounts, the analysis between grants and loans . . . had not been reached'. Government money apparently represented about 77 per cent of the Corporation's resources in 1981 but had declined to 62 per cent by 1987. This change is misleading to the extent that some of the increase in capital and revenue reserves is actually interest due to the government which is effectively capitalised.

The financial relationship with the government is further complicated by the Corporation's belief that some of the money it has injected into industry consists of funds 'managed' for the government. Hence it makes no loss provision against these funds but it is not clear that the government sees it that way. To quote the Auditor again, 'As in the past, there has been no confirmation that Government would underwrite any losses that ultimately accrue on these investments' (Annual Report, 1984–5, p. 24). In 1987 these managed funds came to KSh 100.5m. Another source of funds for the ICDC has been certain West German loans via the Kenya government, which have become grants. In 1987 these 'loans' amounted to 11 per cent of total funds. In general, interest due is capitalised as further debt rather than returned to the Government.

Turning now to current sources of funds, it is clear from Table 15.5, that very little money was available from the sale of investments. The years illustrated are not exceptional. 'Capital and Revenue Reserves' is a complex item, and its construction yields several surprises. First of all it includes 'profit' – the difference between income and expenditure.[4] 'Income' includes dividends, interest, application fees, management services, capital gains and a few other items. Interest on small loans never seems to be paid, and it is unclear how much other interest is actually received. Indeed, as is pointed out in the 1981–2 Annual Report (p. 5), 'The bulk of this income (referring to interest) is on an accrual basis and does not represent cash received'. And to some extent dividends come into the same category, for, as the 1984–5 Annual Report (p. 3) states, '. . . substantial amounts of interest and dividend arrears . . . had not been realised in cash as at the close of the year'. Furthermore, capital gains are only book profits so they do not represent liquid assets.

Set against 'income' is 'expenditure', which consists of interest payments, administration fees, write-offs and provision for losses. Interest payments remain largely unpaid. Administration costs, though, are real enough: on average during the 1980s they have been rising more than twice as fast as loans outstanding. Added to the profit are various 'adjustments' – 'depreciation', 'increase in interest on government loans' (interest waived), and 'amounts provided for losses on equity investments and loans'. This money is returned to the general pool of available funds. Finally, profits from sales of investments are included. All this gives the final 'capital and revenue reserves' figure.

To summarise and comment further on the financial performance of the ICDC is not easy, as much supporting detail is lacking in the available published information.[5] With regard to the profit and other capital and revenue reserves, these seem to be created not so much from the figures as listed as from off balance sheet transactions dependent on amounts of interest actually received and paid.

Application of funds

Since the beginning of the 1980s, the portfolio of ICDC companies has not changed much. In US $ terms, equity at cost and loans outstanding has remained static at around $ 50m. Funds invested appear to be mainly for support rather than expansion. For example, the 1985–6 Annual Report (p. 1) states, 'The Corporation's rehabilitation programme continued to be given emphasis in the 1985/6 financial year'. Net investment for recent years are summarised in Table 15.6. The total value of the shareholding at cost in subsidiaries at the end of June 1987 was nearly KSh 311m, and in associates over KSh 295m. The directors put the market valuation of unquoted shares at KSh 722m, but how much credence can be put on this figure is an open question as the dividend experience of many companies is

TABLE 15.5　*Current sources of funds (KSh m)*

	Government funds	Small loan repayment	Other loan repayment	Disposal of inv.	Cap and rev reserves	Total
1980–81	43.2	32.4	12.7	0.1	34.9	123.3
1984–85	39.0	33.9	23.9	0.1	57.3	154.2
1986–87	7.9	33.1	14.3	2.7	96.4	154.4

SOURCE: *ICDC Annual Reports.*

TABLE 15.6 *ICDC investments and large loans portfolio (KSh m)*

Portfolio	1982			1985			1986			1987		
	Eq	Lo	Add Eq	Eq	Lo	Add Eq	Eq	Lo	Add Eq	Eq	Lo	Add Eq
Associates	302	42.7	12%	285	40.4	(5%)	286	47.2	0.4%	295	47.5	3%
Subsidiaries	212	75.5	21%	288	150	10%	297	165	3%	311	189	5%
Total	514	118		573	190		583	212		606	237	
(US $ m)	49.6			46.9			49.6			51.0		

Notes: Eq = equity; Lo = loans; Add Eq = additional equity that year.

SOURCE: *Annual Reports of ICDC.*

so abysmal that their shares must in reality be virtually worthless.

Subsidiaries receive proportionately more loans than associates. Some repayments due are automatically turned round and treated as further loans, and it is not known how much interest is ever actually paid. The total principal outstanding in June 1987 was over KSh 189m for subsidiaries and KSh 47.5m for associates, though over KSh 20m of this had been openly written off, and a considerable additional amount – over KSh 121m, was being treated as a current asset, that is as loans receivable. Probably much of this debt should sensibly be written off as well.

The financial analysis presented above is depressing.[6] It suggests an institution facing severe cash flow difficulties and severe restrictions on lending operations. Disbursements appear to be largely directed to propping up existing ventures rather than initiating new ones, and to the sterile business of capitalising repayments and interest.

Performance

The ICDC investment portfolio is divided between fourteen subsidiaries and forty-five associates. The former include a very mixed bag of companies ranging from mining ventures to business services but by far the largest recipients of equity investment and large and medium-sized loans have been textile firms. Funds committed to this sector alone totalled KSh 489.5m in 1987 and constituted nearly half the total investment portfolio of the ICDC. Regular dividends came from just three subsidiary companies – Kenya Wine Agencies, General Motors and Minet ICDC (Insurance Brokers). Total dividends as a percentage of total capital subscribed equalled 6.7 per cent in 1985–6 and 6.9 per cent in 1986–7, an unspectacular return even assuming dividends were actually paid over.

Seventeen associated companies declared a dividend in 1986–7. Many of the others have yet to declare a dividend. The consistent profit earners are heavily weighted towards the subsidiaries of international companies engaged in manufacturing import substitutes, such as Eveready Batteries, Chloride Exide, East African Industries (Unilever) Firestone and Metal Box. A few firms not in this category, such as NAS Airport Services, the monopoly holder of the airline catering concession, also appear to do well. Total dividends as a percentage of nominal capital, at 18.1 per cent in 1985–6 and 30 per cent in 1986–7, are better than those received from ICDC subsidiaries. Even so, calculation of financial rates of return need to be treated with caution because of delays in actual payment of declared dividends. For example, the 1986–7 Annual Report (p. 3) stated, 'As at 30 June 1987 dividends amounting to KSh 86.7m were in arrears'.

By any normal commercial criteria the ICDC is not viable. Its continuation in a state of apparent financial solvency is due to the magnanimity of creditors, and various off-balance sheet transactions. Such dividend and interest income that does accrue is from a minority of companies, some yielding very high dividends. From a very narrow base total return on total investments is made to look more or less satisfactory. A robust development finance institution might sell off successful investments so as to raise useful finance for new projects, but the ICDC clearly dare not do this. In order to bolster its own weak position it must hang on to the profitable shares it does hold. 'Profit', as seen, is very much a manufactured figure, since it is derived from calculations involving interest not received, interest waived and so on. What, then, has gone wrong?

First, the ICDC as a financially 'soft' institution (Kornai, 1980), is hardly fitted to induce the sort of disciplined reorganisation of both itself and its commitments that might lead to effective solvency. Its shareholder, the government, does not lay down how its lending policy should be organised between loans and grants, is not explicit about the funds the ICDC claims to be managing on its behalf, regularly waives interest payments and never insists on repayment of loans: all seems designed to discourage rigorous management of the Corporation's own financial operations. Thus the ICDC appears untroubled about its obligations to service its own debt, is coy about the interest and dividends that it actually receives and is ready to capitalise unpaid interest and capital repayments without requiring radical restructuring of recalcitrant enterprises. In short, the ICDC's ability to assess the long term viability of new ventures, to monitor progress and take proper action in cases of failure to service loans leaves much to be desired. And all this while administrative costs rise – between 1981 and 1987, they more than doubled, reaching nearly KSh 60m.

As has been pointed out above, a sad feature of the ICDC's investment portfolio is that concerns which ought in theory to do well because they (a) produce goods that consist of or are based on local materials, (b) make import substitutes or (c) provide local services, often do not. Thus the Annual Report 1985–6 (pp. 7–11) notes that Kenya Taitex Mills 'continued to perform poorly because of production difficulties and rigid market conditions'; that in Sokoro Fibreboards 'profits declined due to a general increase in costs'; and that Kenya Bowling Centres 'made progress towards raising funds for its rehabilitation programme'. Paradoxically the concerns which did well were sophisticated manufacturing concerns such as motor vehicle assembly and accessories firms. But these were branches of multi-national enterprises who 'know how to do it'. The disastrous investments in the textile industry, by contrast, no longer involve significant foreign participation.

Thirdly, severe exogenous shocks might be expected to damage even the best planned investments. Domestic demand in Kenya is very much influenced by fluctuations in agricultural production and in the price of commodity exports, particularly that of coffee and tea. Undoubtedly the sudden switch in Kenyan monetary policy in 1981, from a regime of overvalued exchange rates and repressed interest rates to more realistic exchange rates and positive interest rates caused severe financing problems for companies only established a few years and with high exposure to foreign exchange loans. The change in policy also coincided with low commodity prices which further depressed domestic demand. With the benefit of hindsight we might ask why the ICDC's project appraisal process did not recognise this fatal weakness in the cash flow projections of many of its investments, particularly in the textile industry.

CONCLUSION

This paper offers an assessment of the performance of development finance institutions operating in the industrial and commercial spheres in Kenya and Zimbabwe. Obviously there is a deep-rooted crisis in the largest DFI in Kenya, the Industrial and Commercial Development Corporation. In our view, the root of the problem lies in the operationalisation of Patrick's 1966 concept of a 'supply-leading' development finance institution. Kenya's post-independence development strategy was published under the title *African Socialism and its Application to Planning in Kenya* and is generally referred to as 'Sessional Paper 10 of 1965'. This document advocated a fairly moderate form of state intervention. The main feature of 'African Socialism' of significance for DFIs operating in the industrial sector was the assertion of the need to transfer economic resources to the indigenous population (Africans) and the strategic role assigned to the development finance institutions in achieving this aim. More prosaically, the government was acutely aware of a financing gap in the balance of payments as well as a shortage of industrial capital and high level managerial manpower. However, it did not perceive the need to offer significant general incentives beyond the Foreign Investment Protection Act, 1964, which merely guaranteed investors against arbitrary nationalisation. No tax breaks or enhanced depreciation allowances were offered to attract foreign investors.

Basically, the government wanted to attract inward investment but at the same time wanted to control the activities of foreign companies. As Sessional Paper 10 of 1965, paragraph 120 states: 'Government expects the private sector to play a large role in development, subject, however, to firm guidance, and explicit controls when necessary. This approach will permit Kenya to attract private capital and management which could not otherwise be obtained for development'.

Instead of developing an effective regulatory agency capable of assessing investment proposals, whether local or foreign, and monitoring existing ones, it fragmented regulatory responsibility between a vast array of ministries. By restricting the local borrowing capacity of foreign investors to 20 per cent of the investment (Exchange Control Notice No. 19), the government increased the foreign exchange risk exposure of Kenyan subsidiaries. Under these conditions of perceived political risk – an administration, at least publicly, oriented towards national ownership and control, an opaque regulatory environment and severe restrictions on reducing foreign exchange exposure – foreign investors were mainly willing only to set up joint ventures with the ICDC.

By and large, first wave import substituting industries operating behind protective tariff barriers and import quotas and managed as part of the global network of transnational corporations have proved quite profitable for the ICDC. The disasters came with the second wave of investments after 1975. This time the expansion of activities was into industries where markets were competitive, particularly textiles. This development was stimulated by a rush of money into the economy in the wake of the 1977 coffee boom. An aggressively expansionary chief executive of the ICDC authorised loan and equity participation in a number of joint venture contracts. These projects were permitted much higher debt equity ratios than had previously been the case. Foreign equity participation was on a minority basis and sometimes consisted of little more than capitalised management or technical services fees. No sooner had many of these ventures opened for business than Kenya was forced to take the structural adjustment medicine in the wake of the 1980 recession and balance of payments crisis. None of these latter companies has recovered from the devaluation of 1981 and subsequent process of creeping devaluation. Each company has been locked into a downward spiral of under investment and severe cash flow problems. Foreign joint venture partners have departed. Several ventures have gone into receivership or liquidation. Some have never traded.

One of the lessons to be learned from the experience of the Kenyan ICDC seems to be that when a DFI becomes involved in a joint venture as an equity investor it seems to encourage a dangerously uncritical attitude of the specific investment amongst the regulatory agencies of the state. Clearly it is unwise of the state to assume that one of its DFIs always has the capacity to evaluate an investment opportunity correctly.

Is there an iron law at work which will inexorably lead to a similar fate for Zimbabwe's currently more modest DFIs? No certain answer can be given to this question, for despite some general similarities of colonial economic history, recent history has diverged (see Mosley, 1983). In relation to nearly all other African territories Zimbabwe was comparatively late in achieving official independence. Though socialist rhetoric surrounded the achievement of independence, pragmatism has been the dominant characteristic of economic policy. There have been few cases of nationalisation of private enterprises and no strong pressure from government to indigenise the private sector or to provide soft loans to African businessmen. Thus the economic environment in which Zimbabwean DFIs operate is very different from that prevailing in Kenya in the 1970s.

In the 1990s, with only a modest expansion of domestic demand in African countries in prospect, it is appropriate that financial institutions should be demand following where they are financing import substitution industrialisation. As Kenya's experience has demonstrated, whatever illusions occurred in the 1970s, industrial investment in this sector is validated by domestic demand. The lesson of the 1980s is that domestic demand expansion depends to a large extent on the export sector. Unfortunately, it is inherently more risky, so that scarce foreign exchange resources may need to be preferentially lent to export-oriented industries while effective rates of protection for domestically-oriented industry remain high. Nevertheless, financial caution in lending policies needs to be maintained.

In this paper we have seen examples of 'cautious' supply-leading by DFIs, as in Zimbabwe, and 'adventurous' or even 'rash' supply-leading, as in Kenya. In the one case the effect on the economy has been limited, in the other the effect on the DFI itself has been disastrous. The DFIs appear to be damned whatever they do. Unsustainable macro-economic policies, and the compulsions of structural adjustment drive home the lesson that there is no primrose path of economic growth and DFIs tend to compound the problem by creating their own internal debt crises. Ironically they are needed more than ever to finance efficient import substitution and export-oriented industries to offset the perceived political risk that deters foreign investors. Yet they remain weighed down by past mistakes.

NOTES

1. The senior author would like to acknowledge the support of the Leverhulme Trust through a project grant to Professors John Stopford and Susan Strange titled 'Partners in Production'. Views expressed in this paper are those of the authors alone. An earlier version was presented at the Development Studies Association Annual Conference, Belfast, in September 1989.
2. Of course, during the 1970s and early 1980s, many African countries pursued policies that seriously over-valued their currency which, in turn, sucked in imports until foreign exchange resources were exhausted and also discouraged exporting.
3. At a conference organised by the Confederation of British Industry in London in May 1989, to promote foreign investment in Zimbabwe.
4. It is a little surprising that profit and other capital and revenue items become sources of funds in the same twelve months that they accrue, but that is how the reports treat the figures.
5. A substantial source of funds item which is referred to in the accounts, but which receives no elaboration, is 'long term loans'. This was KSh 19.1m in 1981, KSh 69.3m in 1984 and KSh 22.7m in 1987. It is not apparent where this money

comes from, or on what terms it accrues. As this money does not appear in the main statement of sources of funds in the annual reports but is found obscurely tucked away elsewhere, it has not been listed in Table 15.5. This money is essential in making up the balance between receipts and payments.

6. Notwithstanding the substantial qualifications to the financial performance of the ICDC made in the published accounts and, in particular, whether repayments of principal and interest due on loans and dividends actually occurred, Barbara Grosch (July 1987, p. 10) makes the claim that the ICDC 'had average returns (on loans and equity) that were only slightly below the commercial bank lending rate in most years'. She arrives at this heroic conclusion by calculating the rate of return by adding interest and dividends receivable and dividing by loans plus equity investments.

REFERENCES

Bates, R. H., (1981) *Markets and States in Tropical Africa* (Berkeley: University of California Press).

Bhatia R. J., and D. R. Khatkhate, (1975) 'Financial Intermediation, Savings Mobilisation and Entrepeneurial Development: The African Experience', *IMF Staff Papers*, 22 132–58.

Gerschenkron, A., (1962) *Economic Backwardness in Historical Perspective* (Cambridge, Mass.: Harvard University Press).

Grosch, B., (1987) 'Performance of Development Finance Institutions in Kenya: 1964–84', Working Paper No. 450 (Nairobi: Institute for Development Studies, July).

Hyden, G., (1983) *No Shortcuts to Progress: African Development Management in Perspective* (London: Heinemann).

Industrial and Commercial Development Corporation of Kenya (1982, 1985, 1986 and 1987), *Annual Reports* (Nairobi: ICDC).

Industrial Development Corporation of Zimbabwe, 1980 and 1987, *Annual Reports* (Harare: IDC).

Kane, J. A., (1985) *Development Banking* (Lexington, Mass.: Heath).

Kenya Government (1965), *African Socialism and its Application to Planning in Kenya*, Sessional Paper 10 of 1965 (Nairobi: Government Printer).

Killick, T., (1979) *Development Economics in Action* (London: Heinemann).

Kitchen, R. L., (1986) *Finance of Developing Countries* (London and Cluchester: Wiley).

Kornai, J., (1980) *The Economics of Shortage* (Amsterdam: North Holland).

MacKinnon, R. I., (1973) *Money Banking and Economic Development* (Washington: The Brookings Institution).

Mosley, P., (1983) *The Settler Economies* (Cambridge: Cambridge University Press).

Patrick, H., (1986) 'Financial Development and Economic Growth in Underdeveloped Countries', *Economic Development and Cultural Change*, 14 174–87.

Zimbabwe Development Bank (1988) *Annual Report* (Harare: ZDB).

APPENDIX

TABLE 15.A1:   *Rate of Exchange for US Dollar in Kenya Shillings and Zimbabwe Dollars*

Year	K Sh	Z $
1979	7.33	0.674
1980	7.57	0.631
1981	10.29	0.717
1982	12.73	0.919
1983	13.80	1.105
1984	15.75	1.502
1985	16.25	1.641
1986	16.04	1.678
1987	16.52	1.663
1988	18.60	1.943

16 Credit as a Policy of Agricultural Development with Reference to its Operation in Jordan

Talib Younis

INTRODUCTION

The purpose of this paper is to discuss the problems of agricultural credit institutions in developing countries with specific reference to Jordanian institutions. A credit institution will often be set up by a government of the Third World to provide investment for the rural sector. This investment is seen as a means of promoting innovation and, therefore, efficiency in the agricultural sector. Through improved efficiency, it is also seen as a means of abating the poverty of farmers.

Easy credit, however, does not often lead to the desired end results, but instead to ever-increasing indebtedness of farmers: and examples of bankrupt institutions are common. For ease of reference, factors contributing to these results are divided into two categories: (i) those which are external to the credit agency, and (ii) those which are concerned with the practices of the agency itself. External problems which are discussed briefly include: (i) the use of land for urban development (often necessary as farm workers migrate to industrialised areas in search of work) as a contributing factor to reducing available land for agricultural use and, therefore, to reducing the incomes of farmers; (ii) problems of land fragmentation, which decreases efficiency of land use; (iii) wastage of pasture land by deforestation, soil erosion, etc; (iv) inefficient water distribution networks; (v) difficulties in supplying agricultural inputs; and (vi) deficiencies in supportive services, for example, poor market information or a lack of storage facilities. Internal problems are often unique to the agency or country involved. However, more general lessons may be learned from the identification of problems within a specific situation.

The example which will be used is that of Jordan, where three separate semi-governmental agencies exist to disburse credit to the agricultural sector; the Agricultural Credit Corporation (ACC), the Jordanian Co-operative Organisation (JCO) and the Jordan Valley Farmers Association

(JVFA). The existence of three agencies is quite unusual and with this arises unusual difficulties.

For the purpose of this paper only those areas which have been identified as being 'problem areas' shall be discussed, and we shall evaluate how far it is possible for the credit institutions to operate successfully against the external problems, and indeed whether credit is simply an easy option, i.e. to be seen to be doing something, rather than actually providing a solution.

EXTERNAL PROBLEMS

The use of land for urban development

One of the common problems of the Third World is that farmers and farm labourers have low incomes. This can ultimately force them to leave rural areas and move into the cities in search of employment in industry. This creates a greater demand for housing, and arable land is bought up for urban development. In addition, landowners may leave land fallow in pursuit of the high prices of real estate. This situation exists in Jordan and is demonstrated in Table 16.1. In 1975, the total area of land held for agricultural purposes was 3.904 thousand dunums; by 1983 this had been reduced to 3.642 thousand dunums.

Land fragmentation

As the amount of arable land decreases, the problem of land fragmentation is exacerbated. This can occur when a landowner dies and divides up his land amongst his successors; with each generation smaller portions of land are available to each farmer. In Jordan in 1975 the number of holdings of up to 100 dunums totalled 40 874; by 1983 this had increased to 49 036. Conversely, the number of holdings over 100 dunums was 9913 in 1975 and was reduced to 8402 by 1983.

The implication of this phenomenon is clear; in order to generate a higher income the farmer requires more land; the more land the farmer has, the better the ratio of income per dunum. The opposite is also true.

Wastage of pastureland

The problems of deforestation and soil erosion are perhaps the most common throughout the Third World. The results were all too apparent in the Sudan and Bangladesh last year. Flooding is one of the most serious effects and in Jordan in 1987 this presented a serious problem when the districts of Al-Shaa and Al-Karana were flooded. Farmers had to receive assistance from the government in order to survive.

TABLE 16.1 *The size of agricultural land holdings*

Size of holding (dunums)	Number of holdings in		Total area of land held (000)	
	1975	1983	1975	1983
Less than 5	8522	9050	16.04	23.72
5– 10	3825	5451	25.70	36.70
10– 20	6922	9655	92.20	128.70
20– 30	5337	6609	121.90	151.30
30– 40	4666	5743	150.80	185.90
40– 50	2968	3547	125.80	150.30
50– 100	8634	8981	570.80	592.10
100– 200	5479	4947	701.80	631.90
200– 500	3359	2610	933.80	727.10
500– 1000	719	569	452.10	355.60
1000– 2000	253	191	299.70	238.90
2000– 5000	84	65	220.50	181.00
5000–10000	10	13	58.90	75.00
10000–25000	9	4	133.80	60.80
More than 25000	0	3	0	103.50
TOTAL	50791	57436	3904.00	3642.00

SOURCE: 'The Size of Agricultural Land Holdings', Subhi Qasem in *Agricultural Policy in Jordan*, ed. Alison Burrell (London: Ithaca Press, 1986) p. 23.

Inefficient water distribution networks

At present up to 90 per cent of arable land in Jordan is dependent on rainfall (Al-Habab and Arabiat, 1988, p. 23). The Five Year Development Plan of Jordan identifies investment in the area of water resources as one where actual investment compares poorly with planned investment. In the period 1981–5 some 521 JD million was planned for irrigation whereas actual investment amounted only to 245 JD million. This has represented a pattern since 1973. (See Table 16.2.)

The implication of this for the farmer is clear; the amount of land required to generate an income of 2000 JD per year, where the land is cultivated with stone fruits, varies from 10 dunums where the land is irrigated, to 21 dunums where the farmer relies on rainfall (Qasem in Burrell, 1986, p. 27).

Difficulties in supplying agricultural inputs

Fertilisers, pesticides and veterinary medicaments are often imported from abroad. The problem is to disburse imports and domestically-produced inputs to those who require them in the right quantity and at the right time. Problems of distribution can, therefore, affect the ability of the farmer to

TABLE 16.2   *Planned and implemented expenditure for 1976–80 Plan and 1981–5 Plan*

	1976–80 Plan		1981–85 Plan	
Sector	Planned *mnJD*	Implemented *mnJD*	Planned *mnJD*	Implemented *mnJD*
Agriculture and co-operatives	40.1	51.7	234.5	182
Water and irrigation	97.4	73.8	521.7	245.5

SOURCES: 'Water Supply for the Agricultural Sector', Falid Salih Natur in *The Agricultural Sector of Jordan, Policy and Systems Studies*, ed. A. B. Zahlan (London: Ithaca Press, 1985), p. 252; Ministry of Planning, HK of Jordan (n.d.) *Five Year Plan for Economic and Social Development of Jordan* (Hashemite Kingdom of Jordan: National Press).

generate income. In Jordan, this problem has been lessened with development and growth in agribusiness firms and the efforts of the co-operative movement.

Deficiencies in supportive services

Supportive services are those which are necessary once the crop has been produced: marketing, distribution and storage.

Market information in Jordan is traditionally focussed on a 'one trader to another' basis. Alternatively, there is the Agricultural Marketing Organisation (AMO) which produces monthly plans to encourage import or export of certain goods at certain times. The farmer, however, is at the mercy of the world and traditional markets. The latter, which include the Gulf States, Syria and Iraq, have deteriorated in recent years as a result of home-grown produce and limited availability of hard cash due, to some extent, to the Iran/Iraq war. In some areas, because of the deterioration in markets, there is surplus production and there are insufficient storage facilities or processing plants for perishable goods. It is ultimately the farmer who suffers the effects.

DEFECTS IN THE CREDIT ORGANISATION

Co-ordination

The ACC, JCO and JVFA appear to have different areas of responsibility; the ACC concentrates on the building up of livestock reserves, the JCO on the provision of basic foodstuffs such as wheat and barley, and the JVFA on vegetable crops. The lines of responsibility are not, however, so clearly defined: for example, the JCO and ACC can both lend money for the purpose of purchasing machinery. This raises the possibility of the farmer receiving a loan for the same purpose from more than one source and making an insufficient increase in profit to allow him to make the necessary repayments.

Loan recipients

Those who receive loans and the manner in which loans are disbursed are other problem areas for the agencies in Jordan. The ACC lends to individual farmers; the JCO to co-operatives and the JVFA to farmers who are members of the association and co-operatives in the area. One of the problems of lending to the rural community is that it is an expensive sector to service; small transactions cost as much in administration as larger ones; high expenses lead to reduced available capital and this, combined with low interest rates, actually reduces accessibility to credit. The JCO advocates lending to co-operatives, hence reducing costs. However, the co-operatives then pay out to the individual, taking commission on the loan. The advantages of lending to small groups in terms of pressure from peers is lost to the ACC, JCO and the JVFA, since they either lend on an individual basis or lend to a large group.

Lending procedures

The processes which the farmer must go through in order to gain a loan are complicated, burdensome and expensive. At the first stage, required collateral is usually land and the amount of the loan will depend on the size of the holding. Lending to an innovative farmer on the basis of his expertise as opposed to his material possessions is the exception rather than the rule, and credit agencies are therefore caught in the same trap as other sources of credit such as banks or suppliers; they lend on a low risk basis.

The individual farmer approaching the ACC or JVFA to request a loan can expect to have to provide exhaustive information initially to officials at the local level. However, the higher the amount requested, the more officials and/or committees debate and consider its granting, since it is referred upwards through each of the organisations and must be approved at each level for referral to the next. This can be a deterrent to applying for a loan; the farmer experiences loss in terms of time and expenses and the bureaucratic machinery may not move quickly enough to grant the loan when it is needed.

Types of loan

Loans which are granted to farmers can be either seasonal, where the repayment period is approximately twelve months with the loan being used for operational expenses or seasonal inputs; medium term, where repayment is over two years or up to as long as ten years, and loans are used to purchase machinery or finance irrigation projects; and long-term, such as loans for the building of offices or storage facilities or, in some cases, of industrial plants which will aid the agricultural sector.

The ACC and JCO offer all types of loan, the JVFA only seasonal loans. In 1986, the proportion of loans was such that the ACC granted 50 per cent of its lending capital for intermediate loans, 25 per cent for seasonal loans and 25 per cent for long-term loans. The JCO used 64 per cent on seasonal loans and 36 per cent for intermediate loans (Arabiat, 1977, p. 22). Repayment rates are extremely low; in 1985 repayment to the ACC stood at 53 per cent, to the JCO at 13 per cent and to the JVFA at 15.7 per cent. By 1986, the JVFA could offer only JD32 000 (approximately £12 000) in seasonal loans (Arabiat, 1977, p. 25).

As Nimal Sanderatne states '[W]ithout productive investment, the short-term credit leads only to greater indebtedness to the lending agency' (1983, p. 187), one would question the wisdom of the JVFA and JCO concentrating on seasonal loans when the primary aim of extending such credit is to increase efficiency in the agricultural sector, thereby increasing the incomes of farmers. The different emphasis in lending on the part of the ACC must be considered to be a factor in its achieving a significantly higher repayment rate.

Savings and insurance

In terms of reducing default, it has been the experience of credit agencies that provision in terms of a savings scheme or loan insurance can be effective. Warren F. Lee argues that low financial savings rates in rural households is not so much an indication of an inability to save as a lack of deposit services which meet the needs of the rural sector (in Von Pischke, 1983, p. 107).

Savings schemes assist the farmer since they allow him to make provision for the fluctuations in his income which occur throughout the cycle of producing his crop. The JCO is the only one of the three institutions which operates such a scheme and the growth in deposits has made a major contribution to its working capital; an important factor if credit is to be accessible to all. Loan insurance schemes, whereby debts may be settled from a claim, thereby reducing the default rate, are not in evidence in any of the three agencies.

The above are indications of the types of problems which exist; whereas good practices are apparent (in such aspects as the careful monitoring of projects and payment by instalment on the basis of progress, easily accessible field agents to whom repayment can be made, stringent powers to seize property without recourse to the law courts in the case of the ACC and the JCO, encouragements to pay the loan on time by reducing the interest by 1 per cent and good levels of farmer representation on the various Boards of Directors of the agencies) repayment rates remain low (indicating that farmers' incomes are not sufficiently increased) and the efficiency of the agricultural sector is declining: its contribution to GDP was about 9 per cent for the years 1973–5, 8.6 per cent for the years 1976–80 and 7.9 per cent for the years 1981–5 (Five Year Plan, p. 532).

Having briefly examined the problems which affect the credit agencies and the performance of the agricultural sector as a whole, the question then arises whether those problems which are internal to the agency/ agencies, having been overcome, will lead to an improvement in efficiency and to securing reasonable incomes for farmers, in the face of problems over which the agency has no control.

CREDIT AS A SOLUTION

We began by stating what the general aims of a Third World government would be in establishing a credit agency to service the rural sector. These are: to provide investment to promote innovation and efficiency, and to reduce the poverty of farmers. There can be added other general aims, for example, ensuring food security in the nation.

However, the stating of general aims does not constitute a strategy for dealing with the problems of the agricultural sector in the Third World. It can be argued that the provision of cheap and accessible credit is a useful tool for development, but only where it forms part of an overall strategy to lead to improvement in the performance of the agricultural sector and, therefore, to the generation of income for farmers.

Howell and Bottrall state:

The precise role of credit in agricultural development is not always easy to determine. Even though credit has often been regarded by governments as a primary factor in promoting agricultural development, it is now more generally recognised that credit can only have an ancillary role following the establishment of some basis for new investment, probably new technical knowledge and possibly also a degree of structural change in rural society (in Howell, 1981, p. 5).

Howell and Adams go further:

The popularity of agricultural credit programmes is due, in part, to the ease with which most of them can be carried out. For the political leader it is easy to announce a new lending policy, or to establish a new credit agency, or to increase the amount of funds available for lending in response to some pressing problems in rural areas. Lending, particularly on concessionary terms, allows government to show an immediate concern for the problems of small farmers (in Howell, 1981, p. 2).

On the one hand, we see a view that credit is seen as the panacea for the problems of the agricultural sector due to some misplaced faith in what it can do, whilst, on the other hand, we see the view that governments, being fully aware of the limitations of credit as a policy for agricultural development, adopt it nonetheless so that it appears that they are addressing the problem without having to take any unpopular or radical action. Which of these is the case will obviously depend upon the politicians concerned.

If we return to the example of Jordan, which has been quoted throughout, it is clear that credit, as a response to the problems of agriculture, is inadequate. Most of the serious problems contributing to default lie out with the realm of the agencies: whilst greater co-ordination, group lending, simplification of procedures, the encouragement of productive investment and the provision of loan insurance and/or saving schemes would almost certainly lead to improvement in performance of the agency, these efforts are worthless if flooding occurs because of insufficient investment in forestation and dam-building; or if drought occurs because of insufficient investment in water reservations and networks; or if farmers must farm their small pieces of land on a subsistence basis; or if, quite simply, the farmer having borrowed and invested in new technology and having dramatically increased his productivity, finds it is difficult to sell his produce because of inadequate marketing arrangements.

The answers to these problems do not lie simply in providing credit to farmers; nor perhaps is it acceptable that such a burden should be placed on them. When we look to Jordan we see that numerous conferences of the Ministry of Agriculture and a mass of literature debate the impediments to development in the agriculture sector. (See reports of 1980, 1983, 1985 conferences under the auspices of this ministry.) However, there remains a significant absence of long-term planning for agriculture, water resources and land resources, and whereas time and again the recommendations begin with a statement of the necessity of research into existing resources, we note with disappointment that a proposal to establish a National Centre for Agricultural Research received only 55 per cent of planned expenditure during the period 1981–5. The Agricultural Marketing Organisation also still has to be further developed in order to usefully provide information to farmers on what they should be producing and in what quantity. Further, there is, at present, no single governmental agency responsible for the provision of water resources; no significant research has been done on what natural resources there are; and there is no indication as to the requirements of the agricultural, industrial or commercial sectors.

Research, planning and, most importantly, implementation of policy, as the areas in which problems lie, are matters which government need attend to. Resources and expertise having been made available in these areas, credit can play a useful role in the development of the agricultural sector; without such action, credit serves only to further burden those whom it should help.

REFERENCES

Al-Habab, S., and S. Arabiat, (1988) 'The Change in Agriculture in Jordan', paper prepared under the auspices of the Jordanian National Conference for Human Habitation.
Arabiat, S., (1977) 'The Role of Agriculture Credit Institutions and Commercial Banks in Financing Agricultural Projects in Jordan', working paper presented at the Conference 'Finance by Banks of Agricultural Projects in the Arab World', Khartoum, Sudan, 15–17 December.
Burrell, A., (1986) (ed.), *Agricultural Policy in Jordan* (London: Ithaca Press).
Howell, J., (1981) (ed.), *Borrowers and Lenders* (Leeds: Bonnby, Hollingworth and Moss).
Von Pischke, J. D., (1983) (ed.), *Rural Financial Markets in Developing Countries*, EDI Series in Economic Development (Maryland: John Hopkins University Press).
Planning, Ministry of, HK of Jordan (n.d.) *Five Year Plan for Economic and Social Development of Jordan* (Hashemite Kingdom of Jordan: National Press).

17 The International Transfer of Institutional Innovations: Replicating the Grameen Bank in Other Countries

David Hulme

INTRODUCTION

The Grameen Bank of Bangladesh has been the most widely acclaimed development 'success story' of the 1980s. It has grown from a micro-project into the country's fourth largest bank by providing poverty-alleviating loans to a clientele conventionally regarded as 'unbankable'. Such experiences are rare, and in consequence the Grameen Bank has been seized upon as a potential model for transfer and replication. It has received high level official delegations from China, Nepal, Malaysia, the Philippines, Indonesia, Sri Lanka, the Solomon Islands and other countries; has been subjected to detailed studies by several bilateral and multilateral aid agencies; and has been the basis for scores of study tours from non-governmental organisations (NGOs). Many visitors, some of ministerial status, have subsequently announced that the Grameen Bank should be replicated in their own countries.

However, the experience of earlier attempts to transfer high-performing institutions between nations suggests that this should be approached with some caution. The admirable results achieved by the Etawah project in India were not reproduced when it was used as the model for the Indian Community Development Programme and similar programmes in sixty other countries (Holdcroft, 1982). Likewise, the much-acclaimed Comilla project provided the 'paradigm' (Robertson, 1984, p. 55) for a spate of donor-funded integrated rural development projects (IRDPs), many of which subsequently achieved very disappointing results (Crener *et al.*, 1983).

Opinions about the feasibility of using the Grameen Bank as a model for institutional development differ markedly. For analytical purposes it is useful to categorise these opinions as falling into one of four possible propositions.

(1) Replicate the Grameen Bank on a large-scale basis through a public sector agency (as was attempted with the Etawah and Comilla models). To date, this position has only been publicly proposed by a small number of politicians seeking to gain popularity through rhetoric.

(2) Use the Grameen Bank as the initial model for a small scale action research project that can be gradually modified to suit different socio-economic and physical environments. When, and if, this research project can be shown to be achieving its goals it should be institutionalised and its operations expanded by organic growth. This is the strategy favoured by the Bank's founder (Yunus, 1986), by the directors of a Malaysian replica (Gibbons and Sukor, 1989), some international NGOs (Redd Barna, 1988) and the International Fund for Agricultural Development (IFAD). Those taking this position usually emphasise that the key to success is not simply replicating Grameen Bank structures and procedures, rather it is adopting the 'approach' or 'philosophy' of the Bank – a commitment to the poor and an orientation to learning from experience.

(3) The Grameen Bank is not directly replicable in other countries, but certain of its structures, procedures and policies are transferable and could improve the performance of institutions in other countries. These include the organisation of borrowers into cells and centres, basing operations close to the borrowers' residence, concentrating on off-farm investment, increasing the intensity of loan supervision, having interest rates that are close to market rates, concentrating on female borrowers, and using loan insurance schemes (Fuglesang and Chandler, 1986; Hossain, 1988; Mosley and Dahal, 1987).

(4) The Grameen Bank is an interesting case but little can be learned from it and it is not a suitable model for use in other countries. This position has been taken by central bankers and bankers in government-controlled banks interviewed in Sri Lanka, Indonesia and Malaysia. The grounds cited for non-transferability include: (a) a belief that unique features of Bangladesh's social and economic environment determine Bank performance; (b) that the Bank is totally dependent on the charisma and contacts of Professor Yunus and he cannot be 'replicated'; (c) the high degree of subsidy that underpins Grameen Bank field operations.

In this paper the validity of these contrasting propositions is examined. The first section briefly describes the methods and achievements of the Bank to give the reader an idea of its main features and substantiate claims that it has been successful. (For a fuller description see Hulme and Turner, 1990, pp. 207–15). Following this, three recent attempts to use the Grameen Bank as an institutional model are compared. The conclusion analyses the ways in which the notion of institutional replication appears to have been modified in recent times and comments on the promises and pitfalls faced by those trying to transplant the Grameen Bank to new soils.

THE GRAMEEN BANK

Background

The Grameen Bank started out as a small action-research project in the village of Jobra, Chittagong District. It is the idea of Muhammad Yunus, a professor of economics at Chittagong University, who believed that the poor could be reliable borrowers and could make wise investment choices. The project sought to provide small loans (£20 to £40) for low-income households with no access to formal sources of credit for self-selected micro-enterprises that would raise household incomes and create employment. The Bank charges an interest rate of 16 per cent per annum, which is closer to commercial rates than the heavily-subsidised government rural credit schemes. (If compulsory contributions to the 'Group Fund' are included in interest rate calculations then the effective rate is around 22 per cent.)

By 1979 the experiment had identified what was believed to be a viable model for credit delivery and the project was expanded with loans from the Bangladesh Bank and later from the International Fund for Agricultural Development (US \$3.4 million in 1980 and US \$23.6 million in 1984). Currently the Grameen Bank has loans totalling US \$105 million from a number of aid donors. Sweden and Norway are the largest contributors and each has advanced around US \$30 million. Since 1983 the Grameen Bank has had the formal status of a 'specialised credit institution'. After considerable negotiation with the Government of Bangladesh (GOB), members now control 75 per cent of the issued shares and the GOB 25 per cent.

By February 1990 the Bank was running 677 branches and had 694 067 members organised into 28 156 borrower 'centres'. Total loans disbursed per annum have risen from less than Tk 1 million (£1 = 53.40 taka in January 1990) in the early years, to Tk 542 million in 1986 (Hossain, 1988) and are likely to exceed Tk 1750 million in 1989. Although the bulk of loans are made in rural areas it should be noted that only 45 per cent of total loans extended have been used for agriculture, livestock, forestry and fish farming.

Structure and procedures

The Grameen Bank evolved out of an explicit action-research project in which Professor Yunus experimented with organisational structures and procedures to overcome the challenge of lending to the poor. Trial and error led to the favouring of a 'group within group' structure of cells of five members and centres of thirty members; groups organised on the basis of proximity rather than loan use; and a concentration on female borrowers, who are currently around 87 per cent of Bank membership.

A summary of some of the major characteristics of the Grameen Bank is provided in Table 17.1. The Bank's main activity is to provide small loans to individuals for investment purposes. For a loan to be sanctioned the individual concerned must persuade her/his fellow 'cell' members that s/he has a good proposal and intends to repay the Bank as, if one member of a cell defaults, no other member of that cell can get a loan until the default is cleared. This relatively simple device has aided the Grameen Bank in overcoming the problems of 'imperfect information' that other lenders have faced and creates a set of social pressures and supports that serve as an incentive to repayment. The centre, ideally comprising of six cells, meets at a regular time every week at a centre meeting house to which a Bank fieldworker has come. The meeting involves flag-raising, songs and physical exercises before members discuss business in hand and undertake their banking transactions in the open. Each cell and the centre itself are led by elected chairpersons who have to step down after one year of service. Some centres have established larger-scale group enterprises, but many of these have faced problems because of a lack of technical and managerial expertise, and the Bank has scaled down its lending for such activities, except for fish farming and deep tube wells (DTWs).

In the last few years the Bank has extended its activities into making larger, low-interest, long-term loans (Tk 7000 to 12 000) in a UNDP-funded Rural Housing Programme (Islam et al., 1989) and into the 'direct management' of 700 DTWs and a large fisheries project. It is too early for detailed results of these programmes to be available but it must be noted that they present the Bank and its members with a different set of problems to overcome.

Performance

Hossain (1988) has produced a detailed analysis of the economic results achieved by the Grameen Bank. In summary these are as follows:

(1) The Bank is successful in terms of lending on an increasing scale to households which meet its criteria. Only 4.2 per cent of investment loans go to borrowers with more than 0.5 acres of cultivable land. (However, there is cause for concern that agricultural labouring households are poorly represented in the borrower population.

They comprise more than 60 per cent of the Bank's target group, but provide only around 20 per cent of the membership.)

(2) The incomes of a sample of Grameen Bank members were 43 per cent higher than that of comparable groups in non-Grameen Bank villages and 28 per cent higher than non-Grameen Bank members in the same villages.

(3) The Bank has an outstanding repayment rate record. Out of 975 loans surveyed only 0.5 per cent were overdue beyond one year and only 3.3 per cent had an overdue weekly premium.

(4) The Bank has declared an annual profit on its overall operations since 1984. However, the administrative costs are very high and are cross-subsidised by interest rate earnings from depositing concessionary loans with other banks. The implicit rate of subsidy on loan operations is around 39 per cent.

In addition to its economic achievements the Bank also argues that its mobilisation and organisational activities 'empower' the poor. The qualitative nature of 'empowerment' makes it difficult to measure the achievement of this objective. Although there is some limited evidence that some Grameen Bank groups have extended their activities into labour markets, and also that they have made demands that the legal system should operate properly and not be abused (Fuglesang and Chandler, 1986), detailed accounts are not available. Indeed, it should be noted that there are potential contradictions between notions of empowerment and an institutional approach that has been determined by the 'non-poor', and which focuses on individual enterprise rather than group activities.

While some external observers have analysed Bank performance in terms of specific policy decisions (Mosley and Dahal, 1987), Yunus and his staff argue that it is the overall approach that is the principal explanatory variable. This 'approach' is closely akin to Korten's (1980) learning process. Procedures and structures evolve from small-scale experiments designed by Bank personnel who have access to continuous feedback from intended beneficiaries. The Bank is highly disdainful of conventional technical assistance, which emphasises the expertise of outside specialists. Staff commitment is fostered by careful staff selection, extended in-the-field induction training and performance-related promotion. The membership is subjected to a rigid discipline (in terms of a set of obligations laid down by the Bank but largely 'policed' by members), but also enjoys active involvement in a range of important decisions (who chairs the group, who gets loans, what loans are used for). There is a great emphasis on the training of staff and members. Potential borrowers undergo a seven-to fifteen-day induction course and are tested on their knowledge of Bank rules, procedures and principles. Both field staff and centre representatives

TABLE 17.1 *A comparison of selected characteristics of the Grameen Bank and three schemes that have used it as a model*

	Grameen Bank	Amanah Ikhtiar Malaysia (AIM)	Savecred	Malawi Mudzi Fund (MMF)
GENERAL				
Country	Bangladesh	Malaysia	Sri Lanka	Malawi
Date of commencement	August 1976	September 1987 (based on an experiment from late 1986)	June 1988	December 1988
Was it modelled on the Grameen Bank?		Yes – staff have studied the G.B. and project documents state it is to replicate G.B. AIM uses GB staff as consultants	Yes – 18 Red Barna (SL) staff visited GB before plans drawn up. Director of SAVECRED studied GB for 6 months	Yes – IFAD states that this is an experimental pilot project to test if GB can be replicated, MMF staff to visit GB.
Who designed the scheme?	Prof.Md. Yunus	Prof. Dr Gibbons and Prof. Sukor Kasim of Sains Universiti, Penang, Malaysia	Resident Representative and staff of Redd Barna (SL)	Consultant to IFAD
Relationship of designer(s) to scheme manager(s)	Designer is Managing Director	Designers are Managing Director and Director of Loans Division	Designers are Chairman of Board and Co-ordinators	Designer prepared profile and job specification for recruitment of manager
Location of Operations	5 of Bangladeshi's 21 districts	Northwest Selangor-State	9 small areas	Southern Region
STRUCTURAL FEATURES				
Institutional status	PVO experiment now a formal Specialised Credit Institution	Non-profit, Registered- Trust	Programme operated by a charitable NGO	To be determined-not to be run by a ministry or parastatal

	Board (75% member reps and 25% GOB reps)	Board, (Selangor state Gov't, YPEIM Univ Sains and others)	Board (5 Redd Barna staff appt'd by RB Resident Rep.)	Committee of GOM ministry/agency reps – app't by GOM
Controlling Board				
Responsibility for day-to-day operations	Managing Director (Founder)	Managing Director (Founder)	Resident Rep. (Initiator)	Scheme Administrator (Appt'd)
Major source of capital	IFAD	YPEIM (Islamic Development Foundation)	Redd Barna (from donations from Norway)	IFAD
Do members have to form groups/planned size?	Yes/30	Yes/30	Yes/30	Yes/30
Do groups have to form cells/planned size?	Yes/5	Yes/5	Yes/5	Yes/5
Is membership restricted to the poor?	Yes	Yes	Yes	Yes; To be determined by Scheme Administrator – the landless and near-landless
Criteria for loan eligibility	Landholding of less than 0.4 acres of cultivable land	Monthly income of less than M$250 (per family) or M$50 (per person)	Landless families with 3 or more children/dependents with income of less than RS1000 p.m. Smallholder families whose net income from Land is less than RS500 p.m.	
Will member groups be single sex?	Yes	Yes	Yes	To be determined
Are loans to women to be favoured?	Yes	Yes	Yes	Not known

PROCEDURAL FEATURES

Interest rate (for loans)	16%	No – a management fee of M$75 per loan	Not known-policy states scheme must cover costs-that suggests 20 to 25% p.a.	15% (or more) p.a.
Loans made to	Individuals	Individuals	Individuals	Individuals
Are group pressures used to assist with repayment?	Yes – other cell members cannot borrow if a default occurs	Yes – other cell members cannot borrow if a default occurs	Yes – other cell members cannot borrow if a default occurs	To be determined
Maximum loan size	TK5000	Yes	RS5000	Yes – To be determined
Average loan size	TK3040 (1985)	M$ 1130 (1988)	N/A	MK200 (1988 planned)
Repayment frequency	Weekly	Weekly	Weekly	Weekly
Length of loan	52 Weeks	50 Weeks	52 Weeks	52 Weeks
Loan use	Any income generating	Any income generating	Any income generating	Any income generating
Loan must be invested within	14 days	7 days	14 days	To be determined
Loan supervision	By cell and centre	By cell and centre	By cell and centre	To be determined
Compulsory savings in Group Fund	Yes, TK1 per week	Yes	Yes, RS3 per week	To be determined
Emergency/Risk Insurance Fund	Yes	No	Yes	Yes
Where are transactions conducted?	At centre (i.e. in village)	At centre (i.e. in village)	At centre (i.e. in village)	To be determined

Transaction procedure	Open	Open	Open	
Do members have to undergo initial training?	Yes, 7 to 14 days	Yes, 7 to 14 days	Yes, 7 days	To be determined
Are members tested on their knowledge of procedures before admission?	Yes	Yes	Yes	To be determined
Use of procedures to foster member commitment	Yes – flag, salute, songs, exercises	Yes – pledge, religious identity	Yes – special greeting, 1 minute meditation or prayer, reading of SCF guidelines	Nothing stated in plans – to be determined
Rotation of cell & centre leaders	Yes, annually	Yes, annually	Yes, annually	To be determined
OTHER FEATURES Empowerment of the poor as an objective	Yes	Yes	Yes	No statement
Use of Government extension/support services	No	Yes	No	Yes

SOURCES: Asia and Pacific Development Centre, 1988; Fuglesang and Chandler, 1986; Hossain, 1988; Redd Barna, 1988; Sukor, 1989; World Bank, 1987; and, field interviews

are regularly 'rotated' to minimise opportunities for oligarchic practices.

Does the Grameen Bank experience provide a model suitable for transfer to other countries?

TRANSFERRING THE GRAMEEN BANK TO OTHER COUNTRIES

Research for this paper has identified seventeen attempts to use the Grameen Bank as a model for transfer to twelve countries. As far as can be determined, all of these 'replications' are grounded in the proposition that the Grameen Bank should be taken as the basis for a small-scale experimental project which is closely monitored and modified during implementation. In the following pages three of these attempts are reviewed in some detail. This reveals that while they have many common features (Table 17.1), each also has distinctive characteristics.

AMANAH IKHTIAR MALAYSIA (AIM)

AIM has its origins in Project Ikhtiar, an action-research project which sought to alleviate poverty in Northwest Selangor by providing loans, the first of which were disbursed in December 1986. This project lent M$422 000 (£1 = M$4.59 in January 1990) to its 448 members up to June 1988 when it was closed down, having been judged to be successful. Amanah Ikhtiar Malaysia (AIM) was established in September 1987 to institutionalise the Project Ikhtiar experiment.

By September 1989 AIM had six branches which had disbursed M$388 044 to 762 members. It was operating in Kedah and Pulau Pinang as well as Selangor. At the time of writing it was intended to open a further nineteen branches by the end of 1990 which should be able to provide loans to 50 000 households by the mid-1990s.

The schemes operated by Ikhtiar have been very closely modelled on the Grameen Bank (Table 17.1). However, some modifications were made at the outset of Project Ikhtiar 'to adapt [the] Grameen Bank to the Malaysian context' (APDC, 1988, p. 11). The Project and AIM have utilised capital made available by the Islamic Economic Development Foundation of Malaysia (YPEIM) and, in deference to Islamic values, a fixed management fee is levied, rather than interest. This decision is not merely a token gesture to religious sentiment, as AIM has identified its major loan programme, *Ikhtiar Al Qardhul Hassan*, with Islamic principles. The YPEIM funds are derived mainly from voluntary donations from salaried Muslims, and the scheme emphasises the spiritual obligation of borrowers to repay loans. A religious identity is thus used as an additional factor helping to ensure commitment to AIM. Also, and in contrast to the

Grameen Bank, AIM does not emphasise the exploitative nature of the linkages between rich and poor. Rather, it has a conciliatory stance and stresses that the rich have an obligation to help the poor. The main reason for this appears to be the analysis of AIM's designers that poverty-alleviation is possible in rural Malaysia without prior socio-political structural change.

Other early modifications to Grameen Bank practice include the decision not to utilise salutes and physical exercises during meetings; and a much more intensive and coordinated use of Malaysian government support services (particularly agricultural and technical extension) and administrative infrastructure (Gibbons and Sukor, 1989). The scheme's designers believe that changes to Grameen Bank practice should be made with great care, as they encountered severe problems with the modifications they attempted. For example, the introduction of 'emergency loans' in Project Ikhtiar was associated with severe repayment problems as some members took out loans that they could not service (for other examples see, ibid., 1989, pp. 19–40).

Overall, this experiment has produced favourable results, although some of the early Project Ikhtiar loans did not run smoothly and their repayment rate was only 77.4 per cent. Lessons from this experience (particularly that of concentrating on female borrowers) were rapidly learned and the repayment rate for loans advanced by AIM was running at 99.86 per cent in November 1988 (Sukor, 1989, p. 18). In addition AIM members had collected group funds of M$38 700, much of which was being lent out to cell members without charge.

An 'in-house' impact study of a sample of 178 of AIM's borrowers found that some 70 per cent of the group had experienced a positive change in their income as a result of the Ikhtiar loan (Table 17.2). The study found that average household income for this sample had risen by M$78. Significantly, loans to female borrowers are associated with a much greater impact on household incomes than loans to male borrowers (Table 17.2).

In terms of financial viability AIM acknowledges that the establishment of new branches will require external support, which has been provided by the state government of Selangor in its start-up phase. However, the AIM management calculate that after five years of decreasing subsidy branches should be financially viable by charging a management fee of M$75 per loan (AIM 1989). This would represent an implicit annual interest rate of 13.3 per cent for an average size loan. They believe that outside support during the establishment phase is readily available for institutions that alleviate poverty and need not compromise plans for becoming self-financing.

These results have impressed the Malaysian government, which is now studying whether the AIM approach should be supported under the Sixth Five Year Plan or adopted by state-owned banks.

TABLE 17.2　*Net increase in monthly household income as a result of Ikhtiar loans (by gender of borrower), December 1986 to August 1988*

	Female borrowers		Male borrowers		Female and male borrowers	
	%	Average Change (M$ per month)	%	Average Change (M$ per month)	%	Average Change (M$ per month)
Loan had a positive impact on household income (n = 125)	84	$136	65	$65	70	$119
Loan had a negative/no impact on household income (n = 53)	16	–$1	35	–$21	30	–$20
TOTAL/AVERAGE	100	$113	100	$63	100	$78

SOURCE: Gibbons and Sukor, 1989, p. 10.

SAVECRED (Sri Lanka)

The SAVECRED scheme, operated by Redd Barna (the Norwegian branch of the Save the Children Fund) is an action-research project attempting to establish a credit programme for the poor in Sri Lanka. The scheme started operations in mid-1988 in areas where Redd Barna has been working for many years. It is closely modelled on Grameen Bank structures and procedures. SAVECRED utilises the same single gender, cell and centre structures, has criteria that make membership exclusive to the poor, explicitly favours lending to women, uses group pressures to foster high recovery rates, collects loan repayment instalments on a weekly basis over one year, permits borrowers to determine loan utilisation, has a compulsory savings scheme and emergency insurance fund, requires all prospective members to undergo training and oral testing and has all financial transactions occur in the open at weekly meetings (Table 17.1). Less tangibly, but just as importantly, the scheme attempts to foster the spirit of the Grameen Bank, especially in terms of discipline, group solidarity and participation.

There is a major difference, however, in that the Redd Barna experiment does not seek to create a distinct financial institution. Instead, it is intended to establish an economically viable credit scheme alongside other Redd Barna activities. As a result of this SAVECRED meetings are directly linked to 'non-credit' activities and after financial business has been transacted SAVECRED members form a 'Development Circle' which discusses broader community development initiatives, particularly the maintenance of Redd Barna-supported pre-schools.

The close similarity of the features of the SAVECRED scheme to the Grameen Bank is surprising as the Sri Lankan experiment has been guided by Andreas Fuglesang and Dale Chandler who reviewed the Bank for the Norwegian Ministry of Development Corporation (NORAD) in 1986. In their study they explicitly warned of the dangers of attempting to replicate the Grameen Bank in other cultures and contexts, and argued that the preferred approach was to take specific lessons from the Grameen Bank as appropriate. This appears to have been the original intention in Sri Lanka when the decision was taken to redesign Redd Barna's poor-performing credit programmes. The initial stage of redesign involved seven Redd Barna staff undertaking a study-tour of the Grameen Bank. Subsequently, a group of five senior staff produced a detailed proposal for the SAVECRED scheme. In April 1988 eleven Redd Barna staff studied specific features of the field level activities of the Grameen Bank. Parallel with this a consultant prepared a report on the lessons that could be learned from two of Redd Barna's more successful credit projects. In May 1988 a conference was convened which finalised the details of the SAVECRED scheme. In the event, the modifications that have been made to make the Bank's approach suit 'Sri Lankan cultural conditions' are minimal. The scheme has been launched with the dissemination of a detailed operations manual (Redd Barna, 1988) and the training of seventy-five staff. While the manual notes that 'individual rules cannot be easily changed without disrupting the coherence of the whole' pressures for change will arise from 'essential' action research directed by the Colombo Office (ibid, p. 8–10). The initial SAVECRED scheme, although planned in great detail, is seen as 'the first step or two. The rest of our way is a matter of trial and error, of learning from our experience and modifying the direction of our work accordingly' (ibid). By mid-1989 nineteen centres had been established with a total of 491 members. Total loan disbursement had reached Rs 250 000 (£1 = Rs 67.85 in January 1990) and the repayment rate was reported as 100 per cent (personal communication, R. P. Wijewardene and Henk Hendriks).

Malawi Mudzi Fund (MMF)

This scheme has only recently been established and many of its details are not yet finalised. However, given that the project is to 'operate on the lines of the Grameen Bank', it is likely that the MMF will be closely modelled on Grameen Bank structures and procedures. The International Fund for

Agricultural Development (IFAD), which is financing MMF, sees it as a pilot project to test the possibility of replicating the Grameen Bank in other countries (World Bank, 1987). In consequence, the MMF is targeting small loans, up to 200 Kwacha (£1 = 4.40 Kwacha in January 1990) on landless and near-landless households in a densely-populated rural region of Southern Malawi. It does not require collateral, but borrowers must join cells of five which aggregate into centres of thirty members. Loans are to be repaid on a weekly basis over one year and their use is determined by the borrower and screened by cell members.

The major difference between this project and the Grameen Bank (and also AIM and SAVECRED) is that it is government-initiated and will not enjoy the independence and autonomy that characterised the Grameen Bank's early years (and now characterises the AIM and SAVECRED experiments). It is under the control of the Office of the President and Cabinet, and is supervised by a committee of civil servants from 'interested agencies'. This latter committee does not have the day-to-day field level experience that has been the hallmark of those taking decisions about the Grameen Bank's evolution (and indeed, those now guiding AIM and SAVECRED). The capacity of the project to redesign itself in the light of experience will not only be determined by the quality of the project manager (who is appointed rather than being self-selected) but also by the activities of an influential but remote body of interested agencies. Whilst, in theory, a supervisory committee can provide useful advice and support for a pilot project, the arbitrary and/or self-interested decisions and morale-sapping influences of such inter-departmental committees should not be underestimated.

Another difference is that the MMF has had to adopt a time-bound frame of reference related to the achievement of short-term output objectives. The requirements of multilateral lending are such that, even for an innovative donor like IFAD, the MMF has to have a 'two-phase' seven-year timetable with predefined targets for the establishment of branches, the number of borrowers and the average size of loans. This creates pressures to spend and achieve short-term output rates which can affect the quality of lending, especially in relation to repayment rates and targeting. Added to these funding-related problems is the fact that, as multilateral agencies find it necessary to make loans and grants in relatively large-scale packages, the MMF is a minor sub-project (US $0.95 million) of a much larger loan (US $14.4 million), and so there are doubts about the attention and priority that the MMF will receive from the Government of Malawi and multilateral agency staff.

Finally, MMF has to test whether the Malawian context is fundamentally different from that of Bangladesh (and Malaysia and Sri Lanka). Can a Grameen Bank-type institution operate in areas with lower population densities, where the rural economy has a different structure, and where effective low-paid clerical and administrative staff are more difficult to recruit?

FROM 'INSTITUTION BUILDING' TO 'INSTITUTION BREEDING'

It is too early to make any firm pronouncement on the degree of success achieved by recent attempts to replicate the Grameen Bank. However, both the AIM and SAVECRED schemes provide evidence that the Grameen Bank may be transferable. Further support for this comes from the recent experiments of Accion Comunitaria del Peru (ACP) and El Instituto de Desarrollo del Sector Informal (IDESI), both in Peru which have attained 98 per cent rates of repayment in credit programmes operated along Grameen Bank lines (Thomas, 1990). A number of important points, relating to the four propositions in the Introduction, emerge from these experiments.

A 'learning process approach'

Whilst theories of institutional replication and transfer are almost non-existent, the evidence gathered from AIM, SAVECRED and MMF indicates that there has been a fundamental shift in the metaphor that informs the practice of replication and transfer. In contrast to the notion of using successful experiences as blueprints for establishing new institutions on a large-scale in other countries that was evident in the 1960s, the three cases examined here have been informed by what Korten (1980) has termed a 'learning process approach'. This is underpinned by a biological analogy. In essence a good, foreign seed stock (a high-performance institution from another country) is used in a small-scale experiment in a new environment. The results of this experiment are closely monitored and the original stock is modified until an environmentally-suited stock is produced. This 'new variety' is then gradually disseminated and the new institution extends through organic growth.

Such an approach contrasts markedly with the attempts to replicate the Comilla and Etawah projects by creating large-scale bureaucracies to promote an untested, foreign blueprint. This second generation of institutional transfer recognises the inherently experimental nature of transfer and sees transfer as a long-term activity for which success is not guaranteed. Such transfers are aided by economic and social analysis, but ultimately the experimental institution's ability to learn from field experience is the critical factor in determining success or failure. While many factors influence this change in approach to institutional transfer, the fact that NGOs and non-official aid agencies are now prime movers in the activity is of great significance.

Refutation of the 'unique situation' theory

The proposition that the performance of the Grameen Bank is dependent on unique features of Bangladesh's socio-economic environment or the personality and charisma of its founder, and therefore that it is not a suitable model for transfer, appears refuted. The way in which AIM has identified itself with Islamic principles, and in this way fostered member and staff commitment to the organisation, illustrates that there are a variety of mechanisms by which commitment can be fostered in addition to the personality of the leader. David Gibbons, the managing director of AIM, argues that the personality factor has been overemphasised and that the nature of field level operations in Grameen Bank-type initiatives, exposing staff to the plight of the poor, builds up the dedication of project staff.

High repayment rate, low running costs

Much of the Grameen Bank's performance relates to its ability to reduce the costs incurred by itself as a lending agency (in comparison with other lenders) and to provide loans to borrowers at rates that they find attractive. The former property has been achieved largely by having high repayment rate (Mosley and Dahal, 1987). This is closely associated with the 'group within group' structure which overcomes problems of information and creates an incentive system that fosters repayment. The experiments in Malaysia, Sri Lanka and Peru (Thomas, 1988) indicate that this relatively simple device may have a high degree of transferability. This device also permits agencies to keep costs down as it permits field officers to handle relatively high account loads, up to 300 per loan agent.

The latter property, acceptable costs to borrowers, is determined not so much by interest rates (as the Grameen Bank charges higher rates than government schemes) but by keeping down the transaction costs that borrowers incur. This is done by having all transactions close to the residence (so that travel and food costs and wages foregone are kept to a minimum), timing them so they do not disrupt work schedules, and by operating a service that does not require the payment of unofficial bribes or commissions. (Field researchers report that in Bangladesh, as in other countries, many government-delivered loans entail the payment of a 'fee' of around 10 per cent to the field agent.) The transferability of these features may be more problematic. In particular, in areas with more dispersed rural populations the average distance of meeting sites from borrower residences is likely to be much greater. In addition, where schemes are government-initiated it may be less easy to foster the level of commitment that favours the elimination of unofficial 'fees'.

The role of subsidy

During the initial phase of experimentation, and the subsequent stages of branch creation, it is evident that poverty-focused credit agencies will require subsidy. Scheme designers must recognise this and identify sources of concessionary finance to fund institutional development. However, such support needs to be treated with caution and branch-level operations should be designed so that once they are running at a steady level they should be able to cover the running costs and a proportion of the costs of services provided by higher levels of the organisation. If this objective is not achieved then the expansion of a successful experiment can only be achieved by a corresponding expansion of concessionary finance. The Grameen Bank still has to face this issue of whether it should continue to expand its network by relying on cross-subsidising its field operations with earnings from donor-provided concessionary finance, or whether it should modify its programmes, along the lines identified by Hossain (1988).

The role of official agencies

The procedures and policies of official aid agencies mean that they encounter greater difficulty in running pilot replication programmes than indigenous non-government organisations (such as AIM) and international non-government organisations (such as Redd Barna). The need to make budget estimates for several years ahead, to absorb planned disbursements, to meet targets for branch establishment and to receive supervision from committees composed of public servants from 'interested agencies' are not conducive to experimentation and learning from mistakes. The peripatetic expatriate management common to official aid agency programmes make the institutionalisation of experimental results less likely. The Grameen Bank has already come into conflict with aid agencies requesting that it provide 'experts' to plan schemes in other countries. Instead, it argues that those who will run the schemes should come to study the Grameen Bank and subsequently implement their own 'learning' rather than an external consultant's 'knowledge'.

Interestingly, in Asia there appears to be no lack of non-governmental agencies and individuals coming forward to attempt to establish Grameen Bank-type institutions. By contrast, in Africa there appears to be a relative dearth of NGOs and individuals able or willing to launch such action-research projects. In consequence, a greater reliance on official development agencies (international and domestic) to initiate pilot projects seems likely to continue.

CONCLUSION

The Grameen Bank has already had a significant impact in alleviating poverty in some parts of Bangladesh. Its main contribution to development, however, may not be what it achieves in Bangladesh but whether it can diffuse to other countries and can promote the development of a more effective model for transferring knowledge generated from successful experiences in one context to other situations.[2] The three cases reviewed in this article, illustrating the concept of 'breed your own institution from good foreign stock', provide some grounds for cautious optimism.

NOTES

I should like to acknowledge the financial support of the Nuffield Foundation for research related to this article; and acknowledge the assistance of valuable comments on an earlier draft from John Farrington, David Gibbons, Syed Hashemi, Henk Hendriks, Paul Mosley, Jim Thomas and R. P. Wijewardene. Thanks also to Muhammad Yunus and Mazammel Huq of the Grameen Bank for providing information and advice.

1. These are the Native Self Employment Program (Canada), CONTIGO (Chile), Karya Usaha Mandiri (Indonesia), Mudzi Fund (Malawi), Amanah Ikhtiar Malaysia (Malaysia), Projekct Usahamaju (Malaysia), Women's Development Unit Credit Programme (Nepal), Waste to Wealth (Nigeria), GTZ Rural Development Programme (Pakistan), Accion Comunitaria del Peru (Peru), El Instituto de Desarrollo del Sector Informal (Peru); Projec Dungganon (Philippines), Ahon Sa Hirap (Philippines), Center for Agricultural and Rural Development (Philippines), SAVECRED (Sri Lanka), Good Faith Fund (USA) and Full Circle Fund (USA).

2. In addition, the Bank has a profound impact within Bangladesh on the credit activities of NGOs, such as Action Aid, Bangladesh Rural Advancement Committee (BRAC) and Proshika, and official programmes, such as DANIDA's (Denmark) Rural Poor Programme.

REFERENCES

Amanah Ikhtiar Malaysia 'Reference materials' (1989). Memos available at AIM, Sabak Bernam, Malaysia.

Asia and Pacific Development Centre (1988) 'Study Tour: Grameen Bank and Project Ikhtiar', *APDC Newsletter* 8–11.

Crener, M. A., G. Leal, R. Le Blanc, and B. Thebaud, (1983) *Integrated Rural Development: State of the Art Review 1982–3* (Quebec: Canadian International Development Agency).

Fuglesang, A., and D. Chandler, (1986) *Participation as Process: What we can learn from the Grameen Bank, Bangladesh* (Oslo: Norwegian Ministry of Development Cooperation).

Gibbons, D. S., and M. Sukor Kasim, (1989) *Reducing Extreme Rural Poverty Through Benevolent Loans* (Penang: Center for Policy Research, University Sains Malaysia, 1989).

Holdcroft, L. E., (1982) 'The Rise and Fall of Community Development in Developing Countries, 1950–1965: a Critical Analysis and Implications' in G. E. Jones, and R. Rolls (eds) *Progress in Rural Extension and Community Development*, vol I (Chichester: Wiley, 1982).

Hossain, M., (1988) *Credit for Alleviation of Rural Poverty: the Grameen Bank in Bangladesh*, IFPRI Research Report 65 (Washington, D.C.: International Food Policy Research Institute).

Hulme, D., and N. M. Turner, (1990) *Sociology and Development: Theories, Policies and Practices* (London: Harvester-Wheatsheaf and St. Martin's Press, 1990).

Islam, N., A. I. Chowdhury and K. Ali, (1989) *Evaluation of the Grameen Bank's Rural Housing Programme with UNDP Funding* (Dhaka: Centre for Urban Studies, University of Dhaka).

Korten, D. C., (1980) 'Community Organisation and Rural Development: a Learning Process Approach', *Public Administration Review* 40 (5) (1980) 480–511.

Mosley, P., and R. P. Dahal, (1987) 'Credit for the Rural Poor: a Comparison of Policy Experiments in Nepal and Bangladesh', *Manchester Papers on Development*, 3(2) (1987) 45–59.

Redd Barna, Sri Lanka (1988) *SAVECRED: a Handbook for Project Staff* (Colombo: Redd Barna).

Robertson, A. F., (1984) *People and the State* (Cambridge: Cambridge University Press).

Sukor Kasim, M., (1989) *Pendekatan Pinjaman al-Qardhul Hassan di Dalam Menquranqkan Kemiskinan*. Paper delivered at the Institute for Strategic and International Studies, Kuala Lumpur, 1989.

Thomas, J., (1990) 'Credit programme for the informal sector in Peru', *Appropriate Technology*, 16 (4) 20–3.

World Bank, (1987) *Malawi: Smallholder Agricultural Credit Project (IDA/IFAD Credit)* (Washington D.C.: World Bank).

Yunus, M., (1986) 'Grameen Bank As I See It', paper delivered at the International Labour Organisation, Geneva.

18 The Female of the Species: Women and Dairying in India

Shanti George

INTRODUCTION

As this chapter [1] studies the intersection of various subordinate categories, we begin by noting that dairying is itself a subordinate activity in rural India, ancillary to agricultural production and drawing on crop wastes and residues for milchstock nutrition. With male labour in villages usually directed to agriculture and other primary activities, it is generally the subordinate gender which puts labour into the subordinate activity of dairying. Baviskar (1988) discusses the preconditions for household dairying, and stresses the presence of an able-bodied woman, in addition to finance to purchase a milch animal, land to grow fodder or resources to otherwise acquire it, and suitable shelter.

The subordinate gender's contribution to a subordinate activity has for long been almost unacknowledged in the literature on rural development. The only full-length book on women and dairying in India (itself quite recently published), says: 'It is indeed curious to note that relevant statistics about labour inputs in dairying are not found either in the census or in dairy-related data' (Chen *et al.*, 1986, p. 50). When in 1979 I compiled an annotated bibliography on dairying in India, only twenty-six of more than 500 entries said anything significant about women's involvement. However, the entries on females of such other species as cows or she-buffaloes ran into hundreds!

More recent work attempts to compensate for such neglect of women's work in dairying. Here we try to build on this work by relating subordinate gender and subordinate productive activity to other subordinate categories.

WOMEN AND DAIRY POLICY: THE SUBORDINATE GENDER

In 1985 India's Planning Commission broke its hitherto almost perfect silence on the subject of women and dairying, in the seventh plan's section on animal husbandry and dairying, with four words at the end of the last remedial measure suggested, viz. 'making arrangements for training of farmers *and their women folk*' (GOI, 1986, p. 34). Thus women reached the periphery of a five-year plan's section on dairying, if only as append- ages to their menfolk.

It might be argued that the sixth plan had already broken this silence. A chapter on 'Women and Development' (the first such in a five-year plan document) stated: 'Efforts would be made to offer larger employment for them in the schemes for public distribution system, rural godowns, Oper- ation Flood II, dairy development and social forestry and in armed forces' (GOI, 1981, p. 426). However, no mention of women in dairy develop- ment spilled over from this chapter to the earlier one which discussed dairying.

As for the fifth, fourth, third, second and first five-year plans, their only reference to females in dairying were to cows and she-buffaloes (GOI, 1952, 1956, 1961, 1969 and 1973). Here officials in independent India differed little from those of British India. The report of the Royal Com- mission on Agriculture, and the bulletins from agricultural departments (e.g. Keatinge, 1917), referred to women in dairying – if at all – as the family labour which lowered milk production costs.

There is, however, an honourable exception in Wright, who provided policy guidelines for Indian dairying at the Imperial Government's request, and stressed the role of women:

I strongly recommend that serious consideration should be given to the provision of dairy training for women. Women have a natural aptitude for dairy work: moreover they are already largely responsible for the handling of milk and the manufacture of milk products such as *ghee*. If improvements are to be effected in the handling of milk and milk products under village conditions, the cooperation of the women of the village is essential (Wright, 1937, p. 103).

Dairy policy in India has otherwise not addressed itself to the central role of women in milk production and processing – to the detriment both of the dairy economy and of women. A policy that apparently ignores women can yet affect female involvement in dairying through its technological decisions and choices. We argue below that the sixth five-year plan which talked of 'greater involvement of women in science and technology' (GOI, 1981, p. 323), and the seventh plan which proposed providing women with 'skill manuals and training aids in . . . animal husbandry' (GOI, 1986, p. 327), embodied a dairy policy which substantially eroded women's participation.

On the other hand, Wright matched his appreciation of women's contri- bution to dairying with policy recommendations which consolidated female participation. Such a policy might have enhanced India's dairy economy through women's efforts at the same time that it increased female employment and income through dairying – but it was implemented neither in colonial nor independent India.

WOMEN AND DAIRY TECHNOLOGY: THE SUBORDINATE SCIENCE

The logic and practice of dairying in rural India differs from the dairy science imported from Europe/North America and imparted at educational institutions in India. Dairy scientists from these institutions dismiss as unscientific the milk production and processing practices of 'illiterate', 'uneducated' village women. Rural dairying is thus not only a subordinate economic activity carried out by a subordinate gender, but a subordinate science.

Practitioners of the dominant dairy science deplore 'unscientific' breeding among Indian milchstock, and the absence of detailed records of each cow's parentage and milk yields.[2] Is it then accidental that India boasts the world's best tropical dairy breeds? Portrayals of unsystematic milchstock breeding in rural India arise because most village men do not keep written records of the fluid milk output of cows. However, *women* keep a *mental* record of how many tins of *ghee* they make from a *buffalo*'s surplus milk – and use such criteria to decide which breeding bull to patronise next time (Khurody, 1974).[3]

Similar pronouncements about the absence of 'scientific' milchstock feeding in rural India[4] are based on the premise that industrially compounded cattle feed should be combined with specially cultivated green fodder, in proportions varying with the lactation cycle. While this feeding system tries to maximise milk yield, the subordinate dairy science of rural women seeks to minimise the use of purchased inputs and to maximise that of residues and by-products. Thus, instead of cultivated green fodder (which would reduce the land available for food and cash crops), grass is laboriously collected from fallow land and road sides, and added to such agricultural waste as the green tops of harvested sugarcane.

'Compounded' cattle feed is also used by rural women, processed by them at home from oilcakes and other agricultural residues. Their ingredients vary with the lactation cycle as well as the marketing outlet, with oilcake emphasised where milk is sold as a fluid, and cottonseed where *ghee* is the marketable product, because cottonseed enhances fat content (Kelkar, 1915). The dominant dairy science ignores such domestic compounds as they are not factory produced or standardised according to some written formula. Even where they buy mill compounded feed, milk producers may find it inadequate and make a compound of their own by adding oilcake and other ingredients to the factory product (IIM, 1968).

In a tribute to the subordinate dairy science, Crotty (1980) remarks that

India's milk production uses extremely constrained agro-economic resources and is yet surprisingly productive, matched in the output of milk per hectare of grassland only by the European Economic Community (that high temple of the dominant dairy science). This is an indirect tribute to the women who 'man' India's dairy sector.

It can be argued that the dominant dairy science displaces women while the subordinate science integrates them. The subordinate dairy science is woman-integrating not because it was developed *for* women, but because it was developed *by* them, with its locus in their sphere of the household:

> Although there are no official statistics available as to the degree of participation of women in dairying, experience and observation show that women play a major role in dairying [, a]lthough women's labour inputs into livestock maintenance vary to some degree by region, age or caste . . . In the . . . project area [Yellamanchili taluka, Visakhapatanam district, Andhra Pradesh], the typical routine of women who maintain cows or buffaloes is as follows:
>
> | | |
> |---|---|
> | 4.30–5.30 a.m. | – cleaning the animal shed |
> | | – collecting dung |
> | | – watering the animals |
> | 5.30–6.00 a.m. | – milking |
> | [6.00–9.30 a.m. | – other household chores] |
> | 9.30 a.m. | – animal sent for grazing either through woman's own child or . . . paid labour |
> | 5.30 p.m. | – animals return from grazing |
> | 5.30 p.m. | – feeding and watering the animals |
> | 6.00 p.m. | – milking. |
>
> (Chen et al., op. cit., p. 50)

What requires deeper study is how decision-making powers are related to the female labour input into milk production. Given that the household women are responsible for milchstock, how do they decide when in its dry period a milch animal will be serviced, and by which local breeding bull? Within the household's feed resources, how do they determine ingredients and proportions for milchstock in various phases of the lactation cycle? Available literature suggests that the subordinate gender which labours at the subordinate activity of dairying is also able to make some decisions, but with variations according to region, caste, class and age.

Also requiring study is the rural women's culture which centres around milch animals and milk products. Through responsibility for milchstock, they develop some expertise in handling dairy animals, compounding cattle feed domestically, recognising the nutritive value of grasses, choosing breeding bulls, and maintaining milchstock health. However, that most animal healers and handlers of breeding bulls seem to be men (e.g. Batra,

1987), suggests the limits within which this female milch animal culture operates. Rural dairy women should be studied as decision-makers and as sources of expertise, and not only as providers of labour.

Women's work in dairying continues from producing milk to processing it, a critical matter in a tropical and low income economy, where milk spoils easily at the same time that expensive preservation technology is not widely feasible. These constraints have been overcome through kitchen technology which generates a range of less perishable dairy products.

Simple *heating* to boiling point extends the life of milk and can be repeated. Simmering after boiling yields *rabadi* (condensed milk) and ultimately *khoya/mava* or milk solids. These solids are used in confectionery, keep for a longer period than milk, and can be stored and transported to an urban market at little expense.

Souring is another elementary but effective method of prolonging milk's life and marketability. *Dahi* (curds) keeps better than milk. A little *dahi* introduced into a container of milk sets within hours and is edible (and saleable) for more than a day. If longer keeping turns *dahi* very sour, it can be cooked with garnishing into *kadhi*. Souring can be combined with heating: *dahi*, introduced into milk boiling over a fire, splits the milk, and after draining, the split solids form a slab of *paneer* (cottage cheese). This, wrapped in a wet cloth, is transported to nearby markets for use in confectionery or savouries.

Agitation is the third process which transforms perishable milk into longer life products, with *malai* (cream) churned into *makhan* (butter). Household churns are generally made of wood, their size varying with the amount of milk handled, so that a small churn is manipulated between the palms of two hands and a larger one may require a rope attachment overhead. *Makhan* keeps longer than milk, especially if floated in cold water in an earthen pot. Surplus *makhan* is 'clarified' into *ghee* through heating on a low fire, followed by straining. *Ghee* has a shelf life of several months that can be further prolonged by reheating and straining, and travels long distances to urban markets.

Churning separates milk into butterfat and a liquid byproduct (*chhas* or buttermilk) containing the other lactic solids plus some fat. Unlike *makhan* or *ghee*, buttermilk is easily perishable and must be disposed of within the household. In certain areas, e.g. Kerala, buttermilk is sold by women within the village at half the price of milk. Elsewhere, buttermilk is customarily not sold but given away to those without milchstock or whose animals are dry (e.g. ISAE, 1957). Again, women distribute the buttermilk, as in the following case from Haryana:

> the traditional big landowners, who owned large herds of milch cattle, produced milk and *ghee* on a large scale; long queues of landless low caste people with their utensils were accepting buttermilk from the

female relatives of the big landowners (Batra, 1981, p. 102, emphasis added).

Women, then, tend milch animals, and process and dispose of milk. Their commercial outlet is the private trader who comes to the kitchen door. While the main household income from the primary activity of agriculture is controlled by the male, subsidiary income from dairying is handled by the woman (Nath, 1960).

The statement that the dominant dairy science propagated by formal institutions is woman-displacing is often contested. Do not programmes embodying the dominant science, such as Operation Flood,[5] affirm women's economic contribution by encouraging dairying? Do not these programmes enhance female participation by focussing on the crossbred cow, which needs more attention and care than indigenous stock? A crossbred cow's vulnerability to tick-borne infections necessitates stall feeding, not exposure to insects through grazing. Does this not support women's role, as stall feeding is generally female work while grazing is a male responsibility?

A closer look at the breeding and feeding procedures of dairy development programmes based on the dominant science, reveals some displacement of women's labour and some erosion of their decision-making scope. With crossbreeding through artificial insemination with liquid or frozen semen, women can no longer choose breeding bulls for their milch animals. Decisions on breeding are made elsewhere, by personnel at the local artificial insemination centre, or at the breeding station which allocates semen to it.

During fieldwork in Kerala, I saw women take their milchstock to the breeding bull in a village household's backyard, but shrink from the aggressively male space of the government's artificial insemination centre. Ironically, reproductive efficiency could be lowered by artificial insemination, if heat periods were missed because men were too busy to take the animal to the centre.

Similarly, programmes which recommend that the green component in milchstock diets should come from specially cultivated fodder, shift control over that part of animal diets to the field, which is the male domain. (In contrast, when green feedstuffs are gleaned from agricultural byproducts and residues and gathered grass, green fodder is a female responsibility.) Dairy development strategies which use factory compounded cattle feed replace women's home-made compounds, and by presenting women with prepackaged feed, erode female decision-making and skill in domestic compounding.

Does the transfer of decision-making in milchstock care from 'ignorant' village women to 'trained ' scientific personnel represent progress? Papers presented at the National Conference on Crossbreeding drew attention to

(1) the unscientific introduction of crossbreeding programmes without proper breeding plans or rigorously tested breeding bulls (e.g. Bhat, 1978 and Shukla and Desai, 1978), and (2) inadequate quality control of compounded feed, exemplified by the toxic content in samples (Shukla and Desai, *op. cit.*)

As for the argument that crossbred cows increase female employment in dairying, a policy based on crossbred cows certainly tends to exclude *poor* women from participation, for crossbred stock are expensive to purchase, risky to maintain because of vulnerability to disease and climate, and need costly nutrients and veterinary care (Nyholm, *et al.* 1975).

Moving to dairy processing, programmes based on the dominant science usurp women's work by using machines to make milk products. Some products like dried skimmed milk are unfamiliar to Indian women. Others are western variants of familiar products like butter and cheese. There are also Indian milk foods, notably *ghee* and sweetmeats like *shrikhand* and *gulab jamun*, for which machines did not exist but were developed. In villages which supply Amul, India's largest dairy plant, home manufacture of *ghee* has dwindled and households in fact buy *ghee* from the dairy (Amin, 1964). The Gujarat Association for Agricultural Sciences has noted that *ghee* made with indigenous techniques has superior qualities to that produced in dairy plants.

Further, under such programmes, the market does not come to the household to do business with women as the private vendor does. Instead, milk must be carried to the village dairy cooperative, and men do this in areas of India where women are restricted to the household. Even where women deliver milk to the cooperative, payment is often claimed by men, especially where it is made every week or fortnight and thus becomes a lump sum.[6]

In brief, rural women have some – if circumscribed – scope for decision-making where the indigenous and now subordinate dairy science prevails. By contrast, the now dominant western dairy science reduces village women from doers-and-deciders to doers only, who contribute labour while decisions about cattle diets and breeding are taken elsewhere. In dairy processing, the dominant dairy science reduces women from milk product manufacturers to consumers of machine-made foods. In milk marketing, the policy which shifts procurement from the household to a cooperative may diminish women from producers-and-receivers of income to producers alone. To strengthen female participation and control, dairy development programmes must make use of the indigenous dairy science.

This is not to say that in order to protect women's economic status, dairy development should be non-development, frozen in time and unchanging. Dairy development should build on the female-centred indigenous dairy science and technology, and introduce innovations from western science in a manner that enhances female involvement or is complementary to it.

This links to wider criticism of programmes embodying the dominant dairy science, and to arguments that effective and egalitarian dairy development would be decentralised, small scale, labour intensive and low cost (George, 1987). Thus, Nair (1981) has suggested decentralised agro-industrial processing in rural areas, so that byproducts and residues such as bran or oilcake become more easily available for animal nutrition. Some decentralised processing of animal feed could take place in rural workshops, preferably women's cooperatives, which build on village women's long experience and expertise. In the early 1980s, cattle feed factories' average capacity utilisation was only 40 per cent (Jha Committee, 1984), and the problems which undermined their performance included insufficient furnace oil and frequent breakdowns in electric supply (FAO, 1981). Why not then use womanpower, of which so much is underemployed and in need of income?

Again, India undeniably requires *some* industrial dairy plants to manufacture such products as dried skim milk. But why manufacture *ghee* through industrial methods and take employment out of rural women's hands? Instead, rural women's *ghee*-making cooperatives could extend household technology in a workshop situation (GOI, 1947). The value added in *ghee* manufacture would then be by women, and nutritious buttermilk residues would be theirs to dispose of. (Similar cooperatives could manufacture the *shrikhand* and *gulab jamuns* at present produced by machinery in large dairies like Amul and Sugam in Gujarat.)

We noted above that among dairy policy makers in both imperially-ruled and independent India, only Wright appreciated women's contribution and recommended technology and organisations to encourage rather than erode it. He suggested that changes should be evolutionary rather than revolutionary, that dairy processing be based on village industries rather than factories, that indigenous milk products be stressed more than western counterparts, and that an adequate supply of milk and its products be ensured for village populations. He also recommended that dairy education and research in India should centre around native milk products, low cost equipment, village cooperative enterprises, and on local stock rather than crossbred/exotic dairy animals. He urged female involvement in dairy education and training.

In the half century since Wright's document, Indian dairy policy has gravitated towards the opposing principles of revolutionary restructuring, industrial processing, western dairy products, urban supply, expensive equipment, imported and hybrid milch animals – and strategies which increasingly displace women.

WOMEN AND DAIRY COOPERATIVES: THE SUBORDINATE CLASS

The arguments so far presented come from one side of a sharply polarised debate, neatly summarised by Van Dorsten (1984) through competing hypotheses about women and dairy development based on imported technology and organisation:

Endorsing Hypotheses
1. Women continue to bear the main responsibility for dairying, with much extension activity directed to them.
2. Dairy cooperatives free rural women from traditional isolation, enabling them to manage these cooperatives.

Critical Hypotheses
1. Westernisation and commercialisation convert some dairying activity from women's work into men's.
2. Women remain excluded from managing dairy co-ops, whose payments for milk tend to reach men.

(Van Dorsten, 1984).

The 'endorsing' hypotheses would counter this chapter's arguments thus: (i) The shift from domestic to industrial compounding of feed and manufacture of products allows over-worked women some leisure for activities more fulfilling than processing residues or churning milk. (ii) If milk cooperatives established under dairy development programmes reduced women from producers-plus-income-receivers to producers only, this was temporary. Any negative effects are being redressed by encouraging dairy cooperative membership among women rather than men, and by establishing milk cooperatives with all-female membership.

These counter-arguments can be contained by using the category of subordinate class which crosscuts that of 'subordinate gender', and by studying the involvement of various classes of rural women in dairying. Mitra (1984, 1986a, 1986b, 1986c and 1986d) conducted a survey, elaborated by case studies, of 715 women milk producers in three districts of Andhra Pradesh, viz. Krishna, Chitoor and Nalgonda, followed by similar research in the Banaskantha district of Gujarat. Her respondents, classified into women from landless, small farmer, medium cultivator and largeholder households, reveal some sharp contrasts with reference to dairying (see Table 18.1).

Mitra notes a few commonalities underlying the contrasts. In all households, men were more likely than women to drink milk. However, women had more access to milk in largeholder households, all of which consumed milk, than in landless milk producing households of which only 9 per cent retained milk for consumption. Again, while the time spent by women of landless and medium cultivator households in dairying appears similar,

TABLE 18.1 Women and dairying by landholding group

Households	Average annual consumption expenditure (rs.)	Gross annual income from dairying (rs.)	Average daily sale of milk (litres)	Percentage of households consuming milk	Time spent by women (hrs/day)		
					Dairy activity	Agricultural labour	Domestic work
1. Landless	4300	1999	2.6	9	2.5	7	2.5
2. Small farmer	4800	2400	3.25	76	3.5	6.5	3.5
3. Medium holder	6900	2950	3.39	84	2.5	–	2.0
4. Large	9000	5000	6.00	100	0/4.0*	–	6.5

* 57 per cent of women in largeholder households reported no labour in dairying and 43% reported four hours a day on dairying, but mainly on supervision.

SOURCE: Data from Mitra (1984, 1986a, 1986b, 1986c and 1986d).

landless women performed all chores associated with milchstock, but medium-holder women who cleaned cowsheds and fed and milked stock, could delegate the tasks of collecting grass, cutting fodder and caking dung.

The starkest contrast was between a landless woman who daily put in 2.5 hours of dairy work (along with seven hours of agricultural labour) to earn an annual income of Rs. 2000 from the sale of 2.6 litres a day, and more than half the women in largeholder households who contributed no labour to the dairying that brought their families Rs. 5000 a year with a daily sale of six litres. With such contrasts, can the category of subordinate gender unite the divisions of dominant and subordinate classes? Development programmes based on the dominant dairy science have a differential impact on dominant and subordinate classes within the subordinate gender. Machines which manufacture animal feed and milk products *do* replace tedious labour with leisure and convenience for women – but only for some women.

Programmes disseminating crossbred cows benefit the households which can maintain and profit from these animals, and thereby benefit women in these households. Where development programmes encourage specially cultivated fodder for milchstock rather than green crop waste and grass, women in households with sufficient land for fodder cultivation *do* gain respite from gleaning. They gain similarly when home processed feed is replaced by purchased compounds, and when domestic manufacture of *ghee* declines with milk surpluses sold in liquid form. While purchased inputs and commodities increase both production and consumption costs, this is not of paramount concern to households with a regular cash flow, who can exploit economies of scale, and can afford to spend on production and consumption. Indeed, households with an adequate resource base welcome the shift to commercialisation.

But have these women suffered a loss because of this shift, with trade in dairy products located outside the household and the income no longer under female control? Where all-women dairy cooperatives are established, or where some managing committee positions of 'mixed' milk cooperatives are reserved for women, it is usually women from dominant castes or from largeholder households or both who thereby gain some status and power (as we see below), and this could be a trade-off against such a loss.

In contrast, the acquisition and maintenance of crossbred cows (or even the less expensive milch buffalo) are usually beyond the means of poorer households, as we have seen. Landless households cannot grow green fodder, and those with marginal holdings will not divert land from subsistence crops. Their limited cash constrains purchase of such inputs as mill-compounded feed. If the private trader who visits the house is replaced by a cooperative to which milk has to be carried, male hands as well as female may collect dairy income. For subordinate class women, the shift is rarely compensated for by positions on managing committees to which women of the dominant class have access. (One of Mitra's case studies is of a marginal landholder's wife. Although a managing committee member of the all-woman dairy cooperative in the village, her working day from 4 a.m. to 9 p.m. left her little time or energy for committee meetings.)

Indeed, let alone not benefitting women in the most subordinate class, commercialised dairying can negatively affect their lives. For example, agricultural labourers' access to crop waste and weeds from their employers' holdings has sometimes allowed them to maintain milch animals despite their inability to grow or purchase fodder. When dairying is commercialised, the landowner often expands his milch herd and feeds his weeds and waste to milchstock. Thus if landless labourer households continue to keep milchstock, women must expend more time and energy in gleaning green waste from elsewhere (Sambrani, 1980). In fact, women in landless households *without* milchstock suffer from commercialised dairying, when labourers' reduced access to crop waste decreases their supply of domestic fuel, forcing women to cover greater distances in search of substitutes (Sambrani, *op. cit.*).

If we consider the class divisions which crosscut the unity of gender, the dichotomy between competing hypotheses begins to disintegrate. For example, one hypothesis 'endorses' commercialised dairying as follows: 'Women invest more of their underutilised labour in dairying and are rewarded with higher incomes and increased social status within their families' (Van Dorsten, *op. cit.*) The competing 'critical' hypothesis holds that commercialised 'dairying induces the women to increase their workload or drudgery (at the expense of their health), while the benefits from dairy farming both in terms of nutrition and of cash income accrue mainly to men' (*ibid.*).

A perspective combining gender with class acknowledges the simultaneous validity of both hypotheses, but for different classes of women. Commercialised dairying may well increase employment opportunities, income and status for women in the middle ranges of the rural class structure, but at lower socio-economic levels can substantially increase the already heavy female workload (Mitra, *op. cit.*) As Singh *et al.* (1979) put it, poor rural women who keep a milch buffalo toil under a three-fold burden of animal care, home management and agricultural labour, while their counterparts who cannot afford to participate in dairying also carry three arduous loads, viz. housework, field labour and jealousy of those with milch animals.

Tensions between the categories of 'subordinate gender' and 'subordinate class' emerge sharply when current dairy development programmes attempt to control for the principle of gender by establishing all-female milk cooperatives. Thus, the procurement of milk is relocated from the household to the cooperative, but to compensate a space within the public domain is cordoned off and labelled 'For Women Only'. Does this create a collectivity with strong bargaining power, where women deal with each other rather than with exploitative private traders?

Khadgodhra village's milk cooperative has attracted attention as the first with an all-female membership. It is attached to the Kheda district co-operative, which owns Amul Dairy and is treated as a dairy development model. Early reports hailed the Khadgodhra cooperative as a 'managerial shift', whereby 'modern dairying has effectively related itself to women of rural India by helping to break through the barriers of their seclusion and change the status that traditional society has accorded to them' (Somjee and Somjee, 1976).

Later investigations revealed that 'while the cooperative remains an exclusively female organisation, the staff members are all males' (Singh *et al.*, 1979), and that the female managing committee depended on male employees to handle the cooperative's affairs. Along with limited favour-able observations came a sharp question: 'Was the Khadgodhra cooper-ative meant to be a gimmick and a showpiece, the initiative for which did not arise from any deep conviction on the part of the authorities of the need for bringing women more into the decision making process?' (Sundar, 1981: 87). Sundar pointed out that beyond Khadgodhra village, the Kaira cooperative's female membership was less than 7 per cent.

At that point, attention focussed on whether the subordinate gender could hold its own against the dominant one, rather than whether within that subordinate gender the dominant and subordinate classes could work together for mutual benefit. A later analysis related membership in and control over dairy cooperatives to gender and class (Figure 18.1).

Moving from left to right, the figure shifts from using only gender to combining gender with class. But the combination is used only for the female gender, without reference to membership and control of dairy cooperatives by rich or poor men, or by rich men and women, or by poor men and women. We shall return to this later.

Empirical material to flesh out this typology comes from Mitra's work (*op. cit.*).[7] Of the thirty-five dairy cooperatives in Andhra Pradesh, Bihar and Gujarat that she studied, twelve were women's cooperatives, one in Bihar and eleven in Andhra Pradesh. (She explains that some seventy-two women's cooperatives were established in Andhra Pradesh under a special project involving the Ford Foundation.) Among the twelve, Mitra dis-tinguishes between what she calls women's cooperatives as such and 'genuine' women's cooperatives, the six in the former category being undermined by male resistance or control, unlike the latter. She then subdivides the six 'genuine' women's cooperatives into two dominated by upper caste women, and four in whose management women from back-ward or scheduled castes participated effectively:

Membership	1. Men only	2. Men and Women		3. Women only		
		2a. Men in majority	2b. Women in majority	3a. Rich women in majority	3b. Poor women in majority	3c. Only poor women
Control	Men	Men with some women	Women with some men	Rich women	Poor women	

FIGURE 18.1 *Membership in and control over dairy co-operatives*

SOURCE: M. Chen, M. Mitra, G. Athreya, A. Dholakia, P. Law and A. Rao, *Indian Women: A Study of Their Role in the Dairy Movement* (New Delhi: Shakti, 1986).

Mitra's classification of women's cooperatives in 12 villages
(1) Women's cooperatives opposed by men – in villages Samanatham, Chowtapalli and Nomula.
(2) Women's cooperatives controlled by men – in villages Ootuvanku, Amnabolu and Sadullapur.
(3) 'Genuine' women's cooperatives dominated by upper caste women – in villages Siddantham and Challapalli.
(4) 'Genuine' women's cooperatives with low/scheduled caste participation – in villages Gongulamuddi, Polavaram, Kangarivarripalli and Phanigiri.
(Sadullapur is in Vaishali district of Bihar. All other villages are from the Chitoor, Krishna and Nalgonda districts of Andhra Pradesh).

A closer look at Mitra's categories is revealing.

Male and upper caste dominance

She notes that women's cooperatives tended to be formed only where other (i.e. male) cooperatives malfunctioned or were strangled by factionalism or competition – or where canny males realised the special assistance that a women's cooperative would receive from outside agencies. This was so even with two 'genuine' women's cooperatives.

Where women's cooperatives were covertly manipulated by powerful men, some collaboration by female relatives is apparent. E.g., in Amnabolu the village headman supported a women's cooperative, of which his wife became president, and she scrupulously followed caste proscriptions when dealing with the cooperative's few Harijan members. Again, in Sadullapur the chair'man' of the women's dairy cooperative was the mother of an affluent orchard owner, and the secretary was the *sarpanch*'s daughter-in-law.

In the 'genuine' women's cooperatives dominated by upper caste women, their behaviour sometimes parallelled that of upper caste men in cooperatives. In Siddantham, the female dairy cooperative's president was an ex-*zamindar*'s wife, a member of the ruling political party and had a college degree. She organised 250 women members in the cooperative, with a managing committee that represented all castes in the village. However, no committee meetings were held, and her affiliation to the dominant family ensured concurrence with her decisions. The ex-*zamindar* himself could not have done better! This was hardly a genuine cooperative, let alone a 'genuine' women's cooperative. Does the Siddantham case differ in kind or only in degree from Amnabolu (see above) where a powerful man's wife also presided over the women's dairy cooperative? Yet Mitra categorises Siddantham – unlike Amnabolu – as a genuine women's cooperative.

Backward and scheduled castes

Among subordinate caste women, Mitra generally treats women from backward and scheduled castes together. The need for differentiation emerges in the Ootuvanku case, classified as a male-influenced women's cooperative. Ootuvanku seems composed mainly of backward castes, scheduled castes and scheduled tribals, with all three groups represented in the female dairy cooperative's managing committee. Male control of the cooperative aside, the relations of the backward caste women members to those from the scheduled caste and tribe are of interest. Mitra reports backward caste opposition at the election of scheduled caste or tribal women to the managing committee, and a negative reaction to extension workers' support to these women.

Of the four women's dairy cooperatives described as having successfully involved low caste women, the Phanigiri case was presumably included as the only one in Andhra Pradesh with a paid secretary who was female and from a backward caste. Yet this double triumph turns out to be somewhat hollow: the woman secretary's limited training meant that a male employee tested the milk, and the managing committee was dominated by upper caste women.

Inclusion of the Polavaram women's cooperative in this category is also questionable, for the village is dominated by the Reddy caste and a Reddy woman is the cooperative's president. Perhaps this was considered to be counterbalanced by the fact that, unlike the ladies described in Siddantham or Amnabolu above, the Reddy president was not arbitrary or coercive in her dealings with low caste women, and was assisted by one of them. All the same, only five out of 121 milk producers in the village belonged to a scheduled caste or tribe.

Two women's dairy cooperatives in this category remain, viz. Gongala-muddi and Kangarivarripalli. However, distinguishing between backward castes and scheduled castes – as suggested above – we mark the small number of scheduled caste households in the two villages (as few as two out of ninety in Kangarivarripalli), and that these villages held no assetless group of numerical significance. (But see further comments below on Gongalamuddi.)

Successful cooperatives

Although Mitra's framework focusses on caste, her observations on the class situation are useful, e.g., in the Kangarivarripalli women's dairy cooperative, she attributes the good working relations between women members from the dominant Kamma caste and from a backward caste, and the latter's active managerial participation, to the fact that most members belonged to smallholder households, regardless of caste.

Of the twelve villages, the most promising seems to be Gongalamuddi where an already existing women's milk cooperative was reorganised, and both the earlier and the present institutions worked reasonably well. Further, the scheduled castes were effectively represented in the cooperative's management, and although the small number of scheduled caste households in the village has been alluded to, their proportion of seven out of 50 is not insignificant. A group savings scheme was initiated so that poorer members could obtain bank loans, including ones for the purchase of milch buffaloes.

Mitra's brief description allows little speculation about why this women's dairy cooperative succeeded with subordinate castes and classes. One reason might be the village's demographic composition, with only some fifty households of which forty belong to the Kamma caste. Another could be the female extension personnel attached to the special project mentioned earlier. Kangarivarripalli had these personnel, as well as a similar demographic situation to Gongulamuddi, with Kammas constituting almost seventy out of eighty households. In the Ootuvanku case, however, despite the presence of female extension personnel, the larger number of scheduled caste and tribal households in the village seemed to make the dominant (backward) caste insecure, and this had an adverse effect on the women's dairy cooperative.

GENDER, CLASS AND TECHNOLOGY

If the conclusion suggested is that women of dominant and subordinate castes cooperate only when the latter are in a minority, this does not promise much for the subordinate in women's dairy cooperatives. The same is true of another of Mitra's findings, that women's dairy cooperatives seemed neither more nor less effective in encouraging milk production in poor households than male or mixed cooperatives: she particularly mentions the two most successful of her cases, Gongalamuddi and Kangarivarripalli. (Especially interesting is Mitra's use of the term 'paternalistic' to describe the attitude of upper caste women in all-female dairy cooperatives to fellow members from subordinate castes. We need to develop appropriate terms for subjugation patterns between classes within the female gender, rather than merely extend the terms already applied to patterns of dominance by males.)

Mitra's findings not only illuminate the intersection between the categories of subordinate gender and subordinate class, but relate to our earlier discussion of a subordinate dairy technology. Earlier we noted that when milk procurement shifts from the female sphere of the household to the public domain, as when the private trader at the door is replaced by a cooperative's office, control over milk income may move from female hands to male. Mitra corroborates this in Ghantashala, a village with a largely male milk cooperative, chosen to contrast with women's dairy cooperatives. In Ghantashala, women indeed complained that they had lost control over household earnings from milk after the dairy cooperative's establishment.

Here, the differences between women from dominant and subordinate groups are interesting. Among landless households, women tended to deliver milk to the cooperative, and an equal number of men and women collected the fortnightly payments. With small farmers, both genders brought milk to the cooperative, but men were more likely to collect the returns. Among medium cultivators, more men than women delivered milk to the cooperative and men also made the fortnightly collections. With largeholders, a still greater proportion of men carried milk to the cooperative and took charge of the returns. We noted (pp. 276–7) that in the last two categories increased income from milk is matched by a decrease in the labour contributed to dairying by the household's women.

Mitra's case studies suggest that it is women from subordinate sections who prefer alternative commercial outlets for milk. Her interviews with women in large and medium holder households do not generally suggest use of such outlets. On the other hand, in a Gujarat village, a small farmer's household produced eight litres of milk daily during the rainy season, of which five were carried to the cooperative by the man, who kept the income thus generated. Of the other three litres, a third to one half remained after household consumption, and the woman made this into *ghee* to sell to a private trader, saving the money for her daughter's marriage. While the man was full of praise for the cooperative, the woman (in his absence) said she knew little of the cooperative but was glad that *ghee* manufacture provided her with some independent income and savings.

What of alternative outlets and all-female cooperatives? Mitra's description of such a cooperative in Sadullapur village tells us that before the cooperative was established, members from the ex-untouchable Dusadh caste had sold their milk to *dahivars* or pretty traders. These members said that they could deal better with *dahivars* than with the cooperative's office bearers who were from a dominant caste, and that they did not know what pricing system the cooperative followed so just took whatever was paid to them. They pointed out that the *dahivar* provided cash advances, unlike the cooperative.

CONCLUSIONS

The material now available on Indian women and dairying is a welcome addition to the literature, which previously had little significant reference to the womanpower which keeps milk flowing – although women often appeared on the covers of books or in the illustrations of articles on dairying in India. Such superficiality of coverage (pun intended) is being redressed, and as suggestions for further study I underline two issues raised above.

The relationship between gender and class must be examined more closely, both the divergent and convergent interests of women from different classes, and overlapping and opposing interests of the genders within a class. Chen *et al.*'s typology of membership and control of milk cooperatives (Figure 18.1) referred only to classes within the female gender, not within the male or across both genders. Mitra's findings are again useful here. In certain landless households with milch animals, men withdrew from agricultural labour to tend these animals, while women continued to work in the fields yet also bore the brunt of milchstock care. These cases were found especially in the Krishna and Chitoor districts of Andhra Pradesh, and were related to local agrarian relations. Labour's bargaining power was weakened by the mechanisation of agriculture, which not only took over activities performed by male labour (such as ploughing) but allowed landowners to opt for the lower-paid labour of women. Mitra contrasts this with areas where labourers' bargaining ability was strengthened (e.g. with assistance from voluntary agencies), and where women then withdrew from wage labour to take care of dairy animals. An analysis which is restricted to the female gender alone, or even to both genders within a class, could not do justice to such situations.

Again, while dairy policy should focus on the subordinate gender, it should do so with reference to the subordinate science of rural dairy women. Chen *et al.*'s policy recommendations arise from concern for rural women and among these the poorest, but are structured according to present dairy development programmes based on the dominant dairy paradigm. By recommending that 10 per cent of all dairy cooperatives should be female cooperatives or that one-third of managing committee members in all dairy cooperatives should be women, Chen *et al.* can only succeed in wresting a few seats for women within the dairy industry that is eroding female participation (and it has been suggested (pp. 281–2) that these seats will be occupied by the dominant class within the subordinate gender).

In contrast, we recommended (pp. 273–4) that dairy development programmes build on the subordinate dairy science practised by village women, e.g. by locating some cattle feed manufacture in rural areas to make use of village women's expertise in processing residues into feed (especially given the problems faced by India's compound feed industry), and by entrusting the manufacture of indigenous dairy foods to women's cooperatives. The reasoning here is that subordinate paradigms allow subordinate groups to assert themselves (as with dominant paradigms and groups).

Such a reorientation requires better understanding of the subordinate dairy science, ideally by participant observers residing in villages for at least a year and closely studying the part of women's culture that deals with dairy animals. (Such work would resemble Batra's doctoral study of the livestock system of a village, but with a female focus.) It is striking that the few studies now available of women and dairying in India are from areas where some dairy development 'intervention' has taken place. (This parallels the earlier observation that policy recommendations on women and dairying are always located within the framework of existing development programmes.) It is time that women's work in dairying was studied in its own right. While the literature on Indian dairying relates gender among bovines to species, breed, function, technological change and policy trends, it has, until very recently, neglected the female of the human species.

NOTES

1. A preliminary version of this chapter was presented at a conference on 'Women in Agriculture' (Centre for Development Studies, Trivandrum, February 1988). This version is part of work funded by a Bernard Conyers Rural Communications Fellowship from the Arkleton Trust.
2. An early twentieth century example: 'The ordinary village cultivator in India is usually poor and ignorant . . . It would be difficult to convince him of the benefits of modern breeding and dairy farming' (Joshi, 1917, p. 158).
3. E.g., Hogle (1970) attributed difficulty with milk production estimates partly to the fact that he interviewed farmers and not their wives.
4. According to one dairy official, a milk cooperative is necessary to teach 'a poor producer . . . that you get a better calf if you give better food to a pregnant cow' (Kurien, 1974, p. 718).
5. India's Operation Flood is the world's largest dairy development programme. See George, 1987, for a critical discussion.
6. See Mitra's case studies, also discussed on p. 284.
7. Since Mitra has used caste rather than class in her analysis, some blurring of the categories is necessary here.

REFERENCES

Amin, R. K., (1964) *Mogri: Socio-Economic Study of a Charotar Village* (Vallabh Vidyanagar: Sardar Patel University).
Batra, S. M., (1981) 'The Place of Livestock in the Social and Economic Life of a Village in Haryana' (Ph.D. thesis, Department of Sociology, Delhi University).
Batra, S. M., (1987) 'Socio-Cultural Aspects of Cattle Diseases and Veterinary Medicine in a Village in North India' (paper at a seminar on India's Livestock Economy, Centre for Development Studies, Trivandrum, 26–8 March).

Baviskar, B. S., (1988) 'Dairy Cooperatives and Rural Development in Gujarat', in D. W. Atwood and B. S. Baviskar (eds), *Who Shares? Cooperatives in Rural Development* (New Delhi: Oxford University Press).

Bhat, P. N., (1978) 'Problems of Stabilising Crossbred Cow Population Under Field Conditions in India', in NDDB, 284–9.

Chen, M., M. Mitra, G. Athreya, A. Dholakia, P. Law and A. Rao, (1986) *Indian Women: A Study of their Role in the Dairy Movement* (New Delhi: Shakti).

Crotty, R., (1980) *Cattle, Economics and Development* (Slough: Commonwealth Agricultural Bureau).

Dogra, B., (1981) 'The White Revolution: Who Gets the Cream?', *The Economic Scene*, 67 10–19.

Food and Agriculture Organisation (1981), *World Food Programme Terminal Evaluation Report on Project India 618*, (Rome: FAO).

George, S., (1987) 'Stemming Operation Flood: Towards an Alternative Dairy Policy for India', *Economic and Political Weekly*, 22 (39) 1654–64.

Government of India (GOI) (1947), *Report on the Marketing of Ghee and Other Milk Products in India*, (Calcutta: GOI Press, 1947).

GOI (1952), *The First Five Year Plan*, (New Delhi: Planning Commission).

GOI (1956), *The Second Five Year Plan*, (New Delhi: Planning Commission).

GOI (1961), *The Third Five Year Plan*, (New Delhi: Planning Commission).

GOI (1969), *Draft Fourth Five Year Plan* (New Delhi: Planning Commission).

GOI (1973), *Draft Fifth Five Year Plan* (New Delhi: Planning Commission).

GOI (1981), *The Sixth Five Year Plan* (New Delhi: Planning Commission).

GOI (1986), *The Seventh Five Year Plan*, Vol. II (New Delhi: Planning Commission).

Gujarat Association for Agricultural Sciences (n.d.), '*Reports of Agricultural and Animal Husbandry Study Groups*', mimeo.

Hogle, H., (1970) *The Influence of Agricultural Extension in Selected Villages of Kaira District (Gujarat, India)* (Ann Arbor: University of Michigan).

Indian Institute of Management (IIM) (1968), *Milk Procurement in Baroda*, mimeo (Ahmedabad: IIM).

Indian Society of Agricultural Economics (ISAE) (1957), *Bhadkad: Social and Economic Survey of a Village, A Comparative Study (1915–1955)* (Bombay: ISAE).

Jha, L. K., S. K. Rau, I. Z. Bhatty, N. N. Dastur, P. Bhattacharya and A. R. Shirali, (1984) *Report of the Evaluation Committee on Operation Flood II* (New Delhi: Ministry of Agriculture).

Joshi, L. L., (1916) *The Milk Problem in Indian Cities with Special Reference to Bombay* (Bombay: D. R. Taraporewala and Sons).

Keatinge, G. F., (1917) *Note on Cattle in the Bombay Presidency* (Bombay: Department of Agriculture, Bulletin No. 85).

Kelkar, G. K., (1915) *Notes on Cattle of the Bombay Presidency* (Bombay: Department of Agriculture, Bulletin no. 75).

Khurody, D. N., (1974) *Dairying in India: A Review* (Bombay: Asia Publishing House).

Kurien, V., (1974) 'The Larger Dimensions of Dairy Development in India', *Milchwissenschaft*, 29(12) 714–19.

Mitra, M., (1984) *Mata Aur Gau-Mata: The Women and the Sacred Cow – A Study of Women in Dairy Production* (The Hague: Institute of Social Studies).

Mitra, M., (1986a) *Bihar: The Land of the Unfinished Revolution and the White Revolution* (The Hague: Institute of Social Studies, Working Paper No. 5, Dairy Aid and Development Series (DADS)).

Mitra, M., (1986b) *Impact of Dairy Cooperatives on Selected Areas of Banaskantha District, Gujarat* (The Hague: Institute of Social Studies, Working Paper No. 10, DADS).
Mitra, M., (1986c) *Women in Dairying in Andhra Pradesh* (The Hague: Institute of Social Studies, Working Paper No. 19, DADS).
Mitra, M., (1986d) *Case Studies of Women's Dairy Cooperatives from Andhra Pradesh* (The Hague: Institute of Social Studies, Working Paper No. 20, DADS).
Nair, K. N., (1981) *An Alternative to the Operation Flood II Strategy* (Trivandrum: Centre for Development Studies, Working Paper No. 134).
National Dairy Development Board (NDDB) (1978), *Proceedings of the National Conference on Crossbreeding* (Anand: NDDB).
Nath, Y. V. S., (1960) *Bhils of Ratanmal: An Analysis of the Social Structure of a Western Indian Community* (Baroda: M. S. University, Monograph Series 1).
Nyholm, K., H. Schaumburg-Muller and K. Westergaard, (1975) *Report on Livestock (Dairy) Development in the Bangalore Milk Shed Area* (Copenhagen: Institute for Development Research).
Royal Commission on Agriculture in India (1928), *Report* (London: His Majesty's Stationery Office).
Sambrani, S., (1980) *Transforming the Rural Poor: The Big Push in Action* (Anand: Institute of Rural Management).
Shukla, P. C., and M. C. Desai, (1978) 'Feeding of Crossbred Cows in Gujarat State: Problems and Need for Solutions', in *NDDB 1978*, 215–21.
Singh, N., D. Jain and M. Chand, (1979) *Milkmaids of Kaira District: Some Notes*, (New Delhi: Institute of Social Studies Trust).
Somjee, A. H. and Somjee, G. (1976) 'Managerial Shift: Indian Women Acquire a New Role in Dairying', *World Annual Review*, 18, 28–33.
Sundar, P., (1981) 'Khadgodhra: A Case Study of a Women's Co-operative', *Social Action*, 31.
Van Dorsten, F., (1984) 'The Rural Impact of Operation Flood: Viewpoints and Hypotheses' (The Hague: Institute of Social Studies, Working Paper No. 4, DADS).
Wright, N. C., (1937) *Report on the Development of the Cattle and Dairy Industries in India* (Simla: Government of India Press).

19 Utilising Bank Loans as an Organisational Strategy: a Case Study of the Annapurna Mahila Mandal

Dina Abbott

INTRODUCTION

During the 1970s, India has seen unique new forms of women's organisations. Whilst during their embryonic stages such organisations were viewed with an element of surprise both in India and the West, they are now regarded as exciting and firmly-rooted, articulating the needs of women from the most suppressed of social and economic classes. Examples include the Self-Employed Women's Association (SEWA) based at Ahmedabad, the Working Women's Forum (WWF) in Madras and the Annapurna Mahila Mandal (AMM) in Bombay.

Many Indian 'Mahila Mandals' (women's organisations) are founded on attitudes of 'social welfare' or charity towards women from improvished backgrounds. The leadership usually derives from elitist, middle-class women who control the organisation 'from above'. What differentiates SEWA, WWF and the AMM from these women's organisations is (a) a conscious move towards a political understanding which allows them to address class and gender-related social issues; (b) an awareness of the economic value of the membership, who despite contributing significantly to the household's total income and, on a wider scale to the national economy, remain 'invisible' due to the nature of their income-generating work and their social positions; and (c) the composition of leadership, mainly made up of more experienced members, emerging 'from below' at a grass-roots level. Such an approach has allowed the women to adopt a new collective identity, one which challenges isolation and redefines their economic and political 'invisibility'.

It is beyond the scope of this paper to enter into discussion of the number of complex factors that contribute to achieving the set goals of these organisations. Out of these, therefore, I will focus on the organisational strategy which has been of primary importance to SEWA, WWF and AMM – that which involves ideas of 'social banking' and credit access for the poor.

In this paper, I propose to take the AMM as a case study to examine how such an organisational strategy has not only given birth to the AMM, but has had significant influence in its consequent growth. It is argued that whilst 'bank loans for the poor' make for a powerful organisational strategy, this is nevertheless a very demanding one, especially on limited resources that may otherwise be constructively utilised addressing the long-term political goals of the organisation.

A CONSTANT NEED FOR CREDIT

Perhaps one of the reasons SEWA, WWF and AAM have been able to organise where conventional trade unions and political parties (such as the Congress and Communist Parties) have failed is that they have recognised that the most pressing need of their membership is access to ready cash and credit.[1] Membership consists of women at the lowest levels of social and economic ladder, often illiterate, coming from households with a minimal level of consistent employment. Whilst the woman is expected to take on much of the domestic unpaid work, there is also a pressing need for her to provide some form of income to the household. This contribution often amounts to up to 50 per cent of the total family income ('Sharamskati', 1987; Government of India, 1989). Illiteracy, lack of training, lack of skills, lack of employment opportunities, need to combine domestic and dependent care along with paid work, social norms that restrict mobility together with caste and class position are only some of the factors that restrict entry to the labour market.

The women, therefore, have a minimal choice. Even putting-out, subcontracted work or labouring is only obtained through fierce competition. The women are thus often forced to enter the already overcrowded 'informal sector' labour market, carrying out a range of jobs such as buying and selling goods, and constantly innovating new ideas for differing types of petty commodity production or petty entrepreneurial activities. What form these latter activities take often depends on the capital investment available, which is more usually than not a very small amount. In turn this produces low returns (Bhapat and Crook, 1988; Bardhan, 1985; Joshi, 1976; Baud, 1989).

In its struggle to survive and deal with daily living and crisis situations, the household's paramount and constant ready cash needs are met by various forms of complex borrowing and credit arrangements. Every possible source is explored and often a new loan is used to pay off another more pressing one. Access to credit sources is also socially differentiated, with some groups having better access than others. For example, those who have family members working in factories or textile mills will be able to borrow from employee funds (known as 'societies'); others may have a 'pooling' system in the slum district which allows them access to the pooled money in rotation. During emergencies, ornaments and brass pots and other valuables are pawned. Those who do not have such items have to resort to moneylenders who charge high interest rates and recover monies owed by violence.

Within this cycle of borrowing, cash is first allocated to the household's daily and crisis consumption needs. The primary need is that of the household's immediate survival. Long-term needs have to take secondary place. Allocation of working capital for women (no matter how small) thus depends heavily on the immediate financial circumstances and needs of the total household.

Studies have shown that such allocation also depends on the working capital requirements of the men in the household (Buvinic, 1985). Men's work is usually considered to be of more importance and of larger economic value, thus, their share is prioritised both in terms of heirarchy and the amount allocated. The allocation is also biased in their favour because they often control the household income. Larger and more regular working capital allows men to invest in activity which will produce higher returns (such as scooter-rickshaws or stalls). However, the essential amount that women require to begin or continue their income-generating activity is not easily or regularly available. In the face of this, the operation often becomes so difficult that women give up and change to another form of income-generating work that requires lower working capital but brings in lower returns.

It is at this point that women's organisations can provide a strategic intervention. Their aim is to make credit available, specifically as working capital, thus allowing the woman to continue (and in some cases start-up) her operation. However, there is a major practical problem attached to this kind of intervention: where can women's organisations, developed and run by women from below poverty-level backgrounds, find money to lend to others? An answer for SEWA, WWF and AMM lay in the banks, newly nationalised and advocating policies of 'social banking'.

SOCIAL BANKING AND DRI LOANS

The State Bank of India was nationalised in 1955, followed by fourteen of the largest banks in 1969. By 1980, 91 per cent of deposits were held in public sector banks (Savara and Everett, 1983). Nationalisation was intended to replace an elitist image by a populist one. The Government of India wanted to develop a 'mass' banking system which would be accessible to the rural and urban poor, including scheduled castes, women and other 'weaker section' borrowers requiring small amounts for their income-generating projects.

A variety of 'weaker section' lending programmes were formed (Government of India, 1986). This paper is primarily concerned with the Differential Rate of Interest Scheme (DRI) which allows the urban poor access to a maximum of Rs 1500 for working capital and Rs 5000 for fixed assets at a minimal interest rate of 4 per cent per annum (present figures). Eligibility is dependent on family income being below Rs 5000 per annum in urban areas. Each bank is expected to meet at least 1 per cent DRI lending target worked out on previous year's advances, a target which the government hopes will increase (Savara and Everett, 1986).

In order to meet the government's target, each bank is obliged to loan various amounts to 'weaker sections' through its main branches. However, in view of the administrative problems involved in loaning and recovering such small amounts, bank managers do not consider these to be viable transactions. Often the transaction cost to the bank is greater than amounts lent. Further, the borrowers do not fit with the conventional image of 'business' lending. The DRI borrowers are illiterate, sometimes have no fixed abode or proof of 'family-income' and 'self-employment'. Also, in caste/class-ridden India, higher status bank employees can show overt prejudice against such poor, lower-caste/class clients. The bank's half-hearted attitude to weaker-section lending programmes is reflected by the minimal level of resources allocated by some branches. The clients themselves are fearful of bureaucracy and officialdom and often frightened by the implications of non-payment. Altogether, this adds up to a reluctance on behalf of the clients to borrow and the banks to lend. It is small wonder, therefore, that many such schemes remained paper schemes in the early 1970s and still do in some banks.

The beginnings of all three organisations (SEWA, WWF and the AMM) lie in the ability to turn these 'paper schemes' into workable schemes that allow their members rightful access to credit. The small cumbersome amounts that bank staff find difficult to handle are of crucial importance for a woman requiring working capital for her income-generating project. By adopting an alternative approach to banks for DRI loans, i.e. through group rather than individual loans, women have also discovered an organisational strategy which reaches those previously seen by many as 'unorganisable'. This is illustrated by the AMM, which is discussed in the next section.

HISTORY AND GROWTH OF THE AMM

The *khannawalli*

The history of the AMM is linked closely with that of male migrants to

Bombay, who for a variety of reasons (discussed below) are unable to cook for themselves. In turn this opens up an opportunity for a number of women (known as *khannawallis*) to provide meals for these men and earn some income. Bombay is a city of migrants and every year more and more (often from surrounding districts such as Ratnagiri, but sometimes as far as Madras) are drawn to Bombay in the face of rural poverty and starvation. As a result, Bombay is congested and overcrowded and lacks adequate housing facilities. In 1981, it was estimated that as many as 8.3 million people live in slum housing (Census of India, 1981).

Although both men and women migrate to Bombay, it is the men who utilise the services of the *khannawallis*.[2] Men from surrounding districts tend to migrate without their families because of (a) the need for the family to continue farming any land in the village and (b) lack of cash and the need to save maximum amounts, uncertainty of employment and lack of housing in Bombay (Dandekar, 1986; Jetley, 1987; Savara, 1987).

Stronger caste groups such as the Hindu Marathas from Kolapur will pool money to buy/mortgage a room (known as *kholi*) in Bombay. Other Kolapur migrants of the same caste group will then share this room for a lower than average rent (10 to 15Rs a month). Up to forty men will share one *kholi* at a time. The *kholi*, therefore, literally just provides a roof over the head. There are hooks for the men's clothes and sleeping mats that are rolled away when not in use. There is no room for cooking facilities.

At a simple level, a low income, together with the need to send regular amounts to his village, inhibits the migrant from 'eating out' regularly at cafes, for example. At a more complex level, the migrant not only needs cheap food, but that which is nutritious, corresponds with his work schedule, caters to his orthodox food habits and taste, meets with his religious and caste norms and satisfies his psychological need to be with his ethnic grouping or with people from his own or a neighbourly village (Singh, 1976; Dandekar, 1986).

The very real food problems of male migrants provides a gap in the market and a chance to make income for many working-class *khannawallis* – some wives of textile mill workers, others widowed or deserted, or in rare cases, unmarried mothers. These women usually share the social and poverty backgrounds of the migrants. Their 'clients' are usually men from the same native village and same Bombay locality. Many of these will be close or distant relatives. Some idea of the numbers involved can be gleaned from the fact that Thorner and Ranadive (1985) found eighteen *khannawallis* in a sample of 173 households (Mahtre *et al.*, 1980).

There are a number of factors that contribute to social differentiation amongst the *khannawallis*, including caste, religion, level of village links, composition of household, number of children, age and marital status, household income level, to name but a few. However, generally those *khannawallis* who feed the type of rural migrant worker I refer to here, are from low-income, sometimes below poverty-line, groups. The differentiation, therefore, has to be seen in relative terms with some being even poorer than others.

The women will often cite the needed to combine child-rearing and domestic work with that of income-generation as the main reason for entry to this type of work. Further reasons lie in the lack of skill in other areas and the lack of capital needed to explore other opportunities. It is easier for them to merge a traditional familial duty and transform it into a valid way of generating income by utilising informal migrant support systems.

However, the woman's initial entry to the work and the level at which she deals with the clients is considerably influenced by her social position and religious affiliation. She has to choose between providing meals to be eaten at her home; providing packed meals (known as *daba*); or accepting clients who board as well as eat with her. Social norms governing behaviour for single women, especially those in a younger age group, are radically different to those who are married and older. It is considered improper, for instance, for a widow to allow strange men to board with her. Often Muslim women, married or not, have to restrict the activity to *dabas* only because of the religious norms governing their association with men. Further restrictions to the level at which the work is entered is determined by factors such as space, the men's work schedules, size of the household and the labour available. Depending on these, the men will eat at the woman's home or will be provided with a *daba* twice a day. Both will usually include five to six chappatis, vegetable curry, *dhal* (lentils) and rice, with fish, eggs or meat occasionally. Those who board will also be given breakfast.

The *khannawalli's* primary resource, her home, is usually an over-crowded, badly-ventilated one-room tenement (average 12 × 8 feet), often with no running water, electricity or proper sanitation. Here, the woman cooks meals for migrant 'clients' as well as her family. Usually there are less than twenty clients, but my recently completed fieldwork shows that the client numbers can be as high as fifty or seventy.

This type of work involves a constant struggle to acquire raw materials as well as cash for daily purchases, to retain clients and combine paid and unpaid home-based work. The *khannawalli's* day is long and hard, beginning with queueing for water, sometimes as early as 4 a.m. Often there will only be two or three shared water taps (which may run for two or three hours only) for up to forty households. The women have to fill and carry water pots to meet the family and clients' water needs for the day. Secondly, there is a constant shortage of basics such as cooking oil, sugar, rice and kerosene. Although the Government of India has introduced a ration-card system devised to allow fairer access to these commodities, people complain that shopkeepers hoard goods, later selling them at black market prices. Buying from ration-card shops means queueing for hours daily, or else turning to other shops that sell at higher prices – an option that is not available to many.

Severe competition for clients often leaves the *khannawalli* in a weak bargaining position. She is sometimes unable to negotiate meal times, for instance. This means that she is obliged to feed the clients at their convenience, rather than at hers. Undercutting from other *khannawallis* also means that she cannot raise her charges even if the prices of raw materials increase. The *khannawalli* usually ends up with a long day constantly supplying and serving food. Yet, more often than not, she is unable to show any cash income or profit for her hard work. Nevertheless, she continues this work as cooking for others allows her to save some food and guarantees regular meals for her own family. Her children will receive regular food. In this way, she continues to provide a valuable service to the migrant workers (whose wages she subsidises) and the factory or mill owners (who continue to maintain low-wages and sub-standard housing).

The value of this service to the migrant worker was recognised by Prema Purao, a full-time textile trade union official and a member of the Communist Party of India (Marxist) (CPIM). In 1974 during the forty-two-day textile mill worker's strike, she realised that despite lack of wages and money, the men were turning up well fed for strike duties; she discovered that the *khannawallis*, who were themselves often wives of striking workers, continued to feed the men by pawning whatever they could. Other CP activists and trade union officials informed her that this trend was a general one in many textile-mill localities.

From talking with the women, two points began to emerge: first, that the women were desperate for working capital, and secondly that they were getting themselves deeper into debt due to the high interest rates charged by moneylenders. With the help of her husband, himself a CPIM member and a banking official, Prema Purao thought of approaching the bank for a DRI loan. This idea was frightening to the women not only because of its novelty, but more so because of the perceived consequences of non-repayments. Already there were rumors of imprisonment started by money lenders who foresaw a decline of their lucrative business in slum localities.

The Annapurna

In order to overcome these initial psychological barriers, considerable organisational skills were required. Prema Purao's political background gave her a good grounding in this. Adopting a Ghandian strategy where the first approach to social reform is through the challenge of negative language, the 'job title' of *khannawalli* was replaced by the word 'Annapurna'. According to folklore, Annapurna is a self-reliant woman who, when her husband deserts her, not only feeds her household but the whole world, earning herself a name that literally means the 'Goddess of food'. She represents an 'organised, socially aware and economically independent woman' (AMM Annual Report, 1988). Thus, association with the AMM (first registered in 1975) immediately identified the Annapurna with a dignified and valuable income-generating occupation.

AMM's immediate aim was to acquire credit for its members that would act as their working capital. However, banks were still reluctant to lend to individual Annapurnas. Following the earlier example of SEWA, therefore, Prema Purao suggested a radical change in the approach to the banks. The new strategy included forming a group of about fifteen Annapurna who would then approach the bank collectively. Organisationally this meant that (a) the women would not be isolated in their relationship with the banks and officialdom; (b) group-formation would encourage solidarity, committment, accountability and loyalty to the organisation and ideas of team work; (c) such groups would develop qualities of leadership at the grassroots levels which would in turn help form other groups, thus increasing the membership of the organisation; and (d) committment to the AMM together with peer group pressure would encourage a higher rate of repayments of loans in the hope that the banks would then adopt a more lenient view towards lending.

The pilot group consisted of fourteen women, also CP members and wives of active textile trades unionists. These women therefore received considerable support from their men relatives and families. In 1975, the first applications were submitted to the Dena bank following form-filling sessions that lasted four days and nights. These took the bank six months to process and each of the fourteen women received her first loan of Rs 1500 as working capital, officially according her 'self-employed' status in her own right. Despite the lengthy procedures and the long wait, the success of the initial group can be seen as a major breakthrough in organisational terms. Today, after thirteen years, the AMM continues to adopt the same tactics, and by 1988 the number of loans obtained has risen to some 25 011 (AMM Annual Report, 1988).

Membership is automatic with any loan application. However, because some members have received up to eight loans, the latter cannot be used as an accurate guideline and unfortunately, the AMM are not able to release accurate membership figures at present.

PRESENT STRUCTURE

The organisational structure of the AMM as depicted in Figure 19.1 aims to reflect a 'grassroots' leadership and a democratic participation which begins at the membership level. The executive committee consists of sixty representatives, fifteen of whom are elected or appointed to office (such as secretary, treasurer – elected; lawyer – appointed). The remaining forty-five are elected representatives from local committees. The executive committee meets once a month and make all the major decisions. The office holders hold a weekly meeting at the AMM centre at Dadar with

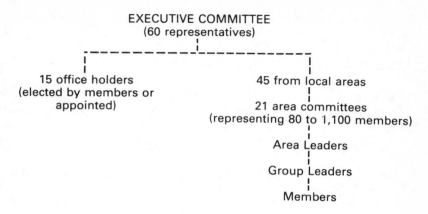

SOURCE: Adapted from AMM handout.

FIGURE 19.1   The organisational structure of the AMM

other area and group leaders. Prema Purao is the secretary and is still regarded as the main motivational force both by the executive committee and by the membership.

The idea of a 'grassroots' leadership begins to take on real meaning at the group and area leader level. These roles are arguably the most pivotal in the organisation. As the original group of fourteen women gained more experience, they became 'group leaders' for others who needed loans. This worked in two ways – either the woman approached the group leader, or the group leader herself identified a woman she felt would benefit from a bank loan. Having collected names of another eleven to fourteen women in her immediate locality, she then visited each woman several times in order to assess the applicant's need, reliability and ability to repay, and to examine evidence of 'self-employment' (such as customer's ration cards) as required by the bank.

Her association with the AMM allows the group leader to develop (a) leadership and organisational skills; (b) awareness of democratic structures and participation; (c) literacy and numeracy skills necessary to keep account of numbers of payments collected; and (e) skills which help articulate the needs of her immediate group by acting as an intermediary between women she represents (women from the same social and econ-omic background as herself) and the AMM.

As the number of groups increases in a certain locality, an 'area leader' is elected by the group leaders. With the assistance of one or two group leaders, the area leader takes on the central role of communicating her area's borrowing requirements to the AMM. Success in acquiring loans for her area depends on each area leader's negotiating skills and capabilities.

She also plays a major role in making sure repayments of loans are met.

PRESENT RELATIONSHIP WITH BANKS

Throughout the years, AMM's relationship with the banks has changed radically, and the AMM has developed consistent relations with a number of banks. Ironically, the banks now regard AMM as an enforcing agency that not only helps them administer their DRI quota but guarantees a high rate of repayments. The group and area leaders who gather information required by the banks and regularly collect repayments are in fact reducing the most expensive and cumbersome part of the bank's work without receiving any payment. It is not surprising, therefore, that branches of the State Bank of Maharastra, the Bank of Baroda and the Dena Bank (to name but a few) now approach the AMM to assist them in dispersing their quota, rather than the other way round.

Yet the AMM has had to develop its own Co-operative Credit Society in 1986. The primary reason for this is that whilst their relationship with the banks is affable, the banks take too long to administer applications and cannot meet urgent loan needs. The Credit Society was founded in order to meet these needs, not only for the Annapurna, but also for other low incomes groups (such as vegetable vendors, rag pickers, *bidi* workers) on much on the same lines as the SEWA bank, which intervenes in times of crisis when the only other resort would have been the moneylender. By 1987 the Credit Society share capital exceeded Rs 1 400 000. With a 100 per cent recovery rate and a 4 per cent per annum interest rate, the Society showed a profit of Rs 8000 in the first year.

LOOKING AHEAD

In 1981, a long and bitter struggle over union recognition, industrial legislation and bonus payments cost hundreds of textile mill workers their jobs. An estimated 58.42 million mandays lost. Employers victimised strikers and took advantage of the conflict by introducing new technology (with a further reduction in jobs) without negotiations or agreement with the unions. The result was a drastic reduction in the workforce from 224 000 to 140 000. Out of those taken back, most lost their 'permanent' status and were re-employed as casual workers on a daily basis, often only finding enough work for ten days per month (Factsheet 1, 1983; Bakshi, 1986).

All this had direct repercussions on the work of the Annapurnas who lost many customers. The future of this activity is, therefore, of prime consideration to the AMM and it has dealt with this in a number of ways.

In December 1983, towards the end of the textile strike, the AMM initiated a catering training section aiming to upgrade cooking and catering skills. Women are taught to follow new recipes, sell food across the counter, price, keep stock and cost accounts, all of which enables them to expand their activity and explore new opportunities. This section is based at the Dadar area in Bombay and seventy to eighty women are undergoing in training at one time.

The Dadar centre has also gained contracts for canteen catering at the Nurses' Training Institute (for 300 people) and supplies packed lunches to two office blocks (300 *dabas* a day). Unfortunately, a recent contract with the Telecom's canteen became commercially non-viable because of competition from a private firm. In the face of this kind of competition, the AMM argues that government institutes should prioritise catering contracts to women's organisations like themselves.

The AMM centre also began a vocational training section in 1983, training women to machine. Fifteen Annapurna, who for health or other reasons can no longer cook, have been trained to produce bags and other handicraft items for sale. An Air-India order for napkins was also taken on for a short time.

The administration and the day-to-day running of the Credit Society also acts as a training ground for teenage daughters of the Annapurna. The administrative and financial skills learnt here help these young women to explore alternative employment and income-generating opportunities that might otherwise be denied to them.

Local areas also run literacy programmes for the Annapurna, and tutorial classes for their children in order to help them with their schooling. A circulating library is being planned at the moment.

Health as a working-woman's issue is taken up at local level by area leaders, whilst regular check-ups are available at the AMM centre. Also, a lawyer (who has unfortunately now left) provided legal services for a variety of cases.

CONCLUSION

The AMM model exemplifies that by directly addressing the most pressing and primary need for women's income-producing work and by discovering alternative organisational strategies, it is possible to collectivise women who have been often dismissed as 'unorganisable' in the past. A collective approach has allowed the Annapurna to redefine her 'invisible' role. Her ability to confer with others in the same 'trade' and her ability to gain credit in her own right facilitates an understanding of the 'market value' of that work (despite its relatively low profile). The increasing awareness of her economic worth, in turn, influences her growing awareness of her political and social worth.[3] The resulting confidence is apparent in women with the longest association with the AMM, especially group and area leaders.

Whilst there is little doubt about the effectiveness of utilising credit programmes as an alternative organisational strategy, especially at the embroynic stages, questions need to be raised about the influence of credit programmes on the long-term goals of the organisation. Directly related to this is the demand on resources credit programmes make. At present much of the AMM's time and effort is taken up with matters relating to the bank loans. This applies to both AMM office holders and group and area leaders. Continuously collecting repayments, completing application forms, and so on means that the AMM is not only doing a job for the banks, but doing it without any reimbursement. Further, the pressure from banks wanting to disperse their DRI quota means that there is a constant need to form new groups. This means that resources are diverted from any quality input into those groups that already exist. Although it can be argued that forming new groups further increases membership, it can also be argued that too much emphasis on credit programmes can in effect hinder the organisational development.

Credit requirements are not the only problem the women face. Whilst their struggle for survival may well relate to their lack of money, the women encounter a multitude of other problems arising from their position in the household and wider society. These include insecure tenancy arrangements, lack of education and health facilities for themselves and their children, domestic violence, dowry demands, desertion, caste ostracism and so on. These multiple needs are complex, involving gender-related social issues which require a politically-planned programme in order to adopt a systematic approach. At present, whilst the AMM makes an attempt to address these issues, this is done on an ad-hoc basis as there are simply not enough resources to deal with both the credit programme administration and the rest of the needs of the membership.

AMM as an organisation has the potential of addressing as well as representing member's concerns and needs, for pressuring Government agencies for policies appropriate for the needs of its members (as exemplified by SEWA: 'Sharamshakti', 1987; Bhatt, 1989). It has to be seen by its current and potential members as a *women's* organisation, a catalyst of empowerment and political visibility, rather than an organisation that gives credit.

Credit remains a useful tool of organisational strategy, but needs to be treated with some caution. Ultimately, emphasis on credit as a short-term remedy which focusses on individual 'problem-solving' has to shift towards longer-term broader political needs if the organisation is to achieve any success in challenging the subordination and vulnerability of its members.

NOTES

1. It is important to note, however, that neither of these examples shy away from the ideas of trade unionism. SEWA is a registered trade union providing an alternative model to conventional trades unions. All three also include active Communist Party and Congress party members and follow Ghandian principles of inter-castism and egalitarian values.
2. To detail why migrant women do not eat with the *khannawallis* requires lengthy consideration of issues which are beyond the scope of this paper. This include: gender attitudes towards cooking, differing types of employment such as live-in domestic or prostitution, migration which includes children as opposed to single male migration and so on.
3. Although studies on 'evaluation' or the impact of credit programmes are virtually non-existant, other programme-specific studies have shown that women experience an increase in self-esteem, amongst other economic and social benefits (Berger 1989).

REFERENCES

Baksi, R., (1986) *The Long Haul* (Bombay: BUILD Documentation Centre).

Bhapat, M., and N. Crook, (1988) 'Duality of Female Employment', *Economic and Political Weekly of India*, 30 July 1591–5.

Bardhan, K., (1985) 'Women's Work, Welfare and Status: Forces of Tradition and Change in India', *Economic and Political Weekly of India*, 14 December, xx, 50.

Baud, I., (1989) 'Forms of Production and Women's labour: Gender Aspects of Industrialisation in India and Mexico' (Eindhoven University: PhD thesis).

Berger, M., (1989) 'Giving Women Credit: Strengths and Limitations of Credit as a Tool for Alleviating Poverty', *World Development*, 17 (7) 1017–32.

Bhatt, E., (1989) 'Towards Empowerment', *World Development*, 17 (7) 1059–65.

Bunivic, M., (1985) 'Helping the Third World's Poor Women', *Christian Science Monitor*, July 5.

Dandekar, H., (1986) *Men to Bombay, Women at Home: Urban Influences in a Sugao Village 1942–1982* (Ann Arbor: University of Michigan Press).

Factsheet No. 1, (1983) Factsheet Collective, *Bombay's Historic Textile Strike* (Bombay: Centre for Education and Documentation).

Government of India, (1989) *National Perspective Plan for Women 1988–2000* (New Delhi: Ministry of Urban Development).

Government of India, (1986) *The Twenty-Point Programme, Perspectives and Strategies* (New Delhi: Ministry of Programme Implementation).

Jetley, S., et al., (1985) *Women's Work and Family Strategies: Utter Predesh, Bihar and West Bengal* (New Delhi: ICSSR).

Joshi, H., (1976) 'The Case for Employment of Women in Indian Cities', *Economic and Political Weekly of India*, Special Number, August,1303–8.

Mahtre, S., S. Brahme and G. Kelkar, (1980) *Bank Credit to Women: a Study of Khanavals* (New Delhi: ICSSR).

Savara, M., (1987) *Women in Food-Processing – a Study in Bombay and Pune cities* (Bombay: Centre for Studies in Decentralised Industry).

Savara, M., and J. Everett, (1983) *Bank Credit to Women in the Informal Sector – a Case Study of DRI in Bombay city* (Bombay: SNDT Women's University).

Savara, M., and J. Everett, (1986) 'Institutional Credit as a Strategy Towards Self-Reliance', in *Invisible Hands* (London: Sage Publications).

Singh, A., (1976) *Neighbourhoods and Social Networks in Urban India* (New Delhi: Marwah Publications).

Sharamskati – a Report of the National Commission on Self-Employed Women in the Informal Sector (New Delhi).

Thorner, A., and J. Ranadive, (1985) 'Household as a First Stage in a Study of Working-Class Women', *Economic and Political Weekly of India* 31 October 47–53.

20 Fundamentalism and its Female Apologists

Haleh Afshar

> Religion is both a problem (or *the* problem) where its structures of dominance have oppressed women, as well as a solution where its vision of liberation or equality has generated powerful movements for social change.
>
> (Eck and Jain, 1986)

It is the contention of this paper that feminist and Muslim fundamentalist women both begin from similar premises where the subordination of women is concerned; it is in their conclusions that the two groups vary considerably. It is therefore necessary to consider the analysis offered by Muslims and consider seriously whether the feminist solutions remain valid even in the cultural and political context of countries such as Iran.

In the hundred years that preceded the Islamic revolution Iranian women had slowly and painfully struggle for and gained access to education in 1910, obtained the abolishment of the veil in 1936 and the right to vote in 1962. During the last decade of the Shah's rule even the domain of personal laws was eroded, with a curb on the unequivocal male right to divorce and custody of children in 1973, a ban on polygamy and right to alimony after divorce in 1976, as well as legal abortion on demand in 1974. But many women remained critical of what they saw as enforced liberation. The unveiling of women, though rooted in more than a hundred years of struggle, had been forced on them by royal decree. It is true that the first recorded attempt at liberation from veil was staged by the famous feminist Qoratolayn in the 1840s.[1] Nevertheless, there was some reluctance on the part of many women to abandon the decency of the *hijab* for what they saw as the abandonment and nakedness of unveiling. The extension of capitalism and gradual inclusion of women in the labour market did not, in the long run, bring the hoped-for equality, and did create a double burden, shared by women everywhere, of paid and unpaid labour. In this context, some of the criticisms of Muslim fundamentalists concerning the involvement of women in work and the public domain remains pertinent.

THE CRITIQUE

Both Iranian and many Western feminists agree that participation in the labour market has not resulted in the undisputed liberation of women. That so long as capitalism continues to carry the pre-capitalist ideological conceptions of women as bearers of inferior labour, then women will remain poorly-paid and undervalued. Similarly, so long as the reproductive activities of women and the burden of child-raising remain in the private and feminine domain of unpaid labour, then this double or triple burden will prevent women from breaking out from their subordinate position.[2]

Prominent Iranian ideologues such as Ali Shariati and Ayatollah Mottahari and many women writers concur with this analysis. They argue that the penetration of capitalism and its values failed women totally and left them bereft of honour and dignity. One of the best-known Iranian exponents of this view, Zahra Rahnavard, considers Marxism and the labour analysis to be as oppressive to women as capitalism and the cult of female beauty:

> these depraved ideologies prefer to push women out of their nests and their homes and make them abandon their children to nurseries and boarding schools and line up to serve in the offices, factories, shops and up streets and down alleys (Rahnavard n.d., p. 52–3).

But, Rahnavard argues, in the unequal struggle in the labour market, women lose out physically and psychologically: they are exploited by the market and degraded in every sense. Furthermore, Rahnavard shares the Western feminists' view that, on the whole, neither communism nor capitalism have effectively solved the dilemma of paid and unpaid employment of women. Both have failed to accommodate motherhood and social reproduction:

> the Marxists say women are equal to men in every respect. The only exception is the specific requirements of maternity such as giving birth and suckling new born babies, but these only last one to three months. Otherwise, women are no different and must, like the men, the youths and the children, serve the production process . . . The only road to freedom for women is by cutting the classical familial bonds and joining the great process of industrial production. . . . These steps lead to the same ends as capitalism (Rahnavard, pp. 52–3, 27–36).

The view that state child care would inevitably lead to anomie, alienation and the emergence of a dislocated social order, is one that is shared by Rahnavard and Khomeini,[3] and not endorsed by Western feminists. But the opinion that both capitalism and socialism have come to exploit women as sex objects is one of the many common conclusions of feminists and fundamentalists.

> Now under this universal control . . . she too has become one of the many sources of exploitation, of disempowerment and of paralysis, of stealing and hoarding from all . . . and the very essence of her life is sucked out.
> How?
> From her, now with the help of sociologists and psychologists they have built a scented, arousing, undulating, naked doll who wriggles through beauty and fashion journals to make herself ever prettier.
> But why?
> To improve the sale of their useless surplus products, old stocks which if left much longer on the shelves would bring about their total ruination and the downfall of their filthy order. So she advertises for them and sells for them.
> They have made her into a common doll (Rahnavard, pp. 11–12 and 27).

Similarly, Ayatollah Morteza Mottahari is of the view that capitalism has made women into mere mannequins:

> If you wish to see the rented woman then you must drop in at the cafes and nightclubs and see how . . . for an insignificant wage . . . women have to surrender their body, soul and honour to men . . .
> The rented woman is the one who, for the benefit of a commercial concern, has to contort herself in a thousand different forms so as to lure a client for the goods. She has to appear in indescribable ways on our television screens to advertise their products (Mottahari, 1980, p. 49).

Feminists accept that the emphasis on objectification of women in turn makes many vulnerable to the projected images of femininity and sends them in pursuit of fashion and beauty, a process that is deplored by feminists and fundamentalists alike.

Although, on the whole, there is universal agreement on both the failure of the labour market to liberate women and the objectification of women, it is in their strategies in dealing with these issues that feminists and fundamentalists differ extensively. In part, these are based on differing views of women and femininity, and in part on too optimistic a view of Islam. In the classic mould of revivalism, fundamentalists chose an idealised, timeless, static interpretation of Islam and its benefits for women in their writings.[4] The problem is that, in practice, the world they live in is organised by men whose interpretations are different, detrimental to women and backed by man-made laws. In their bargain with patriarchy,[5] fundamentalist women have lost sight of the dynamics of economics and political reality. Hence their differing reasons for the endorsement of the veil and the Islamic views of motherhood and domesticity.

WOMEN AND ISLAM

Intellectually, Muslim women scholars have a great advantage in their current efforts to re-interpret Islam in favourable terms; it is the undoubted love and admiration that the Prophet of Islam had for women in general and for his first wife, Khadijah, in particular. If we accept the well-known fact that all religions endorse a patriarchal structure and discriminate against women, we may be able to argue that, in terms of degrees of oppression, Islam may be one of the better faiths.

Muslim feminist scholars substantiate this view by returning to the origins of Islam and disregarding its current practices, and the evolution of its views and ideas about women. Thus they denounce the well-known *hadith* that women were created from the left rib of Adam, which happened to have been bent. They argue that such views go against the very text of the Qoran, which after all is the sacred word of God. Accordingly, they note that man and woman were created by God from the same essence.

> Men, have fear of your Lord, who created you from a single soul. From that soul He created its mate, and through them he bestowed the earth with countless men and women (4:1).

Hassan (1985) and Rahnavard (n.d.) point out that, in Arabic, this single soul is a feminine noun and conclude that obviously it was the man who has been created from the rib of woman. Thus they argue, in terms of equality of sexes, at least at the point of creation, Islam does seem to do better than most other world religions.

> Then Satan whispered to them that he might manifest unto them that which was hidden from them of their shame, and he said: Your Lord forbade you from this tree only lest you should become angels or become immortals (7:20).

> Thus did he lead them with guile. And when they tasted of the tree their shame was manifest to them and they began to hide [by heaping] on themselves some of the leaves of the Garden (7:22).

Islam also accords considerable economic autonomy to women and curtails the power of parents and spouses in disinheriting them or abusing their property rights. Thus Muslims point out that although women obtain half as much as men in terms of inheritance, their entitlement is inalienable, as is their independent right of ownership:

> Men shall have a share in what their parents and kinsmen have, and women shall have a share in what their parents and kinsmen leave: whether it be little or much, they are legally entitled to their share (4:7).

Those women who participate in the current Islamic resurgence have much to support their cause.

WOMEN AND MARRIAGE

Women do not lose their identity or their wealth on marriage. In Qoranic terms, marriage is, in fact, a flexible arrangement arrived at by mutual consent where women are expected to be 'obedient'[6] but in return they can expect to be kept in the style to which they had been accustomed before their marriage. Marriage itself is negotiated in terms of a contract which is binding on both parties, and for the consummation of marriage the contract includes an obligatory payment, *mahre*, by the husband to the wife (4:4 and 4:24). Even if the marriage is not consummated and the husband divorces his wife, he is still expected to pay half the *mahre* (2:238). Within marriage, not only are men expected to maintain their wives (4:34 and 2:236) but also they must treat them with kindness (2:238). Furthermore, they must pay an additional fee for mothers who agree to suckle their babies (2:233).

As an institution, marriage is praised and celibacy on the whole seen as undesirable. In fact, marriage is one of the signs of the goodness of Allah:

> Among His signs is (the fact) that he has created spouses for you among yourselves so that you may console yourselves with them. He has planted love and mercy between you; in that are signs for people who reflect (30:21).

Thus, marriage is seen as a refuge of love and kindness for both men and women, a domain of mutual intimacy, comfort and protection. Women commentators tend to underline the importance of both partners in securing this haven of happiness:

> They are expected to find tranquility in each other's company and be bound together not only by sexual relationship, but by 'love and mercy'. Such a description comprises mutual care, consideration, comfort and protection (Lemu and Hareen, 1978, p. 17).

Given this analysis, it is not surprising to see that a number of women fundamentalists argue forcefully for the separation of spheres and for women locating their work and energy in the domestic sphere. To them, such a choice is not an indication of subordination, but rather one of complementarity of genders, each with their own equally important domain of duty and obligation. The proponents of Islam remain convinced that it is the recognition of the marital and reproductive obligations of women and the earthly and heavenly rewards allocated to these that makes Islam so very special and appreciated by many women the world over. It is a heavenly duty, Islam abhors celibacy and celebrates married life. ˜

For all its differing facets and concepts of mutual obligations, marriage is not seen necessarily as a once-and-for-all event but as an institution that can change; men and women alike are allowed to choose different partners at different times of their lives. Divorce is extremely easy for men, and possible for those women who have the necessary foresight to include a right of divorce for themselves in their marriage contract. Failing that, women are allowed by the Qoran to negotiate (4:128) or 'ransom themselves out of the relationship' (2:229). Although the Qoran advises believers to seek reconciliation within marriage whenever possible (4:35, 2:28), when such efforts fail, it requires that Muslim men should make reasonable provisions for their divorced wives (2:342), retain them in honour or let them go in kindness (2:229). There is no shame attached to divorce and divorced men and women can meet and remarry (2:235). At no time are they permitted to take back the *mahre*: 'Do not take from her the dowry you have given her even it be a talen of gold' (4:21).

Thus, Muslim scholars have for long argued that Islam does not shackle women within marriage, does not bind them to domesticity and by allowing them a separate property entitlement makes them economically independent of their husbands and therefore well able to fend for themselves. Of course, much of this is owed to Khadijah, Muhammad's first and most remarkable wife, who was considerably older than him. A rich widow, Khadijah initially appointed him as her trade representative and he travelled the world on her behalf. Subsequently she asked him to marry her. When Muhammad refused, she merely referred him to his uncle and more or less commanded him to marry his nephew off to her. The marriage was a success; Khadijah was the first convert to Islam, and it was thanks to the protection of her very powerful tribe that Muhammad survived the early turbulent years of Islam when he was hunted out by the people of Mecca. So long as Khadijah was alive, Muhammad took no other wife and the verses of the Qoran advocating polygamy (4:3) and the need for the relatives of the prophet to cover their finery *zinat* (33:33) all date from after Khadijah's death.

POLYGAMY

But even the most submissive of converts has difficulties in accommodating the question of polygamy. The new emerging school of revivalist feminist Muslims, assisted by scholars such as Eqbal in Pakistan and Ali Shariati in Iran, all emphasise these positive aspects of Islam and explain away the negative ones. Hence the verse about polygamy is read in its totality, whereby it states:

> But if your fear that you cannot maintain equality among them, marry one only or any slave girls you may own. This will make it easier for you to avoid injustice (4:4).

Rahnavard argues that polygamy is only permitted as a means to protect orphans and is a fall-back position when, for reasons such as a war, large numbers of men have been killed and women and particularly children are left unprotected; and Lemu sees it as a way of dealing with 'the surplus of unattached women in the society' (Lemu and Hareen, p. 24).

Mahboubeh Rezayi prefers to emphasise that the Qoran indicates that God viewed monogamy to be the norm and polygamy the exception, and that this respect for monogamy under normal circumstances is one of the firm pillars of women's rights and the respect for them (Rezayi, n.d., p. 94).

However, Lemu is of the view that, in times of war and shortages of men, women should agree to polygamy: 'under these circumstances . . . if given the alternative, many of them would rather share a husband than to have none at all' (Lemu and Hareen, p. 28).

But one of the leading ideologues of the Islamic revolution in Iran, Ayatollah Mottahari, applauds temporary marriages, whereby a man may marry a woman for as long or as short a period as he wishes. Furthermore, he recommends polygamy as a 'social necessity', required to deal with depravity as well as an assumed gender imbalance. Hence he argues that men should approach polygamy 'as a necessary duty . . . just like the duty to do one's military service' (Mottahari, 1980, p. 348). Thus the scholarly interpretation of Muslim women and their conditional accord with polygamy is dismissed by a leading religious expert whose views echo those of the law makers in Iran. The intellectual debate loses its relevance in the context of actual fundamentalist laws and their purveyors.

DOMESTICITY AND MOTHERHOOD

It is not so much marriage as motherhood that is seen by the devout as the particular privilege of women. It is argued that there has been a divine division of labour and that women have been made for domesticity and motherhood and thus should adopt this role willingly. Rahnavard states:

> Does motherhood, wifehood, lack of responsibility for earning a family income . . . imprison the Muslim woman in her home, tie her down with familiar ties?
> Never! Never . . .
> This is the road to freedom, to the liberation of women to her growth and achievement . . . She has the revolutionary responsibility of showing the right path and prohibiting the wrong deed, decrying the false and teaching the right . . . It is women who teach the future generations and it is women who must endorse or reject any political agenda (Rahnavard, n.d., p. 103–10).

But of course such an eternally sanguine view of motherhood, rooted as it is in the biological being of women, denies any choice to women; they are to confine themselves eternally to reproduction, and any deviation from such a path would apparently prove fatal to both the particular woman and the whole society. Mottahari explains:

> The replacement of the father by the government, which is the current trend in the west, will undermine maternal sentiments, alter the very nature of motherhood from an emotional tie into a form of waged employment with money as an intermediary between mother and her love, motherhood then is no longer a bond, but a paid employment.
> It is obvious that this process would lead to the destruction of the family and the unavoidable and total annihilation of womankind (Mottahari, 1980, p. 214).

FORMAL EMPLOYMENT

Commentators such as Rahnavard argue that it is the nature of women that dictates such division of labour:

> There are physical and emotional differences that are ignored at their peril. Communism undoubtedly oppresses women by denying the specifities of the feminine, the woman whose nature has burdened her with the heavy and difficult task of motherhood . . . But Islam praises motherhood, orders men and women to bring love and peace to each other and recognises the centrality of this biological specifity which means that . . . she, as a human being, is entirely responsible before God and society. To fulfil this responsibility, her obligations are

channelled in accordance with her physical and emotional characteristics. Because of these and the heavy burden of child bearing and birth and after that the social duty of child rearing, she is not expected to be a full participant in social production and Islam does not give her a primary role in the process of production (Rahnavard, n.d., p. 100).

In many ways, fundamentalism is a ratification of motherhood as a paid and respectable role for women to be performed within the domestic sphere, and certainly part of its appeal is rooted in its validation of this role. Much fundamentalist writing is directed against feminists, Marxists, or capitalists, all of whom in their different ways are seen to be attacking the central role of motherhood, and to be denouncing domesticity as women's chains. Those who accept Islam see motherhood both as a task and a reward:

What a spirit of mutual kindness, this lowering of the wing of mercy on us while we are helpless. And later on, our protecting tenderness to our children and our elders when they are in need of it! If we are good and patient, understanding and encouraging in our behaviour towards our family members, thus bringing forth the very same virtues in them as well, we are sure to carry these virtues forward into human society as well (Lemu and Hareen, 1978, p. 44).

That motherhood is a sacred duty and that 'mothers of believers' have a special corner of heaven designed specially for them is not contested by any of the fundamentalist theorists. The many verses of the Qoran commanding motherhood include the following:

We have enjoined man to respect his parents; his mother bears him with fainting after fainting, while his weaning takes two years. Thank me as well as your parents; towards me lies the goal. (31:14)

Thus in thanking their mothers, Muslims are thanking God and fulfilling a religious duty. There is also the oft-quoted statement of the prophet that 'paradise lies at the feet of mothers'. Islam ratifies a division of labour with women as the guardians of the cradle and men as the breadwinners. It is, however, the causes of such division of labour, the rewards thereof and the length of time devoted to it which is open to discussion. The Qoranic verses commanding believers to love and respect their mothers are too numerous to mention. Although it is thus accepted that motherhood is a worthwhile and important task, some commentators, such as Ali Shariati, believe that women can only achieve success in terms of their men folk, be it through marriage, motherhood or daughterhood. He holds the daughter of Muhammad, Fatemeh, as an exemplary person for all women to follow and these are the qualities that Shariati sees as worthy of notice:

> As a mother she raised a daughter like Zeinab and sons like Hosein and Hassan. In a different aspect as an exemplary wife, one that stays every inch of the way with Ali through his loneliness, difficulties, problems and great moments. (Shariati, n.d., p. 40)

If women are the bastions of the family, if their failure to remain good mothers is perilous to the whole social wellbeing, then of necessity they will become dependent on men for their livelihood. This is accepted by all believers who refer to the Qoranic verse stating that 'Men have authority over women because Allah has made the one superior to the others, and because they spend their wealth to maintain them' (4:34). Using the very diverse and extensive meanings of each word, Hassan argues that the interpreters of this verse have merely chosen the wrong meaning. What is implied here is merely a permission granted to men to spend their wealth on women for the short period of childbearing. Besides, authority here is not one that is given to men, absolutely and forever, but one that is accorded to them for a specific purpose and a limited period. Accordingly, this verse may be interpreted to mean that at the time of childbearing men have the responsibility to spend their wealth on the superior women who are capable of reproduction and must be provided for at this time.[7] Thus a correct translation would read:

> Men are the maintainers of women with the bounties which God has bestowed more abundantly on some of them than on others; and with what they may spend out of their possessions (4:34).

Rahnavard also makes the point that the word 'authority' is a misinterpretation and what is meant by the Qoran is a specific allocation of responsibilities. Men have not been appointed to rule over women, but are given the heavy responsibility to secure their livelihood while women get on with the important task of motherhood. So, like Hassan, Rahnavard interprets the verse to mean that men are given a duty and not an authority, and that the notion that one is superior to the other means each one of them is superior to the other in different respects (Rahnavard, n.d., pp. 79–82).

But different scholars make different judgements on the implications of this responsibility. Riffat Hassan argues that this is a very temporary obligation: she sees the episode of economic dependence as a short-term one, maybe lasting while the mother is caring for the baby, as a means of avoiding the terrible problems of being an impecunious single mother, or having to combine full-time work with child care. But Hassan emphasises that the bounties abundantly bestowed by God are not merely bestowed on men. Nor are they gender specific in kind, in terms of intellectual ability or artistic talents. In Hassan's view, some men and some women have been gifted in preference to others. That is to say there is no impediment on the formal employment of women in any field and they may have the same abilities as men.

SEXUALITY AND THE VEIL

Sexuality in general and female sexuality in particular has been a major concern amongst Muslim theologians since the time of the prophet (Abbott, 1985, p. 22). As far as sexuality in general is concerned, Islam, in common with Hinduism, celebrates sexual union and does not ascribe a high religious value to celibacy and sexual abstinence. At the same time, however, Islam, in common with other religions, condemns overt female sexuality. Some feminist writers have suggested that it is male fear of female sexuality which underlies this condemnation.[8] Traditional ideologues, on the other hand, take the view that restraints on women are necessary because women have learnt to exploit the ever-present desire of the male.

In her fascinating study *Woman in the Muslim Unconscious*, Fatna A. Sabbah argues that there is a deep seated-fear of the omnisexual woman amongst Muslim men who are convinced that:

> Her desire is a force so irresistible, so biological, so animal, that she is fatally impelled to rebel against the constraints, the barriers that are supposed to try to impair her capacity for sexual pleasure. She is by definition in rebellion against all the care taken for hierachization and classification as the foundation of the spiritual Islam, which is based on the control of biological forces and their subordination to an order designed by and for man and his glorification in the male god Allah. (Sabbah, 1984, p. 32)

Hence the need to hide women, to protect men, since in the Muslim unconscious, all women are potentially omnisexual. This perspective makes it considerably easier to understand much of the writing of many male Muslim leaders which otherwise would seem much too full of hatred for women to be rational. It also helps to explain the introduction of the veil and polygamy.

There is, however, an interesting difference between male and female analysis of the process. Whereas Sabbah sees the unconscious male fear of the omnisexual woman as the source of the perceived need to restrain her, men prefer to depict women as exploiting male desire for love. According to Mottahari:

Woman, with her natural cleverness . . . has noticed the weak point that nature has given to men and has made him the seeker of love and the pursuer and has made woman the sought one and the pursued. . . . when woman realised this situation and her position where men are concerned and recognised his weak point, she resorted to make up and ornaments and luxury to help her capture the man's heart and at the same time she distanced herself from man in the knowledge that she must not give herself for nothing, but must inflame his desire and passion and thus raise her own status (Mottahari, 1984, p. 52).

The views put forward by Mottahari and other Muslim ideologues have been criticised by women such as Mahboubeh Rezayi. Rezahi warns against

these seemingly religious leaders who have pretension to understanding Islam but who in the guise of Islam knowingly or unintentionally inter-pret Islam according to their own wishes and interests and seek to enrich themselves from such misleading interpretations (Rezayi, n.d., p. 96).

Such criticism may be valuable in itself but it can have little effect in a society where men alone can influence decision-making and formulate the policy of the Islamic republic.

What is worth noting, however, is that in the context of Islamic fun-damentalist discourse, whereas women see marriage as a partnership between equals, the men tend to see it more as a financial transaction between the body of the female believer and the purse of the male – but a transaction that must remain the sole undisputed private property of one man. So that it is not the minis and see-throughs *per se* that are objection-able, but the wearing thereof in public that is seen as problematic. Motta-hari explains why:

To drag out sexual urges and satiate them in public away from the home environment weakens society, undermines its labour power and reduces its production capacity (Mottahari, 1984, p. 77).

Oddly enough, there is no discussion as to why Westerners, with all their corrupt practices, end up having higher levels of productivity and not a totally traumatised male population. It may be true to say that Muslim men are caught in a trap of their own making through their fantasies of sexuality. They have created this notional potent man, in need of a harem full of women to satisfy his eternal lust, but they may well be faced with women who are more sexually active, demanding and voracious than the men. Then it becomes necessary to hide and cover women, to confine them to living in seclusion under the 'authority' of one man, to confine their sexual demands and to protect other men from their allure. At the same time, all this hiding of women makes them appear ever more desirable to the Muslim men who remain eternally obsessed with sexuality and unable to decode it.

> Islam has specifically instructed women to cover themselves since women have an instinctive desire to show themselves off and to be noticed (Mottahari, 1984, p. 73).

The image of woman as the temptress is one that is projected not only by men, but also by some female commentators so that Rahnavard, for example, states:

> Through this woman, this sensitive foothold they have conquered, how easily they get to the men, the other half of humanity and direct his attention to sexuality, to appearances and to lust and divert his attention from major social problems (Rahnavard, n.d., p. 12).

It is the vulnerability of men that demands the hiding of women: 'It must be noted that sexual freedom will arouse lust and turn it into a permanent insatiable obsession' (Mottahari, 1984, p. 98). Clearly, these tempting sex objects should be locked away to allow society to be run properly by clear-headed men.

CONCLUSION

I find it difficult to understand why women choose to accept the veil. Research on the psychology of oppressed persons tells us that one strategy for dealing with their situation is to adopt the rules of the oppressor and obey them unquestioningly. This must certainly be seen as one possible explanation: there is also the need for Islamic women to find their own identity. Islam teaches them that they are the source of culture and traditional values: they must therefore find an alternative identity to the doll-cum-film starlet pattern already rejected by feminists in the west. Where the latter simply stopped wearing the make-up and pretty dresses which Mottahari considers typical of women, Islamic women have either covered them up, or even abandoned them and withdrawn their bodies from the male gaze while at the same time submitting to the will of Allah.

In explaining why women embrace fundamentalism, perhaps the most important factor is the failure of modern social systems to lighten the double burden of these women who take an active part in the formal system employment sector. The ideology of patriarchy and its dictates demands that all women, whether employed or not, should remain the guardians of the home fires, the cradles and the graves. But they are expected to fulfil these roles free of charge, for the doubtful joys of femininity and fulfilment. For Muslim women the burdens are all the heavier since the belief in gender-specific familial demands are part and parcel of their stated religious duties. Furthermore, in practice, many Muslim countries have little public provisions for the care of the very young and the very old. Those women who do work do so thanks to the availability of unpaid familial support, often provided by their children.

Nor are women paid as well as men. The segregation of the labour market firmly discriminates against the work done and skills acquired by women, who are everywhere considered to be secondary wage earners. Given this reality, it is not surprising that Rahnavard is able, quite rightly, to point an accusing finger at Russia and socialism. Nor can one argue that capitalism has done any better: the objectification of the female body, the ever more expensive cult of youth and beauty leave much to be desired in the lives of women in the west. What is more, the fragmentation of the nuclear family, the increasing alienation of the younger generations, the impoverishment and dependence of the old on ever-decreasing public resources makes life in the advanced industrial societies appear less than alluring to many women, including those who choose to convert to Islam in the West. In the context of many Muslim countries, there is also the unavoidable addition of social pressure and the need for what Marie Aime and Hellie Lucas define as 'entremism'.[9] To gain peer approval and to benefit from the practical and emotional support offered by fundamentalists many chose the easier option of entering into the group, rather than fighting for what may in the long-run prove to be illusory benefits. Of course, there is little evidence to suggest that any religious system has ever succeeded in protecting old cultures, traditions and familial values from the advent of industrialisation. Conceivably, post-industrialism, by returning the workers to their home bases may yet change preceding trends.[10] Nevertheless, much as I disagree with the contentions of Muslim fundamentalists on the question of women and their position in society, I can see that what they offer in terms of paid domesticity in the context of a relatively flexible and clearly delineated marriage contract, does have a certain logic and attraction for many women. Given the obvious failure of western-style feminism to bring lasting liberation for Muslim women, for many the only way forward may be through a feminist reinterpretation of Islam itself.

But there is a major difference between male and female Muslim commentators of the new devout generation on the question of nature or nurture. Women see reproduction as natural and subordination as nurtured, while most of the men view women as naturally inferior and physically and mentally unequal. Sadly it is the men who make the laws and women who are subjected to its inequalities.

Within a year of its establishment in Iran, the new regime rejected all the personal law improvements by decree. The veil was reintroduced, abortion made illegal, and a 'bantu' education introduced, with women trained to become good mothers and banned from the faculties of science and engineering.[11] Within three years, the Islamic criminal laws, *Qassas*, introduced in July 1981, formally relegated women to the position of second-class citizens and confirmed their apparent legal subordination. They were entirely banned from practising in the legal profession. Women became legally almost invisible. Their evidence could not be accepted by courts of law, if un-corroborated by a male witness. According to the new laws of retribution, the murderer of a woman can only be punished if her male protector pays the blood money of the killer (articles 5 and 6). Since women are strongly advised not to participate in the public domain, they are assumed to be financial burdens and not assets and are therefore accorded half the blood money of men. In law and in practice women have been defined as subordinate to men in Iran.

Thus in practice, far from bestowing pride and glory on women, Islamic laws have proved considerably more oppressive than the 'unsuccessful' feminist strategies. This is becoming apparent in Iran, despite the intense process of political re-education and Islamic propaganda currently addressed to women. So long as male fundamentalists are making the laws, at best women defendents of Islam can do no more than remain apologists for the regime.

NOTES

1. For further discussion see Mahmoudian (1985) and Afshar (forthcoming).
2. There is an extensive literature on both these points. See, for example, Elson and Pearson (1981, pp. 144–67, Hartman (1981, pp. 1–42), Beechey (1987), Mitter (1987), Afshar (1987a) and Frobel (1980).
3. For further discussion see Afshar (1982, pp. 47–60).
4. I am indebted to Ruth Pearson for referring me to Amrita Chichhi's paper on 'Fundamentalism' in D. Kandiyoti (ed.) *Women and the State* (London: Macmillan, forthcoming) where this point is discussed at length.
5. See Deniz (1988).
6. There is much controversy amongst Muslim scholars about the meaning of obedience and whether or not it is a requirement for good behaviour rather than submission.
7. See Hassan (1985).
8. For a detailed discussion, see for example Sabbah (1984) and El Sadaawi (1980).
9. Hillie Lucas and Maire Aimee, paper given at the Colloquium on the Rights of Subordinated People, La Trobe University, Melbourne, Australia, 1988.
10. See the excellent arguments put forward by Mitter (1987).
11. For detailed discussion see Tabari and Yeganeh (1982), Afshar (1982, pp. 79–90), Afshar (1985), Afshar (1987b, pp. 70–86) and Afshar (1988).

REFERENCES

Abbot, N., (1985) *Aisha, the Beloved of Muhammad* (London: Al Saqi Books).
Afshar, H., (1982) 'Khomeini's Teachings and Their Implications for Women', in A. Tabari and N. Yeganeh, *In the Shadow of Islam* (London: Zed Press).
Afshar, H., (1985) 'Legal and Socio-Political Position of Women in Iran', *International Journal of Sociology of Law*, 13 (February), 47–60.
Afshar, H., (1987a) (ed.), *Women, Work and Ideology in the Third World* (London: Tavistock).
Afshar, H., (1987b) 'Women, Marriage and the State in Iran' in H. Afshar (ed.), *Women, State and Ideology* (London: Macmillan).
Afshar, H., (1988) 'Behind the Veil: The Public and Private Faces of Khomeini's Policies on Iranian Women', in B. Agarwal (ed.), *Structures of Patriarchy Kali for Women* (London: Zed Press).
Afshar, H., (forthcoming) 'The Emancipation Struggles in Iran, Past Expectations and Future Hopes', in H. Afshar (ed.), *Women, Development and Survival in the Third World* (London: Longman).
Beechey, V., (1987) *Unequal Work* (London: Verso).
Deniz, K., (1988) 'Bargaining with Patriarchy', *Gender and Society*, 2 (3) (September) 274–90.
Eck, D., and D. Jain (1986) (eds.), *Speaking of Faiths* (New Delhi: Kali for Women).
El Sadaawi, N.,(1980) *The Hidden Face of Eve* (London: Zed Press).
El Sadaawi, N., (1982) 'Women and Islam', *Women's Studies International Forum*, 5 (2) 193–206.
Elson, D., and R. Pearson, (1981) 'The Subordination of Women and the Internationalisation of Factory Production' in K. Young et al., *Of Marriage and the Market* (London: CSE Books).
Frobel, F., et al., (1980) *The New International Division of Labour* (Cambridge: Cambridge University Press).
Hartman, H., (1981) 'The Unhappy Marriage of Marxism and Feminism', in L. Sargent (ed.), *Women and Revolution* (London: Pluto Press).
Hassan, R., (1985) 'Made from Adam's Rib', *Al-Mushir*, XXVII (3) (Autumn) 124–55.
Hijab, N., (1988) *Womanpower* (Cambridge: Cambridge University Press).
Lemu, B., and F. Hareen, (1978) *Women in Islam* (London: Islamic Council of Europe).
Mahmoudian, H., (1985) 'Tahira: an Early Feminist', in H. Fathi (ed.), *Women and Family in Iran* (Leiden: Brill).
Mitter, S., (1987) *Common Fate and Common Bond* (London: Pluto Press).
Mojahedin, K., (1980) *Zan Dar Massyreh Rahayi* (Tehran: Mojahedin's Publication).
Mottahari, M., (1980) *Nezameh Hoquqeh Zan Dar Islam* (Qum: Islamic Publication).
Mottahari, M., (1984) *Massaleyeh Hajab* (Qum: Islamic Publication).
Rahnavard, Z., (n.d.) *Toloueh Zaneh Mosalman* (Tehran: Mahboubeh Publication).
Sabbah, F. A., (1984) *Women in the Muslim Unconscious* (Oxford: Pergamon Press).
Shariati, A., (n.d.) *Zaneh Mosahman* (Tehran: Shaziafi Foundation).
Tabari, A., and N. Yeganeh, (1982) *In the Shadow of Islam* (London: Zed Press).

Index